COMP/MODS

DISCOVERING WRITING SKILLS

JOHN A. HIGGINS

YORK COLLEGE, CITY UNIVERSITY OF NEW YORK

THOMAS Y. CROWELL COMPANY · NEW YORK

ESTABLISHED 1834

THOMAS Y. CROWELL COMPANY, INC.
666 Fifth Avenue
New York, New York 10019

Typography by Bill Frost

We thank the following organizations and individuals for supplying us with the
Module-opening photographs: 1: United Nations; 2: United Nations; 3: Helena
Frost; 4: United Nations; 5: United Nations; 6: United Nations; 7: United
Nations; 8: United Nations; 9: William E. Frost; 10: United Nations; 11: Salt
River Project; 12: United Nations; 13: United Nations; 14: United Nations;
15: William E. Frost

Library of Congress Cataloging in Publication Data

Higgins, John A
 Comp/mods : discovering writing skills.

 Includes index.
 1. English language—Rhetoric. 2. English
language—Grammar—1950–   I. Title.
PE1408.H479   808′.042   76–4823
ISBN 0–690–00824–4

TO MY MOTHER AND MY FATHER

CONTENTS

TO THE INSTRUCTOR

How to teach it all? Where to start? How to cope with a class of twenty-five developmental writing students having two-hundred-fifty writing problems? There is so much to explain and show that instructors just do not have class time for it all. "If I could spend an hour a day with each student, one on one . . . ."

This book is designed to give the student such one-on-one instruction, for it talks directly to him. It does not tell; it shows and asks and makes him answer. Using inductive techniques, it leads him to discover writing principles for himself and to "execute" them, as coaches like to say, with increasing skill. Flexibly organized in modules, *Comp/Mods* permits you to start with each student wherever is best for *him,* to set up an individual course of study to meet his particular writing needs and to adjust this course for any ratio of individual to group or whole-class instruction. The text's modules on sentence structure and grammar, with terminology minimized and simplified, treat the fundamentals of the English sentence as fully as practical at this level. And by integrating motivation with its inductive approach, *Comp/Mods* lets the student see the reason each writing skill is needed as he is discovering that skill—often discovering it within himself.

Both the content and the method of *Comp/Mods* are based on my twenty years' experience with the kinds of students for whom the book is intended, as well as on research into their writing habits and analysis of the composition texts they have worked with in secondary schools. What to include is a major problem in planning any text for students whose work may contain any or all conceivable writing problems—and occasionally some inconceivable ones. Too many texts concentrate on grammar and mechanics to the neglect of diction and paragraph content. Because this book treats all three main components of writing—words, sentences, and paragraphs—it must be selective. It focuses, therefore, on those problems which arise most frequently in the papers of freshmen in developmental courses. There is, for example, a full section on using noun and verb inflectional endings, a common problem among these students yet one rarely treated in texts.

The book's inductive approach—guided induction really, —operates on the principle that a student will understand and retain a concept much better if he discovers it himself than if it is merely pointed out to him. Discovery is followed by practice and by application. Many of the assignments require revision of previous writing; others involve peer-group evaluation and mutual assistance. The text requires the student not merely to do the practices but also to supply key words in the explanatory matter itself, forcing him to focus on vital passages he too often tends to skim. In fact, the text reads very much like a script for a series of classroom lessons, for really this is how it was designed—as a dialogue between instructor and student.

The text's main divisions are called modules because each is largely an independent unit developing and reinforcing concepts in a single area. Each may be completed by a student working entirely on his own (with evaluation your only role), by conventional full-class instruction, or by a combination of both methods. Many exercises provide for group or team work. Each module ends with a mastery test, which in almost every case requires not merely fill-ins but student writing as evidence of competence. For further individualization, certain more difficult material has been set in boxes for optional assignment, as has supplementary material for the slower student.

Certain modules are designed to comprise, together, the core of the course, whereas others are intended only for students with problems in particular areas, such as spelling or agreement. You may arrange the sequence of modules as you wish, respecting only the stated prerequisites. The Instructors Manual suggests several sequences. At the end of the book there is a prescription page, on which you may lay out an individual course of learning for each student, based on his early writing samples.

So that each student may work on his own, answers have been provided—up to a point—at the end of each module. He can check these answers to see if he is on the right track. You can monitor his progress by examining his other answers—the ones the text does not give. (Suggested answers for these exercises are provided in the Instructors Manual.)

Most deserving my thanks for help in preparing this book are the thousands of college and high school students who have taught me how to teach English—especially the freshmen at York and Queensborough Community Colleges of the City University of New York and Nassau Community College; it is mostly their sentences and paragraphs I have used throughout the book. My grateful appreciation goes also to my colleagues at York, especially Professor Mary Epes, for their assistance and suggestions; to Phil Leininger and Marge Lakin of Thomas Y. Crowell for their editorial advice; and most of all to my wife, Betty, for her constant and invaluable support and assistance.

TO THE STUDENT

This book will not tell you how to write better; it will instead let you discover for yourself how to write better. You will find that becoming a better writer does not mean memorizing pages of rules and definitions, but discovering and using what has been in your brain for a long time. Much of it too is nothing more than common sense. Yet you should not expect good writing to come to you without hard work.

This book allows your instructor to custom-make a course for you as you both see what your writing needs are. Your instructor may write a prescription for the particular modules that you alone need, so that you will not have to spend time on what you can already do well. (A *module* is like a chapter but is more of a mini-course, with its own test at the end.) Your teacher may have you do much of the book on your own, for it is designed so that it can be done that way. Your instructor—and you—will know your progress as you both evaluate the writing and tests you do for each module; and, of course, the instructor will be watching your work along the way and helping you through the difficult spots.

How do you do the book on your own? By writing in all the answers asked for and checking the answer pages at the end of each module to see if you are right. Yes, the answers on each topic are given—but only up to a point; after that you are on your own. Although there is nothing to stop you from glancing at the given answers beforehand, you will not know whether you have really grasped an idea unless you write the answer *first* and only then look to see if you were right. Remember that eventually you will come to the questions with no answers given. How well you do these and the writing assignments that follow them is what your instructor will be concerned with most.

There are also places where you and the others in your class may look over each other's work to help each other out. Writing well is not easy. You will find much sweat and frustration in this course. But you *can* learn to write well, as others have done. And what you learn here you will need and use in every course you ever take, and in whatever you do for the rest of your life.

MODULE 1

GETTING STARTED

Previous modules required: none
(†There are no answers given in this module.)

Since we will be going through these modules together, the best way to begin is to introduce ourselves. My name is on the front of the book. Who are you? Tell a little about yourself:

Hello, my name is _____

and I come from _____ .

As we begin this course I am wondering _____

_____ .

In this class I would like most to learn _____

_____ .

Right now I am a little afraid that _____

_____ .

However, I do hope that _____

_____ .

Students often say that they just cannot think of anything to say or that they cannot get started when they try to write. But you have already completed the first writing assignment of the course! The world is full of things to write about—people, places, experiences, facts, ideas, beliefs, feelings, problems. . . . Take yourself, for example. You may not think so, but you have already gone through experiences that writers of stories, essays, plays, and poems have made masterpieces of: growing up, for example—and perhaps love, violence, loneliness, death of loved ones, and fear. You probably have already had ideas on improving the city or town where you live that make more sense than many schemes that come from the mayor's office. As a child and as a teenager you saw your parents or relatives fight over things you knew were not worth the fuss. You have seen your friends do foolish things; you have done foolish and embarrassing things yourself. You have doubled over laughing at incidents in high school or on your job. You have marveled at spring and cursed your boss or teacher or some stupid machine that would not work. You have had to tell people how to do things the right way. You have had to make agonizing decisions. You have been cheated, lied to, deceived by "friends." You have been laughed at, made to look foolish. You have been given traffic summons or school failures you did not deserve. You have been hurt.

On the other hand, you have had beautiful successes: you made that great play in the big game; you made the cheerleading squad; you finally outsmarted the person who cheated you; you won that big bet or landed that good job; you earned the money to buy your own car; you got the greatest boy/girl in the world to love you. You are going to college. Some of these were all the sweeter because someone had told you you could never do them.

In short, you have lived—and life is what people want to tell others about. For example, how often has a friend "blown off steam" to you—told you very forcefully why he was so angry at something? What have *you* blown off steam about lately? What makes you

most angry? _____

Here are more questions about yourself and your feelings toward the world. You may skip any that you would rather not answer. Write only about one sentence for each now:

What do you find ridiculous about the world you live in?

_____

_____

What gives you great pleasure—something that most people think would not do so?

_____

_____

What "turns you on" most?

_____

_____

What "turns you off" most?

_____

_____

Do you expect to be happier five years from now than you are now?

_____

_____

On what controversial issues are your beliefs opposite to those of most people you know?

_____

_____

If you had to join a cause, what cause would it be?

_____

_____

If there were a knowledge machine that could pour great knowledge of *one* area of human learning into your mind, what area would you choose?

_____

_____

In what ways has life hit you harder than it has hit most people?

_____

_____

In what ways are you more fortunate than most people?

_____

_____

In what other ways are you different from most people?

_____

_____

What have you noticed about the other people in this class?

_____

_____

"People are funny." How true is this?

_____

_____

What did people tell you you could never do that you did?

_____

_____

Your instructor may suggest other questions. Answer them in the spaces below:

a. _____

b. _____

c. _____

Now, from all the ideas you have written so far, pick three that you think you can say more about. For example, you may tell the *why* or *how* of an idea. In the spaces below, expand each of these three answers to three sentences each:

a. _____

_____

_____

_____

b. _____

_____

_____

_____

_____

c. _____

_____

_____

_____

_____

Next, think over these three ideas once more. Which one can you tell still more about—say seven or eight sentences altogether? This one you will be asked to let another student read. When you have chosen one, start again and write all you want to say about it on a separate sheet of paper, double-spaced. Then, if you are in a class, exchange papers with the student next to you.

If you now have another student's paper, read it. When you are finished, write in the space at the bottom of his paper one sentence to the student who wrote the paper. Tell him your reaction—whether you agree or disagree with him, for example, or how you like what he said. (If you want to say something negative, think first of how you will feel if the other person returns *your* paper with a negative comment on it.)

When you have your paper back, read the other student's comment and think about it. Does it make you want to change in any way what you wrote? Did he perhaps misunderstand what you wanted to say? Do you feel that you and the other person have *communicated* with each other, that you know and perhaps understand each other just a little better than when you both first walked into the classroom? That is what writing—in fact, all communication—is about: putting an idea from your mind into another person's mind as closely as possible to the way it was in your mind.

Your final task in this module is to make any changes you think are needed in the paper you wrote. Then, on a separate sheet, carefully recopy your piece of writing, double-spaced. When you have finished, read it over to catch possible slips in copying. Give the finished paper to your instructor. You do not need a title.

MODULE 2

CLEAR WRITING: THE FIRST STEPS

<u>Previous modules required:</u> Getting Started (1)*

INTRODUCTION

There is a story that once during the Russian Revolution a young officer of the czar's army, whom the czar suspected of being a secret revolutionist, was ordered imprisoned and sentence to die. But the czar's daughter, who was in love with the young officer, went to the czar and begged her father to spare him. The czar, moved by her plea, agreed, and, since it was near the hour set for the execution, he hastily scribbled a note to the general in charge of the prison to tell him that the officer's execution was impossible and that he should be pardoned.

The next morning, to their horror, the czar and his daughter received word that the officer had been executed on schedule. "What went wrong?" the czar thundered. "I clearly wrote *Pardon—Impossible to be executed.*" But when the general was brought to the czar to explain, he showed the note, which read *Pardon impossible to be executed,* and said "But sire, you clearly said *Pardon impossible—To be executed.*"

The obvious moral of the story, of course, is that we must be clear when we communicate. But there is more than that in the story. The czar assumed that his message was perfectly clear; he neglected to take time to consider whether it could be read differently by his reader. It is not easy to write clear, simple explanations. Remember the last time you tried to follow a written explanation, such as your friend's directions to his house, a recipe, the assembly instructions for a crated bicycle, the rules of a board game?

WRITING DIRECTIONS

How common is unclear writing? Below are (1) a set of directions a girl sent out with invitations to a big party she was giving at her house and (2) a map of the area. When you finish reading the directions, trace on the map with your pencil the route she has instructed you to follow until you reach the location of her house:

From Collegeboro, take Interstate 32 to Exit 17—Snavely Road. Go along Snavely Road several blocks, past two traffic lights, until you come to a gas station. Go left there to a stop sign three blocks down. Go down this block to the next intersection, and we're the house right on the corner. You can't miss it. See you at 8:30 next Friday! Love, Carol.

Is Carol's house at any of the numbered points on the map of Partyhaven? If so, at what numbered point? _____ If not, put an *x* at the location your direction-following led you to. (At this point your instructor may take a survey of the class to determine which point most students have arrived at, and whether it is the one Carol meant.)

Is there only one point to which Carol's directions definitely lead? _____ If not, why? Did Carol omit any needed information? If so, what?

_____

_____

_____

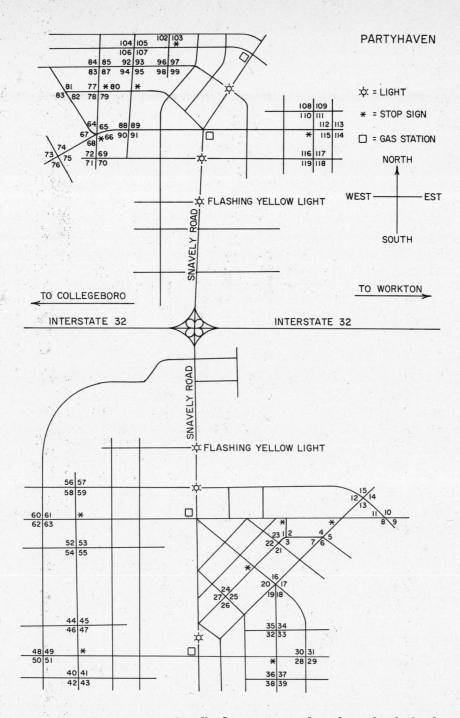

Now, on a separate paper, rewrite Carol's directions so that they clearly lead to only *one* point—let us say point 34. Then do whichever of the following items your instructor indicates:

A.   Give your rewritten directions to your instructor.

B.   Exchange papers with another student. Follow his directions with your pencil on the map. Do they lead to point 34? If not, write on his paper the point (or points) his directions led you to and return the paper. But first be sure the mistake was in his writing of the directions and not your reading of them. If he returns your directions saying they led him to the wrong point, make the needed corrections and give the directions to another student to follow. Repeat this process as often as necessary until your directions are clear enough to lead your reader directly to point 34.

C. Your instructor will name some other numbered point on the map, representing your apartment; he will also tell where your friends are coming from. Write a set of directions that will clearly lead your friends to your apartment.

D. Write a set of directions guiding a stranger from your classroom by foot to a room in a building at least half a mile away and not on the same street as your classroom building.

E. Follow the same directions as in D, but assume they are to be tape-recorded for a blind person to follow.

F. Bring to class an example of unclear instructions you have found such as those for the assembly or use of a product, or those in a recipe book or textbook, or rules explaining how to play a game. Be able to point out why they are unclear.

WRITING AN EXPLANATION

It is time for you to write an original explanation. Choose one of the following topics and in ten to twelve sentences explain it clearly to a person unfamiliar with the procedure. There is only one catch: You must use words in sentences only—no lists, illustrations, or diagrams:

How to cook lasagne (chitterlings, homemade chicken soup, etc.)

How to win at poker (on the horses, etc.)

How to make a person of the opposite sex interested in you

How to make yourself look glamorous

How to cheat successfully on an examination

How to avoid paying the check

How to change a diaper (traditional square cloth type)

The process by which a president can be removed from office

The process of choosing and being accepted at a college

The registration procedure of this college

1‡

Which topic did you choose? _____

Your explanation will not have a title; therefore what do you think your first sentence must

2‡

tell the reader? _____

Now, on a separate paper, write your explanation. When you have finished, exchange papers with another student—one who probably would not already know about what you have explained. Read her paper. How clear and complete was the explanation? On the back of the paper write whatever questions you want to ask about what she said, such as what she meant by a certain word or statement. Also, she might appreciate a few words of praise; if you found the writing clear or interesting, tell her so. Next, return the paragraph, reclaim your own, and read what was said about your writing. As a result of the questions and comments, do you want to make any changes on your paper? If so, do so, as neatly as possible. Your instructor may ask you to submit the paper to him.

By now you should be able to write generally clear explanations. However, there are two more problems that may arise as you try different kinds of explanatory writing. Can you see the first problem in the directions below? Consider how clearly they are written:

To reach my house from Collegeboro, which is two exits west on Interstate 32, about twenty miles—that is, exit 15, you go east on Interstate 32 to Exit 17 South— be sure not to go North—and get off there. You will see a Howard Johnson's on the left and a Sunoco station on your right. Turn right on Snavely Road—it's the only turn you can make. Go along Snavely for about a mile, past a flashing yellow light and two other regular lights to a Gulf station on your right. You will first pass a Shell station, but that's not it. The Gulf station is past several blocks that slant off to the left. Turn left at the Gulf station and go east three blocks—they are pretty short blocks— to a stop sign. Make a left there and after you have made this left go one block north to the next corner. I live in a red brick house, just like all the other houses on that corner. My house is the one across the intersection on the right side, which is the northeast corner. This time I've tried not to leave out anything important in these directions. I hope you find us. Love, Carol.

To what numbered point did Carol's new directions lead you? _____ Do

Carol's new directions lead you only to her house if you follow them exactly? _____
Then what is wrong with them? (Imagine yourself driving through the town and trying to read and follow her directions at the same time.)

_____

_____

Go back and cross out with a pencil everything that is superfluous (not needed) in these directions. Then compare what is left with your latest version of the directions you wrote on page 9. Are they almost the same or are they quite different?

_____

Carol's directions had so much extra information that the *wrong* words might stick in your mind instead of the right ones: Carol's mere inclusion of the unnecessary word *north* might make you wonder whether she had said "Go south, not north" or "Go north, not south." If north were not mentioned, this confusion could not happen. The same is true for *Gulf station* and *Shell station*. Instructions or explanations cluttered with unneeded information only confuse the reader.

Cross out all unneeded words in the following explanation. Assume that the reader is a stranger to subway travel. To determine what is really unneeded, pay attention to the first sentence; it states the writer's central idea—what he really wants to show the reader. Only information that fits under this idea should be in his explanation:

Though there are dozens of routes and about five hundred stations on the New York subways, a visitor will find the route-numbering system really quite simple to follow in traveling around the city. For most of the routes, single letters such as A, D, or F, are used to identify express routes—fast trains that skip some stations. Double letters, such as AA or EE, identify local trains, which make all stops. It was not always like this. The old BMT Division once had its own numbering system—1, 4, etc., although most trains never showed any numbers, just names such as Sea Beach or Culver. Few people know where the name Culver Line came from; there is no station, street, or neighborhood by that name. Then the BMT merged with the newer IND Division and adopted its lettering system. That led to much confusion at the time, and many people complained to the mayor. One part of the system, the IRT Division, uses numbers instead of letters today, since the city has more subway routes than there are letters in the alphabet. The letter-identified trains can never mix with the numbered trains because the IRT's tunnels are too narrow, some of them dating back to the turn of the century. In most cases, trains with letters or numbers close to each other serve the same outlying areas; for example, E, EE, F, and GG all go to the same area of Queens. Riding one of these lines is a unique experience, especially in the rush hour.

Check the answer page to see how you did.[7]

The second problem that may interfere with clear writing can be illustrated by the story of the husband whose wife left a note saying she would be home late for dinner and asking him to please bake a cake for dessert, following the simple recipe on page 63 of the cookbook. The husband dutifully assembled all the listed ingredients and began to read the directions. The first line said, "Separate four eggs." He thought a minute, scratched his head, then took four eggs out of the carton and carefully placed one in each corner of the pan.

Needless to say, this husband's baking adventure never went much further. Why? What did *separate* mean in the baking instructions?

[8]

_____

What did the husband take it to mean?

[9]

_____

Whose fault do you think it was that the cake was never baked—the husband's or the cook-

[10]‡

book writer's? _____

For an idea to be passed clearly from your mind to your reader's, then, you must be

sure the reader [11]u__d_____s the m_____g of the terms you use. Often we are so familiar with the technical terms of the things *we* know well that we forget that "outsiders" probably do not know them. A doctor might unthinkingly explain to a grieving widow that there had been no chance to give her husband an EKG or an IV because he was DOA. A gadget advertised as "so simple to assemble any woman can do it in a few minutes" may have assembly instructions that refer to Phillips-head screwdrivers and lock washers. A man who decides to do his own sewing may buy a machine with instructions that tell him to do this or that with the bobbin without ever telling or showing him what a bobbin is.

The writers of such explanations mistakenly [12]as__ __m__ that the reader understands these terms. Do you know what we call words that are known and used only by "insiders" of a

trade, profession, field of study, sport, etc.? The word is [13]j__ __g__n.

Do as many of the following as you can, without consulting a dictionary or any other reference source:

[14]‡Describe clearly a Phillips-head screwdriver or a lock washer, and tell its purpose.

_____

[15]Describe clearly a fan belt, and tell its purpose.

_____

[16]Describe clearly a bobbin, and tell its purpose.

_____

[17]Describe clearly basting *or* marinating, and tell its purpose.

_____

Your instructor may take a count of how many persons of each sex know the meanings of the above terms customarily known only by the other sex.

Below is an explanation that the writer thought was clear to general adult readers, such as the members of this class. If you think it is clear as it is, hand in a paper to your instructor which simply says *Clear as is*. If you think it needs to be made clearer, rewrite it more clearly on a separate paper and submit it to your instructor. You may consult a good dictionary, encyclopedia, or other reference book. Your instructor may have you work with several students on a group rewriting:

> *It has come to our attention that many citizens are having difficulty understanding the treaty our nation has just concluded with the Republic of Illyria. It is really very simple. All the signatories have agreed to respect the hegemony of Illyria over all its archipelagos, as well as the right of Illyria to maintain all its ancient customs in these areas, including primogeniture, unicameral legislatures, and indentured servitude.*

Check the answer page.[18]

EXPLAINING A SKILLED OPERATION

Each of us has some special skill; we can do something that most people cannot. On your job you may have learned to run a complex machine or complete some intricate operation. Perhaps you can play the guitar, give permanent waves, execute a perfect hook shot, conduct a Seder, tune up an engine, disarm an attacker, administer an electrocardiogram, mix an exotic drink, balance books, make your own dress, tell where the fish are biting, master the "expert" ski trail. You may know the differences between women's and men's basketball rules, the quickest routes to any point in the city, a way to outsmart the establishment. In short, you are an expert at something—probably at several things. Think of one special skill or knowledge you have that probably few or no other people in the class have. It can be as simple as something only persons of your sex would know, such as arranging a hairdo or choosing a good cigar. It should be something that you can explain in about eight to twelve sentences. (To fit this length you may have to explain only one part of a whole skill, procedure, or knowledge.)

¹‡What did you think of to write about?

_____

_____

²‡What will you tell or show the class about the topic you chose?

_____

_____

_____

³‡What jargon or other words will you have to explain?

_____

⁴‡What part of your explanation do you think the average reader in the class will find hardest to understand?

_____

_____

Before you begin, think carefully about how you will handle these difficulties.

As you did with the previous explanation you wrote, write what your first sentence must tell your reader. (There will be no title.)

5‡

_____

_____

Now, on a separate paper, write eight to twelve sentences explaining the topic you chose (without diagrams, drawings, or lists). When you have finished, exchange your paper with another student, following the same directions as you did for your previous original explanation (page 10).

REVIEW Before you take the mastery test for this module, here is a quick review of what you have learned:‡

¹‡Communication must be c_ _ _ _ to be successful.

²‡Clear writing never o_ _ts any n_ _ _ed information.

³‡Clear explanations o_ _ _ all un_ _ _ _ed information.

⁴‡Clear explanations avoid j_ _g_n that the average person does not

u_ _r_ _ _ _d.

MASTERY TEST Choose a topic from A or B:

A. A skill or special knowledge such as those mentioned for the last writing assignment (page 13), other than the one you already explained.

B. One of the following:
   (1) how to drive a standard-shift car (written for persons who can drive only automatic-shift cars)
   (2) how to play _____ (a moderately difficult card game—not one like bridge, which needs a whole book to be explained; write it for persons who know the names of the cards and a few simple card games)
   (3) how to execute some aspect of a sport, such as a certain kind of dive, basketball or football play, method of fishing
   (4) a topic suggested or approved by your instructor

Write a clear explanation of your topic in ten to fifteen sentences—first a rough copy, and then, after checking for clarity and revising, a neat copy. Submit it to your instructor.

ANSWERS

WRITING DIRECTIONS

[2]No

[3]Carol omitted which direction to turn when leaving Interstate 32; whether the flashing yellow signal counts as one of the two traffic lights; whether to make a full left or a half left at the gas station; which direction to go from the stop sign; on which of the four corners to find her house.

WRITING AN EXPLANATION

[3]Point 34

[4]Yes

[5]They contain more information than is needed; this extra information makes the directions seem more complicated than they are and may confuse the reader.

[6]The words lined out below are definitely not needed; the words dotted out may also be omitted:

To reach my house from Collegeboro, ~~which is two exits west on Interstate 32, about twenty miles—that is, exit 15~~, you go east on Interstate 32 to Exit 17 South—~~be sure not to go North~~—and get off there. ~~You will see a Howard Johnson's on the left and a Sunoco station on your right.~~ Turn right on Snavely Road—~~it's the only turn you can make.~~ ~~Go along Snavely for about a mile~~, past a flashing yellow light and two other regular lights to a Gulf station on your right. ~~You will first pass a Shell station, but that's not it. The Gulf station is past several blocks that slant off to the left.~~ Turn left at the Gulf station and go ~~east~~ three blocks—~~they are pretty short blocks~~—to a stop sign. Make a left there and ~~after you have made this left~~ go one block ~~north to the next corner. I live in a red brick house, just like all the other houses on that corner.~~ My house is the one across the intersection on the right side, ~~which is the northeast corner.~~ . . .

Your version and this version should be the same or almost the same.

[7]The words lined out below are not needed, since the selection is merely explaining to a stranger how to find his way on the subways; the words dotted out may also be omitted:

Though there are dozens of routes and about five hundred stations on the New York subways, a visitor will find the route-numbering system really quite simple to follow in traveling around the city. For most of the routes, single letters, such as A, D, or F, are used to identify express routes—fast trains that skip some stations. Double letters, such as AA or EE, identify local trains, which make all stops. ~~It was not always like this. The old BMT Division once had its own numbering system—1, 4, etc., although most trains never showed any numbers, just names, such as Sea Beach or Culver. Few people know where the name Culver Line came from; there is no station, street or neighborhood by that name. Then the BMT merged with the newer IND Division and adopted its lettering system. That led to much confusion at the time, and many people complained to the mayor.~~ One part of the system, the IRT Division, uses numbers instead of letters ~~today since the city has more subway routes than there are letters in the alphabet. The letter-identified trains can never mix with the numbered trains because the IRT's tunnels are too narrow, some of them dating back to the turn of the century.~~ In most cases, trains with letters or numbers close to each other serve the same outlying areas; for example, E, EE, F, and GG all go to the same area of Queens. ~~Riding one of these lines is a unique experience, especially in the rush hour~~.

⁸To break the egg and separate the yolk from the white

⁹To keep the whole eggs as far apart as possible

¹¹understands, meaning

¹²assume

¹³jargon

¹⁸The words that readers might not understand, and that should be replaced, are signatories, hegemony, archipelagos, primogeniture, unicameral, indentured, servitude. What did your dictionary say they mean?

MODULE**3**

THE CENTRAL IDEA

Previous modules required: Getting Started (1)*—Clear Writing: The First Steps (2)*

INTRODUCTION Read the following selections:

SELECTION A

A pilot doesn't feel at home in a plane until he's flown it for thousands of miles. At first it's like moving into a new house. The key doesn't slip into the door smoothly; the knobs and light switches aren't where you put your hand; the stairs don't have proper spacing, and the windows bind as you raise them. Later, after you've used the the key a hundred times, it fits at once, turns easily in the lock. Knobs and switches leap to meet your fingers on the darkest night. The steps touch your feet in perfect timing; and windows slide open with an easy push. My test flights in California, the long hours of night above deserts and mountains of the Southwest, the swift trip over the Alleghenies to New York, have removed the feel of newness from The Spirit of St. Louis. Each dial and lever is in the proper place for glance or touch; and the slightest pressure on controls brings response. My ears have become accustomed to the radial engine's tempo. It blends with the instrument readings and the clearing mist to instill a feeling of confidence and hope.

SELECTION B

Haze thickens behind me until the coastline becomes lost. I know now what my father meant when he warned me, years ago, of depending too heavily on others. The earth-inductor compass needle leans right. How much ice has accumulated on the plane? Can those be the same stars? I've lost command of my eyelids. The very instability which makes it difficult to fly blind or hold an accurate course at night now guards me against excessive errors. I'd almost forgotten the moon. I glance at the chart on my lap. Maybe the steady periods aren't caused by the magnets pointing toward the pole. Here, it's two o'clock in the morning.

Which selection makes more sense to you; that is, in which is it easier to understand

[1]

what the writer is trying to show you? _____ (One of the next two answers should be easy; the other may not be answerable at all.)

[2]The writer of selection A is trying to show us that

_____

_____

[3]The writer of selection B is trying to show us that

_____

_____

Why were you able to understand one selection clearly, but not the other? Both are *about* the same subject: Charles Lindbergh's famous transatlantic flight. What then is the difference? Let us look more closely at each of the selections.

Selection A gives us ten sentences of ideas. Lindbergh talks *about* feeling at home in a plane; moving into a new house; getting keys and windows to work; learning where switches and stairs are; flying over mountains and deserts; becoming familiar with dials, levers, controls, and engine tempo; and feeling confidence and hope. But is there one of the ten sentences that announces what the whole selection intends to show us? If there is, circle that sentence in selection A.‡

Selection B gives us eleven sentences of ideas. Lindbergh talks *about* losing the coastline, not depending on others, the earth-inductor compass, ice, stars, sleepiness, his plane's instability, the moon, his chart, the magnetic compass, and the time. But is there one of the eleven sentences that announces what the whole selection intends to show us? If there is, circle that sentence in selection B.‡

Look again at blank 2; does what you wrote there generally match what you circled in selection A? It should. Now look at blank 3; were you able to state what selection B intends to show us and circle a sentence that generally matches it? If you completed blank 3 and/or circled a sentence in selection B, are you sure that is what the *whole* selection intends to show?

It is time to reveal the secret: Selection A is a whole paragraph taken directly from Charles A. Lindbergh's book, *The Spirit of St. Louis,** but selection B is merely a collection of unconnected sentences from various pages of the same book. Selection B has no single idea that it intends to show us, no point to make. If you could not complete blank 3 or circle any sentence in selection B, your thinking is sharp! Look back at blank 1. Did you choose selection A there? If you did, you were right again; you have already grasped a good part of the central idea of this module: that to make sense, a writer must have in his mind not merely a *topic* he wants to write about but an *idea* on the topic that he wants to show his readers.

Selection B made little overall sense because it had no such idea; selection A made sense because it did, and it announced this idea to the readers in one sentence. Check the answer page to see whether this is the same sentence you circled. It should have been.[4] Even though all the sentences in the selection contain ideas, the idea in this circled sentence is special because it controls what belongs in the paragraph. It sets the boundaries outside of which no sentence in the paragraph may go. It is the umbrella that all the other ideas fit under. It is the center that the paragraph focuses on. Therefore we call the idea in this

sentence the [5]c__ __t__ __l idea.

As you will see in this and future courses, any single piece of writing, from a paragraph to a thousand-page book, needs a central idea. When your high school English teacher asked you to search for the *theme* of a poem or story or told you to improve your *topic sentence,* he was just using other words for *central idea.* In fact, when you hear professors talk about

the *thesis* of some scholar's work, what do you think they mean? [6]C__ __ __ __ __ __ __ __ __ __. Why should you bother about a central idea? Have you heard people say, "I never worry about that stuff? If the teacher says to write about flying, I just put down whatever comes into my head about flying." Such people may unconsciously be developing a central idea in their writing, but more often they are producing writing like selection B.

What seems the most sensible place in the paragraph to put the sentence that

[7]
announces your central idea? _____ Was the central idea of

[8‡]
selection A in that position? _____ That is the usual position for a central idea

---

* New York: Scribner's, 1953, p. 191.

sentence. The simplest way to make your meaning clear to a reader is to tell him right away what you intend to show him.

Here is another paragraph. Find the central idea sentence. Circle it:

SELECTION C

Many state authorities are now supporting strong state regulations to clean up [substandard] vocational schools. For example, after Texas put through a tough new regulatory law, about one-third of the state's private vocational schools shut down. The Education Commission of the States has proposed model licensing legislation, calling for strict standards of financial stability, equipment, and instruction in all states. Congressmen Alphonzo Bell and Jerry L. Pettis, both of California, have introduced a bill requiring the Secretary of Health, Education and Welfare to make a study of the Federal Government's involvement in funding private vocational schools and to adopt new procedures to prevent students from being cheated.

— Jean Cooper, "Career Schools
Aren't Always What They Claim,"
Reader's Digest (June, 1974), p. 145

Check your answer.[9] Incidentally, by now you should be coming to understand what a *paragraph* is. It is a group of sentences—usually from about four to fifteen—developing a central idea.

Now we will move one step further. The central idea sentence has been removed from the following paragraph. Read the paragraph, decide what its central idea is, and then write a central idea sentence for the paragraph: (Caution: You are not being asked to write a *title*, such as "My Brother Charlie" or "An Unusual Person." Write the first *sentence* of the paragraph. If you are unsure about exactly what is or is not a sentence, write something in the form of what you circled in selections A and C.)

SELECTION D

Topic: My Brother Charlie

10‡

_____

_____

_____

He puts mustard on his poached eggs. He paints yellow polka-dots on his green car. Once after reading about how college students used to swallow live goldfish, he tried to gulp down a live caterpillar. Another time he poured catsup all over his chest and staggered into a hospital emergency room; he spent a night in jail for that. His latest idea is to stand outside supermarkets wearing a Little Orphan Annie wig, soliciting money for air fare to find Daddy Warbucks.

When you have written the central idea, do whichever of the following your instructor directs:

A. Exchange central idea sentences with another student. Write in pencil a comment about her sentence and return her paper.

B. Submit your central idea sentence to your instructor.

C. Check your central idea sentence with a model provided by the instructor.

Next, you will use your understanding of *central idea* in a seven-to-nine-sentence paragraph of your own on a topic your instructor suggests or approves. (You may want to pick one from the master list, page 483, or an unused topic from a previous module.) First, choose the topic and write it here:

11‡

_____

Below you will find a drawing of an umbrella. In the space under the umbrella, jot down a list of everything that comes into your head about the topic. (Write only a list, not full sentences, and do not worry now about the order of the items.) Squeeze all you can out of your mind. Do you recall that a few pages back a central idea was compared to an umbrella? After rereading the items on your list, ask yourself what you want to show the class about the topic. The answer will, of course, be your central idea. Write it in the blank at the top of the umbrella.

If we think of the central idea as an umbrella, then what does the space under the umbrella represent? As you may have guessed, it represents the area covered by the central

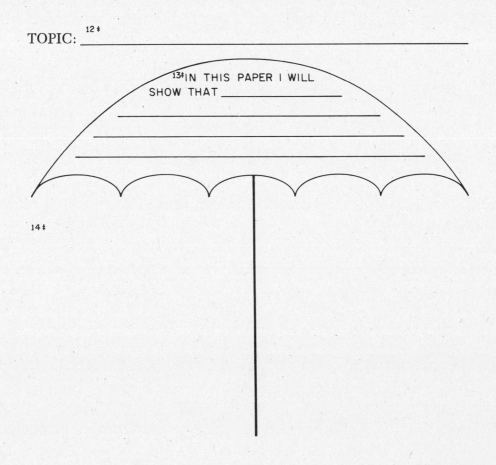

TOPIC: ¹²‡ _____

¹³‡IN THIS PAPER I WILL
SHOW THAT _____

14‡

idea. Examine all the items you jotted down under the umbrella. If any items on your list do not belong under the central idea, cross them out.‡ (These crossed-out ideas may be

suitable for another paragraph with a different [15]c_ _ _ _ _ _ i_ _ _ _.)

Now, on a separate paper write your paragraph. Begin with the exact words you wrote following the word *that* in the blank at the top of the umbrella. This will be your

[16]c_ _ _ _ _ _ _ i_ _ _ _ sentence. When you finish the paragraph, exchange paragraphs with another student for mutual evaluation or submit it to your instructor, as he directs.

FORMING A CENTRAL IDEA

Forming a central idea is not always easy. Students often confuse a *central idea* with a restatement of the topic. For example, Professor Smart asked his class to write a paper comparing today's movie heroes with those of the 1930s and 1940s. They were instructed to write a central idea first. Which of these four students actually wrote a central *idea*?

Student A: *In this paper I will discuss movie heroes.*
Student B: *In this paper I will compare recent movie heroes with older ones.*
Student C: *In this paper I will show how today's movie heroes compare with heroes of the 1930s and 1940s.*
Student D: *In this paper I will show that today's movie heroes are less exciting than the heroes of the 1930s and 1940s.*

[1]

Only one is a true central idea. Which? _ _ _ _ _ _ _ _ _
Why? How is this different from the others?

[2]

_ _

Look again at all four. What does each tell us that we do not *already* know from the words of the topic: "Comparing today's movie heroes with those of the 1930s and 1940s"? What

[3] [4]

does A tell? _ B? _ _ _ _ _ _ _ _ _ _ _ _ _

[5] [6]

_ _ _ _ _ _ _ _ _ _ _ _ _ C? (Be careful. Does C really tell us something or only seem to?)

_ _ _ _ _ _ _ _ _ _ _ _ _ _ _ _ _ _ _ D? _ _ _ _ _ _ _ _ _ _ _ _ _

_ _ _ _ _ _ _ _

Only student D actually wrote a statement telling what he was going to *show* about the topic: that recent heroes are less exciting than older ones. This is what a central idea

must do; otherwise it is not an [7]i_ _ _, but only a repetition of the topic. How can you be sure you have written a real central idea and not just restated the topic? Using a certain word will guarantee that you will write a full idea. What word did D use immediately after

[8]

"The central idea of my paper is . . ."? _ _ _ _ _ Only a full idea can follow this word.

Try writing a central idea. Which party do you believe will win the next presidential election, the Democrats or the Republicans? Assume that you have been assigned to write a paper giving your opinion on the outcome of that election. Write a central idea for such a paper by completing this statement (being sure to keep the word *that*):

[9]"In this paper I will show that _____

_____."

Next, look over any two or three paragraphs you have written so far in this course (except the one you wrote for this module). For each, complete this statement:

[10]*Paragraph 1:* "In this paper I have shown that _____

_____."

[11]*Paragraph 2:* "In this paper I have shown that _____

_____."

[12]*Paragraph 3:* "In this paper I have shown that _____

_____."

Can you circle a sentence in each of these paragraphs that states the central idea you have just written for that paragraph? If so, circle it. If not, write one in where it fits best and then circle it. Your instructor may ask to see these.

Not only for the papers in this course but for every paper or report you ever write, you will need a central idea. You have learned that to ensure writing a real *idea* you need

[13]

what word in your central idea statement? "In this paper I will show _____. . . ."

Assume that you are going to write paragraphs on *five* of the following topics. Think of a central idea for each of those five, and write a central idea statement for each. Each statement should begin with the words "In this paper I will show that. . . ." For example, if you were writing on the topic "School Busing," your central idea statement might resemble this: "In this paper I will show that busing is the only practical way to give inner-city children educational equality."

[14]American sports and money

_____

[15]Preferential hiring of minorities and women

_____

[16]Honesty and success in politics (college, the job, etc.)

_____

[17]Careers I have rejected

_____

18‡Urban renewal in my community

19‡The college (or high school) grading system

20‡Integrated communities

Your instructor may add other topics. He may check the central ideas you have written. Revise any that he tells you to.

FINDING WHICH IDEA IS CENTRAL

Often one item you have jotted down on a list of ideas under a topic will be enough for a central idea by itself. Let us say that your instructor has asked you to write a paragraph describing a place that has been important in your life. You choose Lake Squmpagook, and under the umbrella you jot down these ideas as they come into your head—in no particular order:

TOPIC: _____An important place in my life—Lake Squmpagook_____

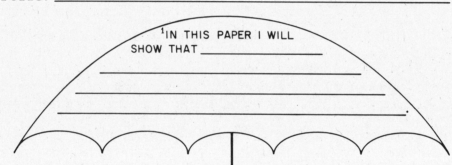

¹IN THIS PAPER I WILL SHOW THAT _____

Lake Squmpagook
towering mountains
state headquarters of Women's
   Conservation League located there
Mount Silvertop overlooks
fifteen miles long
trail to top—rough trip
Robert Smythe new state ecology
   commissioner
over 150 lakes in twenty-mile radius
still go camping with Fatty and Charlie

northeast corner of state
trees start to turn in August
rustic cabins on shores
went to camp for city children there—
   age ten
old Indian arrowheads in sand
legend says bottomless
learned to love natural world there
Fatty Melton upset canoe

From these ideas pick *one* that would make a valid central idea. (Hint: Will it be a single detail or a broad, general statement?) Write your central idea on the top part of the umbrella. Check it in the answer section. Now cross out any ideas remaining under the umbrella that do not seem to belong under your central idea. Check your work in the answer section.[2]

Sometimes, however, you may have to put together several items from your list to form your full central idea statement. Look at the following umbrella. From the jotted-down notes (in no particular order) under this new umbrella, which four items seem to be parts of the main point the writer wants to show us?

[3]

_____

_____

_____

_____

TOPIC: _____ An important place in my life—Lake Squmpagook _____

[4] IN THIS PAPER I WILL
SHOW THAT _____

_____

_____

_____

Lake Squmpagook	icy water—once could see twenty feet down
deep blue sky	went to camp for city children there—age ten
price of outboard motors has tripled in ten years	old Indian arrowheads in sand
towering mountains	legend says bottomless
Mount Silvertop overlooks	returned last year—lake polluted
northeast corner of state	Fatty Melton upset canoe
fifteen miles long	oil slick, dead fish, floating garbage
learned to love natural world there	still go camping with Fatty and Charlie
rustic cabins on shore	state headquarters of Women's Conservation League located there
over 150 lakes in twenty-mile radius	shocked, saddened on revisit
trees start to turn in August	railroad stopped running there twelve years ago
man's thoughtlessness	
Robert Smythe new state ecology director	

What is the writer trying to show us? From the items in this second umbrella, he seems to want to express his sadness and shock at learning how man's thoughtless pollution can destroy a place of beauty that in his childhood had given him a love for the natural world. This thought must be shaped into a central idea sentence. Can you do it? Try:

[5]"In this paper I will show that at Lake Squmpagook, where I once learned

_____, I have also _____

_____

_____."

After you have checked this central idea with your instructor or with the answer page, revise it if necessary; then copy it at the top of the umbrella.

Now that you have your central idea, what is the next step?

[6]

_____

Do that now with the items listed. You should find at least four such items.

Check your answers.[7]

Here is more practice. For each of the following umbrellas, examine the listed ideas and try to find a central idea. (Each list has been taken from a selection by a professional writer.) You may be able to take the central idea directly from one of the listed ideas, or you may have to compose your central idea by thinking of what most of the listed ideas together seem to show:

TOPIC: _____ Tess's face _____

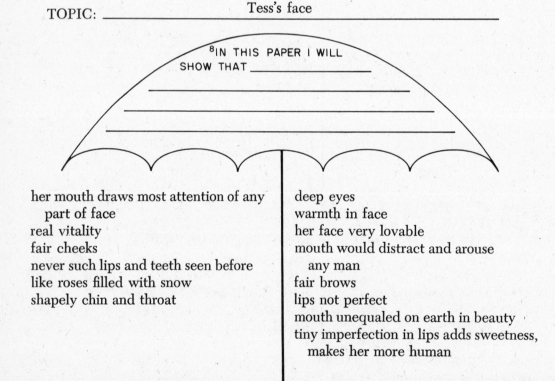

[8]IN THIS PAPER I WILL SHOW THAT _____

her mouth draws most attention of any
    part of face
real vitality
fair cheeks
never such lips and teeth seen before
like roses filled with snow
shapely chin and throat

deep eyes
warmth in face
her face very lovable
mouth would distract and arouse
    any man
fair brows
lips not perfect
mouth unequaled on earth in beauty
tiny imperfection in lips adds sweetness,
    makes her more human

— From Thomas Hardy, *Tess of the D'Urbervilles* (New York: Dell, 1962), p. 173

TOPIC: _____The City of Istanbul, Turkey_____

[9†]IN THIS PAPER I WILL
SHOW THAT _____
_____
_____
_____

Istanbul no longer capital of Turkey
   (Ankara is)
but economic center of nation
7 percent of Turkey's people live there
most trading in bazaars
bazaars much bigger than U.S. shopping
   centers
the Egyptian Market one of major
   trading centers

Egyptian Market 300 years old
city divided into four sections—
   called Galata, Uskudar, Stamboul,
   and Pera
one-third of Turkey's shipping goes through
   Istanbul
the Great Bazaar one of two major
   trading centers
Great Bazaar 2 million square feet and
   500 years old
Great Bazaar and Egyptian Market in
   Galata section of city

— From James Stewart-Gordon, "Immortal Istanbul," *Reader's Digest* (January, 1974), p. 153

TOPIC: _____Blacks in Baseball_____

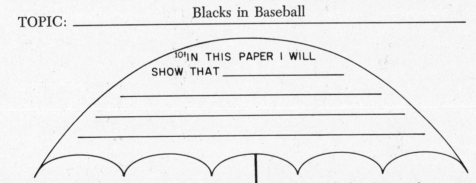

[10†]IN THIS PAPER I WILL
SHOW THAT _____
_____
_____
_____

Bud Fowler—first black on a
   white team, 1860
Moses Walker, a black—American
   Association catcher, 1884
Welday Walker (Moses' brother)
   on the same club later
William Higgins, another black also in
   early major league
Cap Anson, famous white player, led
   antiblack campaign in 1880s—
   had blacks barred from major leagues

white backlash—late 19th century—
   set color line in pro ball
slaves played baseball
black teams in South before Civil War
1880—twenty blacks on minor league rosters
Jackie Robinson not first black major
   leaguer

— From Jack Orr, *The Black Athlete: His Story in American History* (New York: Pyramid
Books, 1969), pp. 65–66

It is now time to write another paragraph of your own. Choose a topic from those your instructor suggests (or, if he permits, from those for which you wrote central ideas on pages 25–26). Follow the same steps as you did last time: (1) Jot down under the umbrella every idea that comes into your head about the topic; (2) from those ideas, form a central idea and write it at the top of the umbrella; (3) check all the remaining ideas under the umbrella against the central idea and cross out ideas that do not belong under the central idea. Then think of the order in which you want to present the remaining details (you may want to number them); now write the paragraph—seven to nine sentences.

When you have finished, do either A or B below, as your instructor directs:

A. Exchange papers with another student. In *pencil*, circle the sentence you think the other student intended to be his central idea. Then lightly cross out any sentences or parts of sentences that you believe do not belong under that central idea. Return papers; consider the other student's thoughts about your paper; make (in ink) any changes you wish and submit the paper to your instructor.

B. Circle in pencil the sentence that contains your central idea and submit your paper to your instructor.

FOCUSING THE CENTRAL IDEA STATEMENT

(If your instructor sees that you are already writing very good central ideas, he may tell you to bypass one or both of the following sections.)

By now you probably have mastered the form of the central idea. You know that the key word is

[1]t _ _ _. But is just the proper form enough? Are your central idea statements really capturing the essence (the heart, the core) of what you want to show? Look at this central idea: "In this paper I will show that widespread political corruption has had an effect on the American

people." Does this have the proper *form* for a central idea? [2] _____ But what question probably comes into most people's minds after reading it?

[3A]

_____

Do you think this writer really wants to show us only that there is an effect, without telling us what that effect is? Assume the writer feels that the corruption has made many Americans distrust all politicians; write an improved version of his central idea statement:

[3B]"In this paper I will show that widespread political corruption has _____

_____

_____."

Let us look further into this problem of writing good central ideas. A student wrote, "In this paper I will show that in the next few years the American people's tastes in cars will

change." Does this have the proper form for a central idea? [4] _____ But does it really state the main point that the writer wants to make? Does he really want to show us just that tastes in cars will change, or does he probably want to tell us *how* and *why* he thinks they will change? Can you rewrite his central idea to include the *how*? Assume that the writer sees a change from today's cars to even smaller cars:

[5]"In this paper I will show that in the next few years _____

_____

_____."

Such a central idea statement zeroes in much more on the author's real main point than the first statement does. But have we really reached the writer's true central idea yet? Will his paper be finished when he has told us *how* he thinks tastes in cars will change? What about *why*? Would you as his reader accept his prediction if he gave you no reason for it? Assume that he thinks constantly increasing gasoline prices will cause this change; rewrite his central idea once more to include the *why*:

[6]"In this paper I will show that _____

_____ because _____

_____."

This is a good, solid central idea statement because it includes the *full* central idea—the main point that the writer will have shown us by the time we have finished reading his paper. To sum up: This writer did not want to show us just that tastes in cars will change, nor just how they will change, but mainly why; thus his central idea statement must stress the *why*.

Many (though not all) central idea statements need a *why*, and the simplest way to

supply that *why* is to include in your statement the word [7]b__c____s__, as we just did in the final central idea statement about cars. You try some. Improve these central idea statements, making up whatever ideas or reasons you need:

Original	*Improved*
[8]In this paper I will show that the structure of family life has changed in the past twenty years.	In this paper I will show that the structure of family life has _____ _____ _____ because _____ _____ _____.

[9]In this paper I will show that my child-hood visit to Lake Squmpagook was significant in my life.

In this paper I will show that my child-

hood visit to Lake Squmpagook _____

_____

_____

_____

_____ .

[10]In this paper I will show that I remember my grandfather's death. (Hint: What significance does this event have for the writer?)

In this paper I will show that my grand-

father's death _____

_____

_____

_____ .

Here is a small modification of what you have just learned. Its purposes are to put first things first and to prevent your central idea from rambling. Let us use the central idea about cars as an example. Our final statement was "In this paper I will show that the American people's taste in cars in the next few years will change to even smaller economy models because of constantly rising gasoline prices." If the *cause*, the gasoline price rise, is going to receive most emphasis in your paper, why not put the cause first in your central idea statement? Try it. "In this paper I will show that

in the next few years [11]c_ _ _ _ _ _ _ _ _ly r_ _ _ing g_ _ _ _ _ _ _ _ _

p_ _ _ _ _ will cause Americans to c_ _ _ _ _ _ to even s_ _ _ _ _ _ _

e_ _ _ _ _ _y c_ _ _s."

Try it now with another one:

Original

[12]In this paper I will show that life in many cities today has become a nightmare because of the corruption of officials in charge of vital services.

Improved

In this paper I will show that c ___

_____

_____

has made l_____

In later modules on sentence structure you will have more practice on putting main ideas into main positions.

There are two more points to make regarding central ideas. To discover the first point, read this central idea statement: "In this paper I will show that life in many cities today has become a nightmare because of lack of federal funds, crime, corrupt officials, greedy municipal unions, overcrowded schools, broken-down transportation, polluted water, decaying neighborhoods, and welfare abuses." What do you think is wrong with this as a central idea statement?

13

_____

Remember that a central idea is *one* idea. The statement above is virtually an outline of the whole paper. How could this statement be revised to focus on *one* central idea? In either of two ways: (1) Can you think of one term which covers all the causes mentioned? What is the root cause of all those causes? Is it lack of money, human greed, indifference of local, state, and federal officials? The writer should not scatter his shot but pick *one* ultimate cause and mention only that in his central idea. Try it with the above central idea statement:

[14]"In this paper I will show that life in many cities today has become a

nightmare largely because of _____."

(2) What if there is no single ultimate cause? Unless you want to write something close to the length of a book, you could not possibly discuss fully all the causes of the urban nightmare listed in the original central idea. You still need a focus. What can you do? Try filling in this central idea statement:

[15]"In this paper I will show that out of the many causes of today's urban

nightmare, _____ is one of the most important."

Whatever cause you pick, you admit there are others and mention them briefly, but you give a detailed discussion of *one* prominent cause; you focus on *one* central idea.

That word *one* leads us to the next question. "In this paper I will show that Roman civilization accomplished many architectural marvels and it was destroyed by internal corruption." What, if anything, is wrong with this central idea that could lead the writer into composing a poor paper?

16

_____

The central idea consists of two statements joined by *and*. What are they?

17A

_____

17B

_____

Other than that they both concern Rome, what connection do they have with each other?

18

_____ Can they, as they are written, form one central idea?

19

_____ The writer actually has *two* central ideas. She probably should write two separate papers. If she wants to write *one* paper, what can she do? There are two possibilities: The first is quite simple; she can [20]el_ _ _ _ate o_ _ i_ _ _. Write what her central idea might become if she did that:

[21]"In this paper I will show that _____

_____."

The second solution depends on whether the writer actually sees a connection between the two statements, even though none comes through in her statement. In such a case, what should she do with her original statement?

[22]Re_ _ _ _ _ _ it so that _____

_____

Let us suppose that she was trying to bring out the tragic contrast that the same nation with brains to produce such technical marvels as the Coliseum, the Appian Way, and the great aqueducts did not have the brains to stop its own destruction from within. Now we can see a way in which those two ideas *can* form a single central idea. Write a good central idea statement showing the connection between these two ideas. The word *and* should not appear:

[23]"In this paper I will show that al_ _ _ _ _gh the R_____

_____

_____."

Remember: If you find that your central idea contains two statements joined by *and* (not just two words, such as *Washington and Lincoln,* or short word groups, such as *in the country and in the city*), you probably have *two* central ideas instead of one. Drop one idea or rewrite the central idea to show how the two ideas are connected.

GAINING EXPERIENCE WITH CENTRAL IDEA STATEMENTS

Now that you have discovered all the basics of writing good central ideas, practice on these. Each of the original central idea statements below contains some kind of weakness. Improve each statement, inventing additional information when necessary:

Original	Improved
[1] In this paper I will discuss my attitude toward equal rights for homosexuals.	In this paper I will _____ _____ _____.
[2] In this paper I will show how an LSD trip affects a person.	In this paper I will _____ _____ _____.
[3] In this paper I will give my opinion of the novel *The House on Glansvere Moor*.	In this paper I will _____ _____ _____.
[4] In this paper I will show that growing up in a ghetto affects your whole life.	In this paper I will _____ _____ _____.
[5] In this paper I will show that radio can be more entertaining than television and radio commercials cost the sponsor less than television commercials.	In this paper I will _____ _____ _____ _____.

Some of the next five may be satisfactory as they are. If they are, just write "satisfactory" on the right. If they are not, improve them as you did the first five:

[6] In this paper I will show that I can look back on memories of spending a

In this paper I will _____

weekend at my grandfather's when I was a child and still remember my feelings.

_____

_____

_____.

7‡In this paper I will show that experiencing the birth of a second child is no less thrilling than experiencing the birth of the first.

In this paper I will _____

_____

_____

_____.

8‡In this paper I will show that college buildings should be designed to accommodate handicapped people because such people are equally entitled to an education, they often do better than non-handicapped students, education will make them productive members of society, and they will be able to share in the fun of college life.

In this paper I will _____

_____

_____

_____

_____

_____.

9‡In this paper I will show that grammar book writers, who tell us to always use the word _he_ when a person's sex is unknown, are male chauvinists.

In this paper I will _____

_____

_____.

10‡In this paper I will show that Senator Flinch's legislative record will earn him reelection this year.

In this paper I will _____

_____

_____

_____.

In Module 1 you were asked to answer questions about yourself. Here are some of the same questions again. This time, however, instead of merely answering them, use the answer as a basis of a central idea statement for a paper you might write on the question. For example, for the question "What makes you most angry?" you might have written in Module 1, "Boys assuming that all girls are gold diggers." This time, under _Central idea,_ you would write, "In this paper I will show that boys are unfair to assume that all girls are gold diggers." Here is that question again, along with seven others. Answer any five:

What makes you most angry?

[11]‡Answer: _____

[12]‡Central idea: _____

_____

_____

What do you find ridiculous about the world you live in?

[13]‡Answer: _____

[14]‡Central idea: _____

_____

_____

What gives you great pleasure—something most people think would not do so?

[15]‡Answer: _____

[16]‡Central idea: _____

_____

_____

What "turns you on" most?

[17]‡Answer: _____

[18]‡Central idea: _____

_____

_____

What "turns you off" most?

[19]‡Answer: _____

[20]‡Central idea: _____

_____

_____

Do you expect to be happier five years from now than you are now?

[21‡]Answer: _____

[22‡]Central idea (Hint: Include the *because*.): _____

_____

_____

On what controversial issue are your beliefs opposite to those of most people you know?

[23‡]Answer: _____

[24‡]Central idea: _____

_____

_____

If you had to join a cause, what cause would it be?

[25‡]Answer: _____

[26‡]Central idea: _____

_____

_____

Your instructor may wish to examine your central ideas.

FINAL TOUCHES

Now that you have become proficient at writing central ideas, it is time for you to learn that the words "In this paper I will show that" are only for you, the writer. They help you form a central idea. They do not appear in the actual paper—only the words after *that* appear. For example, if your central idea statement reads, "In this paper I will show that San Diego has the best weather of any city in the United States," what actually appears in your paper is just "San Diego has the best weather of any city in the United States." Lindbergh did not begin his paragraph on page 20 with "In this paper I will show that a pilot doesn't. . . ." These words are not needed in your final paper. Always use them when you are forming your central idea on your scrap paper, but drop them in the final version. Go back to the last five central ideas you wrote in the exercises above and cross out "In this paper I will show that."‡

Must every paragraph have a central idea? Except for certain special kinds of paragraphs (usually very short ones, such as quotations) the answer is *yes*. But does the central idea statement always have to come at the beginning? As you advance in your study of writing you will see that writers sometimes like to put it at the end or almost anywhere else. Sometimes the central idea is not directly stated at all, but merely implied. For the less experienced writer, however, the simplest and safest place is at the beginning.

If your instructor directs, turn back to Selection D on page 22—the one about crazy Charlie. Look at the central idea sentence you wrote; then cover it with your hand so that the paragraph begins with *He puts mustard* . . . . Now recopy your central idea sentence at the end of the paragraph.‡ Reread this paragraph. Do you like the way it sounds? Is it better this way than with the central idea at the beginning? Many experienced writers might prefer it this way. As you gain in experience and confidence, you might want to try putting some of your central ideas at the end, leading up to them as stories lead to their climaxes.

Do longer pieces of writing need a central idea? As we said near the beginning of this module, *yes*. In fact, the longer the piece, the easier it is for the writer to lose sight of his central idea; thus no matter how extensive his piece of writing is, even if it is a complete book, he must have a central idea. If he is writing a ten-chapter book, the whole book will have its central idea, each of the chapters will have its own central idea, and each paragraph in the body of each chapter will have *its* own central idea. On your level, if you write a paper with a body of three paragraphs, you will have a central idea for the whole paper, and a central idea for each of the three paragraphs in the body of the paper. Naturally, each of those three central ideas will belong under the central idea of the whole paper. (If your paper has short paragraphs of introduction and conclusion, these do not need central ideas.) Here is a full-length essay. Circle the central idea sentence of each paragraph, and put brackets [ ] around the central idea sentence of the *whole* essay:‡

End Privileged Parking

One day last week I had to run a quarter of a mile in pouring rain from the student parking lot to my first class. Just outside the classroom building there were over twenty empty parking spaces in the area marked "Reserved for Faculty Vehicles." Spending the rest of the week in bed with a cold, I concluded that the college must eliminate privileged parking for the faculty and administration as impractical, unfair, and undemocratic. Since over half the students commute to campus by car and all student parking is restricted to the "boondocks" lot beyond the athletic field, the problem is clearly an important one.

Privileged parking for faculty and administration is, first of all, impractical. In contrast to the far-off student lot, the close-in faculty-staff lots are often half empty, since the faculty do not come in every day as the students do. Those dozens of empty spaces could be filled with student cars on a first-come-first-served basis, saving dozens of student-hours of time each week. Our time is as valuable to us as a professor's is to him. The student lot is nearly full at peak periods now, and next year students may have to be turned away. Privileged parking is, therefore, an inefficient use of campus space.

In addition, privileged parking is unfair, because we students, who must use the remote lot, have to pay a $25 yearly fee while the faculty, administration, and even secretaries are given the choice spots for nothing. A friend who works in the business office tells me that the fee money is used to maintain the privileged lots as well as the student lots. I have informed my student senator of this gross injustice; he intends to bring it up at the next College Senate meeting. What will the dean of administration say in response to this charge? I and quite a few other students will be there to find out.

Even if the dean can quote some legal loophole by which the college is allowed to use our funds that way, the underlying argument against privileged parking is that it is undemocratic. The saying "Rank hath its privileges" is no longer valid today. This is not the Middle Ages, when princes and noblemen rode while peasants walked. Even in India the caste system has been outlawed, and the untouchables are no longer banished. The faculty may argue that we students are younger and more energetic while some of the more venerable professors may lack the vigor for such long treks. But remember that our student population includes fifty-year-old housewives as well as athletes of eighteen. Any professor too feeble to make the walk should be given a permit for the disabled persons lot (the only justifiable privileged lot) or perhaps should be retired. There is no reason a student who has to get up for an 8 A.M. course must trudge hundreds of yards to class so that a professor who may sleep till nearly noon can fall out of his car into his office.

The fight for practical, fair, and democratic campus parking regulations will be won, however, only if scores of students shake off their apathy and make their voices heard when the motion to end privileged parking is made at next Thursday's Senate meeting. A short walk by these students to Central Hall for this meeting may save countless future long walks to and from the college's own Siberia, the student parking lot.

REVIEW   Here is a quick review before your mastery test:

1‡Every piece of writing must have a c_____ i____.

2‡The central idea states what the writer intends to s____ the reader in

the wh___ piece of writing.

3‡You will always be sure you have an *idea* in your central idea statement if

you begin with the words "In this paper I w____ s____ t____...."

4‡After you pick your topic, your first three steps in planning your paper are

(1) j__ d___ _____

(2) form a c_____ i___ _____

(3) cr___ o__ _____

5‡A good central idea statement often needs to tell not only *what* but

also h__ and w__.

[6‡]A central idea statement must focus on _ _ _ idea.

[7‡]Not only paragraphs but also _____ must each have a central idea.

MASTERY TEST

Choose a suitable topic from the master list, from topics suggested in this module, or from topics suggested by your instructor. (Do not choose any topic for which you have already written a central idea that you checked with your instructor, with another student, or with the answer pages.) Follow the steps outlined in this module for writing a paragraph. A blank umbrella follows, to help you. Then, on a separate sheet write the paragraph—ten to thirteen sentences. Circle your central idea as it appears in the paragraph. Submit the paragraph to your instructor.

TOPIC: _____

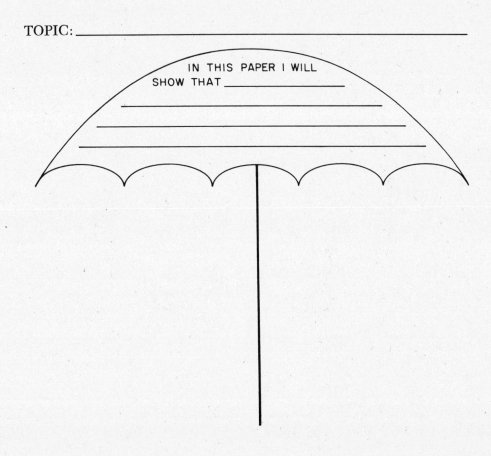

IN THIS PAPER I WILL
SHOW THAT _____

INTRODUCTION

[4]The first sentence, *A pilot doesn't.* . . . The sentence beginning *My test flights* is also a good choice.

[5]central

[6]Central idea

[7]At the beginning

[9]The first sentence

[15]central idea

[16]central idea

FORMING A CENTRAL IDEA

[1]D

[2]Because it states what the writer intends to show us in his comparison

[3]Nothing; it actually tells us less than the topic, since *compare* and *1930s and 1940s* are missing.

[4]Still nothing; it also tells us less than the original topic, since the dates are not mentioned.

[5]Still nothing. The word *how seems* to be telling us more than the topic did. But the writer does not say how they compare: he merely tells us he will show how. We still know nothing about the writer's thinking on the topic.

[6]This tells us that the writer prefers the heroes of the 1930s and 1940s to those of today.

[7]idea

[8]That

[9]". . . the Republicans will win the next presidential election" *or* ". . . the Democrats will win the next presidential election." (Later in the module you will find that these central ideas can be improved by adding "because. . . .")

[13]that

[14]*Sample central idea:* In this paper I will show that today's emphasis on money is ruining professional sports.

[15]*Sample:* In this paper I will show that preferential hiring of minority-group members and women is wrong.

[16]*Sample:* In this paper I will show that being honest works against success in politics.

FINDING WHICH IDEA IS CENTRAL

[1]The most likely item for a central idea is probably *learned to love natural world there.* A sample central idea statement is, "In this paper I will show that Lake Squmpagook has been important in my life because I learned to love the natural world there."

[2]These items probably do not pertain to your learning to love nature at Lake Squmpagook: *Robert Smythe new state ecology commissioner; state headquarters of Women's Conservation League located there; Fatty Melton upset canoe.* It is possible, however, that the writer might see a connection between the last two and his topic.

[3]The most likely are *learned to love natural world there, shocked, saddened on revisit, man's thoughtlessness, returned last year—lake polluted.*

[5]Something like this: ". . . at Lake Squmpagook, where I once learned to love the natural world, I have also learned how man's thoughtless and shocking pollution can destroy nature's beauty."

⁶Cross out items that do not belong under the umbrella—that is, under the central idea.

⁷*Most likely:* price of outboard motors has tripled in ten years, Robert Smythe new state ecology director, Fatty Melton upset canoe; *other possibilities:* state headquarters of Women's Conservation League located there, railroad stopped running there twelve years ago, still go camping with Fatty and Charlie. It is possible, however, that the writer might see a connection between some of these and his topic.

⁸*Sample:* . . . Tess's mouth is the most exciting (attractive, alluring) part of her lovable face. [*Hardy's words:* "when all was thought and felt that could be thought and felt about her features in general, it was her mouth that turned out to be the magnetic pole thereof."]

FOCUSING THE CENTRAL IDEA STATEMENT

¹that

²Yes

^{3A}*What* effect has this corruption had on the American people?

^{3B}". . . made many Americans distrust all politicians"—or similar words

⁴Yes

⁵". . . Americans will turn to even smaller economy models"—or similar words

⁶". . . Americans will turn to even smaller economy cars because of constantly increasing gasoline prices."

⁷because

⁸*Sample:* . . . been loosened in the past twenty years because most older children can be independent with the money they earn instead of having to help support the family.

⁹*Sample:* . . . gave me a lifelong love of the natural world.

¹⁰*Sample:* . . . made me realize how precious family love is.

¹¹". . . constantly rising gasoline prices will cause Americans to change to even smaller economy cars."

¹². . . corruption of officials in charge of vital services has made life in many cities today a nightmare—or similar words

¹³Too many parts; too many ideas

¹⁴*Samples:* "human greed" *or* "indifference of government officials" *or* "intolerably crowded living conditions," etc.

¹⁵*Sample:* "the corruption of officials." Any cause mentioned is just as good.

¹⁶She has two separate ideas instead of one. (She may find herself writing a paper that breaks apart in the middle instead of sticking together.)

^{17A}Roman civilization accomplished many architectural marvels.

^{17B}Roman civilization was destroyed by internal corruption.

¹⁸None, really

¹⁹No

²⁰eliminate one idea

²¹". . . Roman civilization accomplished many architectural marvels," *or* ". . . Roman civilization was destroyed by internal corruption."

²²Rewrite it so that she shows the way in which the two ideas are connected.

²³". . . although the Romans had the brains to accomplish many architectural marvels, they were not smart enough to stop their own destruction from internal corruption"—or similar words

MODULE 4

PARAGRAPH AND THEME DEVELOPMENT

Previous modules required: Getting Started (1)*—Clear Writing: The First Steps
(2)*—The Central Idea (3)

DEVELOPING A PARAGRAPH

Read these two selections. Both were written by freshmen responding to an essay whose central idea was that teenage and college-age youth today want all the freedoms of adults without the accompanying responsibilities, particularly in love and marriage:

SELECTION A

Young people today see how their parents act and how they feel about the world today. Since they feel their parents are wrong they rebel because they do not want to become a "carbon copy" of their elders. Young people want to be treated as persons, not just "kids" who do not know what they are talking about and who should not express their own ideas because they are too young to understand. Young people today want to do and think as they please. They do not want their ideas to be pushed aside for an older person's ideas. They want a free society where there is no such thing that they must do because it is required of them. They want to experience different things and new things. Anything their elders want they do the opposite so as not to be like them. The young people of today are a great generation who want to be heard. They want their ideas on important matters to be able to be heard.

SELECTION B

Young people today are jumping into the adult world for its freedoms and pleasures without thinking of its responsibilities. Let me tell you about Bruce and Kathy. They were the best couple in the neighborhood. All through high school they saw each other and never had an argument. After some thought and advice they decided to take the final step. All went well through the first year; he did not miss the ball playing, and she did not miss the night out with the girls. But soon they bore a child, and the problems began. Here was a young couple, both of whom had never really had too much responsibility. Now with the child it was too much. Bruce left and still cannot be found, and Kathy lives with her mother in regret. Young adults like Bruce and Kathy are impatient to marry because they want the pleasures of the adult world the fastest way they can get them. They do not realize that responsibility goes hand in hand with the pleasures. According to a recent newspaper article, over half of teenage marriages fail. One of the causes of this impatience is that adolescents want to get away from adults. What they feel is really not so much a desire for marriage as just the "generation gap." For instance, I do not get along with my parents. Recently I met a boy who was having the same problem with his parents. The solution he presented to me was marriage. I disagreed with him because I could see that solving one problem would probably create a bigger problem, one like Bruce and Kathy's. Needless to say, I turned him down. Rushing to do the things an adult does does not make a young person more adult or more free, or solve all his problems. As for me, I am going to live the rest of my adolescent life as an adolescent. When I feel I have the maturity to take on a responsibility like marriage, being able to cope with such a responsibility will add to my enjoyment of adult life.

Below the following list are six statements from A and six from B. The list contains five judgments (*a* to *e*) about each statement. In the blank after each statement, write the letter (*a* to *e*) of the judgment you make about it. There are no "right" or "wrong" answers:

(a) I accept this statement because of the evidence the writer gives.

(b) Even though the writer gives no evidence, I accept this statement because I too feel that way.

(c) I accept this statement because it is an obvious, generally known truth which needs no evidence.

(d) I reject this statement because the writer has not shown me that it is true.

(e) I cannot judge whether this statement is true or not, because the writer has given no evidence for it.

FOR SELECTION A

1A‡Young people today rebel. _____

2A‡They rebel because they believe their parents are wrong. _____

3A‡Adults treat young people as "kids" who have no ideas worth listening to. _____

4A‡Young people want a society where there is nothing they are required to do. _____

5A‡They want to do different and new things opposite to what their parents do so as not to be like them. _____

6A‡Today's young people are a great generation who want their important ideas to be heard. _____

Does the writer of selection A seem to be talking about all, most, or just some young people?

7A‡

_____ What in the selection makes you think so? _____

8A‡

_____

FOR SELECTION B

1B‡Young people are jumping into the adult world for its freedoms and pleasures. _____

2B‡They do not think of adult responsibilities. _____

³ᴮ‡Young people are impatient to marry. _____

⁴ᴮ‡They want to marry to get away from adults. _____

⁵ᴮ‡Rushing to do adult things does not make a person more free or solve all
his problems. _____

⁶ᴮ‡A person will enjoy adult life more if he waits to do adult things until he
has the maturity to cope with them. _____

Does the writer of selection B seem to be talking about all, most, or just some young people?

⁷ᴮ‡ _____ What in the selection makes you think so? ⁸ᴮ‡ _____

_____

Now look back at your answers for each selection. See what you can discover from
them. First, were most of your answers for selection B different from those for selection A?

⁹‡ _____ How many answers of *a* did you have for selection A? ¹⁰‡ _____

¹¹‡
How many for selection B? _____ Then which selection gave more evidence to

¹²‡
support its central idea? _____ How many answers of *b* did you have for

¹³‡
selection A? _____ If you had three or more such answers, then was the *selection*

¹⁴‡
doing the job of making you think through your opinions on the subject? _____

¹⁵‡
How many answers of *c* did you have for selection A? _____ If you had four or
more, then almost all of what the writer said was already common knowledge. Then of what
use is the selection? Why did he bother writing if he could say only what almost all his
readers knew already?

¹⁶‡
How many answers of *d* or *e* did you have for selection A? _____ If you

¹⁷‡
had three or more, then how convincing was the writer? _____ Even two *d*'s or *e*'s
would make him pretty unconvincing. Now, ask the same questions for selection B, and you

¹⁸‡
should complete your discovery. Which was the more convincing paragraph? _____

¹⁹‡
Why? _____

_____

²⁰‡ ²¹‡
Which was the more interesting paragraph? _____ Why? _____

_____

As you learned in "The Central Idea," when you write you are usually trying to show
your readers something. Selection A merely made a few general statements about young

people wanting to do as they please. Selection B, on the other hand, focused on young marriages, gave two specific examples of young people who wanted to rush to marriage, and probed the causes and results of such action. Selection B did what effective writing is supposed to do.

In Module 3 you discovered how to write good, clear central ideas. In this module you will discover how to develop your central ideas so that your writing will be convincing and interesting. In this section we will concentrate on smaller units of writing (paragraphs), but in the second section you will see that the qualities that make your paragraphs convincing and interesting will do the same for your longer papers.

FINDING A TOPIC

There is an old saying, "I'm from Missouri—show me." People from Missouri long ago learned not to believe someone who merely *said* something was true; they insisted on being *shown* before they believed. Alert readers are like Missourians; they are not going to believe something is true just because you say it is. You have to show them. How do you do this? How did the student who wrote selection B do it? Was she writing on something she knew

22

about? How do you know she was? _____ The first principle, then, is *Write about something you know well enough to give details on.* In the first column of blanks after the topics below, check every topic on which you think you can write a ten-to-twelve-sentence paragraph:

	23‡	24‡		23‡	24‡
Teenage marriage	_____	_____	Starting college as an over-25	_____	_____
Roadside car repair	_____	_____	Dieting	_____	_____
Preventing pregnancy	_____	_____	Living away from parents	_____	_____
Choosing clothes	_____	_____	The strangest person I ever knew	_____	_____
The world food shortage	_____	_____	Salaries of professional athletes	_____	_____
The Twenty-fifth (presidential succession)			Local crime	_____	_____
Amendment	_____	_____	Civil service careers	_____	_____

Are you still having trouble finding a topic? Think. You probably know more than you realize; for example, think how much you know about

Yourself: the kind of person you are, your experiences, the workings of your mind

Other people: your family, close friends, a person you love(d), one who influenced your life, unusual people that you have known

Places: those which to you are intimate, unusual, famous, beautiful, interesting, or otherwise significant

Ideas you have: ways that parts of our lives or the world can be improved, causes you believe in, injustices that need righting, reasons for certain human behavior

Things you are expert on: doing, making or improving something, knowing how something works, knowing how to act in certain situations

Things you have read about or studied: an incident in history of significance today, a scientific discovery that will affect the reader, a psychological or sociological explanation of some recent occurrence (But should such a paragraph or theme sound to the reader as if you are just parroting an instructor or a textbook?)

The future: some part of your personal future or the future of your college class, of your ethnic group, of the country, of the world

Your instructor and the master list in the back of this book can supply more suggestions. As you discovered in "Getting Started," you know much more to write about than you may think you do.

If you were unable to put a check in the first column for any of the topics listed, write here three topics on which you *can* write ten to twelve sentences each:

²⁵‡(1) _____ (2) _____

_____ (3) _____ Now in the second column of blanks above (24) or in item 25, check the topics on which you think you can write a full-length theme of 25 to 35 sentences. (A *theme* is a paper of about 300 to 500 words developing a central idea. It is the same kind of writing that was called in high school a *composition* and is called in professional writing an *essay*.) Next, in blanks 26 through 28 below, copy *three* of the topics which you checked in item 23 or that you wrote in item 25. At least one of these should be a topic which you also checked in item 24 or 25—one on which you think you can write 25 to 35 sentences. Next, fill in the blanks below for each topic:

²⁶‡Topic: _____

Central idea: I will show that _____

Facts/examples/details

1. _____

2. _____

3. _____

4. _____

5. _____

²⁷‡Topic: _____

Central idea: I will show that _____

Facts/examples/details

1. _____

2. _____

3. _____

4. _____

5. _____

[28]‡Topic: _____

Central idea: I will show that _____

Facts/examples/details

1. _____

2. _____

3. _____

4. _____

5. _____

Now, how interested would you be in reading someone else's paper on any of these topics? What would you expect her to show you about the topic? Would you expect her to show you why the topic was worth reading? Would you expect her to show that she knew more about the topic than you already knew or that she had some new outlook on it? When you write, then, you need to think as two persons at once—the writer and the reader. Who is your reader? If your instructor does not specify a particular audience, assume that you are writing for fairly well-informed adults—for example, the other students in your class.

From these three topics, pick the one you think you can show the most about. (If you had trouble thinking of five facts, examples, or details on a certain topic, that is probably not a good one to choose.) You can guess what you will be asked to do next: Write the paragraph. But you may have more details you want to add, you may want to arrange the

details in a certain order, or you may want to rethink your [29]c_ _ _ _ _ _ i_ _ _. Do that first. Your instructor may supply an "umbrella" sheet as you used in Module 3. Finally, on a sheet of your own paper, write the paragraph, double-spaced. Underline the sentence that states your central idea. When finished, do whichever of these your instructor directs:

A. Exchange papers with another student for mutual evaluation; then revise your own paper.

B. In a group of four or five, constructively discuss and evaluate the papers of all or several group members; then revise your own paper.

C. Submit the paper to your instructor.

DEVELOPING A PARAGRAPH FULLY

How long should a paragraph be? Abraham Lincoln, who towered over most people, was once asked how long his legs were. After thinking a minute, he replied, "Long enough to reach the ground." The answer to the opening question is similar: A paragraph should be long enough to cover the topic. Though some special kinds of paragraphs, such as characters' speech in a story, may have only a single sentence, paragraphs developing a central idea may run from about four to fifteen sentences or more. This book concentrates on paragraphs of between seven and thirteen sentences.

Here is the central idea sentence from a key paragraph of a student theme entitled "Why Are Americans Turning to Smaller Cars?"

The biggest thing that is killing the big car is uncertainty.

In the space below, list several kinds of facts, details, examples, or reasons that you, as the reader, would want the writer to show you as evidence that this central idea is true. List as many as you think are needed:

30‡

Now here is the student's actual paragraph:

*The biggest thing that is killing the big car is uncertainty. People are depressed over the Middle East crisis, inflation, gasoline shortages, and, in general, bad news. These problems cause uncertainty as to where we stand with respect to gasoline availability.**

How well does this paragraph meet your list of needed information? Explain:

31‡

_____

_____

This student's paragraph is an example of an undeveloped, or runt, paragraph. It is under-nourished and weak, like the runt of an animal's litter of young. The last sentence is largely a restatement of the first; that leaves only the second sentence to develop the whole central

_____

* The entire theme can be found on page 303 of "Economy and Clarity."

idea. Does it do so? Does the writer *show* that the Middle East crisis and the other problems have led to uncertainty on gasoline, which in turn has led to fewer sales of big cars? Or does he just *tell* you?

Here is another paragraph developing the same idea. Compare the two:

> *Most of all, it is uncertainty that is killing the big car. Faced with problems like the Middle East crisis, inflation, gasoline shortages, and recession, the average American does not want to go heavily into debt for a car he might rarely be able to drive. The uncertain political situation created by the Arabs and the Israelis has driven the stock market down, sharply reducing many Americans' financial assets. In addition, while the Administration was occupied with the Middle East it ignored inflation, which ran wild. Gasoline prices nearly doubled. This price rise, combined with shortages caused by the Arab oil embargo, forced Americans to use much less gas. The Arabs may renew this cutoff at any time. Since there is no certainty that gas price and supply will ever return to what they were, Americans feel it is safest to avoid the 4000-pound gas-guzzlers, some of which average only seven miles per gallon. New car prices, moreover, are so inflated that the $3000 that bought a full-size car in 1972 now buys only a compact. Finally, there is great uncertainty about employment and wages because of the recession. A worker will not buy a car that he will have repossessed if he loses his job and cannot pay for it. Because of all these uncertainties, then, a million standard-size cars stand unsold in showrooms today.*

What does the revised version do that the original fails to? First, it specifies what the "bad news" is—recession. More important, it shows how each of the four causes has brought about uncertainty and turned buyers away from large cars. Finally, it shows that the writer can tell us how many unsold cars there are, how much a new car costs, how many miles to the gallon it gets. Does he convince you that he knows his subject? _____

Some students even mistakenly shrink the runt paragraph to just a central idea sentence! The following two sentences from the same theme on small cars would have been good central idea sentences for fully developed paragraphs:

> *Many of today's new-car buyers are seriously considering the advantages of small cars and wondering whether they have been driving cars that are bigger than necessary.*
> *The overall sluggishness of the economy is another cause of a purchasing slowdown, especially of the more expensive, large-sized car.*

But each of these was the *only* sentence in its paragraph. These "paragraphs" were not even runts; they were stillborn.

You now know what a good paragraph needs. But knowing what is needed does not always mean that you are able to supply it. If you cannot think of enough details to develop the central idea adequately, what should you do? Naturally, you must ask yourself, "Can I find the needed details? If so, where?" Sometimes the answer to that first question is going to be *no*. If your central idea was that "the majority of professors in this college mark their research papers by weighing them," you would have a difficult time giving anything more than student gossip as evidence, even if the charge were true. But very often there are more details available to you than you think. How?

Suppose you have chosen as your central idea the statement that "college women [or college men—choose the opposite sex] change their clothing styles for different reasons than do noncollege women (men) of the same age," which you are convinced is true. Can you think of four sources you can tap for information and ideas to develop this central idea?

One source would be your own [33]ob_ _ _v_tion. Detectives can look around a room and observe two or three times as much as the rest of us. A little detective work is needed for your paper. What particular changes in styles have you noticed on the women around campus lately? On the noncollege women on the avenue?

A second source would be [34]_th_r p_ _ _le. You must know some women of each type. Ask them why they have made the changes you have noticed. The third source, perhaps the most overlooked of all, is your [35]o_ _ m_ _d. Your first job here is to think of what questions you need to ask yourself. On this topic, you might ask these: What do I remember about past style changes? For what reasons do I change my styles? Could either of these groups do it for the same reason? For what reasons would college styles change differently from noncollege styles—what economic, social, psychological, intellectual reasons? Do I remember reading anything on the topic? Do these reasons I have thought of make sense? Which is the strongest reason? Are there stronger reasons why the two groups' styles would *not* change differently?

You can probably guess the fourth source—the [36]‡li_ _ _ _ _y. On most topics the college or public library will have information in books, magazines, or back newspapers—or perhaps even on tape. How to find such information in a library is beyond the scope of this course, but librarians are always glad to show you how. You will learn much about library research in a future English course.

Here is an experiment to try your powers of observation and thinking. Take a pencil and some paper; go by yourself and sit for about twenty minutes somewhere where you can watch people—not a classroom, but a park bench, a bus, an airport, a waiting room, the college lounge, a museum, a McDonald's, a stadium. Jot down what you notice as you look around. Do not worry now about sentences, spelling, or grammar; just takes notes—several pages of them. Concentrate on the people and what you can figure out about them from their actions and appearance.

Which people were typical of such a place? Which were unusual? Why? Select two or three persons representing different types and observe their actions and appearance in detail. What can you tell about each of these from his actions and appearance? Later, let your mind work over your notes and remembered impressions, seeking some meaning from them. Think first of the questions to ask yourself. What have your observations told you about young people? Old people? Men? Women? College students? About the effect of the place upon the people? About human nature? About the effect of these observations on your view of people and life? Do you now know anything significant that you did not know before your observation? Can you form the answers to some of these questions into a central idea for a paragraph about that place? Do you have enough data to write the paragraph? This experiment should show you that you *can* find facts and ideas to develop paragraphs fully.

Do A or B, as your instructor directs:

    A.   Write a fully developed paragraph from the fact-gathering experiment above.

    B.   Pick one of the following runt paragraphs and turn it into a fully developed paragraph:

        (1) There are many advantages in going to a big-city college. Though many young men and women prefer the rolling lawns of a country campus, many others

prefer to attend colleges right in the heart of New York, Chicago, or Los Angeles. The city offers so much to do that the country campus cannot.

(2) Choosing clothes can become quite a problem. When I go into a clothing store to buy a new outfit, I have trouble making up my mind. There are so many styles to choose from today that I almost hate to do so. Sometimes it takes me hours. Yes, choosing clothes is a big problem today.

(3) The old movies on TV are better than the new ones showing in the theaters today. The new movies are superior technically and much more realistic, but they lack the class of the old Humphrey Bogart or Cary Grant flicks. Some of the new movies are so realistic they are painful to watch.

When finished, do whichever of these your instructor directs:

A. Exchange papers with another student for mutual evaluation; then revise your own paper.

B. In a group of four or five, constructively discuss and evaluate the papers of all or several group members; then revise your own paper.

C. Submit the paper to your instructor.

KEEPING YOUR TRAIN OF THOUGHT ON THE RAILS (UNITY)

Here is a paragraph a student wrote:

(1) Women's lib is moving into so many areas where women do not belong that it is becoming ridiculous and will hurt women's lib in the long run. (2) Last month a woman took the Sanitation Department to court on grounds of sex discrimination because they refused her a job. (3) Actually, she was unable to pass the physical test, which required lifting heavy garbage cans. (4) In another case a girl sued Washboard State University because she was not allowed on their football varsity, even though she weighed only 140 pounds, hefty for a girl but not for a football player. (5) Washboard went on to win the conference championship and a bowl bid without her; this was their third straight bowl game. (6) The most absurd case of all involved a woman who applied for a job as a men's physical education teacher. (7) The college had to hire her because she was the only applicant with a Ph.D. (8) Many other cases like these have been in the papers recently. (9) Women certainly deserve equality with men, but publicity-seekers who go to ridiculous lengths will only start a backlash against women's lib.

37‡

Does anything in this paragraph bother you? If so, what _____
There is something wrong in this paragraph. If you have not spotted it yet, look at the writer's scrap paper. Here is his central idea and his list of details:

Central Idea: I will show that women's lib is going to extremes that will hurt it.
1. woman took sanitation test—couldn't lift cans
2. girl sued Washboard to get on football team
3. girl too small for team
4. Washboard won bowl bid third straight year
5. woman applied as men's physical education teacher
6. she got job—only Ph.D.
7. many other examples
8. conclusion

Do you spot anything wrong in the student's list? If so, what? _____

_____ If not, or to check yourself, answer these questions: Does item 2 fit
under the central idea? _____ Item 3? _____ Item 4? _____
Item 5? _____ Item 6? _____ Item 7? _____ By now you
have probably discovered that one item on the list does not fit under the central idea. What
sentence in the paragraph itself corresponds to this item? _____
Does this sentence fit under the central idea? _____ Was it easier for you to spot
this problem after you saw the writer's central idea and list? _____ Read the
paragraph again, skipping the off-topic sentence. Does the paragraph still show you what the
central idea says it will? Then what should the writer do with that sentence? _____

_____

At this point you may ask, "But what harm does the sentence do? Why not leave it in?"
But what happens to the reader's train of thought when it hits this sentence? His thought
has been cruising along the track of women's lib, but suddenly it is derailed by a sentence
on a football team's record, which has no connection at all with women's lib. The reader has
to try to find the women's lib track again and put his train of thought back on it. The reader's
time and concentration have been lost. An experienced writer will not let this happen.

You have discovered two points. The first is that an off-topic idea can slip into a
paragraph; the second is that it is easier to spot such an idea in the writer's preliminary list
of details than in the finished paragraph. This is one reason you write the central idea and
make the list *before* you start writing the paragraph. Keep in mind that a sentence can seem
to be on the topic while actually being off it. The first sentence below is a central idea; is the
sentence which follows it really on the topic of that central idea?

> *Live opera never succeeded on television because it was too expensive to
> produce.*
> *The great bass Ezio Pinza had ended his operatic career before television sets
> became common.*

The second sentence concerns both opera and television; it *seems* to fit the central idea. But
does it concern the *expense* of televising opera? _____ You need a sharp eye to
catch such intrusions.

Examine each of the following lists. In each, is there one item (or more) off the
topic—not belonging under the central idea? Cross out each such item: (Do not consider
whether you *agree* with any statement—only whether it fits under the central idea.)

[50]*Central Idea:* I will show that more financial aid should be given to low-income
students at this college.
1. cost of living up 20 percent this year
2. tuition and other expenses up 30 percent

3. part-time jobs hard to find
4. available aid up only 10 percent
5. low-income students can't make ends meet
6. college now celebrating its hundredth year
7. students must demonstrate so that the need for more aid will be known

[51]*Central Idea:* I will show that alcohol, not marijuana, should be outlawed.
1. research has shown marijuana not addictive
2. alcohol addictive—five million alcoholics in United States today
3. more marijuana enters United States from Mexico than from Europe or Middle East
4. 5000 killed in drunk-driver accidents each year—only 100 in marijuana-driver accidents
5. alcohol permanently impairs health (liver, heart)—no evidence that marijuana does
6. 90 percent more youths who start on beer go on to be alcoholics than youths who start on marijuana go on to be drug addicts
7. conclusion—outlaw alcohol, legalize marijuana

[52]*Central Idea:* I will show that no math should be required in college.
1. math is hard—takes ten or more hours of students' time from other subjects weekly
2. new methods of teaching math being developed
3. remedial math eats up $100,000 of college budget—this could be used in other areas
4. college-level math of little practical use for most college graduates
5. new college president named yesterday is a former math prof
6. most students dislike math

MAKING YOUR IDEAS HOLD TOGETHER

Read this student paper:

A Memorable Place
(1) We were filled with ecstasy at the thought of coming to the U.S.A. (2) Twelve hours later we were circling Kennedy Airport in New York. (3) For some unknown reason our plane was detoured to Miami, where after refueling we left for New York. (4) We arrived there some hours later, our spirits tired but nonetheless happy. (5) We had come from South America, where the climate is like Florida's, where it never snows. (6) We were received by empty halls and silent rooms. (7) There we were, my mother, my three sisters and I, dead tired, out of our country because we wanted a stable government and economic advancement, in a place that seemed completely dead and covered by a blinding whiteness. (8) The airport did not have the warmth the others had, or so it seemed, because our welcome committee consisted of very friendly but unknown people that were trying to understand my basic English. (9) We were relieved to see my father and our friends coming to the rescue. (10) I have never found the airport as empty as on my first day, and I realize that those few hours we spent in an unfamiliar place showed us what kind of people we would encounter in this promised land.

The student who wrote this indicated that the un-italicized words were his central idea. There is nothing wrong with holding the central idea until the end; however, what *is* wrong

with this paragraph? Does it have details of the trip? ＿＿＿＿＿＿＿ Does it go off the

topic? ＿＿＿＿＿＿＿ Then what, if anything, bothers you about it? ＿＿＿＿＿＿＿＿

＿＿＿＿＿＿＿＿＿＿＿＿＿ Let us follow the writer's train of thought. Who is *we* in sentence 1? Sentence 2 starts with *Twelve hours later. . . .* Later than what? Although sentence 2 has the writer over New York, sentence 3 puts him first where, and then back where? In sentence 6, he was *received by empty halls and silent rooms.* Where? Why? What is the *blinding whiteness* in sentence 7? Snow? If snow was so conspicuous, why did the writer not mention it when he first saw New York in sentence 2? Did the writer intend a connection between *snows* in sentence 5 and *whiteness* in sentence 7? What is the significance of the empty terminal and the snow? In sentence 8, who were the people? What did they do? Why did he think they were friendly? If they were friendly, why did the airport seem to lack warmth? How long was it before his father arrived? Why had his father not been there when he arrived? Was he only *relieved* to see his father? How did his impressions on arrival compare with his expectations when leaving South America? How old was the writer when this happened? (It makes quite a difference whether he was a child or an adult.) How long has it been since his arrival?

Are the above questions just nitpicking, or are they what the reader would naturally ask, to understand clearly what happened and to grasp the significance of the event and the place in the writer's life—in other words, to follow the train of thought developing the

writer's central idea? ＿＿＿＿＿＿＿＿＿＿＿＿＿＿＿＿＿＿＿＿＿＿

Did you ever hear a person's speaking described as incoherent (in ko HEER ent)?

What do you think *incoherent* means? ＿＿＿＿＿＿＿＿＿＿＿＿＿＿＿＿＿＿＿

Many readers would call this writer's paragraph incoherent, because he has left gaps in the tracks of his thought, making it hard or impossible for the reader's train of thought to follow. What he wanted to show was clear in *his* mind, but he never put himself in the *reader's* mind.

Here is the same paragraph again, with blanks for answers to the questions raised. From your own imagination, fill in words which you think would answer most of those questions and make clear what the writer was trying to show:

⁵⁸‡When I was ＿＿＿＿＿＿ years old, ＿＿＿＿＿＿ and I came from

＿＿＿＿＿＿ to the United States. On the day of our departure, we were all filled

with ecstasy at the thought of living in the U.S.A. Twelve hours after ＿＿＿＿＿＿

＿＿＿＿＿＿＿＿＿＿ and after a d＿＿＿＿ to M＿＿＿＿＿

for some unknown reason, we were circling Kennedy Airport in New York.

B＿c＿＿＿＿ we had come from South America, where the climate is like Florida's,

we were amazed to see the city covered with ＿＿＿＿＿＿. Dead tired but none-

theless happy, we ＿＿＿＿＿＿＿＿＿＿＿＿＿; how＿＿＿＿＿, we

oil slick, dead fish, and floating garbage. _____ there was a boys'

₆₄ at top center: 64

camp on the lake at Plopsquat Point. _____ there was a Honda

factory there. _____ the nearest factory was a hundred

miles from the lake. I learned to love the natural world there, _____

because of what I saw there _____,
I will never go back again.

I first went there when	last year	on my return
which	but	when I returned last year
in my boyhood	near	years ago

Now, if your instructor has returned one of your previous paragraphs and indicated that it could be more coherent, rewrite that pargaraph, using signal expressions and your common sense to improve its coherence. (By the way, signal expressions do not always have to come at the beginning of the sentence; we can say either *Furthermore, I believe that . . .* or *I believe, furthermore, that. . . .*) Submit the rewritten paragraph to your instructor.

ARRANGING YOUR IDEAS IN THE BEST ORDER

Read this paragraph:

(1) Lake Squmpagook may be just a plain, ordinary lake to local folks, but to a city boy spending his only vacation in the country, it was paradise. (2) We used to scale the huge outcroppings of granite with only our bare hands for climbing equipment. (3) The lake is fifteen miles long, with two waterfalls. (4) There is a great mountain called Silvertop. (5) There are also some rustic cabins and our boys' camp. (6) We could see twenty feet down into the icy water. (7) It was the remoteness of the camp which made that summer so much fun; it let us imagine we were pioneers. (8) There is also a four-lane highway and a paper mill. (9) During the warm, bright days we would go canoeing amid the pine-covered islands. (10) The village of Squmpagook has a population of 3000. (11) In the cool nights we would roast marshmallows and sing around the campfire. (12) When my friend Fatty Melton upset our canoe, we found out just how cold the water really could be. (13) It is the shimmering waters I have remembered most of all, back in Detroit, in the years since then.

_{69‡}

Did anything bother you about this paragraph? If so, what? _____

_____ As usual, we will examine it. First, does it have an effective central idea

sentence? _____ Then let us look at the development of that idea. Which

sentences describe the water itself? _____ Which sentences mention man-

made structures or places near the lake? _____ Which sentences mention particular activities the writer did? _____ Where were each of the following in relation to the lake? (Use only the information in the paragraph, not your imagination.)

The granite outcroppings? _____74_____ Silvertop? _____75_____ The town?

_____76_____ The cabins? _____77_____ The camp? _____78_____ The highway?

_____79_____ The mill? _____80_____ Detroit? _____81_____

By now you have probably seen what is faulty about this paragraph despite its good central idea and adequate details. When you tried to answer questions 74–81, you may have recognized a problem you learned to overcome in the previous section—the paragraph

without [82]s__g____s. But even if we put in signals, your answers to questions 71, 72, and 73 above indicate that a problem still remains. Look at what you have discovered about how the writer arranged his sentences:

Sentence Content

1. central idea
2. writer's activity
3. natural features of lake
4. natural surroundings of lake
5. man-made surroundings of lake
6. description of water
7. writer's activity; writer's attitude toward camp
8. man-made surroundings of lake
9. writer's activity
10. man-made surroundings of lake (town)
11. writer's activity
12. writer's activity; description of water
13. description of water; writer's present location; sum-up

The details the writer mentions are not in a sensible [83]o__d____. Like quite a few other tasks in writing, arranging details in an order is largely a matter of common sense. Let us consider order in different kinds of papers. First of all, do you have to worry about order when you are telling something that happened or explaining how to do something?

[84] _____ Why not? Because you naturally use time order, the easiest kind of order: After your central idea sentence, you can simply tell the beginning event, then the one after that, and then the one after that, and so forth. Or, if you are explaining how to do something or how some process works, it is just a matter of stating the central idea and then describing how first the operator does A, and then B, and so forth; or how first A happens, which causes B, which in turn causes C, and so forth. Order here is rarely a problem.

What kind of paragraphs *can* cause order problems? The Lake Squmpagook kind, for one—a paragraph describing a place (or a person). Remember what the writer failed to do: tell us where the other objects or places he mentioned were in relation to the lake, and put the sentences describing the same kinds of things together. In the blanks below, rearrange the sentences of the Lake Squmpagook paragraph, putting similar ideas together in an order that makes sense to you. More than one order is possible. Some numbers are filled in as helps toward one sensible order:

Sentence   Content

[85]1.   central idea

3.   description of lake

____.   _____

5.   man-made surroundings of lake

____.   _____

____.   _____

7.   writer's activity; writer's attitude toward camp

2.   writer's activity

____.   _____

____.   _____

____.   _____

____.   _____

13.   description of water; writer's present location; sum-up

Now, on your own paper, write out the actual sentences in the order you just listed, adding any signals you think you need. You may change, drop, or add words as you wish, or even combine sentences, to make the paragraph flow smoothly. Here are some suggestions for signals:

these waterfalls . . .	on the mountain . . .
near . . .	which was located . . .
on the eastern shore . . .	at the southern end . . .
all this was far . . .	once . . .

When you have finished, do A or B, as your instructor directs:
A.   Submit your paper to your instructor.
B.   Check your version against the version your instructor shows you.

What other kinds of paragraphs present problems in order? Suppose you were trying to convince somebody of something; how would you arrange your argument to be most convincing? If you were trying to explain something complicated—something that could not be explained in time order—how would you arrange your facts? Have you ever done door-to-door selling—an occupation where you would have to do quite a bit of persuading? If you had the job of convincing some harried housewife in the lower-middle-income bracket to buy the $200 vacuum cleaner you were selling, in what order would you present the following arguments?

1.   picks up hidden dirt from deep in rugs

2. has attractive chrome-trimmed exterior, available in choice of six decorator colors

3. comes with attachments to do furniture, drapes, crevices, and dusting of delicate objects

4. has a special sale price, this week only, of $130, which is $70 off regular price

5. has light on front to show dirt in dark corners

[86‡]First _____ _____ _____ _____ _____ Last

[87‡]
Why did you arrange them this way? _____

_____ Which of the above selling points would you consider your strongest—the one you would want the housewife to keep thinking about the

[88‡]
most? _____ Where is the best place to put this argument so that it will stay

[89‡]
in her mind? _____

Most salesmen, lawyers, and other persuasive speakers and writers say that they start with their minor points and work up to their strongest argument, which they save for last. There are two psychological reasons for this: (1) The listener feels the speaker's arguments becoming stronger and stronger, so that she is almost convinced just before the speaker delivers his most telling points; (2) What the listener hears last is usually what stays in her mind. Did you arrange your arguments this way? If not, rearrange them into this order and read the selling points to yourself. Are they more convincing this way? (If you have only one reason to convince your reader with, you would arrange your supporting *evidence* from minor points to strongest point.)

Now pick one of the ideas below, or a similar one suggested or approved by your instructor. Using your own sheet of paper or an umbrella sheet, jot down the reasons or evidence you will give to convince your reader. Write your central idea statement. Then number or rearrange the reasons in order of increasing strength, so that you will leave the reader with the strongest reason. (Not every sentence in a paragraph need be a new reason; for some reasons you may want to give a sentence or two more of supporting evidence.) You may argue the opposite of one of these ideas, if you prefer:

The Twenty-fifth (presidential succession) Amendment should be repealed.

Women's lib (or gay lib) has gone too far.

Obtaining a college degree (or high school diploma) has become too easy.

Fewer marriages would fail if. . . .

The United States should seize Middle Eastern oil fields if the need for oil becomes acute.

Professional athletes' salaries are excessive.

Welfare benefits in this area are inadequate.

The courts are too lenient today.

The _____ industry is cheating the consumer.‡

When finished, hold this central idea and list, unless your instructor directs otherwise. You may wish to use it for your next writing assignment.

There is only one more kind of order for you to be aware of in this course. How would you explain a baseball game to an Irishman or gin rummy to someone who has never played cards? How would you explain the organization of the U.S. federal government to a Jamaican? Can we use time order here? Why can we not start explaining baseball by saying "First the pitcher throws the ball to the batter," gin rummy by saying "First you deal the cards," or the federal government by saying "First we elect a president and a Congress"? Think of some game you know well. How *would* you explain it to a nonplayer? How does a good teacher explain a complex idea to you? This paragraph can show you the answer:

A blood corpuscle is a tiny balloon filled with a colored protein; it is called hemoglobin, meaning blood protein. The distinctive feature of the globin is its central iron atom, which is present amidst hundreds of amino acids and other complexes. According to modern theories the iron atom functions by means of electromagnetic forces. It oscillates millions of times a second, and is alternately magnetized and demagnetized in the course of these millions of oscillations. In tune with these oscillations, the hemoglobin constantly acquires and loses an ionic charge. Twenty-two trillion blood cells, each containing several million hemoglobin molecules, each of which contains an oscillating iron atom, charge and discharge ten million times a second—this is what we call "respiration."

— *Fritz Kahn, M.D.*, The Human Body
(*New York: Random House, 1965*), *p. 137*

Put an S in front of what seems to you the simplest, most familiar, or easiest-to-understand sentence in the paragraph.[90] Put a C in front of the sentence that fully explains the writer's complex idea.[91] In what order did the writer present his explanation? He moved from

[92‡] _____ to _____ [92‡]. This is how to explain something when time order cannot be used: Move from the simple to the more complex, from the familiar to the unfamiliar. For instance, explanations of games usually start with "The object of this game is to. . . ." Such a statement gives a simple overall picture of what all the explanation is leading to; the reader thus can see where he is going. An explanation of the U.S. government would probably start with a simple overview like "The U.S. federal government has three branches: one which makes the laws, one which enforces them, and one which judges them." Notice that the order of the paragraph also is set up in

this sentence. A paragraph on this topic would naturally have _____ [93] sections,

one for each _____ [93]. The simple-to-complex movement would take place within each of these three parts. Often your central idea statement will help you by presenting you with such a ready-made order.

Let us take a game both men and women usually know well: basketball. Although some of the fine points are quite complex, the basic idea of the game is not hard to explain.

Assume that you are writing to your cousin living in a foreign country, who will soon visit America, and that you expect to take him to a basketball game. Assume that he is probably familiar with some goal-type games, such as soccer. Write a nine-to-thirteen-sentence paragraph giving him enough of an understanding of the game so that he can enjoy watching it. If you do not know basketball that well, pick some other game; even Monopoly will do. Your instructor may also let you by-pass this assignment and instead write a persuasive paragraph on the topic you chose on pages 64–65. If you choose to explain a game, before you start you might want to peruse this explanation of a sport most Americans do not know well, cricket:

Like American baseball, cricket is a warm-weather game played between a batting and a fielding team on a wide green field, and includes base-running to score more runs than the other team and win. There are only two bases, however, twenty-two yards apart in the center of the field, and no foul lines. The bases (called wickets) are pairs of wooden stumps about two feet high; the pitcher (called the bowler) stands at one wicket and the batsman and the catcher (wicket keeper) at the other. After hitting the pitched ball with a flat bat, the batsman tries to score a run by reaching the other base before the fielder can throw the ball to the wicket. One big difference from baseball, though, is that there are two batsmen, two pitchers, and two catchers on the field at a time—one at each wicket. When the batsman hits the ball and runs, the other batsman runs in the opposite direction, each scoring a run every time he reaches the opposite wicket. A batsman is out if, as in baseball, he hits a ball that is caught on the fly or if a fielder throws any other kind of hit ball to a wicket before a batsman reaches there. The bowler can achieve the equivalent of a strikeout by throwing the ball past the batsman and hitting the wicket. The batsman may guard the wicket by simply stopping the ball with his bat; but after six pitches the other bowler and batsman take up the duel instead. All eleven men on the batting team must be put out before the inning ends and the fielding team comes to bat. There are several other ways of making runs and outs, most of them involving rule violations. Although a game (a match) has only two innings, so many more runs than outs are made that the match may last two or three days. This slowness of play has kept cricket's popularity from spreading much beyond the well-to-do class of England.

When finished with your paragraph, do whichever of these your instructor directs:

A.   Exchange papers with another student for mutual evaluation; then revise your own paper.

B.   In a group of four or five, constructively discuss and evaluate the papers of all or several group members; then revise your own paper.

C.   Submit the paper to your instructor.

DEVELOPING A LONGER PAPER (A THEME)

Are good longer papers written the same way as good paragraphs? Basically, yes. As you learned in "The Central Idea," you need one central idea sentence for your whole paper and central idea sentences for each paragraph in the paper except the introduction and conclusion. Do you recall that at the beginning of this module you were asked to check off which of several topics you thought you could write a 25 to 35 sentence theme on? Before we consider how to put a full-length theme together, keep in mind that the first requirement for writing a 35-sentence theme is that you have 35 sentences worth of ideas!

Let us plan a 25 to 35 sentence theme together. First, pick a topic you can develop to that length—one of those you checked on pages 49–50, one from the master list, or any suggested or approved by your instructor.

¹‡Write the topic here: _____

You start, of course, by jotting down your thoughts and from them forming a central idea for the whole paper.

²‡Write that central idea here: "I will show that _____

_____."

Now you build the outline in two stages. The first stage is to list below the major divisions of your central idea (subtopics). For a theme of this length it is best not to have more than two or three divisions. For example, the writer of "End Privileged Parking" (pages 39–40) had three divisions of her central idea: impracticality, unfairness, and lack of democracy. On a scrap paper, jot down your divisions. Think of the most sensible order for them; then write them in that order in the blanks below. For now, *ignore anything* in the boxes:

Introduction:

    Interest-arouser:

    Central idea as it will appear in paper:

    Importance of topic:

    Other:

First division: _____

    Central idea: _____

    _____

Body

Second division: _____

Body

Central idea: _____

_____

Third division (if needed): _____

Central idea: _____

_____

Conclusion:

Summary sentence(s)(optional):

Reinforcement of central idea:

Final sentence (suggested action, memorable statement—what you want to stay in reader's mind):

Have you guessed what the second stage is? It is to duplicate the first stage on a smaller scale for each division you listed. Each division will be a paragraph of your theme. For each division topic, form a central idea; write it in the box under that division topic. Then, in the space below each of these central ideas, list the details you will give in that paragraph—after you have first jotted them on scrap paper and determined their order.

You have now finished much of the important work of writing this paper. The divisions you have planned—the meat of the paper—are called the *body* of the paper. All that is left is to plan the introduction and conclusion (the slices of bread to go above and below the meat) and then carry out the plan. Put aside for a while the outline you have just worked on and work through the following pages on introductions and conclusions.

WRITING INTRODUCTIONS

Writing on a personal experience, a student opened his paper like this:

> A. *Throughout my life I have encountered many interesting situations and experiences. Some of these have been favorable and others unfavorable. The situation about to be described, I feel, falls into a favorable category. About two years ago....*

Other students started their papers as follows:

> B. *As a child I didn't have many problems but the ones I had seemed very heavy. I remember....*
>
> C. *Facing responsibility to some people is a very difficult thing to do, while for others it is relatively easy. Ever since I can remember....*
>
> D. *There's one room in my house where I spend most of my time. The main reason for this is that there are many different things I can do in this one room....*
>
> E. *It's 7 A.M. this bitter cold December day in 1931, and the line outside the Harmon Employment Agency has grown bigger since I arrived at 5. As it is, I guess I'm lucky; there are only twenty-four men ahead of me....*

3‡

If you had time to read only one of these, which one would you pick? _____

4‡

Why? _____ Which of the openings begin with an everyday statement that tells nothing new—that is obviously true of almost anybody or

5‡

anything? _____ Such a statement is called a *truism* (TROO izm). Which one begins with an indication that the writer is going to show you something new—something

6‡

different from what you already know? _____ Is the answer to this last question

7‡

the same selection you said you would choose to read? _____ Find the last paper you wrote before beginning this module and read the opening sentence or two. Again, try to put yourself in your reader's shoes. If she had time to read only one paper and had to choose from the five openings above and yours, would she pick your paper? If she could choose two, would yours be one of them? If she could choose three? In short, how interesting is the opening of your paper? In A above, what has the writer told you that is not a truism, a

8‡

statement obviously true in almost everyone's life? _____ In B?

9‡   10‡   11‡

_____ In C? _____ In D? _____
If each of these writers in his first sentence has really told you only what you already know or would have assumed, why has he bothered writing that sentence? What reason has he given you for reading on? Now look at E. What do you learn from his opening sentence? Has he started with something different, something that makes you want to read about his

12‡

experience? Is E the answer you wrote for question 3? _____ For question 6?

13‡

_____ Then what have you discovered about how to begin—and how *not* to begin a paper? _____

Themes that begin with commonplace, ho-hum statements like those in A to D make few readers interested enough to read on, just as you have probably tossed aside many books after finding the first few pages dull. When planning your paper, after you have composed your central idea and listed your divisions, facts, and details, ask yourself, "What can I start with that will arouse my reader's interest—that is not a truism?" Open with your answer to this question.

But suppose you find no answer to this question. That must mean your entire paper

is going to contain almost nothing but [15]‡t_ _ _ _ms. In such a case you must ask yourself the unkindest question of all: If I can say nothing but truisms—ideas everyone would agree with already—or facts everyone knows, then why am I writing on this central idea? Hard as it may be, I must drop the central idea or possibly the whole topic, and try another.

Here are the opening sentences of six pieces of writing. Some are from students, some from professional writers. After reading them, rank them in order of interest, from the one that most makes you want to read on down to the one that least makes you want to. Write the numbers of your rankings in order in the blanks at the end, with the most interesting first:

1. There are many problems facing the United States today.
2. Has the earth been visited in antiquity by other forms of intelligence from the vast depths of our universe?
3. To be black in the United States is no longer to be always subordinate.
4. In my short career I have worked in many offices.
5. This is the ominous, behind-the-scenes story of two recent fatal airplane crashes.
6. The maintaining of one's personal property today involves quite a varied field of trades.

[16]‡Most _____ _____ _____ _____ _____ _____ Least

Since the rankings are personal choices, there can be no "right" answer. Two of the six sentences are by professional writers, from *Reader's Digest*. Which two do you think they

are? [17] _____ and _____ When you check the answer page, you may be surprised to find that one of the sentences many students rate best or near best was written by a student in an ordinary freshman composition class.

By now you probably have a good grasp of what is needed to make an interesting opening. Sometimes, as in sentence 3, it is the central idea itself. Other times, as in sentence 5, the writer picks an interest-arousing fact or aspect of his topic. He may also arouse curiosity by a question, as the writer of sentence 2 did.

Incidentally, have you noticed one word that recurs in a surprising portion of weak

openings? [See also pages 54–55 and 69.] It is [18]m_ _ _. The vagueness and wishy-washiness of this word create a bad first impression on the reader, suggesting that a vague and wishy-washy paper will follow. Avoid *many* in your opening sentence. ("Word Choice" treats *many* more fully.)

What else besides the interest-arouser goes into your introduction? Naturally, your central idea—although experienced writers sometimes like to save their central idea for the conclusion, leading up to it throughout the paper. As a less-experienced writer, you will do better to state the central idea somewhere in the introduction.

There is one more item that the reader will look for when starting your paper. As mentioned earlier, she is going to ask herself, "Why should I bother reading this paper?" Sometimes the interest-arouser alone will attract her; however, she will want to know not just how interesting what you have to say is, but how important to *her*.

Here is the introductory paragraph of a freshman paper on the world's increasing population:

(1) The figures are awesome: a world population today of 4 billion, with a million newcomers every week. (2) On the other end, people are living longer thanks to medical science. (3) The number of human beings in the world could double by the year 2000 and reach 16 billion a few decades later. (4) Is the earth ready for them? (5) Indications are it can never be ready.

Which sentence or sentences arouse interest? [19] _____ Which state(s) his

central idea? [20] _____ How does he indicate that his paper is important to

the reader? [21] _____

One of the hardest types of papers to make significant to the reader is a paper on your personal experience. The night the dean caught you attempting to seduce his daughter may be unforgettable in your life, but what significance does it have for the *reader*? A central idea that makes the point of the experience general enough to include the reader will make the paper important to that reader. Which of the following two central ideas does that? Circle its letter:[22]

A. *In this paper I will show that I was almost expelled from the college because the dean caught me trying to seduce his daughter.*

B. *In this paper I will show that a young person can endanger his entire future by letting his emotions overcome his common sense.*

The reader may never have been tempted to seduce the dean's daughter, but he has probably been in conflicts between emotion and common sense, with serious consequences for the wrong choice. He will therefore find your paper significant to him if you use central idea B and use the dean's daughter incident as your chief example to develop that idea.

Take any paper that you have written before beginning this module—if you have any—that the instructor said was weak in arousing interest. Examine it for some interest-arousing fact, idea, or question that you could have begun with, and for a way to make the paper important to the reader. (Your interest-arouser, statement of importance, and central idea do not have to be in separate sentences. The sentence *To be black in the United States is no longer to be always subordinate* arouses the reader's interest ["Is that really true?"], implies the importance of the topic to both blacks and whites, and states the central idea.) In the space below, rewrite the opening paragraph of your paper so that it arouses interest, indicates the topic's importance, and states the central idea. (Introductory paragraphs are usually brief.) If you have no paper to rewrite, try rewriting one of the introductions (A to D) on page 69. Use your imagination:

_____

_____

_____

_____

_____

_____

_____

Now turn back to the outline you are making for the topic you chose on page 67 and fill in the box labeled *Introduction*.

WRITING CONCLUSIONS

How do you end a paper? Do you just stop? Let us look at some famous conclusions:

> *Gentlemen may cry, Peace, Peace—but there is no peace. The war is actually begun! The next gale that sweeps from the north will bring to our ears the clash of resounding arms! Our brethren are already in the field! Why stand here idle? What is it that gentlemen wish? What would they have? Is life so dear, or peace so sweet, as to purchased at the price of chains and slavery? Forbid it, Almighty God! I know not what course others may take; but as for me, give me liberty or give me death!*
> — *Patrick Henry, speech in the Virginia Convention*

> *We, therefore, the representatives of the United States of America, . . . do . . . solemnly publish and declare that these United Colonies are and of right ought to be free and independent States . . . and that all political connection between them and the State of Great Britain is and ought to be totally dissolved. . . .*
> *And for the support of this declaration, with a firm reliance on the protection of Divine Providence, we mutually pledge to each other our lives, or fortunes, and our sacred honor.*
>
> — *Thomas Jefferson, the Declaration of Independence*

> *When we let freedom ring, when we let it ring from every village and hamlet, from every state and every city, we will be able to speed up that day when all God's children, black men and white men, Jews and Gentiles, Protestants and Catholics, will be able to join hands and sing in the words of the old Negro spiritual, "Free at last! Free at last! Thank God Almighty, we are free at last!"*
> — *Martin Luther King, Jr., "I Have a Dream . . ."*

What does each of these three famous conclusions do for the reader? Answer these questions:

What was Patrick Henry speaking about? _____[24]_____

What was his central idea on this matter? _____[25]_____

_____

How strongly did he feel about it? _____[26]_____ Why

was it important to his listeners or readers? _____[27]_____

What was Thomas Jefferson writing about? _____[28]_____

What was his central idea on this matter? _____[29]_____

_____

How strongly did he feel about it? _____[30]_____ Why

was it important to his readers? _____[31]_____

What was Martin Luther King, Jr., speaking about? _____[32]_____

_____ What was his central idea on this matter? _____[33]____

_____

_____ How strongly did he feel about it? _____[34]_____

_____ Why was it important to his listeners or readers? _____[35]____

_____

What, therefore, should a conclusion do? It should remind us of the [36]c_ _ _ _ _ _
i_ _ _. It may also suggest the significance of the topic to us and what we should do about
the matter. It leaves no doubt as to the writer's overall thinking or feeling on the topic. And
there is one more quality of a good ending. What made these paragraphs *sound* like endings?
The answer is hard to put into nontechnical words, but notice that the writers all had a
good "sign-off" line—a statement that stayed in the reader's mind and at the same time
left no doubt that the writer was finished. Just as an introduction should awaken our interest,
a conclusion should leave us satisfied but still interested.

Let us look at some typical student endings. They will obviously not equal Henry's,
Jefferson's or King's, but let us see how well each

1. reminds us of the central idea
2. suggests the significance of the topic to us
3. leaves no doubt as to the writer's attitude toward the topic
4. has a sign-off that sends us away thinking on the topic

Along the way we will discover what else an ending should and should not do.

First, read this paragraph from some part of a student's paper on the inflation crisis of the mid-1970s:

> *Governments will try to stop inflation. Sometimes they will even freeze prices, as the United States did with the beef prices. This does not always work out. The price freeze led into a cutback in supply and there was a beef shortage. Then the prices went up anyway. A government may also pass a heavy taxation law, to take the money away from the people. A government may also reduce its spending money to have less money flowing and stabilize the economy.*

This paragraph seems to be what part of the paper?[37]   ☐ The introduction   ☐ Part of the body   ☐ The conclusion‡

Are there still questions in your mind at the end of this paragraph? For example, does the writer favor any of these government actions? If so, which? If not, then what does he suggest to combat inflation? And whatever way he suggests, how strongly does he feel about its success? Would you expect a writer to answer these questions at the end of a paper on

this topic? [38‡] _____ The paragraph you just read was actually the conclusion of

the student's paper. But was it really a conclusion? [39‡] _____ There is a vast difference between a paper that concludes and one that merely stops. They are like two airline flights that left Seattle for Chicago. One came down to a safe landing in Chicago; the other ran out of fuel over Montana. The first flight concluded; the second stopped. The first require-

ment for the conclusion of a paper, then, is that it must [40‡] c__ __c__ __ __ __, not just stop.

Let us then add a fifth quality of a good conclusion to the four listed on page 73: A good conclusion attempts to answer any major questions raised in the paper, leaving no loose ends. (If you ask yourself whether the student paragraph above has any of those other four qualities, you will see other reasons why it fails to really conclude his paper.) Try writing a two or three sentence conclusion to that student's paper, to follow the paragraph you read. You are free to create any conclusion you wish from his facts:

[41]

_____

_____

_____

_____

_____

_____

Now let us look at conclusions to some other student papers. In the blanks beneath each, write how well you think it achieves the qualities of a good conclusion; you may also list any other strengths or weaknesses you find:

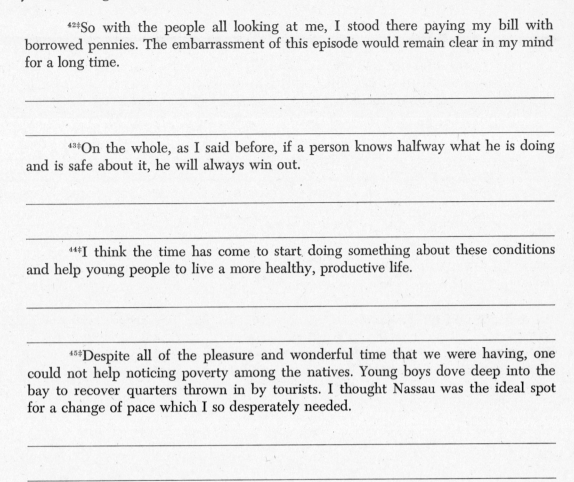

[42]‡So with the people all looking at me, I stood there paying my bill with borrowed pennies. The embarrassment of this episode would remain clear in my mind for a long time.

_____

_____

[43]‡On the whole, as I said before, if a person knows halfway what he is doing and is safe about it, he will always win out.

_____

_____

[44]‡I think the time has come to start doing something about these conditions and help young people to live a more healthy, productive life.

_____

_____

[45]‡Despite all of the pleasure and wonderful time that we were having, one could not help noticing poverty among the natives. Young boys dove deep into the bay to recover quarters thrown in by tourists. I thought Nassau was the ideal spot for a change of pace which I so desperately needed.

_____

_____

Let us examine each of these conclusions. Conclusion 42 is from a paper telling of a personal experience. The first sentence is actually the tail end of the body of the paper. Therefore what does the student's conclusion say besides the fact that she would remember her experience clearly—which is obvious, since she has just told it from memory? This is a typical "nothing" conclusion—just a quick, tacked-on restatement of the topic—no real conclusion at all. What was she trying to show that is significant to us, the readers? What else could she have told us? What did she realize about herself, about other people, about life, from the experience? Did the experience change her attitudes toward money, toward friendship (a friend lent her the money)? Did it affect her self-confidence or her future behavior? (If it did none of these, should she have written about it?) What does she want the reader to take away with him from sharing her experience? Notice how the following conclusion for the same paper gives the reader something to go away thinking about:

I realize now that this experience changed my whole attitude toward money, making me more ruthless in my determination never to be embarrassed by lack of funds again. Thinking back on embarrassing moments, no matter how long ago they were, we all still feel the rush of blood to our faces. Somehow our egos suffer more from these humiliations than from other kinds of defeats, like a physical beating, *a job lost, or a romance gone sour. After hunger and even before sex, the desire to look good, not bad, in the eyes of others may be the most basic of all human motives.*

And here is a professional writer's conclusion to a retelling of a personal experience. It is Justice William O. Douglas's conclusion to his description of how he and another teen-ager once risked death by climbing an extremely dangerous mountain called Kloochman.* He wrote it after he had reclimbed the mountain many years later. Does this paragraph do what a good conclusion should?

> *Those [fears], however, were fleeting sensations. When I came to the top a sense of calm came over me, a deep peace. I knew now what a boy could not know, that fear of death was the compound of all other fears. I knew that long years ago I had begun to shed on Kloochman's walls the great, overpowering fear. Kloochman became for me that day a symbol of adversity and challenge—of the forces that have drawn from man his greatest spiritual and physical achievements.*

Let us look at conclusion 43. This writer does make a general statement that the reader can apply to life as a whole. But what did you think when you read "as I said before"?

He is in effect saying, "I am just ⁴⁶‡r__p__ __ __ing myself." This writer has merely repeated word for word the central idea he had stated in his introduction, leaving the feeling that both writer and reader were back where they had started. You discovered above that the

writer should ⁴⁷re__ __ __ __ you of the central idea in his conclusion; but this does not mean a word-for-word repetition.

What about conclusion 44? Does it remind us of the central idea? In fact, can you determine what the central idea, or even the topic, was? (His topic was "Causes of Juvenile Delinquency.") What is the *something* that the writer wants to be done? And whom does he

want to do it? This conclusion is weak because it is ⁴⁸v__g__ __. It tells the reader only that the writer really had nothing new to show about the topic. Not surprisingly, the writer did

⁴⁹‡

say nothing new in his entire paper. Should he have written on the topic at all? _____

Conclusion 45 presents a different problem. The writer's central idea should not be hard to determine. Circle the sentence that you think contains it.⁵⁰ But what about her other sentences? Does her mention of poverty fit with her idea of Nassau being the ideal vacation

⁵¹‡

spot? _____ Does it seem from the wording that she is mentioning poverty here

⁵²

for the first time in her paper? _____ Do you think a new division of a paper's

⁵³

topic should be introduced in a conclusion? _____ The writer of conclusion 45 does just that. Instead of concentrating on the main ideas she wants you to go away with, she distracts you with a new topic that should have been up in the body of her paper. On top of that, she leaves you hanging by not making clear why she bothered mentioning poverty at all.

---

* Adapted from *Of Men and Mountains* (New York: Atheneum, 1962), pp. 325–326.

Here is a quick review of what you have learned about conclusions. Good conclusions do all or most of these:

1. remind us of the paper's central idea
2. attempt to answer major questions raised in the paper, leaving no loose ends
3. leave no doubt as to the writer's attitude toward the topic
4. suggest or remind us of the significance of the topic to us
5. have a sign-off that sends us away thinking on the topic

Poor conclusions may

1. not be conclusions at all—just the end of the body
2. lack any indication of the importance to us of what the writer tried to show
3. merely repeat the central idea word for word
4. be so vague as to say nothing
5. introduce a new topic that should have been in the body

One more word on conclusions. There are several useful expressions to signal the reader that you are starting your conclusion, such as *therefore, thus, then,* and *consequently.* You do not have to use any of these, but less-experienced writers often feel safe with one of them. Two expressions to avoid, however, are the old student favorites *In conclusion* and *So you can see that.* Why? Simply because they *are* such old student favorites. They are so common that they mark the writers as dull and limited in vocabulary.

Now turn back to the outline you are making on the topic you chose on page 67, and fill in the box labeled *Conclusion.*

REVIEW

[1]To be interesting and convincing, your paragraphs must develop their central idea with _____.

[2]Therefore, in choosing a topic to write on, you must be sure you k_____

_____.

[3]To avoid runt paragraphs, a good length to aim for in your paragraphs (other than introductions and conclusions) is from _____ to

_____ sentences.

[4]Common sources of material from which to form and develop central ideas are o_____tion, o_ _ _ _ p_ _ _ _ _ _, y_ _ _ _ _ _

_ _ _ _, and the _ _ _ _ _ _ _.

[5]The best time to spot off-topic ideas is when you write your l_____

_____.

[6]For the reader to follow your train of thought, your paragraph must contain

s_g_ _ _ _. These will make your paper more c_h_ _ _ _t.

[7]‡When describing a person or place, what must you do about order?

_____

[8]‡When trying to convince the reader, the best order for your arguments is

from _____ to _____.

[9]‡When explaining something that does not fit into time order, such as a

sport, you start with the _____est idea and move toward

the _____.

[10]‡The introduction to a good longer theme usually contains (1)_____

_____, (2)_____, and

(3)_____; it always avoids _____

_____.

[11]‡Each paragraph of the body of a theme has its own _____

_____.

[12]‡The conclusion to a good theme usually accomplishes most of these:

1. _____

2. _____

3. _____

4. _____

5. _____

MASTERY TEST

Do A or B, as your instructor directs:

A. Write a 25 to 35 sentence paper on the topic you chose on page 67, using all the skills you have learned in this and previous modules.

B. Choose three topics from the master list or topics suggested or approved by your instructor. Write a seven to thirteen sentence paragraph on each, using all the skills you have learned in this and previous modules.

ANSWERS

DEVELOPING A PARAGRAPH

[22]She gave evidence from particular cases and from her reading.

[29]central idea

[33]observation

[34]other people

[35]own mind

[45]Sentence 5

[46]No

[47]Most people find it easier.

[48]The writer should remove it from the paragraph.

[49]No

[50]Item 6 is off the topic.

[51]Item 3 is off the topic. (The "facts" in this list are not necessarily true.)

[52]Items 2 and 5 are off the topic.

[53]Yes

[54]No

[55]Most people find it hard to follow exactly what is happening and why it is.

[56]They are what the reader would ask.

[57]Disconnected, the parts not sticking together logically

[59]coherent

[60]near

[61]which

[62]I first went there when

[63]When I returned last year

[64]Years ago *or* In my boyhood

[65]Last year *or* On my return

[66]In my boyhood *or* Years ago

[67]but

[68]on my return *or* last year

[70]Yes: sentence 1

[71]6, 12, 13 (possibly also 3)

[72]5, 8, 10

[73]2, 9, 11 (possibly also 7 or 12)

[74-81]The paragraph does not tell where any of these are in relation to the lake.

[83]order

[85]One suggested order: 1, 3, 4, 5, 8, 10, 7, 2, 11, 9, 6, 12, 13

[90]S: the first sentence

[91]C: the last sentence

[93]three, branch

DEVELOPING A LONGER PAPER

[14]It is hoped you have discovered that your opening needs to arouse the readers' interest by presenting something fresh or uncommon.

[17]3, 5 (sentence 2, which students often rank highly, was written by a freshman)

[18]many

[19]Sentence 1 arouses interest because of the "awesome" facts. Sentence 4 and 5 arouse the reader's curiosity—and curiosity is interest.

[20]Sentences 4 and 5 together state the central idea: that the world can never support the coming population.

[21]In sentences 3, 4, and 5, he implies that this problem will seriously affect his readers, most of whom will be alive in 2000.

[22]B

[24]Whether to fight for liberty.

[25]That we must fight for liberty, because lack of liberty is worse than death.

[26]Very strongly; the force of his words and his "liberty or death" choice tell us this.

[27]Because they had to make the same choice.

[28]The separation of the United States from Great Britain.

[29]That the United Colonies have every right to separate from Great Britain.

[30]Strongly enough to pledge his life and honor to the cause.

[31]Because the birth of a new nation is an important event in the world.

[32]Freedom for all people.

[33]That when all people are free, all kinds of people will live in brotherhood.

[34]Very strongly; the force of his words tells us this.

³⁵Because most of them were yearning for more freedom than they had.

³⁶central idea

⁴¹*Sample conclusion:* Of all these proposed solutions, only the last is both workable and practical. The first has already failed in practice, and no politician would vote for the second. But if the government cuts the money supply, manufacturers must cut prices because otherwise consumers will simply not have enough dollars to buy their goods. The federal government, then, must cut the money supply before it is too late; otherwise, as in Germany of the 1920s, our money soon may literally not be worth the paper it is printed on.

⁴⁷remind

⁴⁸vague

⁵⁰the last sentence

⁵²In her actual paper, she is.

⁵³It should never be.

MODULE 5

WORD CHOICE

Previous modules required: none

INTRODUCTION Read the two selections below:

Well, they had us take a look at the kids every day, and we'd write down a lot of things they did and said. There was this one teacher the kids really did things for. This was because she was damn good at math and could turn the kids on to it. At the end of the week we all got together to talk about what we'd found out since we got there. We all felt that you could pick up an awful lot about how to teach just from watching what the kids did whenever the teacher told them to do something.

SELECTION B

We were assigned to observe the children daily to record their actions and speech. What impressed us most was one teacher that the boys and girls responded to eagerly because she knew her math thoroughly and made it exciting. At the end of the week, when we met to discuss our conclusions, we agreed that anyone can learn a great deal about teaching methods from merely observing the children's responses to the teacher's directions.

Does one of these selections sound more as if someone had *spoken* it instead of

[1‡]

writing it? If you think so, which sounds like the spoken one? _____ What makes you think so? Can you pinpoint the differences between the two? Write below as many differences as you can find:

[2‡]

_____

_____

_____

_____

You should not worry if you had trouble explaining what the differences were, as long as you can see some.

Quite a few people tend to write words on paper just as they come into their minds—just as they would say them to a friend in the student lounge. But the two selections you have just read show that there is a detectable difference between the language of everyday speaking and the language of formal writing.

WORD CHOICE AND SOCIETY

There are several reasons for this difference. First let us look at a reason which you may not like to accept because it has nothing to do directly with the idea you are communicating. Look again at selections A and B. If you were told that neither had been spoken but instead both had been *written*, which writer would you

pick as the better educated? _____ Would you also conclude that he was the
more intelligent? _____

The problem is that writer A may be just as intelligent, just as sharp a thinker, as B—
possibly even sharper. But in our society most people will listen to writer B, since he seems
more intelligent because of the words and sentences he knows how to use. In this module
you will discover how to transform your informal, everyday speaking into formal writing
like that of selection B—a task that will probably be easier than you think, first, because you
already know most of the words that distinguish formal English from informal English and,
second, because you can make this transformation without having to know any rules of
grammar!

To begin with, look back at selections A and B. What *are* the differences? What words,
for example, did writer B use where writer A used . . .

Writer A	*Writer B*
[5]take a loot at	_____
[6]kids	_____
[7]write down	_____
[8]damn good at math	_____
[9]got together	_____
[10]what we'd found out	_____
[11]all felt	_____
[12]pick up	_____
[13]an awful lot	_____
[14]what the kids did	_____
[15]the teacher told them to do something	_____

Look at the words you wrote in the second column. Put a check (✓) to the right of any
word that you never saw before reading selection B or that you do not know the meaning of.

How many checks did you put? _____ You probably know all or almost all the
words in the second column. You see, then, that you do not need a vast vocabulary of fancy
words or a ten-pound dictionary to make your writing more formal; it is just a matter of
spotting in your writing informal words that you can replace with more formal words you
already know.

Look at the two columns again. What is *better* about the words in the second column?
As far as meaning goes, nothing. Most people would agree that selection A is just as clear as
selection B. True, the expressions in the second column are often briefer; but not always.

Then why does writer B sound more impressive to his readers? Why would selection B probably receive an *A* or *B* in a composition class but selection A a *C* or lower? The answer comes best through an old comparison, or analogy, used by countless English teachers. A sweatshirt and dungarees will clothe you at least as thoroughly as a dress suit or a gown, but for a formal occasion such as a church wedding or a banquet, dungarees would be considered wildly out of place, and people there would form a poor impression of the dungaree-wearer. They would probably assume that he either had no other clothes or did not know the appropriate clothes to wear.

In short, the difference is largely social. Rightly or wrongly, people judge us by our language as they judge us by our clothes. If we use only informal words on occasions when readers expect our best formal ones, those readers usually conclude that we know no others or that we do not know we should be using them. Selection A is on an *informal* level—as we would chat with a friend in the lounge. Selection B is on a more *formal* level. This is the level on which most educated people—business executives, teachers, lawyers, personnel directors—expect other educated people to write to them.

You will need to write formal English whenever you write a letter or report of almost any kind on your job; whenever you submit a written assignment to a professor; whenever you express your opinion to a newspaper or at a community meeting; whenever you write applying for a job; in short, whenever you write or speak publicly in the business, professional, or political world—the "educated" world.

(One more word on this matter: The word *formal* should not scare you; it does not necessarily mean *stiff* or *stilted* like the wording of legal documents or wedding invitations. Writing "I have been rendered temporarily impecunious" to someone who has asked to borrow money is almost as out of place as writing "I ain't got no money." "I have no money right now" will do.)

Are all words, then, sharply divided into only two kinds, formal and informal? By no means; what one experienced writer may regard as an informal word, another may consider formal. Also, there are degrees of formality and informality. To determine an exact borderline between these two levels is like trying to tell where the blue ends and the purple begins in a rainbow. Follow your instructor's guidelines in particular cases; it is quite possible he will disagree with some of this book's classifications of words. Perhaps understanding the *ladder of respectability* will make these differences clearer to you.

THE LADDER OF RESPECTABILITY

Remember the word *kids* in selection A of this module? It was replaced by

[17]c_ _ _ _ _ _ _ _ _ in selection B, which most students chose as the more "educated" one. Why? The two words mean the same. We could say that you should avoid *kids* because it really means young goats, but that is not a valid reason because you and all Americans today know the word means *children*. Yet *kids* illustrates an important concept in language, the *ladder of respectability*. Since *kids* did originally mean young (and frisky) goats, it is not hard to see how it came to be used for frisky children—probably among farm families. But at that time nonfarm people would not know that Farmer Jones might be talking about the little Joneses when he referred to his *kids*. At this stage in its development, then, *kids* as a term for children was probably known to only a small portion of the population and would

not be found in dictionaries. We call such words [18]sl_ _ _g; they occupy one of the lowest rungs of the [19]l____er of res_____ity. (Profanity, vulgarity, and obscenity are even lower.) *Kids* was once slang.

If you had been of college age about fifty years ago, you would know exactly what *twenty-three skidoo, the cat's pajamas,* or a *gat* meant. Yet to you then *the fuzz* would have been merely something on the skin of a peach, and *rip off* what a person did to the top of a cereal box. Can you list five other current slang words—words that the previous generation, and possibly the next, would not understand?

20‡

_____ _____ _____ _____

Slang is here today, gone tomorrow. It never stays around long enough to be recorded in dictionaries; if it does make the dictionaries, it is no longer slang. This is what happened to *kids;* it caught on and spread to American schools and cities, even to the "upper classes."

It climbed to a higher rung on the [21]l_____ of r_____y. Today even college professors and judges complain to their wives about their neighbor's kids.

A word on this rung is called a *colloquialism,* which simply means a word we use in *conversing with* someone informally. *Kids* and other colloquialisms, however, have not yet reached (and may never reach) the top rungs of the ladder of respectability: the rungs where they are accepted in *formal* writing. (Words may slip *down* the ladder, too. In the early days of our country, *ain't* was accepted by educated people as a shortened form of *am not.*)

How do we know which words are colloquialisms? Mostly from a combination of reading experience and common sense. For example, at five separate points in the following selection, which is adapted from a college textbook,* the original formal words have been

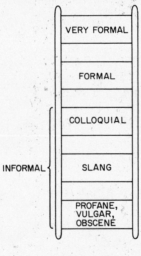

The Ladder of Respectability

replaced by colloquial or slang expressions (one to three words in length). Can you find these five, list them below the selection, and write what you think the original words were?

SELECTION C

One problem that plagues beginning teachers, and older teachers as well, is the seeming lack of self-control of underprivileged children. Because their homes are often

---

* Robert P. Parker, Jr., and Maxine E. Daly, *Teaching English in the Secondary School* (New York: Free Press, 1973), p. 5.

characterized by an awful lot of fragmentation and instability, their behavior reflects their inability to keep real cool in situations involving adults. . . . We think it important, therefore, that the teacher be calm and understanding. For the teacher to be able to exhibit this kind of behavior when confronting a bunch of adolescents, he must have achieved a terrific level of integration and security, so that his own psychic life is completely okay.

Colloquial Expression	Probable original formal expression
22	
23	
24	
25	
26	

If you found all five, congratulations! Double congratulations if you did well in the second column.

Remember: Colloquialisms are not "wrong" or "bad" English. No English that puts the writer's meaning clearly into the reader's mind is "bad." But, as we have said, using slang or colloquialisms, which are for informal situations, in a formal writing situation is regarded by most of the "educated" world as a sign that the writer knows *only* that level of words. Such words stand out like a T-shirt at the Inaugural Ball.

[27]‡Below is a paragraph a student wrote for a class report. He unintentionally sprinkled some slang and colloquialisms into what he intended to be formal English. Try to help him by crossing out each such expression and writing a more appropriate one in the margin. (Partial ‡)

SELECTION D

The Battle of Brickleburg was definitely a turning point in the Civil War. General Grant, with over 50,000 men and hundreds of cannon, waited eagerly for General Lee to dare a strike at his positions. Soon outriders began reporting long gray columns of Confederate soldiers advancing through Brickleburg Valley. When Grant got wind of what Lee was up to, he put down his booze and ordered his commanders to get their butts moving up to the front line. Unknown to Grant, however, a lot of Lee's men had been knocked off by malaria, and Lee knew his men were in for a helluva licking at the hands of Grant's seasoned veterans. But Lee, shrewd soldier and patriot that he was, boldly hurled every available company of infantry directly at the center of Grant's line. These guys charged right into a massacre. Grant, thinking Lee's frontal charge was only a feint in preparation for a main flank attack, did not commit his reserves, who were hanging around a few hundred yards behind the lines. Even so, the charging Confederates got all chopped up by the overwhelming Union artillery. Near tears at the sight of so many Confederate stiffs on the ground, Lee reluctantly ordered the bugler to sound retreat. When the smoke cleared, so great was the devastation visible on the battlefield that more than one hardened Union officer was seen to turn away and puke.

Reread your revised version. Are you finding the "feel" of what formal English is? If your instructor directs, exchange papers with another student. Circle any informal expressions you feel she left in. Return papers. Consider any expressions she circled on your paper. Are they slang or colloquial? She may or may not be right. Make changes if you wish and submit the paper to your instructor.

CONTRACTIONS

On to the next point. Read these two sentences:

a. The president announced today that he won't visit Russia next year if the Russians don't sign an arms treaty before then.

b. The president announced today that he will not visit Russia next year if the Russians do not sign an arms treaty before then.

Which sounds to you more like formal written English? _____ [28]

Which two words from sentence *a* have been changed in sentence *b*? _____ [29]

to _____, and _____ to _____. What is wrong with *won't* and *don't?* Nothing. *Don't,* as sentence *b* shows, is just [30]d__ n___ with the two words slid together. In the same way, *isn't* is a short form for [31]i__ n___, *haven't* for [32]h____ ____, *I'll* for [33]I _____, *he's* for [34]h__ i__, etc. There are several dozen such words in English. Why do you think English has them, when the long forms give the meaning just as well? [35]

_____ Since it takes more time and effort for a speaker to say *we will* than *we'll,* people usually use the slid-together form in informal speaking; but this difference largely disappears in writing, since it takes the eye almost no longer to read one than the other. Look back at sentences *a* and *b*. Which of these versions would you expect to see in your newspaper? [36] _____

Yes, formal writing uses the full forms, not the shortened ones. You should know that the official name for these shortened, slid-together forms is *contractions*. *We'll, won't, shouldn't, could've,* etc., are [37]c_____s. Look back at selections A and B on page 82. In which do contractions appear? [38] _____ Which did we say was the [39] formal selection? _____

At this point you might well pick up a magazine article, a newspaper column, a novel, or even a textbook and say (using informal English), "Look, Professor, you're all wrong.

This person is certainly writing in a formal situation, and he's using contractions!" You would be right, of course; many writers deliberately try to make their writing sound less formal, more like conversation. They often feel that this creates a closeness between themselves and their readers. *You, the writer*, control the level of formality in your writing. However, to be free to exercise this control, you need full command of formal English—just as a weight lifter who can press 400 pounds is free to press only 200, though one who can press only 200 is not free to press 400. That is why this book aims to teach you formal English: so that you will be free to write at that level or any level you choose below that.

Have you figured out yet what the little mark (') between the letters of a contraction means? Notice:

do not	I am	we have
do n't	I 'm	we 've
don't	I'm	we've

What does the mark (') stand for? _____ [40]

Where does it always go? _____ [41] Do you remember

from high school the name of this mark? It is called an [42]ap___t_____e.

Before you are asked to write without contractions, you may need some refreshing on the contracted and full forms. Try to give the full form for each contraction below:

[43]I'm __ ___ ___   I've __ h_____   couldn't _____ _____

you're _____ _____ ___   he's ___ ___   doesn't _____ _____

he's ___ ___   we've ___ _____   don't ___ _____

it's ___ ___   I'd __ wo_____   could've _____ _____

we're ___ _____   aren't _____ _____   should've_____ _____

they're _____ ___   isn't ___ _____   there's _____ ___

I'll __ w_____   weren't _____ _____   let's ____ us

you'll _____ _____   won't wi___ _____   would've _____ _____

she'll _____ _____   wouldn't_____ ____   might've _____ _____

we'll ___ _____

In informal English, *is* and *has* can be contracted to *'s* after almost any word that names something—for example, *The train's here already.* (*The train is here already*); *The train's been delayed* (*The train has been delayed*).

[44]‡Here is a selection that has been made partly informal by having contractions inserted. Cross out each contraction and in the margin write the equivalent formal form. When you finish, reread it to see the difference between the two versions:

Technology has a way of going to extremes. First there were microwave ovens, which don't take more than the blink of an eye to cook a dish. Now there's a trend toward electric pots that cook a dish so slowly you've time for at least forty winks.

Slow cookery, of course, isn't new. Down-Easters have always buried bean pots, and the old cast-iron cauldron hung over a wood fire wasn't a speed demon either.

...The samples we've cooked haven't tasted as good as they should've. What's good about this method? One manufacturer claims that while the heat's destroying bacteria it's keeping the vitamins intact.

— Adapted from Jean Hewitt, "Slow Cooking: An Evaluation,"
New York Times *(June 18, 1974), p. 34*

There are two more points about contractions. First, look back at the contractions on page 88; for which one did you write

⁴⁵‡could have? _____

⁴⁶‡should have? _____

⁴⁷‡would have? _____

⁴⁸‡might have? _____

Because the *'ve* sounds very much like *of* when spoken, some people mistakenly write *could of, should of, would of,* and *might of* instead of the four contractions you wrote above, or even instead of the full forms. Rewrite each sentence below, changing the underlined error first to a contraction and then to a full form:

⁴⁹*Mistaken:*   I <u>would of</u> liked to see *Gone with the Wind.*

Informal: I w_____'__ liked to see *Gone with the Wind.*

Formal: I w_____ _____ liked to see *Gone with the Wind.*

⁵⁰*Mistaken:*   I <u>should of</u> bet on a different horse.

Informal: I _____ bet on a different horse.

Formal: I _____ bet on a different horse.

⁵¹‡*Mistaken:*   I <u>might of</u> been killed in that accident.

Informal: I _____ been killed in that accident.

Formal: I _____ been killed in that accident.

⁵²‡*Mistaken:*   I <u>could of</u> danced all night.

Informal: I _____ danced all night.

Formal: I _____ danced all night.

Here is the second point. While professional writers and teachers may disagree on how far contractions can be admitted into formal writing, they will doubtless agree on one practice to be avoided. Can you discover it in the paragraph below?

SELECTION F

Column 1	*Column 2*	*Column 3*
(1) Do not tell me what I can do and what I can't.		
(2) You don't seem to care whether I am happy or whether I'm not.		
(3) It's tragic that you cannot see the damage you're doing to your own child.		
(4) It doesn't seem to make any difference to you, as long as you are not inconvenienced.		

53‡

Is the author of selection F writing formal English, informal English, or what? _____
54

What is he doing that does not make sense? _____

In column 2, rewrite selection F in formal English.[55‡] (Your instructor may also ask you to write the selection again in *informal* English in column 3.)[56‡] By now you probably have the message of this exercise: Be consistent! A mixture of contractions and full forms is actually worse than a completely informal paper when a formal paper is expected, because it reveals that the writer is not paying attention to his language level at all.

(There are two incidental bonuses from avoiding contractions: one is that you will avoid the error of omitting or misplacing an apostrophe, as in *didnt* or *did'nt;* The other is that there will be fewer occasions when you might confuse two similar words, such as *your/you're.*)

WORD CHOICE AND EFFECTIVE COMMUNICATION

Are there any other differences between speaking and writing besides the social differences you have already discovered? The following questions will lead you to the answer.

When you speak directly to your friend in the lounge, what helps do you have besides your words themselves to put your idea clearly into your friend's mind? For example, when she looks at you speaking, what does she see? _____

_____ From the way you speak to her, what tells her the mood—the

sadness, enthusiasm, worry, or fun—in your mind? Your [2]to___ of v_i___. What can she
[3]

do if something you say is unclear to her? _____

In face-to-face speaking, then, three elements besides the words alone are involved in sending
an idea from your mind to someone else's.

   Now, if instead of speaking face to face you are talking on the telephone, which of
[4]

these three aids vanishes? _____ You must rely

on your voice alone. Next, imagine that instead of telephoning, you are sending your absent
[5]

friend a tape-recorded message. Which other one of these aids do you lose? _____

_____ On tape, you must be much more careful in what you say,
for it must be clear the *first* time. Finally, suppose that you decide to write to your friend
[6]

instead of taping your message. What last aid have you lost? _____

   Now you have discovered the *main* reason that our writing must be different from
our everyday speaking. In writing, our meaning comes through our words only, without the
aid of gestures, facial expressions, or voice tone—and we have only *one* chance to make that
meaning clear. There is still another reason. Most people *expect* us to take more care when
we write than when we talk. In talking, our words usually come out within an instant after
we think of them. In writing, we have time to think of the best words and the best ways
to arrange them—time to cross out and rewrite, time to check for clearness and tidy up. Our
reader may even take it as an insult if we do not take the time to do these.

   Let us examine some of these differences.

FILLERS

   Once more, turn back to selections A and B on page 82. Selection B omits the very
[7‡]

first word of A. What is that word? _____ Why do you think it was dropped in
[8‡]

the formal version? _____ Our conversations are
filled with such expressions, as well as with pauses, *ers*, and *ums*. What do you think is our
[9‡]

usual reason for doing this? _____

   In speaking, our words often run ahead of our thoughts, and we often have to put off
our listener while we think of what we want to say. Since silence in a conversation is
awkward, we usually try to cover the silence with expressions that really mean nothing,
while we are thinking. A politician is doing this when he says, "And, my fellow Americans,
I want to tell you this: . . ." When a minister says, "And so, my dear brethren in Christ . . . ,"
he may be doing the same. How many other such "filler" expressions can you think of?

_____ _____ _____

_____ _____ _____

In writing, our words do not run ahead of our thoughts; in fact, it is often the opposite.

Therefore, do we need filler expressions in writing? _____ [12]‡In the following paragraph, cross out all expressions that seem to be fillers:

SELECTION G

Well, we had quite an exciting incident here yesterday. It seems that a school bus was trying to make a sharp right turn at Beasley Street when it jumped the curb and knocked over a fire hydrant. Let me tell you, the bus found itself in the middle of a huge geyser of water. Boy, the driver had her problems. The bus refused to move, and if she let the children out they all would have been drenched. Anyhow, the fire department finally arrived and shut the water off. Do you know what happened then? Well, the children started yelling for the firemen to turn the water on again. I'm telling you, the bus driver was so disgusted she shouted, "I quit!" and just walked away down the road.

YOU WHO? (POINT OF VIEW)

Once again, here are two selections to read:

SELECTION H

When a person enters a voting booth for the first time, he is faced with a bewildering array of levers and printed names of candidates, most of whom he has never heard of before. He has only three minutes to search the lists for the candidate he has planned to vote for, pull down all the proper levers, and check to be certain he has done everything right. The experienced voter may not find this difficult, but the first-time voter, distracted by the awe of his new power itself, often fumbles his way through the procedure and emerges wondering whether he voted for the candidates he intended to at all.

SELECTION I

When you enter the polling booth for the first time, you are faced with a bewildering array of levers and printed names of candidates, most of whom you have never heard of before. You have only three minutes to search the lists for the candidates you have planned to vote for, pull down all the proper levers, and check to be certain you have done everything right. If you are an experienced voter you may not find this difficult, but if you are a first-time voter, distracted by the awe of your new power itself, you often fumble your way through the procedure and emerge wondering whether you voted for the candidates you intended to at all.

Which selection sounds more formal? _____ What is the difference that makes that version sound more formal? _____

In general, when a person says *you*, is he usually referring to [15]☐ anybody ☐ just the person or persons he is writing or speaking to? Formal writing holds to this meaning of

[16‡]

you—that it refers only to the r＿＿＿＿r; thus the reader will never have to wonder whether *you* refers to him or to anybody. In fact, in fully formal writing, such as research papers, *you* is not used at all. In selection I, which does *you* seem to refer to? [17]☐ Just the persons

[18]

reading the paragraph ☐ Any first-time voter. Then is I formal writing? ＿＿＿＿＿＿＿
There are other traps you may fall into with the use of *you*. Read this sentence:

I like swimming because it develops your muscles.

Whose muscles does the sentence actually *say* are developed? [19]☐ My (the writer's) ☐ Your (the reader's). Whose muscles did the writer *really* mean? [20]☐ My (the writer's) ☐ Your (the reader's). Rewrite the sentence so that it makes logical sense:

[21]I like swimming because it develops ＿＿＿＿＿＿＿ muscles.

[22]Cross out the words that make the selection below inconsistent and illogical. Write the more logical forms in the margin:

SELECTION J

I like nothing better than that first icy splash into a pool after a steaming summer day at work. When your sticky, sweaty body first hits the blue-green water, the sudden refreshing shock of cold swirling around you almost makes me feel that the whole soggy day was worthwhile. You often spend all day at your desk just anticipating that glorious moment.

Submit your revised version to your instructor or check it against the answers, as he directs. A final word on *you:* Is there something a bit silly about each of these sentences?

a. In sixteenth-century England they often executed you for stealing a loaf of bread.

b. When you realize that you are the first man in the history of the world to reach the top of Mt. Everest, you are filled with an indescribable mixture of pride and awe.

Considering that you were not born until the twentieth century, could *you*, the reader of

[23‡]

this book, have been executed in sixteenth-century England—even once? ＿＿＿＿＿＿＿
Unless your name is Sir Edmund Hillary or Tenzing Norkay, could the writer of sentence *b*

[24‡]

be speaking to *you?* ＿＿＿＿＿＿＿ And even if you were the first conqueror of Everest,

[25‡]

would someone else be able to tell you how you felt? ＿＿＿＿＿＿＿ Thus the unregulated use of *you* can lead you into several such difficulties. Rewrite sentences *a* and *b* so that they are consistent and logical:

[26]Sixteenth-c＿＿＿t＿＿＿＿ E＿＿＿＿＿＿＿ men were of＿＿＿＿h＿＿＿＿＿＿

for _____.

²⁷When _____ realized that _____ was the f__ __ __ __ _____

_____

_____

_____

By the way, there is another word that can be used to replace *you* meaning *a person* or *anybody*. It is considered very formal and is used more in England than in America. Can you think of it?

²⁸In England o__ __ must always stop for tea in the late afternoon.

On a separate paper, write a paragraph of seven to nine sentences in formal English, showing how you feel or felt going through a certain kind of experience—for example, skiing from the top of a mountain, watching a horse race on which you have a bet, waking up with a hangover, proposing marriage (or being proposed to), writing an English theme, being mugged, becoming a mother or father for the first time, taking a final exam, visiting a strange place, asking someone you do not know well for a favor. When you have finished, exchange papers with another student for his comment (if your instructor directs); then submit it to your instructor.

A LOT OF THINGS YOU HAVE GOT TO GET STRAIGHT (CRUTCH WORDS)

Read the following:

SELECTION K

A lot of little things get me annoyed when I've got to get ready for school in the morning. The first thing is that when I wake up I get the sun right in my eyes. Next, my mother screeches at me to get down to the kitchen before my breakfast gets cold. By the time I get to the bathroom, my whole family is there ahead of me. This is one thing that really gets me angry because it happens a lot of times. Getting my fair share of food at the breakfast table is getting harder too. Each year my brothers get more greedy, and I cannot even get a piece of food into my mouth. My temper is getting close to the boiling point.

Another thing that annoys me is not getting out of the house and getting to the bus stop on time. Our clocks never seem to get together; I've got to get myself a watch. I missed the bus twice last week and I got a cold from walking to the campus in the rain. It takes me an hour of walking to get to the college when I don't get the bus; it's a very bothersome thing when I get my feet wet.

Last week I got so angry I got into a fight with another student. I punched him in the nose, but he got me right in the eye. The security guard got us both and told us to get out of the building. It gets me how I always get caught whenever there's trouble; a lot of times the other person gets away. It's a funny thing; I can never get away with anything.

Another thing I've got to do is to get out of that math test today. If I can get Professor Schmaltz to excuse me until tomorrow, I can meet Susie and get her to help me with my psych paper. She and I are getting to be good friends. Maybe some day we will get married and then I will get rid of a lot of my problems.

Good written English (even good informal English) means English that sounds alive and interesting. Since you have time to think of words before you write them, if you keep repeating the same simple words your readers will assume that you know no others or that you lacked the ambition to think of them. Your readers may also become so bored that they will toss your paper aside. For example, what is your impression of the writer of selection K? What words has he used so often that we become tired of them? Write three or more words that this writer has used too often and for which you should have found synonyms—other words that mean the same. (Do not list *the, and, I, to,* etc., which have no synonyms.)

²⁹

_____   _____   _____   _____   _____

Such words are sometimes called *crutch* words because the writer leans on them instead of exercising his own mental muscles to find varied or more exact words.

³⁰Now here is part of selection K again; complete the revised version below by substituting more exact words for the crutch words of the original:

SELECTION K (REVISED)

Almost ev____y little inc__d___t an_____ys me when I h_____ to pr_____re for school in the morning. First, when I wake up the sun h____s me right in the eyes. Next, my mother screeches at me to c_____ down to the kitchen before my breakfast i__ cold. By the time I r_____h the bathroom, my whole family is there ahead of me. This really m__k____ me angry because it happens so of_____. Ob_____ing my fair share of food at the breakfast table is bec_____g harder too. Each year my brothers gr____ more greedy, and I cannot even p___ a piece of food into my mouth. My temper is n____r___g the boiling point.

Check your answers. Were there any words in the revised version that you had never heard of before or did not know the meaning of? ^{31‡}_____ If so, which words? ^{32‡}_____

_____ You see, then, that you do not have to learn fancy words to write good formal English; you merely have to pause and think of words you already know. Did you notice another way by which we can avoid tiresome repetition of such words as *get* and *thing*—for example, at the beginning of the second sentence in selection K (revised), what did we do? We simply [33]rew_____ that part of the sentence to [34]o_____ the weak word.

Reread the revised version. Does it sound as if it was written by a more alert, more caring writer than the original was?

[35‡]Try now the next paragraph—this time you should need fewer hints:

SELECTION K (REVISED)

Another an____y____ce is not l_____ the house and a_____

at the bus stop on time. Our clocks never seem to a_____; I really m_____

_____ a watch. I missed the bus twice last week, and I c_____ a cold walking

to campus in the rain. It takes me an hour to _____ to the college, and w___

f_____ really b_____ me.

Besides its increased liveliness, do you notice something else about the revised version?

Is it longer or shorter than the original? [36]_____ Did you notice how often you were able to reduce a two-word or longer expression to a single word, such as *leaving* for *getting out of?* Thus, economy is a bonus by-product of eliminating crutch words. (You will have more practice in this in the modules on economy.)

It is now time for you to try some revision completely on your own. Using your own paper, rewrite the last two paragraphs of selection K, eliminating as many instances of *get* (*got, getting*) and other crutch words as you can. You may be good enough to eliminate them all. Remember that you can either replace them with better words or rewrite sentences to exclude them. Hand the finished paper to your instructor.‡

HOW MANY IS MANY? (VAGUE WORDS)

In selection K we focused on one of the most common student crutch words, *get*, and touched on two others, *thing* and *a lot of*. (*A lot of*, as you have learned, is also colloquial.) Some other crutch words are *many, very*, and *nice*. There is a reason other than mere repetition for avoiding these words. How many is *many?* How many people is *a lot of* people? Are a lot of people waiting outside a telephone booth the same number as a lot of people in Yankee Stadium? How high is *very* high? Can you think of a word that describes such words? [37‡]Va_____. Most of the crutch words are weak because they are not exact; they are vague. In fact, *thing* is just about the vaguest word in the English language. Can you think of anything that is not a thing? Your reader wants to know *exactly* what you mean.

What can you say instead of *many* or *a lot of?* How many people *were* there outside that telephone booth? Replace *a lot of* in this sentence with a more specific word:

[38‡][*A lot of*] _____ people were waiting outside the stage door.

Naturally, if you cannot make an exact count, you can approximate, as in

About a dozen people were waiting outside the stage door.

Your reader still has a much better picture of the group than if you had said *many*.

³⁹In the selection below, try replacing the italicized crutch words with more exact words. (Since you probably do not know the exact figures, make them up or approximate them.)

SELECTION L

Many years ago the Great Depression threw *a lot of* people out of work. Wages of other workers shrank to *very small amounts*. Since people needed jobs so desperately, employers were often *not very nice* to their workers.

Congress passed *very many* bills to bring the country out of the Depression. The 1936 elections showed that though *lots of* the American people opposed these measures, *many many more* favored them. After this election President Roosevelt assured the nation that *nicer* days were ahead.

SELECTION L (REVISED)

_____ years ago the Great Depression threw _____ people out of work. Wages of other workers shrank to u____r $_____ a year. Since people needed jobs so desperately, employers were often c____l to their workers.

Congress passed ov____ _____ _____ bills to bring the country out of the Depression. The 1936 elections showed that though _____ percent of the American people opposed these measures, _____ percent favored them. After this election President Roosevelt assured the nation that more pr___- p___ous days were ahead.

You will find that in your college courses, essay answers written like the original selection L often earn only *C*s, while those written like the revised version, specific instead of vague, earn the *A*s and *B*s.

WHY THREE OR TWO WHEN ONE WILL DO? (ROUNDABOUT EXPRESSIONS)

Finally, there are certain expressions containing two or more words which do not have any special name or type but weaken a person's writing because there are single words with the same meaning—words that he has not thought of.

⁴⁰‡In the revised version below, write single words to replace the italicized expressions in selection M. Some answers should already be familiar to you. (Partial ‡)

SELECTION M

There are countless wonderful *things to see* in London. When you *get there,* you should first *get on* a double-decker bus and *ride around* the city. You will be surprised how many *things to do* there are in a day. You can *walk slowly* through Picadilly Circus, which *looks like* Times Square. You can *go to* the Tower of London, where Henry VIII's wives *got killed* when he *said so.* Another *thing to see* is 10 Downing Street, *the place where the Prime Minister lives.* Chelsea is *where many artists live.* You can *get there* on the subway, which *gets* you anywhere in London for a few cents.

SELECTION M (REVISED)

There are countless wonderful s_____ts in London. When you ar____-____, you should first b_____d a double-decker bus and t____r the city. You will be surprised how many ac____-____t_____ there are in a day. You can st_____l through Picadilly Circus, which res_____b____s Times Square. You can v_____t the Tower of London, where Henry VIII's wives w__r__ ex__c__t__d on his or_____s.

Another at__r__t____n is 10 Downing Street, the Prime Minister's h_____. Chelsea is the h_____ of many artists. You can r_____h it on the subway, which t_____s you anywhere in London for a few cents.

Now reread both selections to see the difference.

REVIEW

Before moving on to the mastery test for this module, you will probably benefit from a review. (Your instructor may choose to make this part of the mastery test instead.)

Each sentence on the left below contains at least one expression that is slang, colloquial, crutch, vague, or otherwise unsuitable for formal writing. Underline each such expression and write a more formal or more exact expression at the right:

1‡He has a lot of nerve.   _____ nerve

2‡We learned five things in his class.   five _____

3‡Many people were injured.

_____ people

4‡There were a bunch of kids outside the candy store

_____ outside

5‡We got out of there in a hurry.

_____ there

6‡The mayor plans to get rid of fifty municipal jobs.

_____

7‡I've got to get a move on.

_____ _____

_____ _____

8‡Sandra is getting married to Mark in the fall.

Sandra is _____ Mark

9‡It's getting dark.

_____ _____ _____ dark

10‡With his wooden leg he couldn't get down the stairs easily.

he _____

d___c___d the stairs

11‡He got his degree in only three years.

_____ his degree

12‡It gets me how he cheats but always passes.

_____

13‡The cops got Louie.

_____ _____

14‡I get a cold every time it rains.

_____

15‡Be sure to get to the hall on time.

_____

16‡My older brother was able to get out of the draft.

a_____ or es_____ or ev_____

17‡Our boss didn't go for the things we did.

our e_____er d_____ _____

l_____ our a_____

18‡He's a pretty nice guy.

[whole sentence] _____

_____

‡19Lots of Americans have very large bank accounts.

[whole sentence] _____

_____

20‡I always vote for the Democrats because they give you more benefits.

_____

21‡Finley got told to get down to New

[whole sentence] _____

Orleans and take a look at the things the branch manager there was doing.

_____

_____

_____

_____

[22‡]Sir, I wish to report that I have investigated the activities of the New Orleans branch manager and that everything is okay.

[23‡]The first thing I will do if elected is to get together with state officials and devise programs to get this burg moving again.

My first a_____ if elected will

be to _____ with state

officials and devise programs to _____

_____

_____

_____

[24‡]My initial reaction upon finishing *War and Peace* was that it's an awfully nice book.

[25‡]In view of the worsening economic situation, the president feels that we should maybe institute price controls.

p__ __ __ __ps.

[26‡]The five things the treaty of 1783 said were . . .

The five _____ of the Treaty of 1783 were . . .

[27‡]Prentiss will try to get the doorman to let us get into the lobby.

Prentiss will try to p__ __ __ __ __de the

doorman to let us e__ __ __ __ the lobby.

MASTERY TEST

On a separate paper, write a paragraph of ten to fifteen sentences, in formal English, on one of the topics your instructor selects from the master list or on a topic he presents. The paragraph will be evaluated on your ability to write in formal English.

ANSWERS

WORD CHOICE AND SOCIETY

[3]Probably B

[4]Most people probably would.

[5]observe

[6]children *or* boys and girls

[7]record

[8]knew her math thoroughly

[9]met

[10]our conclusions

[11]agreed

[12]learn

[13]a great deal

[14]the children's responses

[15]the teacher's directions

[17]children

[18]slang

[19]ladder, respectability

[21]ladder, respectability

[22]awful lot of/great amount of, high degree of

[23]keep real cool/keep (exercise, maintain) their self-control

[24]bunch of/group of

[25]terrific/high

[26]okay/satisfactory, normal, stable

[27]got wind of/learned of, heard of; was up to/was attempting, was planning; booze/liquor, whisky; get their butts moving/hasten, rush; a lot of/a large portion of (better, give a figure—say, nearly a quarter of); had been knocked off by/had been killed by, had died of (You find the rest.)

[28]b

[29]won't, will not; don't, do not

[30]do not

[31]is not

[32]have not

[33]I will

[34]he is

[35]to save time in speaking, to make speaking easier

[36]b

[37]contractions

[38]A

[39]B

[40]a letter (or letters) dropped

[41]where the dropped letter(s) used to be

[42]apostrophe

[43]*Column 1:* I am, you are, he is, it is, we are, they are, I will, you will, she will, we will; *Column 2:* I have, he is, we have, I would, are not, is not, were not, will not, would not; *Column 3:* could not, does not, do not, could have, should have, there is, let us, would have, might have

[49]would've; would have

[50]should've; should have

[54]He is mixing contracted (informal) and full (formal) forms (such as *do not* in sentence 1 and *don't* in sentence 2; *I am* and *I'm* in sentence 2).

WORD CHOICE AND EFFECTIVE COMMUNICATION

[1]the expression on your face (serious, joking, etc.) and the movements of your body (waving hands, shrugging shoulders, etc.)

[2]tone, voice

[3]ask you to make clear what you meant

[4]facial expression and body movements

[5]asking for clarification

[6]tone of voice

[10]*Examples:* Now listen to me . . .; make one thing perfectly clear . . .; Let me tell you (I want to tell you) . . .; Anyhow (anyway) . . .; As I was saying . . .; Yes . . .; Boy . . .; You know . . .

[11]No

[13]H

[14]*You* in the informal version becomes *a person, he,* or *the voter.*

[15]just the person or persons he is writing or speaking to

[17]Any first-time voter

[18]No

[19]Your

[20]My

[21]my

[22]I like nothing better than that first icy splash into a pool after a steaming summer day at work. When my sticky, sweaty body first hits the blue-green water, the sudden refreshing shock of cold swirling around me almost makes me feel that the whole soggy day was worthwhile. I often spend all day at my desk just anticipating that glorious moment.

[26]Sixteenth-century Englishmen were often executed for stealing a loaf of bread.

[27]When I realized that I was the first man in the history of the world to reach the top of Mt. Everest, I was filled with an indescribable mixture of pride and awe.

[28]one

[29]get, got, getting, thing, a lot of

[30]every, incident, annoys, have, prepare, hits, come, is, reach, makes, often, obtaining, becoming, grow, put, nearing

[35]rewrote

[34]omit

[36]Shorter

[39](These answers are not historically accurate; they are only suggestions as to what you might do.) Forty, 10 million, under $1000, cruel, over fifty, 30, 70, prosperous

[40]sights, arrive, board, tour, activities (You do the rest.)

MODULE 6

VOCABULARY SKILLS

Previous module required: Word Choice (5)*—Aid required: a dictionary—paper-back size or larger

INTRODUCTION

A number of years ago a research institute examined hundreds of successful persons in various careers to see whether there was any one characteristic that they had in common, compared with less successful people of the same age in the same occupation. Which of the following do you think the researchers found in more successful persons than any other characteristic? (1) more education, (2) higher IQ, (3) better home life as a child, (4) larger vocabulary.

[1‡] _____ The single characteristic found most often in successful persons was not education, IQ, or background, but a larger vocabulary than the less successful workers.* This does not mean, of course, that memorizing the dictionary will make you a millionaire, but it does indicate how important it is to have a wide command of words both to understand what others say and write and to be able yourself to say and write exactly what you mean. Much of this has already been pointed out in "Word Choice."

YOUR TWO PERSONAL VOCABULARIES

In "Word Choice" you saw that to find the best words for formal writing you do not have to be a "walking dictionary." Most experienced writers rarely consult a dictionary to find just the right words they want. (There is another book better designed for such work, called a *thesaurus* [the-SOR-us], but most good writers try not to rely on that either.) They pull their words from their own [2]m _ _ _ s. In "Word Choice" you saw good formal paragraphs written using such words as *observe, record, response, agree, arrive, eliminate, tour, representative, prepare, obtain, annoyance, activity,* and *stroll.* Unless English is not your native language, you probably knew all or nearly all these words when you saw them. Would you say these words were in your vocabulary or not, before you did "Word Choice"? [3‡] _____

That was really a trick question; the answer is both *yes* and *no,* because each of us has two kinds of vocabulary. The sentence below illustrates the first kind. The sentence tells of newborn twins whose facial features are similar to their father's. What word or words to fit the blank come into your mind *right away?*

[4‡]Everyone says the twins _____ their father.

Most people think right away of *look like.* Words like this, which pop into our heads when we want to say something, make up our first kind of vocabulary. These are all the words we can *recall* when we want to say something. What is the other kind of vocabulary each of us has? Read this sentence:

Everyone says the twins resemble their father.

[5]

Does this mean the same as the earlier sentence? _____ But (honestly!) did the word *resemble* come into your mind at all from the time you read the first sentence until you read the second? [6‡] _____ If you answered *no,* then *resemble* belongs to your second

---

* Johnson O'Connor, "Vocabulary and Success," *Atlantic Monthly,* CLIII (February 1934), 160–166.

vocabulary—the words which you cannot *recall* when you want to say something but whose meanings you can *recognize* when you hear or see them. These then are your two kinds of vocabulary. The words that pop into your head when you want to say something (the words

that you can [7]re____l) are called your [8‡]r_____ vocabulary. The words which you

can not recall when you speak or write but which you can [9]re___g_____ when you see

or hear them are called your [10‡]r_____ion vocabulary. In this module, as in "Word Choice," you will learn how to improve your writing by taking words *you already know* in your recognition vocabulary and moving them up into your recall vocabulary. However, the module will have you putting some meat on the bones of your recognition vocabulary, too, since a word can never be part of your recall vocabulary until it is first in your recognition vocabulary. This is how you learn to use most words:

Word meaning is unknown to you	→	Word enters your recognition vocabulary as you hear or read it one or more times	→	Word enters your recall vocabulary as you start using it yourself

Read the expressions below; rewrite each in one of the three columns below, according to whether you think you (1) know the word to use as part of your recall vocabulary; (2) know its meaning as part of your recognition vocabulary; (3) do not know its meaning at all. The first three items are done for you as an example of what a typical student might write. Of course, the answers will be somewhat different for each student.

poor	depart	work
indigent	jail	illumination
assemble	argue	over
go home	get together	incandescence
happy	penitentiary	employment
dispute	penniless	light
incarceration	drunk	solon

[11]*Recall vocabulary*	*Recognition vocabulary*	*Unknown*
poor	*assemble*	*indigent*

How can you enlarge your vocabulary, either recognition or recall? What do you think of memorizing a page of a dictionary every night? Why might this not be a very efficient

12

method? _____ Then what about memorizing vocabulary lists, as is done in many schools? This is better than memorizing the dictionary because the teacher usually selects only useful words, but such lists are really crutches for students who have failed to learn vocabulary the natural way. What is that natural way? Reading and listening, seeing and/or hearing each word a number of times; this is how you learned nearly all the words you know. For example, write what you think *erstwhile* means.

13‡

Do not look it up. _____ Now read this sentence:

Jimmy Schultz looks like an erstwhile professional boxer.

14‡

Now what do you think it means? _____
You may have hit on the exact meaning, or you may even have the opposite meaning. But, seeing that part of the word was *while,* you may have figured that it had something to do with time. Try again:

Froder's erstwhile friends had testified against him.
The erstwhile town beauty now hustles drinks in a run-down bar.

15‡

What does *erstwhile* mean? _____
This is basically how we learn words—by a combination of (1) seeing and/or hearing them repeatedly in different sentences and (2) recognizing in the words similarities to other words we already know. As with *erstwhile* above, it usually takes several exposures to a word before its meaning becomes clear. Now, check your dictionary to see how close you came

16‡

to the meaning of *erstwhile.* Write the dictionary meaning. _____

The only magic formula for enlarging vocabulary, then, is—read: Read a good newspaper daily. Other excellent sources of vocabulary are the weekly news magazines *Time* and *Newsweek,* and even *Sports Illustrated.* Half an hour daily with the paper or a couple of hours weekly with the magazines will do the job—not in a week or two, of course, but probably over six months or a year. Moreover, you will find yourself well supplied with ideas to write about and the knowledge you need to write about them. Real familiarity with words, through regular reading, makes them float up inside your head from the depths of your recognition vocabulary to the surface of your recall vocabulary, where you can easily find and use them.

have discovered the meaning from this sentence. Much of it hinges on knowing what the word *mutual* means. You can be fairly certain from the sentence that *mutual* and *unilateral* mean ²☐ the same ☐ the opposite. But even without knowing *mutual*, you can figure out that even though the two governments failed to agree to withdraw troops, the United States would withdraw. From just this information, *unilateral* probably means

³‡
_____

Up to now we have been using the most common method of learning words—finding clues in the situation in which the word occurs, which is called the word's *context*. These clues are usually in the other words of the sentence or neighboring sentences. What you see

or hear can also be part of the ⁴c_ _ _ _xt: if an actor in a movie says that the hero is going to the ship's forecastle, you learn *forecastle* just by watching where the hero goes. If your friend says she dislikes the *raucous* music on your stereo, the music itself will give you a good idea of what *raucous* means. At the very least you will know it means something unfavorable.

Besides context, there is another fairly reliable way to find meaning. Look at the word *unilateral* again. Have you seen other words that look like this word or part of it? How about *uni-*? *United, union, uniform, unit*—and of course you know of *unisex* styles. What does

⁵‡
uni- seem to mean? _____ If you are still not sure, you may find help if you recognize the other part of the word. Are you a football fan? Which way does a *lateral* pass

⁶‡
travel? _____ And if you remember your math, you know that a quadri*lateral*

⁷‡   ⁸‡
has four _____. Thus *unilateral* must mean _____. Now check your dictionary for the meaning. A good dictionary will also give you the meaning of the parts, *uni-* and *-lateral*. This information is usually given inside brackets [   ]. Write the dictionary

⁹‡
meaning: _____
If you know Spanish, French, or Italian many words like these will come even more easily to you.

These, then, are the two approaches we use in determining what a word means:

1. by examining the situation in which it occurs (its ¹⁰c_ _ _ _ _ _)
2. by noticing the resemblance it (or part of it) has to words we already know

This is how you have learned nearly all the words you know.

Here is some practice in discovering word meanings from context. What does the

¹¹‡
word *faze* mean? _____ If you are not sure, read this sentence:

> *Merton is not* fazed *easily.*

¹²‡
Faze seems to mean _____. Now read this one:

> *No interruption on the job* fazes *Merton, no matter how annoying it is.*

¹³‡
Faze seems to mean _____. Finally, read this:

Her children were screaming; the washing machine had just broken down;
Elton had just phoned to say he was bringing the boss home for dinner, and she had
only frankfurters in the house; she saw the dog dirtying the living room rug. But none
of this fazed *her; she whistled a tune and went merrily on with her work.*

By now you should have a fairly clear idea of what *faze* means. Write its meaning:
14‡

_____ Now check your dictionary to see how close you came.
15‡

Write the dictionary meaning: _____ Do not be
concerned about how close you came in wording; it is how close you came in *idea* that counts.
Even if you came quite close to the actual meaning on an early try, you probably found that
each following sentence brought you closer to being certain of your answer. Now write a
sentence of your own (not too similar to the ones above) using *faze:*
16‡

_____

Try some other words; first write what you think the meaning is from the word alone,
then what you think it is after reading each sentence:
17‡

    A. *Logistics* (lo JISS tics) means _____.

    The general was concerned about the logistics *of the battle.*

18‡

Logistics means _____.

    The general and his staff sat down and carefully figured out the logistics *of the battle*
    they were planning.

19‡

Logistics means _____.

    The logistics *of the battle presented problems: 50,000 soldiers with their equipment,*
    30,000 tons of ammunition, and 500 tons of food would have to be moved across the
    river on three pontoon bridges in an incredibly short time.

20‡

Logistics means _____. The dictionary meaning
21‡

of *logistics* is _____. Write an original sentence
using *logistics:*
22‡

_____
23‡

    B. *Beleaguered* (Be LEEG erd) means _____.

    The beleaguered *Indian warriors wondered what would happen to them.*

24‡

Beleaguered means _____.

The small, beleaguered *band of Indian warriors had had no food or water for three days.*

25‡

Beleaguered means _____.

The small, beleaguered *band of Indian warriors battled the surrounding U.S. Cavalry regiments to the last man.*

26‡

Beleaguered means _____.

Her children were screaming; the washing machine had just broken down; Elton had just phoned to say he was bringing the boss home for dinner, and she had only frankfurters in the house; she saw the dog dirtying the living room rug. The beleaguered *housewife was ready to scream.*

27‡

Beleaguered means _____. The dictionary mean-

28‡

ing of *beleaguered* is _____. Write an original sentence using *beleaguered:*

29‡

_____

THE SECOND APPROACH

Now we will practice the second approach: noticing resemblances to words you

30‡

already know. What do you think *ingest* means? _____
Probably the word *digest* popped into your mind right away. If people *digest* food in their stomachs, you probably thought, *ingest* must have something to do with food in the body. Up to here your thinking centered on *-gest,* the part of the word that is the same in both the new word, *ingest,* and the familiar word, *digest.* What does the word part that is *different*

31‡

(*in-*) tell us? To *ingest* food most likely means to do what with it? _____

_____ You have just found the probable meaning of *ingest* by noticing resemblances to familiar words. Now we will combine this approach with the first approach,

the ³²c____x__ approach. Read this:

With her broken jaw wired shut, Marian could ingest *nourishment only through a straw.*

33‡

Ingest means _____. The dictionary definition of

34‡

ingest is _____. Write an original sentence using *ingest:*

35‡

_____

Try to discover the meanings of the following words by recognizing similarities to familiar words and using context clues:

A. *Disconsolate:* What does *dis-* usually mean at the beginning of a word? Think of *disappear, disapprove, disallow, discard.* What does *console* (con SOLE) mean? Think of a sentence with *console,* such as "The relatives tried to *console* the weeping widow." Now here is *disconsolate* in context: "The *disconsolate* young widow threw herself, sobbing, on her husband's coffin." "Her friends' expressions of sympathy had no effect on the *disconsolate* [36‡] widow." *Disconsolate* means _____.

B. *Detoxification:* What does *de-* usually mean at the beginning of a word? Think of *derail, descend, desert, depart, detach.* What does *intoxication* mean? What does *toxic* mean, as in "The old lady saved her life by breaking a window and letting the *toxic* fumes blow out of the room"? Now here is *detoxification* in context: "Finding the empty bottle of sleeping pills beside the woman who had collapsed on the floor, the police rushed her to the hospital [37‡] for *detoxification.*" *Detoxification* means _____.

Two points should be made here. First, you may be worried because you did not come close enough to the dictionary meaning in the previous exercise. But do we always need to know the *exact* meaning of a word? Often, of course, we do. But in this sentence from a story,

The lawn was bordered on three sides with brilliant groupings of hyacinths, fuschias, irises, *and* hydrangeas.

we need not know exactly what each of these flowers looks like; it is enough for us to picture rows of brightly colored flowers. Only in a book on gardening would the exact appearance of each flower become important.

We can also often learn the general sense of a word from our knowledge of its parts. For example, in

He spoke with derision *about the new professor.*

you may not know exactly what *derision* is, but from your lifelong familiarity with words beginning in *de-,* do you think the speaker is saying something favorable or something [38] unfavorable about the professor? _____ There are dozens of such word beginnings you have been using for so long that you unconsciously grasp at least the partial meaning of many new words right away, as with *ingest* and *disconsolate.* You know the meaning of *non-,* for example, from *nonsense, nonprofit, nonstop, nonalcoholic, nonpolitical.* [39‡]

What does *non-* mean? _____

> Most words with *non-* may be written either with or without a hyphen (-). All the words above except *nonsense* can be written with a hyphen: *non-profit, non-stop,* etc. In fact, you can often make up your own new words by adding *non-* (with a hyphen) to a word; for example, you might call a very poor actor a *non-actor.*

Let us look at other word beginnings that normally have some kind of negative meaning:

> unhappy   untamed   ungrateful
> unable   unwed   unobserved

[40]‡What does *un-* usually mean? _____

> indecent   inactive   ineligible
> incomplete   incorrect
> inability   injustice

[41]‡What does *in-* often mean? _____

    In- often changes its *n* to another letter to make pronunciation easier, as in *impossible, immodest, immoral, immovable, impassable; illegal, illegible; irregular, irreligious.* Thus *im-, il-,* and *ir-* are really disguises for [42]

_____ and have the same meaning.

(You should also be aware that *in-* often has a very different meaning, as we saw with *ingest.* We will discuss it later.)

> exit   exhale   expire
> expel   exhaust   extract
> exclude   export

[43]‡What does *ex-* often mean? _____

    Sometimes *ex-* is disguised. What has happened to *ex-* in *erase, eject,* [44]

eliminate, emasculate, emit, erosion, escape? _____

_____ Does the disguised *ex-* still have the same meaning? [45]

_____

    Ex- has a slightly different meaning when used with a hyphen. Think of *ex-husband, ex-president, ex-manager, ex-communist.* What does *ex-* [46]‡

mean in such words? _____

    As with *non-,* you can often create your own new words by adding *ex-* (with a hyphen) to a word. What would you call someone who is no [47]

longer a hippie? An _____. Someone who has retired [48]

from being an astronaut? An _____.

The word beginnings that generally have some kind of negative meaning such as *not, down, apart, away from, out of,* or *no longer* are

non- un- in- (im-, il-, ir-) de- dis- ex- (e-)

You also know many other kinds of word beginnings, such as the following:

repeat   reload
readjust   revisit
rebuild

[49]‡What does *re-* mean here? _____

retreat   redeem
return   regurgitate
rebound   revoke

[50]‡What slightly different meaning does *re-* have here? _____

preview   preface   predict
premiere   prearrange   prenatal
preregistration   prewar   preshrunk

[51]‡What does *pre-* mean? _____

This is the time for you to learn what all these word beginnings are called. Since they are attached, or fixed on to the beginning of the word, just *before* the main part of the word, they are called [52]*p__ __fixes*. Now, on to the next prefix:

subway   subdivide   substitute
submarine   subordinate
subtract   substandard

[53]‡What does *sub-* mean? _____

income   infield   include
invest   indoor
inland   inject

[54]‡What does *in-* mean in words like these? (Remember that we said *in-* has

two meanings.) _____

The answers to these prefix questions probably came easily, since you have known them most of your life. The point is to apply them to new words. For instance, see how close you can come to the meanings of these italicized words:

His predecessor *in the job was fired for making* derogatory *remarks about the girls in the office.*

⁵⁵ᴬ*Predecessor* means _____

⁵⁵ᴮ*Derogatory* means _____

The new president promised a policy of nonintervention *in the affairs of African nations; he said he would not treat them as lands* subservient *to the United States.*

⁵⁶ᴬ*Nonintervention* means _____

⁵⁶ᴮ*Subservient* means _____

The child reverted *to bedwetting when his security blanket was taken away.*

⁵⁷*Revert* means _____

Disparaging *remarks came from the audience during Herkimer's speech.*

⁵⁸*Disparaging* means _____

Many U.S. draft evaders *became* expatriates *in Europe.*

⁵⁹ᴬ*Evade* means _____

⁵⁹ᴮ*Expatriate* means _____

Highly important are the number prefixes. Again, you already know many of them from everyday use, as you saw a few pages back with *uni-*. The following sets of questions take you through the common number prefixes. But be careful! Do not assume each paragraph moves on to the next higher number. Some numbers have two prefixes, while other numbers with less common prefixes have been skipped. (One reason we sometimes have two prefixes with the same meaning is that English words come from more than one parent language; most prefixes come from Latin or Greek.)

How many tones does a *mono*tonous voice have? How many persons control a *mono*poly? How many wives does a *mono*gamous man have? How many pieces of stone are used in a *mono*lithic monument? How many persons speak in a *mono*logue? How many eyes

⁶⁰

does a *mono*cle fit? The answer to all these questions: _____

How many wheels has a *bi*cycle? How many pieces is a *bi*sected pie cut into? How many different focuses do *bi*focal glasses have? How many wives does a *bi*gamist have?

⁶¹

How many eyes are *bi*noculars made for? _____

How many people sing a *du*et? How many sets of controls does a *du*al-control car

⁶²

have? _____

How many wheels are there on a *tri*cycle? How many angles in a *tri*angle? How many legs on a *tri*pod? How many colors in the French *tri*color flag? How many prongs on the *tri*dent, Neptune's spear? How many singers in a *tri*o? How many bases on a *tri*ple? How

⁶³

many pieces to a *tri*sected sandwich? _____

How many babies are there in a set of *quad*ruplets? How many sides to a *quad*rangle?

How many languages can a *quad*rilingual person speak? How many feet on a *quad*ruped animal? How many times does my money multiply if I *quad*ruple it at the race track?
64

_____

How many *quart*ers in a dollar? How many *quart*s in a gallon? How many singers
65

in a barber shop *quart*et? _____
How many babies are there in a set of *quint*uplets? How many singers in a *quint*et?
66

_____

67

How many sides does the *Penta*gon Building in Washington have? _____
How many singers are there in a *sex*tet? How many children in a set of *sex*tuplets?
68

_____

How many arms on an *oct*opus? How many singers in an *oct*et? How many notes in
69

an *oct*ave? How many decades has an *oct*ogenarian lived? _____
70A

How many years are there in a *dec*ade? _____ The number after a *dec*imal
70B

point is what part of a whole number? A _____th.*
How many years has a *cent*ury? How many legs has a *cent*ipede? How many *cent*s in a dollar? How many degrees from freezing to boiling on a *cent*igrade thermometer? How
71

many *cent*imeters make a meter? _____
Here is a quick review of the common number prefixes. Fill in each blank with the correct prefix or prefixes for the number given:

72‡1 _____ _____   6 _____

2 _____ _____   8 _____

3 _____   10 _____

4 _____   100 _____

5 _____

A sour note on prefixes: Sometimes what looks like a familiar prefix really is not. For instance, *decide* and *decapitate* have nothing to do with the number ten; they merely have the prefix *de-* added to a word root beginning with *c*. In the same way *decentralize* has

_____

* You may wonder why *Oct*ober is not our eighth month and *Dec*ember our tenth. Actually they were, in the old Roman calendar. But Julius Caesar and Augustus Caesar felt themselves important enough to have months named after them, and put their own months (July and August) into the calendar right after the first six months, which are named for Roman gods. So September (seventh month), October (eighth month), November (ninth month), and December (tenth month) were all pushed back two months.

nothing to do with either *ten* or *hundred, Bible* nothing to do with *two,* and so on. There are many similar-looking prefix-root combinations. Sometimes the same prefix or root has one meaning from Latin and one from Greek. *Homo-* means *man* in Latin but *same* in Greek; *-ped-* means *foot* in Latin but *child* in Greek. *-Aud-* in Latin means either *hear* or *dare.* The best approach in such situations is to try first the prefix meaning that seems to make most sense in the sentence.

Incidentally, have you figured out yet what we mean by the *root* of a word? For each following word, circle the part you think is its root:

[73]de cline   dis turb ance   in abil ity
   bi cycle   faze   luck y

A word's *root* (some books call it a *stem*) is the part that contains the heart of the word's meaning. Sometimes the root is a plain English word, such as *-luck-* in *lucky;* other times the root is part of an old Latin or Greek word, such as *-turb-* or *-cycle-*. All words must have

[74]

a root. Must all words have a prefix? (Check *faze* and *lucky* above.) _____
Note that some words—such as *disturbance, inability,* and *lucky*—also have another part *after* the root. This part has less to do with the word's meaning than with its use in a sentence. Such parts are called *suffixes* (*suf-* is a disguised form of *sub-*).

THE ROOT OF THE MATTER

Science is one area where knowledge of prefixes and roots can be extremely helpful. Here, too, you probably know many of them already. For example, what does *-meter-* mean,

[75]

as in *thermometer, speedometer, gas meter* (What do these instruments do)? _____
Thus when you read of *hydrometers, altimeters,* and *barometers,* you know what kind of objects they are. You also already know what kind of an instrument any word ending in *-scope*

[76]

is, such as *telescope* and *microscope;* it is one used for _____ing.
Let us run through some word parts. Most of them you will meet often in the natural and behavioral sciences. You will probably find you know more meanings than you thought you did. First of all, let us think in terms of opposites: above and below, big and little, etc. (The research study we mentioned at the beginning of this module also found that one of the most common vocabulary mistakes is to think a word means its opposite.) If you think of girls' skirts, two prefixes should come to mind right away: *mini-* and *maxi-*, which you

[77]

know mean _____ and _____, in that order. What other words do
[78‡]

you know that contain *mini-?* _____ _____ _____
[79‡]

Maxi-? _____ _____ _____ There is another prefix
[80]

like *mini-*. A *microscope* lets us see extremely _____ objects such as germs and
[81‡]

cells. What other words do you know that contain *micro-?* _____ _____

_____ _____ Do you see how they all refer to very [82]s_____ things? What would be the opposite of *micro-?* When a microscope makes something appear

very large, we say it _____fies the object. What other words do you know con-

taining this prefix? _____ _____ _____

     Below is a list of some of our most common word parts, most arranged by opposites or near-opposites. In your reading in college you will come across hundreds of words using one or more of these. (In the list are some prefixes we have already met; also, a word part may be listed twice because it is used as an opposite to two other word parts. A hyphen only after a part means that it is usually a prefix; hyphens before and after mean that it is usually a root.) In the blank after each word part you are to try to write a word containing that part. You are not expected to know words for all the blanks. (One more point: Some of these may change their spelling slightly, especially the last letter, in certain words. Sometimes, too, the last letter is dropped.) The first item is done for you as an example.

^{85‡}*Small*   *Medium*   *Large*

^Amini- *minimum*   ^Cmedi- _____   ^Dmaxi- _____

^Bmicro- _____   ^Emagna- _____

                    ^Fmega- _____

^{86‡}*Below, not enough*   *Above, beyond, too much*

^Asub- _____   ^Dsur, super- _____

^Bhypo- _____   ^Ehyper- _____

^Cinfra-, infer- _____   ^Fultra- ("way out") _____

^{87‡}*To*   *From*
^Aad- (often disguised as *af-, ag-, al-, am-, as-, at-,* etc., to match the next letter; for example, *ad + tract* becomes *attract*)   ^Bab- _____

^{88‡}*Forward, in front of*   *Backward*

^Apro- _____   ^Bretro- _____

^{89‡}*Before*   *After*
                    ^Cpost- (words concerning the mail

^Apre- _____   do not belong here) _____

^Bante- _____

^{90‡}*For*   *Against*

^Apro- _____   ^Bcontra-, counter- _____

                    ^Canti- _____

91‡*With, together*

^A^syn-, sym- _____

^B^co-, col-, com-, con- _____

Without, lacking

^C^a-, an- _____

92‡*Same*

^A^sim- _____

^B^homo- _____

Different, other

^C^alter- _____

^D^hetero- _____

93‡*Correct, straight*

^A^ortho- _____

Incorrect, different

^B^hetero- _____

94‡*True*

^A^-ver- _____

False

^B^pseudo- (SUE doe) _____

95‡*Good*

^A^ben-, bon- _____

^B^eu- _____

Bad

^C^mal- _____

96‡*Right*

^A^-rect- _____

Wrong

^B^mis- _____

97‡*One*

^A^uni- _____

^B^mono- _____

Many

^C^multi- _____

^D^poly- _____

98‡*First*

^A^prim-, prem- _____

Last

^B^ulti- _____

99‡*All*

^A^omni- _____

^B^pan- _____

None, nothing

^C^-null- _____

100‡*Hand*

^A^-man- _____

Foot

^B^-ped- _____

101‡*Head*   *Heart*

A-cap- _____   B cor-, -card- _____

102‡*Body*   *Soul, mind, spirit*

A-corp- _____   C-psych- _____

B-phys- _____   D-menta- _____

                                                    E-anim- _____

103‡*Man*   *Woman*

A-vir- _____   C-fem- _____

B-anthro- _____

104‡*Mother*   *Son, daughter*   *Father*

A-mat(e)r- _____   B-fili- _____   C-pat(e)r- _____

105‡*Sister*   *Brother*

A-soror- _____   B-frat(e)r- _____

106‡*Birth*   *Life*   *Death*

A-nat- _____   C-vit-, -viv- _____   E-mort- _____

B-gen- _____   D-bio- _____   F-cide- (kill) _____

107‡*Sun*   *Moon*

A-sol- _____   C-lun- _____

B-heli- _____

108‡*Heat*   *Cold*

A-therm- _____   B-frig- _____

109‡*Water*   *Land, earth*   *Stars, heavens*

A-aqua- _____   C-terra- _____   E-stell- _____

B-hydr- _____   D-geo- _____   F-astr- _____

110‡*Move, go*   *Stand (still)*

A-mov-, -mob-, -mot- _____   E-sta- _____

^B-cede-, -ceed-, -cess- _____

^C-grad-, -gress- (step by step) _____

^D-tract- (pull) _____

^{111‡}*See, eye*

^A-vid-, -vis- _____

^B-oc-, -opt(ic)- _____

^C-spec-, -spic- (look) _____

Hear, ear

^D-aur-, -aud- _____

^{112‡}*Light*

^A-lum-, -luc- _____

^B-photo- _____

Sound

^C-son- _____

^D-phono- _____

^{113‡}*Write, draw*

^A-scrib-, -scrip- _____

^B-graph-, -gram- _____

Speak

^C-dic- _____

^D-loq-, -log(ue) _____

^E-voc-, -voke (call, voice) _____

Now see how many words you can figure out from the list of word parts above. Look at this list as often as you need to. Some words contain two word parts from the list.

¹¹⁴How much land would the territory of *Micro*nesia cover? ^A_____

How large a city is a *mega*lopolis? ^B_____ How good is a *medio*cre movie? ^C_____ What kind of a soul does a *magna*nimous person have? ^D_____ What kind of job is an *infer*ior one? ^E_____ If -*derm*- means skin, where does a nurse inject a *hypo*dermic needle? ^F_____ Where is the *infer*nal region, the home of Satan, where an *infer*no always burns? ^G_____ How tense is a person suffering from *hyper*tension? ^H_____ What kind of waves are *ultra so*nic waves? ^I_____

¹¹⁵What do you do when you *ab sta*in from liquor? _____^A

What does a king do when he *ab dic*ates his throne? _____^B

Where do you go when you are *ad*mitted to a college? _____^C

What does a nation do when it commits *ag gress*ion against another country? _____^D

_____ What happens to you when you are *pro mot*ed? _____ .^E

_____ Would the *pro*ponent of an idea be for it or against it? _____^F

In what direction do a spaceship's *retro*rockets send their power? _____^G

¹¹⁶Who goes to a clinic for *pre nat*al care? _____^A

When does a doctor do a *post-mort*em examination on someone? _____^B

If a soldier *contra*vened an order, what would he do with it? _____^C

If you have *sym*pathy for your friends, for whom would you have *anti*pathy? _____^D

_____ How would you feel if you had *a*pathy? _____^E

Two roads that *con*verge do what? _____ Would someone^F

who *con*curs with your opinion agree or disagree with it? _____^G

Would a group of people living in *con cor*d be friends or enemies? _____^H

Do two words that are *homo*nyms sound the same or different? _____^I
Which pair of words would have the same meaning, a pair of *syn*onyms or a pair of^J

*ant*onyms? _____
¹¹⁷If your generous friend underwent a complete *alter*ation in his attitude toward^A

money, he would become _____. Would a man with^B

*hetero*sexual desires be attracted to men or to women? _____^C

What does an *ortho*dontist do with teeth? _____ Would a^D

church more likely expel a person for *ortho*dox or for *hetero*dox beliefs? _____
What name would John Jones *not* sign if he registered at a hotel under a *pseudo*nym?^E

_____ If your roommate came in smelling like a brewery^F

and said he had drunk only coffee, how would you rate his *ver*acity? _____

Would you rather have a *ben*ign or a *mal*ignant tumor? _____

Would you rather live under a *bene*volent or a *male*volent king? _____

Would a *viva*cious girl probably be invited to many parties? _____

What is *eu genic*s the study of? _____

[118]If the instructor *mis*construes what you say, what has he done? _____

_____ If you wanted to study several kinds of technology, could you do so in a

*poly*technic institute? _____ How many plates might you need

if you were having a *multi*tude of people over for dinner? _____
If your cousin the butcher offered you a choice between two free steaks, one labeled *"prime"*

and one labeled "choice," which would you take? _____
According to the custom of *primo gen*iture, which son in a family receives the father's

inheritance? _____ After Hitler delivered an *ulti*matum to the

Poles to surrender, how many more chances did he give them? _____

If the mayor *nulli*fied a city law, what would he be doing to it? _____

What can you see in a *pan*orama? _____ What is an

*omni*potent king able to do? _____
[119]What would you find in a basket just below the spot where Thomas More was

*de cap*itated at the order of Henry VIII? _____ If your
instructor told you he had written a book but it was still in *manuscript* form, would you

find a copy of it in the library? _____ What is the *pedestal*

of the Statue of Liberty? _____ If you broke your leg, would
you have to undergo *psycho*therapy or *physi*otherapy to restore your leg's *mobility*?

_____ Who would need to go on a diet, a *corp*ulent or a

*psych*otic person? _____ How likely is it that a girl would

take hormone injections to increase her *virility*? _____

Against whom is a *pater*nity suit filed? _____ In the Bible,
Cain and Abel were the sons of Adam and Eve. Cain committed *fratricide;* what did he do

to whom? _____ For over sixty years in the nineteenth century

England was a *matri*archy. What do you know about the country's ruler during that time?
I

_____

[120]When two *dissim*ilar animal species engage in *symbio*sis, what are they doing?
A

_____ When a patient's *vital* signs are *ab*sent, does the doctor send him to the *bio*psy room, the *mor*tuary, the *mater*nity ward, or the *genital* disease ward?
B   C

_____ Where does *solar* energy come from? _____
D

Where is a *lunar* voyage headed? _____ *Helio*tropism in a
E

plant means that its flower always turns its face toward _____.
F

What does a *thermostat* do in a building? _____ A *hydro*plane
G

takes off from what surface? _____ *Geo metry* was first used
H

to do what? _____ *Astro*logers attempt to predict human
I

events from what? _____
[121]If a nation's army trans*gres*ses upon another nation's *terra*in, what has that army
A

done? _____ If you had an *intract*able mule, what would your
B

problem be? _____ A teacher who *motiv*ates a student does
C

what for him? _____ What does an *audiometer* do?
D   E

_____ What does an *optometr*ist do? _____
F

A person who *provide*s for the future is doing what? _____
G

*Lumi*nous paint has what unusual ability? _____
If you underwent *photo*therapy for a skin disease, with what would the doctor be treating
H

you? _____ If you rewrote part of a poem you had composed
I

to give it greater *euphony*, what would you want in the poem?_____
[122]If the state police re*voke* your driver's license, what are they doing to it?
A

_____If two people are engaged in a col*loqu*y, what are they
B

doing? _____ At what part of a play would you find its
C

prologue? _____ When a minister gives a *benedic*tion, what
D

is he doing? _____ What does a *cardiograph* do in a hospital?
E   F

_____ What does a *bio grapher* do? _____

When the druggist demands a *prescrip*tion before selling certain medicines, what does he
ᴳ
want? _____

It will take repeated exposure to these word parts before you will be familiar with
them all. But already you have learned to find or come close to meanings of unfamiliar words
by examining their parts. When you come across such words in your college courses you
will be able to handle them with confidence.

MORE PREFIXES AND ROOTS

Here are more word parts. For each of them try to write a word containing that part
and seeming to have the meaning given:

123‡*Directions*
ᴬbetween—inter-: _____   ᴰthrough—per-: _____

ᴮinside, within—intra-, intro-: _____   dia-: _____

ᶜacross—trans-: _____   ᴱaround—circ-: _____

peri-: _____

124‡*Word parts from natural and behavioral sciences*

ᴬscience, study, speaking — -logy-:   _____

ᴮskin — -derm-:   _____

ᶜnerve — -neur-:   _____

ᴰsuffer, feel — -path-:   _____

ᴱform, shape — -morph-:   _____

ᶠsleep — -dorm-, -somn-:   _____

ᴳfar — -tele-:   _____

ᴴform, mold(able) — -plas-:   _____

ᴵtime — -temp-, -chron-:   _____

ᴶself — -auto-:   _____

ᴷpower — -dyn-:   _____

ᴸrule, authority — -crat-, -cracy-:   _____

^Mpeople — -dem-: _____

^Ncity — -polis-, -politan-: _____

^Ocitizen, affairs of citizens, government —
       -civ-, -polit-: _____

^Pcompanion, group — -socio-: _____

^Qlaw (right, swear) — -jud-, -jur-, -jus-: _____

^Rking, queen — -reg-: _____

^Schief — -arch-: _____

^Tancient — -arche-: _____

^Urace, group of people with same traits and
       customs — -ethn-: _____

^Vcity — -urb-: _____

^Wgod — -dei-, -theo-: _____

^Xworld, universe — -cosm-: _____

^Ybook — -bibl-: _____

^Zname — -nom-, -nym-: _____

^{AA}new — -nov-: _____

^{BB}half — -semi-: _____

^{CC}wisdom, knowledge — -soph-: _____

^{DD}love (general, not sexual) — -phil-: _____

^{EE}dislike, fear — -phob-: _____

^{FF}sexual love or passion — -ero-: _____

Putting together all the word parts you have learned so far, fill in the following blanks. You are free to look back at any list in this module as often as you need to.

A

[125]Where does an *interurban* bus travel? _____

B

Do *intra*mural teams ever play teams from other schools? _____

C

Where does a *trans*oceanic flight go? _____ What do the

D

*circ*umference of a circle and the *peri*meter of a square have in common? _____

_____ What is the *diameter* of a circle? _____
                                                                              E
                                                                                    F
What kind of illness would you have if you went to a *dermatologist?* _____
If this doctor told you your illness was partly *psychological* and that you were somewhat
                                                                        G
neurotic, what would he be telling you? _____
If a scene in a movie contained a great deal of *pathos*, what would it be showing?
        H
_____ What kind of shape would an *amorphous* thing have?
                I

_____ [126]What happens when two people engage in *mental telepathy* with each other?
            A
_____ A *plastic* surgeon can do what to a not-too-beautiful
        B   C
nose? _____ A *chronometer* is a highly accurate _____ .
                                                                    D
How many people share power with an *autocrat?* _____
                                                            E
How many share power with a *monarch?* _____ Annapolis
    F
is a _____ named after Queen Anne. What kind of govern-
                    G
ment is a *democracy?* _____ If you studied the problems of
                                                                    H
modern *urban ethnic* groups, what would you be studying? _____
Would this subject more likely be studied in a *sociology* or an *archeology* class?
    I
_____ If your friend were engaged in *juridical* studies, what
                                                        J
would he be learning? _____
        [127]In 1649 there was a *regicide* in England. Would you like to have been the English
            A   B
king at that time? _____ Why? _____
Just before the *regicide*, the king probably *invoked* his *deity*. Can you discover what he
                                            C
probably did? _____ Russian spacemen are called *cosmonauts*.
                                                                    D
According to this name, where are they trained to travel? _____
                                                                    E
What size library would a *bibliophile* have in his apartment? _____
                                                                            F
How does a person with claustro*phobia* feel about small, closed-in places? _____
                                                                    G
_____ How old is a *novel* idea? _____
Henry VIII broke away from the Roman Church less for *theological* than for *political* and
                                                                    H
personal reasons. What does this mean? _____

The court *ex ceed*ed its *jurisdic*tion in banning *ero*tic magazines throughout the metro*politan* area. What does this all mean? _____

Here is a final set of useful word roots. Again, try to think of one word containing each root and seeming to have the meaning of that root:

128‡Afaith — -fid-: _____

Bbelieve — -cred-: _____

Clead — -duc-: _____

Dsend — -miss-, -mit-: _____

Efriend, love — -ami-, -amo-: _____

Fdisorder, upset — -turb-: _____

Gbreak, burst — -rupt-: _____

Hend — -fin-: _____

Iend — -term-: _____

129When a couple being married pledge to each other their *fide*lity, what are they
A
promising? _____ If you told a very *cred*ulous person that
you had just seen two purple elephants dancing outside the science building, what chance
B
would there be of her believing you? _____ What does an
C
*aque duc*t do? _____ What happens to a person when he is
D
*in duc*ed to do something? _____ Would you like your new
E
neighbors to be *ami*able people? _____ What are you supposed
to do if the finance company sends you a bill and says, "Please *re mit* balance at once"?
F
_____ *E mis*sion controls on cars reduce the car's tendency to
G
_____. How does a young man feel who is en*amo*red of a
H
certain pretty girl? _____ If nothing fazed you, how easily
I
would you become per*turb*ed? _____ What happens when a
J
*rup*ture in a water main dis*rup*ts traffic on Broad Street? _____
K
What has happened to the moral values of a cor*rup*t person? _____

When would an *in fin*ite line end? _____L_____ How long would an

*in term*inable argument go on? _____M_____

RECALLING WORDS YOU KNOW

The previous section emphasized recognition vocabulary; but since this is a writing text, we are concerned with recognition vocabulary mainly as a stepping stone to recall vocabulary. Can you now recall the words you recognized earlier? From the words you have met in this module, recall the word that best fits the blank in each sentence below, replacing the underlined expression. For example:

When Sandy applied the medicated cream to her skin, the pimples *went away* (d *isappear* ed).

¹‡When the rain started, the tourists quickly *went back* (r_____ ed) to their bus.

²‡At the *first performance* (p_____) of the movie, ten people in the audience fainted.

³‡*The man who was president before him* (his p_____ c_____ in the presidency) had a tennis court built in the White House.

⁴‡Ray takes excellent photos because he mounts his camera on a *three-legged support* (t_____).

⁵‡Nancy's husband has been gone for a *period of ten years* (___-_____).

⁶‡The doctor sadly reported that Uncle Will was *going backward* (__g____ing *or* _____g____ing) in his fight for life.

⁷‡That girl of mine will never *change* (_____) her ways.

⁸‡The teller must have *calculated wrongly* (____c_____ed) when she cashed my check.

⁹‡Gail is a terrible speaker; her voice *has only one tone* (is _____ous).

¹⁰‡Hairy-chested Harry is always bragging about his *manliness* (_____ity).

11‡That small building on the corner of the hospital grounds is the

place where they send dead bodies (_ _ _ _ _ary).

12‡Regina did not do well in the tryouts; her performance was only

of middle quality (_ _ _ _ _ _ _ _ _).

13‡Estelle went to the Bateman Clinic for *care before her baby was*

born (_ _ _ _ _ _ _ care).

14‡Ruth's new watch has a *dial that glows in the dark* (_ _ _ _ _-

_ _ _ _ dial).

15‡Alec was so cruel that he had *no feeling at all* (_ _ _ _ _ _ _ _)
toward other people's suffering.

16‡Ben found that rubbing in liniment had a *good* (_ _ _ _ _ _ _-

_ _al) effect on his sore muscles.

17‡The Jensens brought one of those *homes they can move from one*

location to another (_ _ _ _ _ _ _ homes).

18‡Each night Johnny Carson starts his show with *an act where he is*

the only one speaking (a _ _ _ _ _ _ _ _ _ _).

19‡Fred sprayed his kitchen with a *chemical that kills bugs* (an

i_ _ _ _ _ _ _ _ _ _ _).

20‡First came phonographs, then stereos, and now sound *that comes*

from four speakers (_ _ _ _ _ _ _ _ _ _ _ _ic sound).

21‡On the witness stand Beasley *said the opposite of* (_ _ _ _-

_ _ _ _ _ _ _ _ed) what he had first told the police.

22‡Grandma's new glasses *have lenses that focus at two different*

distances (are _ _ _f_ _ als).

23‡Letitia is studying *the chemistry of living things* (b_ _chemistry).
24‡The tides are caused by the pull of *the sun's and the moon's*

(_ _ _ _ar and _ _ _ _ar) gravity.

25‡Jean refuses to use any *device that prevents pregnancy* (_ _ _ _-

_ _ _c_ _ _ive device).

[26]‡The *voyagers to the stars* (_____n____s) discovered that

their ship was being pelted by *extremely tiny meteorites* (_____-meteorites).

[27]‡Vicki is so _____ she will believe anything.

[28]‡We arrived late at the play and missed the *introductory speech*

(___l_____).

[29]‡Sy is such an am___b___ boy that he has no enemies.

[30]‡Some textbook exercises seem *that they will never end* (_____-

_____b__).

MASTERY TEST

Since you have just finished an exercise covering most of what you have learned in the module, you probably do not need additional review. If you did poorly on that exercise, review the appropriate parts of the module. If you did well, begin this test.

Part I. Working from context and your knowledge of word parts, give in the blanks the meaning of the italicized words as closely as you can.

[1]‡Many experts are concerned with what they see as a worldwide *maldistribution* of scarce fertilizer. _____

[2]‡The acting careers of Clark Gable and Gary Cooper were nearly *contemporary*. _____

[3]‡The oil-producing countries *consolidated* their ideas on oil pricing and decided not to lower prices. _____

[4]‡The President urged a policy of *reconciliation* toward army deserters and draft evaders. _____

[5]‡Nitrates reach the ground through rain and help to *replenish* the nitrogen in the soil. _____

[6]‡Miss Cosgrove's lawyer repeatedly declared her innocence, although he could produce little *substantiation* for his claim. _____

_____

[7]‡The professor insisted he would take action to expel the students who had cheated; however, the dean *dissuaded* him in the matter. _____

_____

[8]A new bill in Congress would ensure the *anonymity* of individual taxpayers if the government released their tax records to compile statistics. _____

_____

[9]There was a steady debate over whether the university's open enrollment policy would mean a *diminution* of scholastic standards. _____

_____

[10]The union leader spoke favorably of Mr. Wentworth's *accession* to the presidency of United Motors Corporation. _____

_____

Part II. In each blank, write a word that means the same as the italicized expression. For full credit, use a word with a prefix and/or root learned in this module. If you cannot think of such a word, you may earn partial credit for another word.

[11]Tosca had such a *feeling against* (_____ toward) Scarpia that she stabbed him to death with his own letter opener.

[12]Zarkhov was expelled from the Communist party because of his *beliefs that were different from everyone else's* (_____ beliefs).

[13]In order to escape the FBI, Dillinger used a *false name* (_____ _____) when he traveled.

[14]Mrs. Vanderhoof screamed when she saw the *insect with a hundred feet* (_____) on her collar.

[15]Charlie Flubwell was dropped from the basketball team because his performance on the court was *below* (_____ to) everyone else's.

[16]Dr. Garcia gave Angela a prescription for tranquilizers because she showed signs of *too much tension* (_____).

[17]The doctor also told her to *stay away* (_____) from stimulants such as coffee and cigarettes.

[18]King Claus XI was loved by his people because he was so *good* (_____ent) to them.

[19]Scientists have discovered a new *material that can be molded* (_____ _____ material) which is highly heat-resistant.

[20‡]Even three 275-pound tacklers closing in on him did not *worry* (_____-

_____) the veteran quarterback; he calmly side-stepped them and threw a fifty-yard touchdown pass.

[21‡]The police finally tracked down the *man with two wives* (_____-

_____) just as he was about to marry an unsuspecting third girl.
[22‡]Congressman Wolf sponsored a new law requiring driver trainees to

drive in *cars with two sets of controls* (_____ -control cars) at all times.

[23‡]The next unit in biology was the study of *four-footed animals* (_____-

_____s).

[24‡]Studies in the *science of the mind* (_____ studies) show that people who brag are often trying to cover feelings of inadequacy.
[25‡]The faculty were discontented because the chairman acted too much like

a *person who holds all power himself* (an _____).
[26‡]The sociology class concentrated on the customs of various *racial*

(_____) groups in America.

[27‡]The School of *Study of God* (_____gy) at Calvin University is now accepting women as candidates for the ministry.

[28‡]The Supreme Court ruled that the state court had *gone out of* (_____-

_____ed) its authority in ruling on the Finch vs. Webber case.
[29‡]Since Mrs. Robinson had experienced difficulty giving birth to her

previous babies, the doctors decided to *lead her into* labor (_____-

_____ her labor).
[30‡]The emperor, wanting to keep the people in fear of him, declared that he

was *all-powerful* (_____).
[31‡]The French people often claim that their language *sounds better* (has

greater _____) than any other language in the world.
[32‡]At the climax of *The Scarlet Letter,* the hero admits his *fatherhood*

(_____) of the heroine's child.

[33‡]To the Indians, the *measured distance around* (_____ of) the treaty land was the distance a man could walk in a day.

Part III. (Optional with instructor) Write a paragraph of twelve to fifteen sentences on one of the topics below or on a topic suggested or approved by your instructor. Use the best vocabulary you know.

Fighting City Hall
Careers I am considering (or have considered)
Modern medical care—is it worth its cost?
The college catalogue—is it an aid to intelligent program planning or a hodgepodge
     of confusing course regulations?
Truth in politics

YOUR TWO PERSONAL VOCABULARIES

[2]minds
[5]Yes
[7]recall
[9]recognize
[11]This is a set of probable answers. Your own answers may differ, especially between columns 1 and 2. If your set of answers is very different from this, see your instructor. *Column 1:* poor, go home, happy, jail, argue, get together, drink, work, over, light; *Column 2:* assemble, dispute, depart, penitentiary, penniless, illumination, employment; *Column 3:* indigent, incarceration, incandescence, solon
[12]You would be memorizing many words which you might rarely see or need to use again and which few people would understand if you used them.

RECOGNIZING WORD MEANINGS

[2]the opposite
[4]context
[10]context
[32]context
[38]Unfavorable
[42]*in-*
[44]It has been disguised as *e-*.
[45]Yes
[47]ex-hippie
[48]ex-astronaut
[52]prefixes
[55A]person who came before
[55B]taking away from, or knocking (the girls' character)
[56A]not coming between (the African nations), not becoming involved (in their affairs)
[56B]serving (the United States) in a low position
[57]turn back
[58]"putting down"; lowering the reputation of (the person)
[59A]avoid
[59B]a person who has left his own country to live elsewhere
[60]One
[61]Two
[62]Two
[63]Three
[64]Four
[65]Four
[66]Five
[67]Five
[68]Six
[69]Eight
[70A]Ten
[70B]tenth
[71]100
[73]cline, cycle, turb, faze, abil, luck
[74]No
[75]Measure
[76]looking, viewing, seeing
[77]small(est), large(st)
[80]small
[82]small
[83]magnifies
[114A]A very small amount
[B]Very large
[C]Of middle quality, "so-so"
[D]A large one
[E]One below the level of most others
[F]Under the skin
[G]Hell; under the earth
[H]Too tense; above the normal in tension
[I]Beyond sound; unable to be heard by human beings or faster than the speed of sound
[115A]Stay away
[B]Says he will leave his throne (resign)
[C]Into the college
[D]Steps toward (makes a military move against) the other country
[E]You are moved forward
[F]For it

^GBackward

^{116A}A woman, in the months before the birth of her child

^BAfter the person is dead

^CGo against it, disobey it

^DYour enemies, those you have a feeling against

^EYou would be without feeling, neither for nor against

^FCome together

^GAgree, go along with it

^HFriends, persons whose hearts are together

^IThe same

^JSynonyms

^{117A}stingy—completely changed from generous

^BWomen, the other sex

^CStraighten them

^DHeterodox, different from the accepted teachings

^EJohn Jones; he would use a false name

^FVery poor; he is not truthful

^GBenign, one that is good, harmless, not causing the evil of death

^HBenevolent (good)

^IYes. She would be full of life

^JGood birth—improving the inborn qualities of men or animals

^{118A}Construed it wrongly, taken the wrong meaning

^BYes, they have many technologies there

^CQuite a few

^DPrime—the first in quality

^EThe first-born son

^FNone—that was their last warning

^GDoing away with it—saying that there was no longer such a law

^HEverything there is to see

^IEverything

^{119A}More's head, which was cut off

^BNo; it would exist only in a handwritten (or hand-typed) copy.

^CThe platform on which her feet stand

^DPhysiotherapy—treatment of the body, to restore movement to the leg

^EA corpulent person, one who had a sizable body

^FNot very likely; she would probably not want to become manly

^GThe father (of an illegitimate child)

^HKilled his brother, Abel

^IThe ruler was a woman

^{120A}Two different species are living together

^BThe mortuary; he is dead

^CThe sun

^DThe moon

^Ethe sun

^FRegulates the temperature at which the heat stays

^GWater

^HMeasure the earth, or parts of it

^IThe stars

^{121A}Stepped across, onto the other nation's land

^BThe mule would not let himself be pulled

^CGets him moving

^DMeasures hearing ability

^EMeasures vision

^FSeeing ahead

^GIt glows, lights up

^HLight (such as a sun lamp)

^IA better sound to it

^{122A}Calling it back

^BTalking together

^CAt the beginning; it is a short spoken part

^DSaying good things, giving a prayer or blessing

^ERecords the patients' heart activity

^FWrites of a person's life

^GSomething written (by the doctor) before the customer comes to the drugstore, stating what medicine the druggist should sell him

^{125A}Between cities

^BNo; they play only teams within the school

^CAcross the ocean

^DEach is the measured distance around the figure

^EThe measured distance through the center (from one side to the other)

^FA skin disease

^GThat your illness was partly in your mind (psychology: the study of the mind) and that your nerves were in bad shape

^HA great deal of suffering or emotion (which would arouse sorrow in us)

^INo shape (like a blob)

^{126A}Each feels over a distance what is in the other's mind

^BMold it (into a more attractive shape)
^Cclock, instrument that measures time
^DNo one; he rules by himself
^ENo one; he rules by himself
^Fcity
^GOne where the people rule
^HRacial groups living in cities
^ISociology (the study of groups of people; archeology studies ancient man)
^JThe law (how to speak of the law)
^{127A}Probably not
^BRegicide means the killing of a king
^CPrayed (called in his God)
^DThroughout the universe
^EProbably very large, since he is a lover of books
^FHe fears them
^GNot very old; it is new
^HLess for reasons of religion (the study of God) than for reasons dealing with the affairs of his government
^IThe court went out of the boundaries where it had the right to say what was legal, in banning magazines that arouse sexual passions, throughout the city area.
^{129A}To be faithful to each other
^BA very good chance; she is one who believes almost anything
^CLeads water from a source to its point of use
^DHe is led into it
^EYes, they would be friendly, likable
^FSend the money back to the company
^Gsend out pollutants
^HIn love
^INot very easily; it would take a real catastrophe to upset you
^JA break in the main breaks up the flow of traffic
^KThey have been broken
^LNever; it would be without end
^MIt would never end

MODULE 7

BASIC
SENTENCE
PARTS

Previous modules required: none

INTRODUCTION

Here is a little challenge at which you may be more successful than you think at first. In the selection below, fill in each blank with any word that seems to make sense. (Do not spend time searching for the *one* perfect word; any word that fits will do; you may even add a little humor if you wish.)

[1]When we came _____ to Paris it was _____ and cold and lovely. _____ city had accommodated itself to winter, there _____ good wood _____ sale at the wood and coal place _____ _____ _____, and _____ were braziers outside of many of the good cafes so that you _____ keep _____ on the _____. _____ own apartment _____ warm and cheerful. . . . Now you were accustomed _____ see _____ _____ trees against the sky and you _____ on the fresh-washed gravel _____ through the Luxembourg Gardens in _____ clear [,] _____ _____.

— Ernest Hemingway, *A Moveable Feast*
(New York: Scribner, 1964), p. 11

Submit the paragraph to your instructor or compare your answers with those he provides. If you did well on it, you are making one of the most important discoveries of this course—a discovery not so much about writing as about yourself. It is that you *already know* all or nearly all the basic sentence parts. In that paragraph you showed that you know how to write not only nouns and verbs but nearly all the other parts of speech—words that the grammar books have labeled adjectives, adverbs, prepositions, conjunctions, determiners, modals, and expletives! Just as important, you have discovered that you do not need to know any of the grammatical names of these words in order to write them in sentences. (In fact, this book avoids grammatical terms as much as possible.) Thus in this module you are working in an area where you are not weak but strong.

WHAT MAKES A SENTENCE?

The word *sentence* was used just above. What is a sentence? What does it look like? You may already know that it begins with a [2]c_____ letter and ends with a [2]p_____. But how do we know what belongs in between? Many people have a *sentence sense* through which they can tell whether a string of words is a sentence or not *without* inspecting it grammatically—or even knowing how to do so. (A string of words, or word string, means just what it says—any number of any kind of words in a row.) You may have more sentence sense than you realize. Can you tell which of the following strings of words are sentences? Recopy each in the proper column below the list: *Sentence* or *Not sentence*. (Write the ones in the *Sentence* column with capitals and periods.)

A. I play poker
B. tall and slender
C. a million soldiers served in the war
D. Johnny rode the pony

E. my hardest job
F. dogs with distemper bite children sometimes
G. near Anaheim on the freeway
H. saw him last night

I. Johnny on the pony
J. my ancient car stalled on the freeway
K. Frank Sinatra a great singer
L. Belcher fell through a manhole

Sentence	*Not sentence*
3‡	
_____	_____
_____	_____
_____	_____
_____	_____
_____	_____
_____	_____

Your instructor will check your answers or provide them for you to check. If you had most of the word strings in the proper columns, you have an excellent sentence sense. Like other skills—athletics, singing—a sentence sense comes to some people more or less naturally. Others have to sweat for it. Either way, it is essential for writing that communicates clearly.

Look back at the two columns you filled in above. Cross out any strings of words you wrote in the wrong column and rewrite them in the proper column, according to the answers you were given. Now examine the columns very carefully. What difference do you see or hear between the strings of words in the *Sentence* column and those in the *Not sentence* column? In other words, what makes a sentence?

How about length? Are all the items in the *Sentence* column longer than the items

4‡

in the *Not sentence* column? _____ Then is it length—a certain number of words

5

or more—that makes a string of words a sentence? _____ This is important. You would be surprised how many students feel that they must put a period whenever they find they have written twelve or fifteen words since the last period; as you have already discovered, they are mistaken. Notice that the sentence just before this one you are now reading contains 36 words but the sentence before that only three. One is just as much a sentence as the other.

If length does not make a string of words a sentence, then what does? Of all the twelve word strings above, which ones mention some person(s) or thing(s) near the beginning? 6‡Put a check in the margin in front of all the word strings that do this. Now, of the items you checked, which tell that the person or thing was *doing* something (or is doing it now)? [7]‡Put another check in front of all the word strings that do this. Next, to see how accurate you were in checking, do the following for all the strings you checked *twice*.‡ Mentally divide each string into two parts: (1) the part that mentions the person or thing that was doing something; (2) the part that tells what he or it was doing. Underline part (1) once and part (2) twice. Now try to underline a part (1) and a part (2) for each string you did *not* check twice. How many strings in the *Sentence* column have both [8]

<u>once-underlined</u> and <u>twice-underlined</u> parts? _____ How many in the [9]

Not sentence column have both these parts? _____ Check the answer page now.

Therefore, what have you discovered about what makes a sentence? _____ [10]

_____

_____

What you have just discovered is the most important concept in all writing: that the sentence, our basic unit of thought, has two parts: (1) a part that mentions some person(s) or thing(s) and (2) a part that tells what the person or thing was doing. The sentence cannot merely name the person or thing; it must tell what he or it was doing (or is doing now). As you have discovered, none of the strings in the *Not sentence* column has *both* parts (1) and (2).

Have you ever used Epoxy glue, the kind that comes in two tubes? Each tube contains a different substance which has no gripping power by itself; but when the two substances are combined they form a mighty cement. A sentence is like Epoxy: Neither part separately has the power to make a thought—to be a sentence. Names of persons or things alone (such as *Sebastian, acid*) do not make a thought; neither do words of doing alone (such as *sneezed, burns*). Only when the two parts (the person/thing part and the doing part) are put together does a thought exist (*Sebastian sneezed, Acid burns*). That is what a sentence is, and that is what this module is about.

Here are two Epoxy tubes for you to combine into sentences. The first contains five person/thing parts of sentences. The second tube contains five doing parts, in scrambled order. Combine each item in the *Person/thing* tube with an item it makes sense with from the *Doing* tube, to make five genuine sentences. Write the sentences in the blanks below. (There is more than one possible way to combine some of the items.)

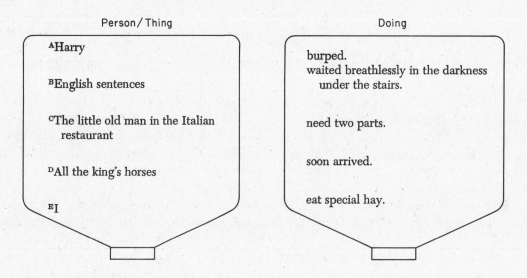

Person/Thing

ᴬHarry

ᴮEnglish sentences

ᶜThe little old man in the Italian restaurant

ᴰAll the king's horses

ᴱI

Doing

burped.
waited breathlessly in the darkness under the stairs.

need two parts.

soon arrived.

eat special hay.

B
_____

C
_____

D
_____

E
_____

Below are some word strings that have only one of the two parts needed for a sentence. On a separate paper, use words of your own to complete the other part, to make a sentence. When you finish, underline <u>once</u> the part of each sentence that mentions the person or thing that was doing something, and underline <u>twice</u> the part that tells you what he or it was doing. The first two items are done for you as examples:

    a.   Alice (Sample answer: <u>Alice</u> <u>went to Dallas.</u>)

    b.   propped her against a tree (Sample answer: The <u>doctor</u> <u>propped her against a tree.</u>)

12‡Our priceless freedom

13‡Desperate and hungry, the killer

14‡probed deeper and deeper

15‡The last train to Clarksville

16‡expect racial peace in the North

17‡frightened both the heroes

18‡rose sharply today

19‡The junkies in our neighborhood

Show your paper to your instructor.

    It is time to give names to these two sentence parts. Perhaps you remember them from elementary or high school. When a book or movie is about war, we say that war is the

20s___j_____ of that book or movie. We say that young love is the 21‡s___j___t of *Romeo and Juliet*. Then the part of a sentence that tells the person(s) or thing(s) the

sentence is about must be the 22s_____ part of the sentence. In the exercise above, the part given in items a, 12, 13, 15 and 19, the part you underlined once, is the

23
_____ part. It tells the person or thing that was doing something—the person or thing the sentence is about.

    The second part of a sentence, the part that tells what the subject was doing, has a

name that exists only in grammar. Do you recall? It is called the 24v_____ part. In the sentence *A million soldiers served in the war*, *A million soldiers* is the subject part (the persons that were doing something) and *served in the war* the verb part (what they were doing). Here are some other examples:

Subject part	*Verb part*
<u>Alice</u>	<u>fell down the rabbit hole.</u>
<u>The last train to Clarksville</u>	<u>left late.</u>
<u>The temperature in Alaska</u>	<u>rose sharply today.</u>
<u>Government officials</u>	<u>expect racial peace in the North.</u>

THE TWO MOST IMPORTANT WORDS IN A SENTENCE

Now let us sharpen our focus on these two parts. Turn back to page 141. In the *Sentence* column, examine the subject part of each item (the part you underlined once). Which *one* word in each subject part actually names the person or thing that was doing something? Write that word in the proper blank below:

[25]A. _____

C. _____

D. _____

F. _____

J. _____

L. _____

Check your answers. Then do the same for the sentences on page 142.

[26]A. _____

B. _____

C. _____

D. _____

E. _____

The word you picked for each sentence is called the *subject word*, or simply the *subject*. The subject part of every sentence, then, contains a single word which mentions the

person or thing that was doing something. This word is called the [27] _____. The other words in the subject part merely give further information about the subject.

Turn back to page 141 again. In the *Sentence* column, examine the verb part (the part you underlined twice) of each item. Which one word in each verb part actually tells what the subject was doing? Write that word in the proper blank below:

[28]A. _____

C. _____

D. _____

F. _____

J. _____

L. _____

Check your answers. Then do the same for the sentences on page 142.

²⁹A. _____

B. _____

C. _____

D. _____

E. _____

The word you picked for each sentence is called the *verb word,* or simply the *verb.* The verb part of each sentence, then, contains one word which actually tells what the subject was

doing. The word is called the ³⁰_____. The other words in the verb part merely give further information about the verb.

To sum up:

Subject part	*Verb part*
The temperature in Alaska	rose sharply today.
Subject (word)	Verb (word)

In the rest of this section we will concentrate on the subject and verb words rather than on the whole subject and verb parts.

To be a sentence, then, a string of words must tell us that some person or thing was doing something (or *is* doing it). This is not a definition of a sentence, nor is it even fully accurate. But we will work with it for now and add to it along the way. Here is some reinforcement of what you have just discovered. Decide whether each string of words below is a sentence or not. Look for the two essential parts, the subject and the verb. In each item, put one line under the subject, if you find one, and two lines under the verb, if you find one. If both the subject and the verb are there, the string is a sentence; and, of course, if either the subject or the verb is not there, it is not a sentence. Write an S in the blank before each string that is a sentence; if any string is not a sentence, rewrite it in the blank below it, adding the word(s) it needs to be a sentence. Use any words that make sense:

³¹_____ Mona Huckleberry wore two different socks yesterday

32 _____ one pink and one orange

33 _____ Mona dresses in the dark

34 _____ saves electricity

35 _____ her boy friend yelled

36 _____ called her stupid

37 _____ she cried

38 _____ he apologized to her

39 _____ the boy friend Horace

40 _____ a flashlight at the store for her

41 _____ the right socks go on her feet now

42 _____ Mona and Horace happily ever after

If you had some trouble with this, do not be discouraged. There is much more you will discover about subjects and verbs in this module. By the end of the module you will probably understand them quite well.

"So now I know what subjects and verbs are. So what?" you may ask. "I never think about sentences when I speak; why fuss about them when I write?" Actually you *do* think about sentences when you speak. In fact, in your speaking, you naturally, mostly unconsciously, stop whenever you complete a thought. (Listen to anybody speak; you will see it right away.) And that is just what a sentence is—a unit of thought. The periods that end sentences signal places where, if you were speaking instead of writing, you would lower your voice and come to a stop. (The module "Punctuation" goes into this in more detail.) Most people have some trouble figuring out just where all these places are in their writing. Being able to spot subjects and verbs is a great help in identifying where your written sentences should begin and end.

A sentence is not our *only* unit of thought. Words (sometimes even parts of words) and word groups are smaller units; paragraphs, compositions, chapters, and books are larger units. But the sentence is our *central* unit of thought.

WORDS THAT NAME PERSONS OR THINGS

Let us take a closer look at those two parts of every sentence, the [1]s_____ and the [1]v____. What is the first part like? Look back at the words you wrote in the first set of blanks on page 141:

I   soldiers   Johnny   dogs   car   Belcher

Each of these refers to some person(s) or thing(s). You have already learned that this kind of word is called the *subject* when it names the person(s) or thing(s) that was doing something. But you may have noticed that there are other persons or things mentioned in many sentences, such as:

A *million* soldiers *served in the* war.
The junkies *in our* neighborhood *bribe the* police.

Since only one of these words in each sentence is the subject, we need another name for a word that mentions *any* person(s) or thing(s) anywhere in a sentence. Do you remember what your schoolbooks called this kind of word—the name of a person or thing? It is called

a [2]n_____. Which of the following words do you think are nouns, words that name persons or things? Write each word in the proper column below:

planet   go   very   George   never   enormous   bridge   beach

Nouns   *Not nouns*

[3]

_____   _____

_____   _____

_____   _____

_____   _____

Now try these:

aunt   excited   college   class   classy   Chevrolet   almost
whenever   program   music

Nouns   Not nouns
    4

_____   _____

_____   _____

_____   _____

_____   _____

_____   _____

Check your answers. If you had more than one wrong in each set, see your instructor before going on.

All of the nouns above name things we can see, hear, or touch. But what about things we cannot? How many of the following words do you think are nouns? Cross out any that are not:

[5]love   happiness   death   philosophy   liberty   rejection   height

A noun, then, can name things we cannot see, hear, or touch (*abstract* things) as well as those we can (*concrete* things).

There is another way to tell whether a word is a noun: Does it fit where only a noun can fit in a sentence? Mentally, try putting in the blank below any five of the words we have so far listed as nouns: (Some of them will need an *a, an, the,* or *my* in front.)

[6‡] $\begin{pmatrix} A[n] \\ The \\ My \end{pmatrix}$ _____ may surprise you.

For example, *The beach may surprise you* and *Love may surprise you* sound sensible, but *(The) very may surprise you* or *(A) go may surprise you* does not.

Remember that sentence:

$\begin{pmatrix} A[n] \\ The \\ My \end{pmatrix}$ _____ may surprise you.

Let us call it the *noun master sentence;* any word that sounds right in the blank can be a noun. Now, on your own paper write the noun master sentence ten times, each time with a noun that you think of on your own. (Avoid nouns you have already identified in this module.) Put *a, an, the,* or *my* in front if you have to. ‡As your instructor directs, exchange papers with another student to discuss your lists together and/or submit the paper to your instructor.

One more word on nouns. Just as a football coach may send in a substitute when his quarterback is tired from playing too much, a writer has a substitute kind of noun to use when repeating a previous noun would sound tiresome or silly. Can you rewrite the following sentence, replacing needlessly repeated nouns with substitute words that come to your mind?

Maxine wanted Jerry to give Maxine Jerry's ring.

[7]Maxine wanted Jerry _____.

There are several sets of such words in English, all of which you are already familiar with. You need to be able to recognize these words as a type of noun. For instance, one set (which includes the words you just substituted above) substitutes for nouns that the reader already knows:

I	you	he	she	it	we	they
me		him	her		us	them

and sometimes

this	that	these	those*

Other sets are used for persons or things that the reader does not know by name or does not want to name:

someone	no one	anyone	everyone	who
somebody	nobody	anybody	everybody	what
something	nothing	anything	everything	

These are not *all* the words that can substitute for other nouns; your instructor will point the others out to you if the need arises.

As a wrap-up on nouns, try the following:

A. Put a check (✓) in front of any word that you think is a noun. Use your common sense first; then mentally use the noun master sentence to check.

[8‡]
☐ of	☐ in	☐ who	☐ cassette
☐ chestnut	☐ it	☐ robbed	☐ heroin
☐ promoted	☐ somebody	☐ nothing	☐ the
☐ fact	☐ Julius Caesar	☐ freedom	☐ what
☐ we	☐ then	☐ normally	☐ recognition

B. Write any nouns that make sense to you in the following blanks. (Add *a, an, the, my*, etc., where necessary.)

---

* The traditional term for these words and the words in the following sets is *pronouns*.
You may have noticed that *me, him, her, us,* and *them* do not fit the master noun sentence. This will be explained in "Noun and Verb Problems." *Who* and *what* will fit the master sentence if you change the period at the end to a question mark.

9‡_____ makes me sick.

10‡_____ relieves pains of headaches, neuritis, and neuralgia.

11‡Recently, _____ has been acting strangely.

12‡Last night in the moonlight, _____ happened.

13‡All of a sudden _____ appeared.

14‡_____ didn't stand a chance.

15‡According to latest reports, _____ has passed the critical point.

16‡_____ really gives off some weird sounds.

17‡Millions of immigrants have come to this country seeking _____ .

18‡_____ may surprise you.

WORDS OF DOING, BEING, OR HAVING

You know that the subject of a sentence is always a noun. Let us turn to the other essential part of every sentence, the 1‡v_ _ _. Remember what the verb does: It tells what the subject was doing. In *Charles bit the dog, bit* tells what the subject (*Charles*) was doing. Examine again the words you picked as verbs in the first sentences you discovered, back on page 141. Notice how each verb (underlined twice) tells what its subject noun was (or is) doing.

I play   dogs bite
soldiers served   car stalled
Johnny rode   Belcher fell

Which of the following words do you think are verbs? Write each word in the proper column below:

student   eat   happy   mystery   depart
flunk   soul   write   investigate   departure

Verbs

2

_____   _____

_____   _____

_____

Not verbs

_____   _____

_____   _____

_____

To test whether you are right, mentally put each word from the *verb* column above into the blank in this sentence:

[3]‡They may _____ (it) soon.

If *every* word from the verb column and *no* word from the other column makes sense in the blank, you are a superb verb-identifier! Now check your answers.[2]

Because there are many different kinds and forms of verbs, there can be no one master verb sentence into which all verbs will fit; but the master sentence used above—*They may*

_____ *(it) soon*—will serve you to identify most verbs.

Here is more practice on verbs. Write each of the following words in the proper column below:

| read | book | in | listen | sometimes |
| modern | modernize | quickly | multiply | transfer |

Verbs

4‡

_____   _____

_____   _____

_____

Not verbs

_____   _____

_____   _____

_____

Check your answers by seeing whether only the words in the *verb* column fit in the verb master sentence.‡

Just as it was easy to spot a noun that named a concrete physical object—*car, Mount Fuji, dog*—it is fairly easy to spot verbs that tell physical actions—*steer, amble, jump, see, fall.* Likewise, as it was harder to spot nouns that named abstract ideas—*freedom, friendship, religion*—it is harder to spot verbs that tell mental action or what seems to be lack of action.

5‡

For example, what is the verb in the sentence below? _____

Charlie just lies in bed till noon.

Lies may not seem like doing anything, but if someone asked Charlie "What are you *doing?*" he would have to answer, "Just lying here." *Lies* is the verb. The same is true in these sentences:

> Einstein *pondered* the universe. [Mental action]
> The Aleutian Islands *extend* into the Eastern Hemisphere. [Just lying there]

If you feel you need further help, here is another way to spot many verbs—by their ending. The words below are all verbs; write the two endings (the last three letters) you find on them: _____[6]

_____

simplify	recognize	magnify
popularize	standardize	dignify

Remember these two endings. You definitely have a verb if you see either one. Another very common verb ending is *-ate*, as in *activate*, *regulate*, *investigate*. It usually (but not always) indicates a verb.

REGULAR VERB ENDINGS

Are you ready for the next point on verbs? You have probably noticed that the verbs we have been using can change their forms:

> The Aleutian Islands *extend▨* into the Eastern Hemisphere.
> Alaska *extend⬚s* into the Eastern Hemisphere.
> The Aleutian Islands once *extend⬚ed* to Siberia.

What is the difference among these three forms? See if you can discover it. First, examine these two sentences:

a. Today the Washington express depart⬚s from Track 5.
b. Today the Washington expresses depart▨ from Track 5.

In both sentence a and sentence b, we are telling what some thing is doing. But why do we need the *-s* ending on one verb? How many expresses are we talking about in sentence a? _____[7] How many expresses are we talking about in sentence b?

_____[8] Therefore, when we are telling that the subject is doing something *now*, we add the *-s* to the verb when the subject noun names [9]⬚ one person or thing, ⬚ more than one person or thing. In the sentences below, put the *-s* ending only in the box of any verb that needs it:

¹⁰Cecelia Wombat drink☐ bloody Marys.
¹¹Sophomores fail☐ fewer subjects than freshmen.
¹²Jagged mountains rise☐ high above Lake Gitchee Goomi.
¹³My stereo set need☐ a new speaker.
¹⁴Veal parmigiana give☐ my boy friend indigestion.

When the subject does something regularly over a long period of time, we consider this the same as if he were doing it *now*, and we use the same verb forms.

Every day the Washington *express* depart⟨s⟩ from Track 5.
Every day the Washington *expresses* depart⟨⟩ from Track 5.

Here are sentences a and b again, with two more sentences:

a.   Today the Washington *express* depart⟨s⟩ from Track 5.
b.   Today the Washington *expresses* depart⟨⟩ from Track 5.
c.   Yesterday the Washington *express* depart⟨ed⟩ from Track 5.
d.   Yesterday the Washington *expresses* depart⟨ed⟩ from Track 5.

Why do we need the *-ed* ending in sentences c and d? In what one way are sentences c and d

¹⁵

different from sentences a and b? _____
Therefore we add the *-ed* when   ¹⁶☐ the subject *is* doing something now, in the present, ☐ the subject *was* doing something at some time before now, in the past. In the sentences below, put the *-ed* ending only on the verbs that need it:

¹⁷When I went to college, sophomores fail☐ more subjects than freshmen.
¹⁸Today, sophomores fail☐ fewer subjects than freshmen.
¹⁹Last month my stereo set need☐ a new speaker.
²⁰The repair man told me that nowadays all stereo sets need☐ new speakers.
²¹The plane to Houston depart☐ ten minutes ago.

So far, then, you know that a verb may appear in any of three forms:

jump⟨⟩

I jump every day   You jump every day.
We jump every day   They jump every day.
Groucho and Harpo jump every day.   The puppies jump every day.
                                          The Mexican beans jump every day.

jump⟨s⟩

He jumps every day.   She jumps every day.
It jumps every day.   The puppy jumps every day.
Groucho jumps every day.   The Mexican bean jumps every day.

The two forms above are both called the *present* form, since they deal with the subject doing something now or regularly.

jump|ed|

I jumped yesterday.

We jumped yesterday.

He jumped yesterday.

It jumped yesterday.

Groucho jumped yesterday.

Groucho and Harpo jumped yesterday.

The Mexican beans jumped yesterday.

You jumped yesterday.

They jumped yesterday.

She jumped yesterday.

The puppy jumped yesterday.

The Mexican bean jumped yesterday.

The puppies jumped yesterday.

This form is called the *past* form, since it deals with the subject doing something at some time in the past. Add the appropriate ending in whichever boxes need one:

²²I jump☐ with joy when I see Randolph.

²³The stock market jump☐ ten points last week.

²⁴My heart jump☐ whenever the professor calls on me.

Now give the three forms for the verb *cover:*

²⁵cover☐   cover☐   cover☐

Add the appropriate ending in whichever boxes need one:

²⁶The pay from my weekend job cover☐ only a small part of my college expenses these days.

²⁷Some profs always cover☐ too much material in one class hour.

²⁸Dagmar cover☐ her head with a shawl when she entered the church.

More practice in these endings is available in the module "Noun and Verb Problems" if you need it.

IRREGULAR VERBS

You can now recognize three forms of most verbs. But what about the following verbs?

I *run* today.

He *runs* today.

²⁹‡

I _____ yesterday.

Every day I *forget* my math book.

Every day she *forgets* her math book.

³⁰‡

Yesterday she _____ her math book.

What goes in the blanks? *Runned? Forgetted?* Of course not. I *ran* yesterday. Yesterday she *forgot* her math book. As you may remember from elementary school, some of our most common verbs have unusual past forms in place of the *-ed.* We call them *irregular* verbs, because that is just what they are. Everyone uses them so often that you should have little trouble with them; for example:

³¹In last night's game Rogers _____ his ankle. [Not *breaked*, but what?]

48That music s_____s good.

49That sun on my back f_____s good.

50That perfume s_____s good.

51That steak t_____s good.

Notice that these verbs, and a few others, such as *appear* and *become*, are all somewhat like *be*. Could you substitute the verb *is* in the five sentences above and get something close to

the same meaning? 52 _____

Besides verbs that show *doing* and those that show *being*, are there any other kinds? Which verbs would you put in these sentences?

53Aretha Franklin's singing h____ soul.

54We h_____ liftoff!" said Mission Control.

55Lincoln h____ two sons.

Check your answers. When you see one of these three words in a sentence, you are seeing a form of the verb *have*.

The verb *have:*

Present form	Past form
have (has)	had

Some other verbs with meanings like *have* are *possess, own, contain*. Like *be*, *have* is one of our most frequently used and most important verbs. *Having* is not exactly *doing*, and it clearly is not *being*. We need to include all three of these verb types in our description of a sentence. Do not concern yourself with memorizing this description; rather, try to grasp the idea behind it:

A sentence is a string of words telling that some person or thing was

56d_____g, 56h_____g, or 56b_____g something.

REVIEW OF VERBS

It is time for review and practice. Underline the subject noun once and the verb twice, in each of the following sentences:

57The doctor probed deeply.

58The only structure was a one-room chicken house.

[59]A snuffleupagus has a shaggy body.

[60]Often Calvin Hoogiban rode in the caboose.

[61]Rancid turnips smell terrible.

[62]‡Some very important people attend our club meetings.

[63]‡Veterans of the Vietnam war receive modest educational benefits.

[64]‡Honest politicians rarely become successful.

[65]‡Sometimes students invent wild stories as explanations for incomplete papers.

[66]‡The slithy toves gyred in the wabe.

Items 67 to 71 below contain one of the two parts of a sentence: either the subject part or the verb part. You make up an original *other* part to make each sentence complete. For items 72 through 76, write *both* parts, making original complete sentences. After you have written all ten, go back over them, underlining the subject noun once and the verb twice:

[67]‡Most Super Bowl games _____ .

[68]‡Politicians _____ .

[69]‡ _____ makes me really sad.

[70]‡ _____ signed the new contract.

[71]‡Community colleges in this state _____ .

[72]‡ _____   _____

[73]‡ _____   _____

[74]‡ _____   _____

[75]‡ _____   _____

[76]‡ _____   _____

VERBS OF MORE THAN ONE WORD

What is the verb in the sentence below? Do not be surprised if something confuses

you: [77]‡ _____

The train has stopped at the junction.

How many words did you find that you recognize as verbs? [78]‡ _____ You have just learned that *has* is a verb; but *stopped* tells what the train was doing and has the *-ed* ending.

It must be a verb too. Can we have two verbs in a sentence? Yes, but let us not say *two* verbs here. Two verbs would mean something like this:

The train *had* brake trouble and *stopped* outside the city.

Here the train did two separate things. In the first sentence, since the train did only *one* thing, we consider *has stopped* one verb. As you see, the verb can have more than one word. In fact, it may have three or occasionally even four words, as you will discover.

Before we go any further, you need to reacquaint yourself with two other forms of verbs. You already know them, of course; you have been using them all your life. So far we have learned the *present* form of the verb (*walk, walks; sing, sings*), and the *past* form—(*walked; sang*). Now think of the words *walking, singing*. Are they verbs too? They would seem to be; they tell an action. But are they really verbs? You can say *Mervin walks to class* and *Mervin walked to class;* however, if someone asked you *What is Mervin doing?* would you answer *Mervin walking to class?* Your familiarity with English will probably tell you that this is ungrammatical in standard English. Which words would you add in these sentences?

[79]Mervin _____ walking to class right now.

[80]Charlene _____ singing "Because" when the lights went out.

[81]We _____ running low on milk.

[82]When I arrived, the ushers _____ throwing Bernie out the door.

[83]I _____ growing tired of the same meals every day.

Thus a verb can have two words. The first word is a form of *be* (*am, is, are, was, were*); the second is a form made by adding *-ing* to any verb. Here are more examples:

Len and I <u>were backpacking</u> on the Appalachian trail last summer.

You <u>are growing</u> more beautiful every day.

The governor <u>is calling</u> the legislature into special session.

Put two lines under the *whole verb* (both words) in these sentences:

[84]The president was vacationing in Florida.

[85]After the first of the month electricity rates are going up again.

[86]Senator Nelson is making no statement to the press on his involvement with Toodles La Fleur.

[87]Miss La Fleur and her lawyers are proceeding with a defamation suit against the Washington *Post*.

Since this third form of the verb always ends in *-ing*, let us call it the *-ing*-form.
The three verb forms you have discovered so far are

Present form	Past form	-Ing-form
sing(s)	sang	singing
walk(s)	walked	walking
run(s)	ran	running
get(s)	got	getting
[*of* be] am (is, are)	was (were)	being

There is one more important form of the verb. Which two words do you think are the verb in this next sentence? Underline them twice:

88‡Zarkhov has broken the Olympic pole-vault record.

You recognize *has,* no doubt, as one part of the verb. Which other word helps tell what

Zarkhov did? 89B_____. Which two words make up the verb in the sentence below? Underline them twice:

90Zarkhov had taken two pep pills before the event.

In both the sentences above, what two-letter ending does the new word in the verb have?

91

_____ This is an ending that appears on the fourth and last form of a verb; we will therefore call this last form the *-en*-form. *Broken* is the *-en*-form of the verb

92b_____, and *taken* is the *-en*-form of the verb 93t____.
Underline twice both words in the verb of each of the following sentences:

94George has chosen the wrong road again!

95Professor Philpot has spoken for over two hours now.

96Wilt's ankle has swollen to twice its normal size.

97The pirates have hidden somewhere on this island.

If you feel fairly confident that you can spot an *-en*-form of the verb, here is the bad news: The *-en*-form is so irregular that it has several completely different endings. The best way to spot such irregular *-en*-forms is by the pattern of their use in the sentence. See if you can discover that pattern; fill in each blank:

98I hope I never lose this bracelet. I have l____ three this year.

99Madame Scrici will never sing again; she has s____ her last aria.

100Marcia didn't let her boy friend drink any more. He had already d_____ far too much.

101Sergeant Kilroy has l__ his men out of the desert wilderness. He can lead them anywhere.

102We have w__ three of the first five games. We have to win only one more.

¹⁰³The ranger has sp_____ three forest fires this month. He is very good at spotting them.

In the sentences above, what verb always came just in front of the word you filled in?

¹⁰⁴‡H____ (h__, h__).
The -en-form of any verb, then, is the form that you use after *have* (or *has* or *had*) in a sentence. The -en-form is often disguised with endings like just -n (as in *sworn, flown*), -e (*gone, done*), -g (*sung, dug*), -t (*brought, lost*), -k (*struck*), -d (*found*), -m (*swum*), and most of all, -ed—the same ending as the past form (*jumped, terminated, decided*)! Even so, if you remember this new master sentence,

She has _____ (it) already

you will be able to find the -en-form of almost any verb. Try it with the verbs in brackets:

¹⁰⁵A[do]   She has d____ it already.

ᴮ[bite]   She has b_____ it already.

ᶜ[take]   She has _____ it already.

ᴰ[choose]   She has _____ it already.

ᴱ[steal]   She has _____ it already.

ᶠ[forget]   She has _____ it already.

ᴳ[show]   She has _____ it already.

ᴴ[have]   She has _____ it already.

ᴵ[sell]   She has _____ it already.

ᴶ[teach]   She has _____ it already.

ᴷ[ring]   She has _____ it already.

ᴸ[terminate]   She has _____ it already.

ᴹ[bring]   She has _____ it already.

ᴺ[surrender]   She has _____ already.

ᴼ[fly]   She has _____ already.

ᴾ[speak]   She has _____ already.

ᵠ[go]   She has _____ already.

ᴿ[leave]   She has _____ already.

ˢ[walk]   She has _____ already.

ᵀ[decide]   She has _____ already.

The four forms of a verb, then, are

Present form	Past form	-Ing-form	-En-form
do(es)	did	doing	done
break(s)	broke	breaking	broke
jump(s)	jumped	jumping	jumped
[be] am (is, are)	was (were)	being	been
sink(s)	sank	sinking	sunk

Besides following *have* (*has, had*), will the *-en*-form appear anywhere else? Examine the sentences below. Underline twice the word or words you think make up the verb.

¹⁰⁶Three lawyers were taken off the case.

¹⁰⁷The strike is set for Monday morning.

¹⁰⁸Ryan was named Secretary of State.

¹⁰⁹All classes are canceled until further notice.

110

Thus the *-en*-form can be used not only after *have* but also after ____.

Here is a very important point about *-ing-* and *-en*-forms. Remember what you learned about the *-ing*-form? Can it be a verb by itself? For example, do we write *Mervin*

111

walking to class? What word must be added? *Mervin* _____ *walking to class.* If the *-ing*-form cannot be a full verb without another verb (some form of *be*) in front of it, is the same true for the *-en*-form? Find out. Are all of the following sentences grammatical standard English? If any are not, rewrite them in the space below, adding whatever is needed:

¹¹²Jim taken the early bus.

_____

¹¹³In the third act Siegfried slain by Hagen.

_____

¹¹⁴Across the world malnutrition stricken millions of people.

_____

¹¹⁵Early in the war Long Island captured by the British.

_____

Both the *-ing-* and *-en-*forms, then, are only *parts* of verbs; to make them into full verbs you must add another verb word in front of them: Add some form of *be* to the *-ing-*form; add some form of *have* or *be* to the *-en-*form.

It is time for some practice. Underline once the subject noun and underline twice all words that make up the verb in the following sentences:

[116]Mighty Casey was advancing to the bat.

[117]The sneer has gone from Casey's lips.

[118]His teeth are clenched in hate.

[119]Now the air is shattered by the force of Casey's blow.

[120]Mighty Casey has struck out.

Each item below gives you a subject. Starting with that subject, write an original sentence containing a verb of two words. Underline both words of the verb. Remember that the first

word of the verb must be a part of [121]h_ _ _ or b__, and the second word must be the
[122]

_____-form or the _____-form of any verb:
[122]

[123]‡Girls _____.

[124]‡The telephone company _____.

[125]‡A big-time TV entertainer _____.

[126]‡A strange noise _____.

[127]‡The Admissions Office _____.

So far you have met verbs of one word or of two words. What words do you think make up the verbs in the sentences below? Underline twice all verb words you find:

[128]Ellen had been sleeping through the whole class.

[129]‡Notre Dame has been stopped on the one-yard line!

[130]

How many words are there in each verb above? _____ You see that both *have* and *be* may appear before the *-ing-* or *-en-*form. Thus some verbs have three words. Which of the three words do you think is the main word of the verb? For example, in this sentence,

The giant airliner had been circling overhead for an hour

[131]

what was the plane doing? _____ Thus *circling*, the *last* word in the verb, is the *main* word in the verb. The main verb word is always the last verb word. The other verb words help the main word by telling the time or other conditions of the verb. What are these helping words in the verb called? Does your city or town have an [132]‡a__x_____ry police force that helps the regular force when it has a big job? Does your local hospital have an

[133]‡a__x__l____ry generator to help provide electricity in case of a power failure? As you have probably guessed, the verb words that help the main verb word are called *auxiliaries*. For this sentence,

Leopold has been taken to a psychiatrist

write the main word of the verb: [134] _____ Now write the auxiliaries: [135] _____

Besides *have* and *be* there are several other auxiliaries that in one way or another change the conditions of the main verb. What new auxiliary—a very common one—do you spot in this sentence? Put two lines under it and the main verb word.

[136]I do brush my teeth every day, Mom.

Do you recall other forms of *do?*

[137]He d_____ brush his teeth every day.

[138]He d___ brush his teeth yesterday.

Add *do* (*does, did*) to your mental list of auxiliaries. Now here comes a whole barrage of others. In each sentence below put two lines under the main verb word and the word that you think is the auxiliary.

[139]A Ernie will pass math.

B Ernie would pass math.

C‡ Ernie shall pass math.

D‡ Ernie should pass math.

E‡ Ernie can pass math.

F‡ Ernie could pass math.

G‡ Ernie must pass math.

H‡ Ernie has to pass math. (Consider *has to* as a single word.)

I‡ Ernie ought to pass math.

J‡ Ernie may pass math.

K‡ Ernie might pass math.

L‡ Ernie used to pass math.

That should not have given you much difficulty.

At this point you have learned just about all you need to know to recognize the verb—the most important part of a sentence—and to write sentences that you are sure contain verbs. Remember what you discovered earlier—no verb, no sentence.

Just a few fine points on verbs:

A. We have seen as many as three words in a verb: two auxiliaries and a main verb word. Can we have more than three? Put two lines under all the words in the verb in the following sentence:

140The driver must have been drinking before the accident.

141

How many auxiliaries are there? _____ That is the limit of words in an English verb: four—three auxiliaries and the main verb word.

B. What about words like *not* and *never*, as in *I have never tried vodka*? Are they parts of verbs? No, but they and other words may appear between parts of the verb. Examine the following sentences:

He has never arrived late in five years.

My husband must never know about our meeting.

The witness could hardly not have noticed the gun in the defendant's hand.

REVIEW OF SUBJECTS AND VERBS

Now you can show your understanding of the two essential sentence parts. Put one line under the subject noun and two lines under every word in the verb of each of these sentences:

142‡Lake Superior once stood as a prime example of pure water.

143‡Lakeside dwellers have often drunk their water directly from the lake.

144‡Such drinks may have been poisonous.

145‡The blame for the lake's pollution has been placed on the Ironrite Mining Company.

146‡Recently an injunction has been issued against the company.

Think of any verbs that make sense in the blanks below, and write them in—one word for each blank:

147‡"The Planet of the Apes" _____ my favorite TV show a couple of years ago.

148‡Ever since I _____ a child, I _____ _____ science-fiction programs.

149‡Tonight I _____ _____ "Godzilla" for the tenth time.

150‡Those monster movies _____ _____ _____ millions of dollars to make.

151‡Last night I sh_____ _____ _____ _____ing

a research paper, but I _____ "The Wolf Man" instead.

Decide whether each of the following is a sentence—whether it has a subject and a full verb. If it does not, rewrite it in the space below, making up and adding the part(s) it needs to be a sentence.

152‡Many memorable moments in sports.

_____

153‡For instance, Bobby Thompson's home run won the 1951 baseball playoffs.

_____

154‡In the 1920s, Red Grange six touchdowns in one game.

_____

155‡Mark Spitz captured seven gold medals in the 1972 Olympics.

_____

156‡Hank Aaron, Wilt Chamberlain, O. J. Simpson all famous.

_____

157‡Babe Didrickson, Billie Jean King, and Althea Gibson set many women's records.

_____

Write five original sentences of seven to twelve words each telling some interesting or amusing incidents that have happened to you or others you know since college began.

158‡
_____
_____

159‡
_____
_____

160‡
_____
_____

161‡
_____
_____

162‡
_____
_____

WHAT FOLLOWS THE VERB

Recall our description of a sentence—*a string of words telling that some person or thing was doing, being, or having something*. You know that the word mentioning the person or thing is called the *subject noun* and the word or words telling the doing, being, or having are called the *verb*. This description can also be written as a pattern:

S V

S, of course, means *subject*, and V means *verb*.

Now we want to look at the word *something* in our description of a sentence:

. . . doing, being, or having *something*.

In this sentence

The old man sneezed

the old man is obviously doing something: sneezing. Do we need any other word(s) after the verb to tell us the thing the old man did? _____[1] But how about these sentences?

The old man faced
The old man had
The old man was

Do the verbs tell us fully what the old man faced, had, or was? Do they tell us the thing he was doing, being, or having? _____[2] Finish these sentences:

[3]‡The old man faced _____.

[4]‡The old man had _____.

[5]‡The old man was _____.

Some verbs, then, complete the thought of the sentence in themselves (*The old man sneezed*). We *can* add other words, such as

The old man sneezed violently in his bed

but we do not *have* to. *The old man sneezed* makes complete sense by itself. But many verbs need another word after them to complete the thought (*The old man faced. . .*). In which of the sentences below is the thought complete in the verb itself? In which *must* we add one or more words to make a complete thought? Add the completing words only where you *must*. Otherwise, put nothing in the blank:

[6]In 1865 Lincoln died _____.

[7]In the accident I broke _____.

⁸The sun has just set _____ .

⁹My girl friend found _____ .

¹⁰Sibyl wanted _____ .

Do the words you added in the second, fourth, and fifth sentences name persons or things?
¹¹
_____ Then they must be ¹²n____ ____ ____s. Since nouns like these complete the meaning of the verb, let us call them *completers*.

Do you know that you are a linguistic scientist? In the same way that linguistic scientists did, you have now discovered the basic pattern of English sentences. You examined a number of individual sentences, noticed a pattern, and reached a general conclusion. This book provided the sentences and the questions, but *you* reached the conclusion. With your new understanding of the *completer* of the verb, we can now expand our basic sentence pattern to this:

$$S \quad V(C)$$

We put the *C* for *completer* in parentheses because not all verbs have to have a completer.

In each of the following sentences, put <u>one</u> line under the subject and <u>two</u> lines under the verb. Then, if the verb is followed by another noun as the completer, put <u>three</u> lines under that completer:

¹³Coal is a dirty fuel.

¹⁴The jury has reached a verdict.

¹⁵Jones acknowledged his terrible mistake.

¹⁶Negotiations should soon begin.

¹⁷Many people have never smoked.

¹⁸Collaborators will be executed.

¹⁹California almost always has fair weather.

²⁰Max might have been taking the late train.

²¹Long ago the United States became a nation.

There is a variation to this S V(C) pattern that appears fairly often. Look at these sentences:

Vicky gave a party.
Vicki gave Jay a party.

The camp counselor told a horror story.
The camp counselor told the boys a horror story.

The nation elected Roosevelt.
The nation elected Roosevelt president.

What appears in the second sentence of each set that was not in the first? Another _____.
You see then that it is possible to have *two* nouns after the verb—two completers. Therefore
we will expand our basic sentence pattern once more, to include this. Since you are a
budding linguistic scientist, try writing this expanded sentence pattern yourself:

[23]S   V(C)_____

This is our final, complete pattern. It fits all possible English sentences. Later in this book
you will learn how to write sentences far more complicated than the ones in this module;
but no matter how long or involved a grammatical sentence is, it has at its core a simple
S   V(C)(C).[*] This is why you are being asked to spend so much time on mastering the
pattern. Being able to identify the pattern in your own writing is as important to you as a
writer as knowing how to dribble is to a basketball player.

In each of the sentences below, put one line under the subject, two lines under the
verb, and three lines under any completer(s) you find:

[24]Lombardi gave the rookie some encouragement.

[25]Lately we are getting more customers.

[26]The keeper threw the chimp a banana.

[27]That bum called my girl a creep!

Now write sentences of your own fitting the parts of the pattern that have blanks. You may
want to add other words like *the, swift,* etc. between the parts. The first one is done for you
as an example:

S	V	(C)	(C)
[28]‡*Aunt Tillie*	*gave*	*the mugger*	*a swift kick.*
29‡			
30‡			
31‡			
32‡			
33‡			

There are three not-too-difficult curve balls to watch for when looking for the subject,
verb, and completers.

First, look at the subjects of these sentences:

---

[*] Some sentences are made up of *two* S V(C)(C)'s; but these sentences are actually two separate sentences,
two S V(C)(C)'s, joined by a link, such as *and.*

The twins were married on the same day.
Jane and Jean were married on the same day.

The subject of the first sentence, of course, is *twins*. What is the subject of the second?
³⁴

_____ You see, then, that we can have a double (or triple) noun in the subject. *And* is the usual link between the parts, although you might sometimes see *or*. And, of course, if there can be a double noun in a subject, there can be a double noun in a completer; and there can be a double verb.

Underline the subject, verb, and completer of these sentences in the usual way, but be sure to catch all the words of each part:

³⁵Bonnie and Clyde robbed many men.

³⁶Bonnie and Clyde robbed and killed many men.

³⁷Bonnie and Clyde robbed and killed many men and women.

If you find doubles confusing, just remember that they act exactly the same as singles. Perhaps bracketing them in a sentence will make the pattern clearer to you:

S	V	(C)
[John and Al]	[buy and sell]	[guns and ammunition].

The next curve ball is not hard at all. You have known since you were about three years old how to turn a statement into a question. What happens to the order of the subject and the verb in most questions?

S V	V S
He <u>is</u> here.	Where <u>is</u> he?

S V	V S V
Ziggy is going.	Is Ziggy going?

Underline the subject and verb of each of the following in the usual way. Watch for verbs of two or more words:

³⁸Charlie was waiting for three hours.

³⁹Was Charlie waiting for three hours?

⁴⁰How long was Charlie waiting?

⁴¹The encyclopedia contains the answer.

⁴²Does the encyclopedia contain the answer?

And the *last* curve ball—the easiest—concerns sentences that tell someone to do something:

⁴³Shut the door.

⁴⁴Submit your papers by Friday.

⁴⁵Fly Pan Am to the Pacific.

⁴⁶Hit that line!

⁴⁷Return all books promptly.

It should not be hard for you to find the *verb* in each of the sentences above. Underline each verb twice. Now where is the subject in each of these sentences? If I say *Shut the door*, to whom am I saying it? To ⁴⁸‡_____. Yes, to *you*. When I say *Submit your papers* or *Hit that line!* I mean that who should do these things? The person I am talking to—you. *You* is the subject, though it is not even in the sentence! Some times we actually say it, as in *You get home on time!* but customarily we omit it. It is *understood* by you and me that *you* should do the action. Thus such an unsaid subject is called *you* ⁴⁹un_____oo___.

What is the subject of sentence 43? ⁵⁰_____ Sentence 45? ⁵¹_____

REVIEW OF SUBJECTS, VERBS, AND COMPLETERS

You are at last ready for a final review on nouns, verbs, and the S V(C)(C) pattern. Decide whether each item from 52 to 58 is a sentence or not; that is, whether it contains the S V(C)(C) pattern. Write "sentence" for each item that is a sentence already. Rewrite each item that is not a sentence, making it a sentence. (Remember that to be a sentence, a string of words needs only an S V(C)(C). It does not have to give you all the information it possibly could. For example, *He saw it* is a complete sentence, with a subject, verb, and necessary completer, even though we do not know who *he* is or what *it* is. The *speaker* knows, and the *listener* probably knows. By contrast, in this string of words, *Foster Croker, governor of Idaho from 1826 to 1830 and one of five sons of a Scottish immigrant*, we are told a great deal about the subject, Mr. Croker; but is this a sentence? Where is the *verb*? No verb, no sentence!)

Now go ahead:

⁵²‡You can modernize a basement for very little money.

_____

⁵³‡Draw lines on the basement wall for door openings.

_____

⁵⁴‡All loose floorboards and cracks in walls.

_____

⁵⁵‡Your electrician can help.

_____

⁵⁶‡Vinyl tiles, indoor-outdoor carpet, carpet tiles, or inlaid linoleum.

_____

⁵⁷‡It will look gorgeous.

_____

^{58‡}Will envy your new basement.

Next, write five original sentences of seven to twelve words each, telling five unusual facts you have learned since coming to college:

59‡

60‡

61‡

62‡

63‡

WORDS THAT CHANGE THE PICTURE

WORDS THAT CHANGE THE PICTURE OF NOUNS

Nouns and verbs are the meat and potatoes of our speaking and writing. But obviously there are more kinds of words. How many kinds? The answer depends on how deeply a person wants to study the English language. Linguistic scholars, like biologists with insects, divide and subdivide word types far more thoroughly than we need to do in order to write well. Traditional "schoolroom" grammars named eight kinds of words: the "parts of speech." Many recent grammar books subdivide some of those eight. We will move in the opposite direction and reduce that number to four, two of which you have already learned—nouns and verbs. Thus you have only two more kinds of words to discover.*

See what you can discover about the first of these two. Let us start with an incident. Your friend Lesley meets you in the hall and tells you she has just bought a convertible at Honest John's used-car lot. "Wait till you see the car I bought!" she tells you. In your mind you begin to picture the car: the make, the color, the model, the year, the condition. Do this in your own mind now: Clearly picture the car you imagine Lesley bought. Now Lesley is going to tell you the kind of car she actually did buy, as you keep *your* picture of it in your mind.

I bought a Ford convertible.

Had you pictured a Cadillac? A VW? An Alfa-Romeo?

I bought a purple Ford convertible.

Had you pictured blue? White? Tan? Two-tone?

---

* Actually, there is a third kind: words like *Aha! Damn it! Yecch! Sonofagun! Holy Cow! Well, oh,* and many of the common "four-letter words." Since words like these usually have no grammatical connection with the rest of a sentence, there is no need for us to study them.

I bought a purple 1927 Ford convertible.

Had you pictured a '75? A '65? A '53?

I bought a rusty purple 1927 Ford convertible.

Now, honestly, was your original mental picture of Lesley's car that of a rusty purple 1927 Ford convertible? Probably not. Now what did you have to do to your mental picture of Lesley's car every time we added another word describing Lesley's actual car? You undoubtedly had to change, or modify, your mental picture as each new word was given to you.

You have just discovered an important concept: There is a kind of word that

[1]ch___g__s, or m__d_____s, our mental impression of a noun. We use words of this kind to bring the reader's mental picture of that noun as close as possible to our own picture of it. In each sentence below, form a mental picture of the noun following the blank. Then add words to change (modify) the reader's possible mental picture of that noun to bring it closer to your mental picture of the noun:

[2]‡The _____ _____ man ambled up to the counter.

(If you think commas are needed, use them. You will learn exactly where to put them in the module "Punctuation.")

[3]‡_____ _____ boys [or girls—take your choice] don't appeal
         to me.

[4]‡You should see the _____ house they live in!

[5]‡Enjoy a _____ _____ weekend at Lechery Lodge.

[6]‡Whitlow certainly lived a _____ life.

Since the words you wrote modify the reader's mental impression of the words they describe,

we call such words [7]m_____s.

Let us look now at some other words which modify nouns. First, what about those pesty little words we have been largely ignoring so far: a (an) and the? Do they modify nouns? Is there a difference in meaning between these two sentences?

   a. You should find a girl and marry her.
   b. You should find the girl and marry her.

In which sentence am I telling my friend to marry any suitable girl he meets? [8]_____

In which am I telling him to marry one particular girl that he knows? [9]_____
Whether I use a(n) or the does modify my friend's idea of the girl I mean. Thus a(n) and

the are [10]m_____s.

By the same thinking, what about *this* and *that*? Does *this* door mean the same as
that door? _____[11‡] As *some* door? _____[12‡] As *any* door? _____[13‡]

As *either* door? _____[14‡] And what about the following? Does *little* talent mean the

same as *much* talent? _____[15‡] As *enough* talent? _____[16‡] As *surplus* talent?

_____[17‡] Is *my* car the same as *your* car? _____[18‡] Are *three* dollars the

same as *five* dollars? _____[19‡] What does each italicized word above do? It

[20‡]ch_ _ _ _s, or [20‡]m_ _ _ _ _ _s, our idea of the noun after it. Therefore all these

italicized words are _ _ _ _ _ _ _ _ _[21]s of those nouns.

    In each sentence below, the subject noun, verb, and completer noun(s) are under-
lined in the usual way. Circle the modifiers of each noun:

    [22]The yellow <u>submarine</u> <u>sailed</u> the seven <u>seas</u>.

    [23]Any two strong young <u>men</u> <u>can push</u> this light <u>truck</u>.

    [24]Our new <u>Prime Minister</u> <u>gave</u> the American <u>ambassador</u> a lengthy <u>interview</u>.

Did you notice that you are becoming quite skilled at understanding the workings of a
sentence? You see how sentences are built up from the basic pattern:

In the sentences below, supply modifiers of your own for the nouns. Use your imagination
where possible. (Add commas as you see fit.)

    [25‡]The _____ course involves _____ _____ work.

    [26‡]_____ _____ clouds indicate _____ rain.

    [27‡]_____ documents became _____ _____ evidence.

    [28‡]_____ jewels have tempted _____ thieves.

    [29‡]_____ team can beat _____ team.

    [30‡]_____ _____ monster devoured _____ _____ demon.

So far modifiers probably seem quite easy, since their position is fixed—they always

come right [31]b_____ the noun. There must be some catch, you say—some curve ball to make things harder. There is, but it is not really hard. Look at this conversation between two girls at a party:

Sue: That weird man offered me a drink.
Linda: He looks okay.
Sue: I'm telling you: That man is weird.

Watch the word *weird.* Is it a modifier in the first sentence? [32]_____

That *weird* man . . .

But in the third sentence, where has *weird* shifted to?

```
      S   V   (C)   (C)
That man  is  weird.
```

It has shifted to the position of the [33]com_____r. Modifiers of nouns, then, can appear in one of two ways:

A.   Before the noun:

     That *weird* man offered me a drink.

B.   As a completer:

     That man is *weird.*

Here are other examples:

[34]You have a green light at the end of your dock.

(Your light is g_____.)
[35]Teddy Roosevelt's tough policy frightened weaker nations.

(Roosevelt's policy was _____.)
[36‡]Poisonous fumes overcame the desperate rescuers.

(The fumes were _____.)

(The rescuers were _____.)
[37‡]Intense physical activity characterized his life.

(The activity was _____ and _____.)

There is one more modifier-like situation to examine:

> Washington's portrait hangs in the National Art Gallery.
> Lincoln's portrait hangs in the National Art Gallery.

Our mental picture of what noun is different in each sentence?

[38]p_____. The words *Washington's* and *Lincoln's* each give us a different mental picture of the noun *portrait*. Thus *Washington's* and

Lincoln's act like [39]mo_____s of a noun. Officially, such words (which end in *'s* or *s'*) are still nouns, but you should realize that they do act like modifiers.

> Here are some other examples:
> *Lesley's* car is a 1927 Ford convertible.
> The *car's* body is rusty.
> Lesley wanted two *experts'* estimates of its value.
> *Honest John's* price for the car was no bargain.

Now it is time for you to show your understanding of modifiers of nouns. Put a circle around each modifier you find in the sentences below. The subject nouns, verbs, and completer nouns are underlined in the first two sentences to help you:

[40]Local <u>consumers</u> <u>are facing</u> higher <u>prices</u>.

[41]The heavy <u>snowfall</u> <u>caused</u> massive urban <u>congestion</u>.

[42]Your new hairdo is hideous.

[43]This revolutionary new product relieves unsightly blemishes.

[44]Some little third-string quarterback might have scored an additional six points.

WORDS THAT CHANGE THE PICTURE OF VERBS

If nouns have modifiers, what about verbs? Look at this sentence:

> The director quickly shut the door.

[45]Subject? _____ Verb? _____ Completer? _____ That should not have given you much trouble. But what about the word *quickly*? Is it a modifier of a noun? Does *the quickly director* or *the quickly door* make sense? If not a noun, verb, or modifier of a noun, then, what is it? What *did* happen quickly? Or to put the question a different way, how was the shutting done? Not slowly, not casually, not fearfully, but

[46]_____ly. And in this sentence,

Robert Jordan thoroughly cleaned his rifle

what word tells how Jordan cleaned the rifle? [47]_____ Notice what happens to our mental picture if we change the word:

Robert Jordan {

hastily
routinely
mechanically
desperately
eagerly

[48‡]

} cleaned his rifle.

[You add one]

Each different word gives us a different mental picture of how Jordan cleaned his rifle. Each

[49]ch ___ g __ s, or [49]m __ d ___ ___ ___ s, our picture—not our picture of Robert Jordan or of the rifle, but of the action of cleaning. Thus *thoroughly, hastily*, etc., modify the word

[50]cl ___ ___ ___ d, which is the [51]v ___ ___ ___ of the sentence.

Verbs, then, can have modifiers just as nouns can. Let us call modifiers of verbs simply *verb modifiers* and modifiers of nouns *noun modifiers*.

In this sentence,

Weary Robert Jordan carefully cleaned his ancient rifle

which word modifies the noun *Robert Jordan*? [52]_____

Which words modify the noun *rifle*? [53]_____ _____

Which word modifies the verb, *cleaned*? [54]_____
Notice the pattern:

(Weary) $\overset{S}{\text{Robert Jordan}}$ (carefully) $\overset{V}{\text{cleaned}}$ (his) (ancient) $\overset{C}{\text{rifle.}}$

Now for more on verb modifiers. First, you have probably noticed that so far all our

verb modifiers have the same ending, which is [55]____. This is one very easy way to spot verb modifiers; nine times out of ten a word ending in an *-ly* syllable will be a verb modifier. Here are some other examples:

The demolition expert *gingerly* lifted the bomb from the wrappings.
General McClellan *cautiously* sent his infantry into the Shenandoah Valley.

What does *gingerly* tell us about the lifting? It tells [56]h____ the lifting was done. What does *cautiously* tell us about the sending of troops? It tells _____ the sending was done. This is one reason we use verb modifiers—to tell our readers *how* an action was done.

Not all verb modifiers have the *-ly* clue, however, and some tell other things about the verb besides *how*. Which word in each sentence below tells something about the verb in that sentence—something about the action? Circle each word that you think does so:

⁵⁸Meteors seldom strike the earth.

⁵⁹Cigars never irritate my throat.

⁶⁰Osmond died yesterday.

⁶¹The police now suspect Rodney.

⁶²He did it then.

What does each of the circled words tell us about the verb? *Seldom* tells us ⁶³wh____

meteors strike the earth. *Never* tells us ⁶⁴wh____ cigars irritate my throat. We use verb modifiers, then, when we want to tell our readers *when* an action was done, as well as *how*. What else might we want to tell about an action besides *how* and *when* it happened? Circle each word in the following sentences that you think is a verb modifier:

⁶⁵We will meet Charlie here.

⁶⁶Inspector Stone found the body nearby.

⁶⁷Both candidates traveled far.

⁶⁸Junior has run away.

Here tells ⁶⁹wh_____ we will meet Charlie. *Nearby* tells ⁷⁰wh_____ Stone found the body. We use verb modifiers, then, when we want to tell *how, when,* or *where* an action was done. (There is other information verb modifiers can tell about verbs, such as *why*, but since *why* cannot be expressed in a single word, we will not consider such modifiers here.)

Circle the three verb modifiers in this sentence:

⁷¹Clyde angrily sent a letter there yesterday.

Which verb modifier tells *how* Clyde sent the letter? ⁷²_____ Which tells *where*?

⁷³_____ Which tells *when*? ⁷⁴_____ Then can we have different verb

modifiers telling *how, when,* and *where* in the same sentence? ⁷⁵_____ Circle each verb modifier you find in the following sentences:

⁷⁶Hurstwood lovingly embraced Carrie.

[77]Hurstwood embraced Carrie often.

[78]Hurstwood embraced Carrie anywhere.

[79]Hurstwood often lovingly embraced Carrie anywhere.

One more point on verb modifiers. You should easily discover it from these sentences:

> Hurstwood lovingly embraced Carrie.
> Hurstwood embraced Carrie lovingly.
> Lovingly, Hurstwood embraced Carrie.

[80]

What have you discovered about the verb modifier *lovingly?* _____

_____ Yes, many verb modifiers are "floaters": They often can be placed at any one of several places in the sentence—any place that sounds sensible. Pick any one verb modifier (like *suddenly, cautiously*) and write this same modifier in a *different* place in each of the sentences below, if you can. (Fill in only *one* blank in each sentence.)

[81] _____ Holden _____ crossed the street _____.

_____ Holden _____ crossed the street _____.

_____ Holden _____ crossed the street _____.

Now make up verb modifiers to put in the blanks in the following sentences, answering the questions in brackets:

[82]‡[how?]   The tall young man waved his arms _____.

[83]‡[when?]   Rick _____ gives the captain free drinks.

[84]‡[where?]   The balloon sailed _____.

[85]‡[how *or* when?]   _____ the announcer delivered his message.

[86]‡[how *or* when?]   Lindy will _____ make it!

[87]‡[where?]   They went _____.

[88]‡[when? how?]   _____ the sun rose _____.

Now it is time to try some sentences with both noun modifiers and verb modifiers. Please keep this important point in mind: Do not worry greatly if you have difficulty telling noun modifiers from verb modifiers. Some borderline cases may even puzzle teachers. What is important is that you can tell the words that are only modifiers from the essential words that form the core of the sentence: the subject, verb, and completers. That is the central purpose of this module.

In each sentence below, there are only three kinds of words: nouns, verbs, and modifiers. Find the subject noun, the verb, and any completer nouns. Underline the subject noun once, the verb twice, and any completer noun three times. Naturally, all the words left after you underline must be modifiers. Circle all of them. (You will find one noun modifier as a completer. Review page 175 if this confuses you.)

[89]Frequently I feel severe pains here.

[90]Nowadays alert police are effectively preventing violent crimes.

[91]Watergate has certainly become famous worldwide lately.

[92]Mary is really a grand old gal.

[93]Tonight Bob Dylan has recaptured his youthful, fanatic audience triumphantly.

[94]This new dishwasher is undoubtedly your personal dream machine.

If you did well on these sentences you are mastering the central concept of this module— in fact, the central concept of all English sentence writing.

Now, if you feel you have really grasped the concept of modifiers thoroughly, go back over the last six sentences and distinguish the noun modifiers from the verb modifiers, by drawing an arrow from each modifier to the noun or verb it modifies.[95-100] If this exercise becomes too confusing, stop; going on will not help you.

The six sentences above form an important checkpoint. If you did not spot the subjects and verbs in five of the sentences, see your instructor without delay.

Just one more item on verb modifiers. There are some other important verb modifiers that you should know. They do not exactly tell *how* an action is done, but they certainly modify, or change, our mental image of the action. Which words in the sentences below do you think are verb modifiers? Circle them:

[101]Nancy almost won the state lottery.

[102]Nancy has not won the state lottery.

[103]Nancy has even won the state lottery.

[104]Nancy has just won the state lottery.

[105]Nancy has only won the smaller state lottery.

Do these words modify our mental image of the action? Is there a difference between *not won* and *just won*? Between *almost won* and *even won*? Remember the words you circled; they are common verb modifiers.

WORDS THAT CHANGE THE PICTURE OF MODIFIERS

What other kinds of modifiers could there be besides noun modifiers and verb modifiers?* Look at this sentence:

c.   The very fat man wore an incredibly dirty suit.

What word modifies *man?* _____[106] But there is another word in front of this word: *very*. Does *very* modify *man* too? We can have a *fat man,* but can we have a *very man?*

_____[107] *Very,* then, cannot be a modifier of *man.* What does it modify? Let us look at what *very* is doing. What word is it telling us something about? It is telling us

how _____[108] the man is. Since it is changing our picture of *fat* (the man is not

slightly fat or *rather fat* but *very fat*) it must be a [109]m_____er of *fat.* And since *fat* itself

is a modifier, you have just discovered that modifiers can have their own [110]m_____ers. We will call such words *modifier modifiers.* (Modifiers having modifiers may sound complicated, but it is really no more complicated than children growing up and having their own children.) Can you spot another modifier modifier near the end of sentence c above?

_____[111] Notice how and why we use a modifier modifier: We feel that the original noun or verb modifier—in this case, *dirty*—does not convey our idea to the reader clearly enough; therefore we add a word to make the modifier stronger (or weaker)—to tell *how* dirty the suit was. Here are other examples:

Never go to Ugo and Carlo's restaurant; their portions are (unbelievably) small.

That (frightfully) ugly boy is her fiance.

Arthur was (truly) sorry for making Hester pregnant.

The campus bus is (almost) (always) late.

(This last one is triple-header: *Late,* in the completer position, modifies the noun *bus; always* modifies *late,* and *almost* modifies *always.*)

In the sentences below, add modifier modifiers in the blanks. Do not use the same word more than once.

[112‡]Blabwell, our _____ energetic salesman, sold 50,000 Snoopy buttons in

February, a _____ slow month.

---

* As you studied modifiers here, you may have asked yourself: "Aren't these what we learned in grammar school as *adjectives* and *adverbs?*" Yes. *Adjective* is another word for *noun modifier,* and *adverb* another word for *verb modifier.*

¹¹³‡Professor Zizz, a _____ tiresome lecturer, is _____ never absent.

¹¹⁴‡Kyoto, a _____ lovely Japanese city, is smaller than San Francisco.

Before we leave modifiers, here is an important caution. Read the following two sentences. (A *crag* is a sharp out-cropping of rock.)

Old Lionel's craggy face broke into a smile.
Old Lionel's rough, weather-beaten, gray, bony face broke into a smile.

Does the first sentence give as good a picture of Lionel's face as the second?

¹¹⁵‡

(Think before you answer; recall what a crag looks like.) _____
Most people who know good writing would say that the first sentence describes the face at least as well as the second, and since the first uses only one modifier instead of four, it is a better sentence. The best way of giving your reader a mental picture that is closest to your own is not by piling up four or five modifiers in front of words but by thinking of one or two words that mean *exactly* what you want to say. Then you will often find that your words need only one modifier or none at all. In the following, can you think of a single noun to replace all the italicized words?

¹¹⁶Farnsworth lived in a *large, imposing, elegant house with many rooms.*

Farnsworth lived in a m_____n.
¹¹⁷The man left the bar and *walked hesitatingly, moving from side to side,* down the street.

The man left the bar and s___gg___ed down the street.
¹¹⁸After her reducing treatment, Midge looked *extremely skinny, almost starving.*

After her reducing treatment, Midge looked em__c____ted.

The larger your vocabulary, of course, the better you will be at using the exact word. The modules "Word Choice" and "Vocabulary Skills" will help you in this.

Here is a brief review of modifiers. You can use modifiers with each of the three kinds of words you have learned so far—nouns, verbs, and other modifiers. You use modifiers when necessary to bring the reader's picture or idea closer to what is in your mind. Rewrite the sentences below, adding three modifiers of any kind to *each* sentence, wherever they seem to fit best. Do not use the same modifier twice in the exercise.

[119]‡The student read the exam.

_____

[120]‡Questions were hard.

_____

[121]‡Her friends finished the exam.

_____

[122]‡She could understand the questions.

_____

[123]‡The student submitted her paper and left.

_____

WORDS THAT HOLD EVERYTHING TOGETHER

We said at the beginning of this module that there are only four kinds of words. You have already learned three of them: nouns, verbs, and modifiers. Here we go on the last.

We have already met the most common word of this last type, on page 170. In the following sentences, what little word is not a noun, a verb, or a modifier? Circle that word in each sentence:

[1]Jabbar and Walton dominated the game.

[2]The horse bucked and neighed.

Do you remember, or can you figure out, what *and* does? Look:

Abbott and Costello
high and dry
ham and eggs

fast and furious
here and there
rise and shine

The job of *and* is to [3]l___k two words, to show that they should be thought of together. Are there other words besides *and* that serve as links in our speaking and writing? Examine this list:

short but sweet
sink or swim

gone but not forgotten
small yet powerful
your money or your life

[4]‡

The three new links in this list are _____, _____ and _____.

These four common words—*and, but, or* and *yet*—are all used to *link* two other words.*
Can they link *any* kinds of words? Look again at the two lists above:

[5]*Ham, eggs* are ☐ nouns, ☐ verbs, ☐ modifiers.
[6]*Sink, swim* are ☐ nouns, ☐ verbs, ☐ modifiers.
[7]*Small, powerful* are ☐ nouns, ☐ verbs, ☐ modifiers.

Then can a link such as *and* join two nouns *or* two verbs, *or* two modifiers? _____ [8]
Look again at the lists above. Do you think a link can join two *different* kinds of words, like

[9]
high and *eggs*? _____
Sometimes it may not be so easy to see the two words that are being linked:

We were served ham and eggs.
We were served moldy ham and salty eggs.
We were served tough, moldy ham and salty, rubbery eggs.

[10]
In all three cases the two words being linked by *and* are _____ and _____.
When we link two verbs, each may even have its own completer:

Sandy washed and ironed her blouse.
Sandy washed her blouse thoroughly and ironed it carefully.

[11]
In both of these sentences, the two words being linked by *and* are _____ and

_____.
The fourth and last type of word, then, is a *link*.†

In each sentence below, (circle) the link, and underline the two words it is joining:

[12]Professor Piffle bores and annoys me.

[13]You and your silly friend will spoil the whole evening.

[14]You must pass the course or quit the school.

[15]‡JoAnn is small but sexy.

[16]‡Scientists have discovered an inexpensive yet highly potent measles vaccine.

Since *and, but, or,* and *yet* do the same kind of job, let us call them all *and*-type links or

simply *and*-links. The term *and-links*, then, includes [17]‡a_ _, b_ _, o_, and y_ _.

---

* They can also link groups of words and even whole sentences, as you will see in "Combining Ideas."
† Again, if you recall your school grammar books, you may recognize that the links you have learned so far
are called *conjunctions* by these books.

Notice this variation of the *and*-links:

Russia <u>and</u> China wooed the Indian government.
<u>Both</u> Russia <u>and</u> China wooed the Indian government.
<u>Not</u> only Russia <u>but</u> [also] China wooed the Indian government.
Jill <u>or</u> Jan can drive you to the station.
<u>Either</u> Jill <u>or</u> Jan can drive you to the station.
<u>Neither</u> Jill <u>nor</u> Jan can drive you to the station.

You see first of all that we have a new *and*-link: *nor*—the negative of *or*. And you also see that *and*-links can add other words for emphasis. These words, then, are all the *and*-links:

(both . . .) and
(not only . . .) but (also)
(either . . .) or
neither . . . nor
yet

(The parentheses mean the item inside *may* appear but does not *have to*. The dots mean that other words appear where the dots are.) In each of the following sentences, circle each word that is part of the link, and underline the words that the link is joining. The first item is done for you as an example:

18 (Both) <u>Charlie</u> (and) <u>Scott</u> passed math.

19 Give the package to either the mayor or his secretary.

20 My partner or I will handle the case.

21 Either my partner or I will handle the case.

22‡ Neither my partner nor I will handle the case.

23‡ Mariner I explored both Mars and its moons.

24‡ That drink made me not only dizzy but nauseous.

Now write in your own links. Make sense.

25‡ B_____ Roosevelt _____ Kennedy loved the sea.

26‡ _____ the second edition _____ the third contains that crucial error.

27‡ You must _____ confess _____ resign.

28‡ The Jackson Zoo has _____ an aardvark _____ a Tasmanian tapir.

You are now an expert on *and*-links.

You will learn only one more type of link in this module, but it is quite an important type. Notice the difference between the two sentences in each set:

Lenny was a wealthy man.
Lenny was a man of great wealth.

Linda was a blonde girl.
Linda was a girl with blonde hair.

Hornblower was a naval captain.
Hornblower was a captain in the navy.

You should easily be able to identify the nouns, verbs, and modifiers in these sentences. But what words of an unfamiliar kind do you spot in the second sentence of each set that

are not in the first? [29] _____ _____ _____ In the second sentence of each set, notice what has happened to the modifiers *wealthy, blonde,* and *naval.* The idea of each is now said in a *group* of words instead of a single word:

wealthy ⟶ of great wealth

[30]blonde ⟶ with b_____ h_____

[31]naval ⟶ in _____ _____

Up to this point in the module we have been focusing on single words. It is important now that you begin to think in terms of *groups* of words that stick together as a unit, that operate as if they were a single word.

In each of the following sentences there is a group of words beginning with one of the three words you just wrote—a group like *of great wealth, with blonde hair* and *in the navy.* Locate such a group in each sentence below and circle it:

[32]Clean your floors with new Waxo!

[33]Sandra Slade is appearing in a burlesque show.

[34]The principal of the school angrily denied the charges.

Do you see what *of, with,* and *in* do? They signal the beginning of a certain kind of *group* of words. A *group* is not just *any* word string (like *when the be if*). A *group* is a string of words that belong together and make sense together. *With new Waxo, in a burlesque show,* and *of the school* are word groups.

There are about sixty other words that act the same way as *of, with,* and *in.* You will not have to memorize them all, since there is an easier way to learn them. How many words can you think of that would make sense in the blank below?

The bird flew _____ the house.‡

To start you off, here is a house. Think of all the places the bird can fly; the arrows may help you. (The house is on stilts to give the bird more places to fly.) Fill in the blanks:

[35]The bird flew   (1)   t__ the house

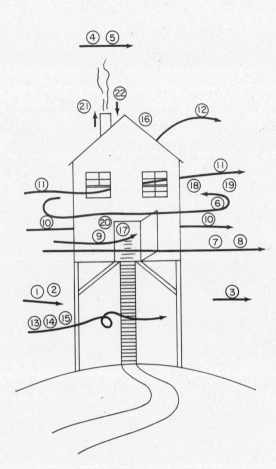

(2)   t_____ the house

(3)   (away) f_____ the house

(4)   o_____ the house

(5)   a_____ the house

(6)   a_____ the house

(7)   p_____ the house

(8)   b__ the house

(9)   i_____ the house

(10)   b_____ the house

(11)   th_____ the house

(12)   o____ the house

(13)   b_____th the house

(14)   b____w the house

(15)   u_____ the house

Now try these variations of the "bird" sentence:

The bird was   (16)   o__ the house

(17)   i_____ the house

(18)   o_____ the house

(19)   n_____ the house

(20)   a__ the door

The bird flew   (21)   u__ the chimney

(22)   d_____ the chimney

And, if there were two houses, we could say *The bird flew* [36]*be_____n the houses;* or if there were three or more, [37]*am____g the houses.* Those are not all the words that act like *of, with,* and *in;* but those will give you a solid idea of how all words of this type act. Now let us look closely at how they do act. You have seen that they begin a group of words. What is that group made up of? Look at the words that *end* some of the groups we have seen so far:

of great *wealth*   to the *house*
with blonde *hair*   up the *chimney*
in the *navy*

All these words are   [38]‡☐ nouns,   ☐ verbs,   ☐ modifiers,   ☐ links. This kind of word group, then, always begins with a word like *of* and ends with a noun. What about the words in between? There can be none, as in *to school,* or many, as in *to the little old red one-room school.* What kind of words are *the, little, old, red* and *one-room?*
[39]

_____ But have we found a verb in any of these groups? _____ Since [40] the words like *of, with,* and *in* join the word group to the rest of the sentence, these words are *links;* and since *of* is the most common word of this type, let us call these words *of*-type links, or simply *of*-links. *Of, with, in, to,* and all the other words you wrote on page 187 are *of*-links. And, to keep things clear, let us call word groups that begin with an *of*-link (like *of great wealth, with blonde hair, in the navy,* and *to the house*) *of*-groups.

Of-links begin *of*-groups; it is not hard.*

But so what? Why do we need to know such groups? There are two important reasons. The first is that they give us a wonderful way of condensing a whole idea into a few words:

Fran met a boy. He has a red beard

can become simply

Fran met a boy with a red beard.

(You will discover how to do this well in later modules.) We will consider only the second reason here. To discover it, first put a circle around each *of*-group you find in the following sentence. (There are five.)

[41]On our new campus, we offer courses in medical technology to students with

fifteen credits of biology.

Check your answers; then write the words that are left in the sentence *after* you have picked
[42]
out all the *of*-groups: _____ _____ _____ Now write the
[43]
subject, verb, and completer of the sentence: _____ _____ _____

That last question was a bit of a trick; the point was to show that if you can identify and set apart the *of*-groups in a sentence, you can much more easily find the main parts of the

---

* In traditional grammar books, *of*-links are called *prepositions,* and *of*-groups are called *prepositional phrases.*

sentence—the subject, verb, and completer. Do you ever feel unsure whether what you are writing is really a sentence? Does the professor often write *Fragment* on your paper, meaning that you have written only a piece of a sentence? In many sentences such as the one above, half to three-quarters of the words are in *of*-groups. Set apart these *of*-groups by circling them, and you will then find it much easier to spot whether you have a subject and a verb. For example, one of the items below is a sentence; the other is not. Which is the sentence? Circle all *of*-groups, and you will find the answer easily; only one of the items will have both a subject and a verb.

44‡In the middle of the night, a small boy in floppy old pajamas sneaked from his bed on the top floor of the orphanage.

45‡At sunset, our cabin in the pines on the shore of Mirror Lake beneath the lofty mountains under the reddish sky of Vermont.

46

Which one is the sentence? _____ This is the second reason for knowing *of*-groups: to ensure that your sentences are really sentences. Think of those circles you drew around the *of*-groups as being plastic bubbles, which make each group a unit in itself and seal it off from the rest of the sentence.

Now think back to the first *of*-groups you met in this section. Remember the kind of words they were made from?

of great wealth	←——————→	wealthy
with blonde hair	←——————→	blonde
in the navy	←——————→	naval

The words in the right-hand column above are all 47‡☐ nouns, ☐ verbs, ☐ modifiers, ☐ links. Now, since you see that *of*-groups originate from modifiers, would you

48

expect them to act the same as modifiers? _____ And can a modifier ever be the

49

subject or the verb of a sentence? _____ Then can an *of*-group or any word in

50

an *of*-group ever be the subject or the verb? _____ This is why it is easy to find the subject and the verb when you isolate the *of*-groups inside plastic bubbles. You know you never look inside the bubbles for the subject or verb. The subject and the verb (and the completer) are always *outside* any *of*-group bubbles.

Before you practice on *of*-groups, here are a few more common *of*-links you need to know. Think of the word that makes sense in each of the following blanks:

51Get your tickets b_ _ _ _ _ _ the game.

52I'll meet you at Zelda's a_ _ _ _ _ the game.

53I'll look for you in the stands d_ _ _ _ _g the game.

54Keep this play secret u_ _ _ _ _ _ the game.

⁵⁵He has been jubilant s_____ the game.

⁵⁶I bought this necklace just f___ you.

⁵⁷I could never live w_____ you.

⁵⁸I came to you d__sp___e countless obstacles.

⁵⁹Everyone is contributing to the fund ex_____ Humphrey.

⁶⁰John Kennedy had a Harvard accent, just l_____ Franklin Roosevelt.

⁶¹He who is not with me is ag____s__ me.

Sometimes the *of*-link may actually be two or three words. If you can think of the ones below, you are fast becoming an *of*-group expert:

⁶²I am sending Follingsbee on the expedition i_____d o__ you.

⁶³I will send Filchingham i__ a_____tion t__ Follingsbee.

⁶⁴In fact, I will send Fitzworthington a__ w__l a__ Filchingham.

⁶⁵The battalion assembled i__ f_____ o__ the barracks.

⁶⁶The men were angry b_____s__ o__ the colonel's harsh discipline.

⁶⁷Colonel Fotheringay strode o____ o__ his headquarters.

To reinforce your new knowledge, examine each item below to determine whether it is a sentence or not. First, isolate each *of*-group by drawing a circle—the plastic bubble— around it. *Then* see if you have a subject and a verb. Only if the item has these, of course, is it a sentence. In each blank write *yes* if the item is a sentence, *no* if it is not:

⁶⁸After the storm the ground was covered with ice. _____

⁶⁹After the storm in the northeast end of the state during the first week of this month. _____

⁷⁰In the gloomiest corner of the musty old library, behind a monstrous pile of books. _____

⁷¹‡In the gloomiest corner of the musty old library, behind a monstrous pile of books, Jack snored quietly. _____

⁷²‡Pizza, with all those anchovies in all that sauce over all that cheese. _____

[73‡]The life of Merton Pudby, in hundreds of vivid pictures. _____

[74‡]A man of unique political skills, with compassion for the common people, with knowledge of political realities and with the guts for the job of Senator. _____

Now write *of*-groups of your own in the blanks in these sentences. Here is an example:

The man __*with*__ __*the*__ __*beard*__ is an FBI agent __*in*__ __*disguise*__.

[75‡]The little girl w_____ _____ _____ _____

gave a bouquet _____ _____ _____ to the

governor o_____ _____ _____.

[76‡]The Recreation Division offers a course i_____ twice

a year f_____.

[77‡]Registration _____ will be held _____

_____.

[78‡]Then I awoke; I sat bolt upright _____ and peered

_____ as I thought _____

_____.

[79‡]I wandered _____ and continued _____

_____ _____. When I arrived

_____ I saw the traffic moving _____

_____.

Besides *of*-links and *and*-links, there are several other kinds of links; however, these two kinds are enough for now. You will discover the others in the "Combining Ideas" and "Economy and Variety."

NAIL-DOWN

You have just about passed your initiation into the mysteries of the English sentence. You have discovered the basics of the four kinds of words—nouns, verbs, modifiers, and links. There is one final section needed to nail all your discoveries down.

Look at this sentence:

The caretaker will light the lamps.

What is the verb? _____ _____ But in this sentence,

The caretaker will adjust the light

what type of word is *light*? _____ And in the following sentence,

A light rain fell in the evening

light is a _____. The point should be clear: The same word can be different parts of speech at different times, depending on its job in the sentence. Here are other examples. Write the kind of word each underlined word is:

[4]Morley's death <u>shocked</u> me. _____

[5]The faulty wire gave me a <u>shock</u>. _____

[6]I need new <u>shock</u> absorbers. _____

[7]‡Today I will <u>walk</u> to work. _____

[8]‡Today I will take a <u>walk</u>. _____

[9]‡Wait for the <u>walk</u> signal at the intersection. _____

There is a special situation you should be aware of. You have learned that *thinking* is a part of the verb *think*, and *broken* a part of the verb *break*. But look at these sentences:

I want a thoughtful man for this job.

Thoughtful is a   [10]☐ noun,   ☐ verb,   ☐ modifier,   ☐ link.

I want a thinking man for this job.

Thinking is a   [11]‡☐ noun,   ☐ verb,   ☐ modifier,   ☐ link.

You should return shoddy merchandise to the store.

Shoddy is a   [12]☐ noun,   ☐ verb,   ☐ modifier,   ☐ link.

You should return *broken* merchandise to the store.

Broken is a   [13]‡☐ noun,   ☐ verb,   ☐ modifier,   ☐ link.

Thinking and *broken* are modifiers that have been made from parts of verbs. Sometimes students mistake such words for the real verb in a sentence.

One way to tell what they really are is to notice their position in the sentence. Read these:

The _____ car passed a stop sign.

In this blank we would expect a   ¹⁴☐ verb,   ☐ modifier.

The car was _____ along the boulevard.

In this blank we would expect a   ¹⁵☐ verb,   ☐ modifier. Now write the word *speeding* in both blanks. These modifiers made from the *-ing-* or *-en-* form of the verb (like *speeding* or *stolen*) are treated more fully in "Economy and Variety."

A last word: In this module you have learned the *basic* parts of the simple sentence and *some* words of each of the four types. Since there are many more complicated ways in which words can be put together to make sentences, you should not expect to be able now to figure out every sentence you meet. But you have made a good start.

REVIEW   Before you begin the mastery test, it would be good for you to run through this review:

SENTENCE: a string of words telling that some person or thing was doing, being, or having something

Subject part   *Verb part*

A tiny spider   was spinning its web in the corner.
        ↑   ↑   ↑
     subject   verb   completer

The basic sentence pattern:

        S   V   (C)   (C)
The spider   gave   Wilbur   a   bite.

The four kinds of words:

(1) NOUNS: car, George, I, us, someone, Germany, independence, death . . .
The noun master sentence:

$\begin{pmatrix} A(n) \\ The \\ My \end{pmatrix}$ _____ may surprise you.

(2) VERBS: go, try, think, be, have, attempt, copulate, intensify . . .

The verb master sentence: They may _____ (it) soon.
Verb forms:

Present form	Past form	-Ing-form	-En-form
break(s)	broke	breaking	broken
start(s)	started	starting	started

The -en-*form master sentence:* She has _____ (it) already.

Verbs including auxiliaries: did go, has broken, had been, was mentioned, is being charged, could have been chosen . . .

    (3) MODIFIERS

Noun modifiers: big, my, intense, gorgeous, this, some, the . . .

Verb modifiers: [*arrived*] here, [*is*] not [*arriving*] now, never [*arrived*], quickly [*hid*], [*studied*] intensely . . .

Modifier modifiers: very [*gorgeous*], too [*intense*], slightly [*unclear*], almost [*dead*] . . .

    (4) LINKS

And-links: and, but, or, nor, yet

Of-links: of, in, with, to, by for, from, around . . .

The first kind of word group—the of-*group:* of the country, at work, with standard shift, during the game, from his bank account . . .

MASTERY TEST

Part I. For each sentence below, do these, in the order given:

  A. Circle each *of*-group.
  B. Draw one line under the subject noun.
  C. Draw two lines under each word of the verb.
  D. Draw three lines under any completers.

1.†The old man with the wooden leg deserves better treatment from the workers at the nursing home.

2.†In the game of tag, they made Fred "it."

3.†One thoughtful act by a young person can restore adults' faith in American youth.

4.†In a bargain store, the friendliest salesman on the floor is sometimes the most dishonest employee of the company.

5.†Behind the woodshed at his old farm in Starkfield, Ethan is greasing his sled runners.

Part II. In the blank after each item, write *yes* if it is a sentence or *no* if it is not. If it is not, rewrite the item in the blank below it, adding one or more words of your own to make it a sentence:

6.†Man fears something about the sea. _____

_____

7.†The fury of the waves, the emptiness of the oceans, the mystery of the depths. _____

_____

[8]‡Since ancient times man has gone to sea and returned with strange stories of ghost ships. _____

_____

[9]‡In one such story, the *Marlborough* was found off South America with a full crew of skeletons. _____

_____

[10]‡Each skeleton at its proper place, in its complete uniform, without a shred of flesh, for 25 years. _____

_____

Part III. Write original sentences of at least ten words each around the words given. You may put words between the given words if you wish (e.g., *the busy ghetto*).

[11]‡The ghetto . . .

_____

[12]‡. . . changed . . .

_____

[13]‡. . . election . . .

_____

[14]‡Happiness . . .

_____

[15]‡. . . could make . . .

_____

Part IV. (Do this if your instructor directs.) Write a paragraph of nine to eleven sentences on one of the topics from the master list or any other topic your instructor suggests or approves. Try to show that you can write *of*-groups and modifiers effectively, but above all make sure that each sentence is really a sentence.

INTRODUCTION AND WHAT MAKES A SENTENCE?

[2]capital, period

[5]No. (If length made a word-string a sentence, then all word-strings in the *Sentence* column would have to be longer than all the word-strings in the *Not sentence* column.)

[8]All of them should. See below.

[9]None of them should. See below.

Sentences: <u>I</u> <u>play poker</u>; <u>A million soldiers</u>
<u>served in the war</u>; <u>Johnny</u> <u>rode the</u>
<u>pony</u>; <u>Dogs with distemper</u> <u>bite children</u>
<u>dren sometimes</u>; <u>My ancient car</u>
<u>stalled on the freeway</u>; <u>Belcher</u> <u>fell</u>
<u>through a manhole</u>

[10]That a sentence needs two parts: (1) a part that tells the person (or thing) that is doing something and (2) a part that tells what he (it) is doing

[11]Some possibilities:

[A]Harry soon arrived.

[B]English sentences need two parts.

[C]The little old man in the Italian restaurant burped.

[D]All the king's horses eat special hay.

[E]I waited breathlessly in the darkness under the stairs.

[20]subject

[22]subject

[23]subject

[24]verb

[25]A. I

C. soldiers

D. Johnny

F. dogs

J. car

L. Belcher

[26]A. Harry

B. sentences

C. man

D. horses

E. I

[27]subject

[28]A. play

C. served

D. rode

F. bite

J. stalled

L. fell

[29]These do *not* have to be in the following order: arrived, need, burped, eat, waited.

[30]verb

[31]S; <u>Mona Huckleberry</u> <u>wore</u>

[32]Not S; add a verb

[33]S; <u>Mona</u> <u>dresses</u>

[34]Not S; add a subject

[35]S; <u>(boy) friend</u> <u>yelled</u>

[36]Not S; add a subject

[37]S; <u>she</u> <u>cried</u>

[38]S; <u>he</u> <u>apologized</u>

[39]Not S; add a verb

[40]Not S; add a subject and a verb

[41]S; <u>socks</u> <u>go</u>

[42]Not S; add a verb

WORDS THAT NAME PERSONS OR THINGS

[2]noun

[3]The nouns are planet, George, bridge, beach.

[4]The nouns are aunt, college, class, Chevrolet, program, music.

[5]None should be crossed out; they are all nouns, for they are all names of things.

[7]to give her his ring

WORDS OF DOING, BEING, OR HAVING

²The verbs are eat, depart, flunk, write, and
    investigate.

⁶-ify, -ize

⁷One

⁸More than one

⁹one person or thing

¹⁰drinks

¹¹fail

¹²rise

¹³needs

¹⁴gives

¹⁵Sentences c and d tell something that hap-
    pened in the past; sentences a and b
    tell something that is happening now.

¹⁶the subject was doing something at some
    time before now, in the past

¹⁷failed

¹⁸fail

¹⁹needed

²⁰need

²¹departed

²²jump

²³jumped

²⁴jumps

²⁵cover, covers, covered (these do not have
    to be in this order)

²⁶covers

²⁷cover

²⁸covered

³¹broke

³²sang

³³ᴬbit

ᴮtook

ᶜspoke

ᴰchose

ᴱstole

ᶠflew

ᴳrang

ᴴwent

ᴵleft

ᴶtaught

ᴷsank

ᴸsold

ᴹbled

ᴺswam

ᴼbrought

³⁴take

³⁵excites

³⁶fail

³⁹No

⁴⁰Yes, it is.

⁴¹being

⁴²am

⁴³are

⁴⁴is

⁴⁵was

⁴⁶were

⁴⁷looks

⁴⁸sounds

⁴⁹feels

⁵⁰smells

⁵¹tastes

⁵²Yes. That paint job is good, that music is
    good, etc.

⁵³has

⁵⁴have

⁵⁵had

⁵⁶doing, having, being

⁵⁷doctor probed

⁵⁸structure was

⁵⁹snuffleupagus has

⁶⁰Calvin Hoogiban rode

⁶¹turnips smell

⁷⁹is

⁸⁰was

⁸¹are *or* were

⁸²were

⁸³am *or* was

⁸⁴was vacationing

⁸⁵are going

⁸⁶is making

⁸⁷are proceeding

⁸⁹Broken

⁹⁰had taken

⁹¹-en

⁹²break

⁹³take

⁹⁴has chosen

⁹⁵has spoken

⁹⁶had swollen

⁹⁷have hidden

⁹⁸lost

⁹⁹sung

¹⁰⁰drunk
¹⁰¹led
¹⁰²won
¹⁰³spotted
^{105A}done
^Bbitten
^Ctaken
^Dchosen
^Esto..n
^Fforgotte..
^Gshown
^Hhad
^Isold
^Jtaught
^Krung
^Lterminated
^Mbrought
^Nsurrendered
^Oflown
^Pspoken
^Qgone
^Rleft
^Swalked
^Tdecided
¹⁰⁶were taken
¹⁰⁷is set
¹⁰⁸was named
¹⁰⁹are canceled
¹¹⁰be
¹¹¹is (*or* was)
¹¹²Not standard; should be *Jim has* (or *had*) *taken the early bus.*

¹¹³Not standard; should be *In the third act Siegfried is* (or *was*) *slain by Hagen.*
¹¹⁴Not standard; should be *Across the world malnutrition has* (or *had*) *stricken millions of people.*
¹¹⁵Not standard; should be *Early in the war Long Island was captured by the British.*
¹¹⁶Casey was advancing
¹¹⁷sneer has gone
¹¹⁸teeth are clenched
¹¹⁹air is shattered
¹²⁰Casey has struck (out)
¹²¹have, be
¹²²-*ing*-, -*en*-
¹²⁸had been sleeping
¹³⁰Three
¹³¹Circling
¹³⁴taken (the last word in the verb)
¹³⁵has been
¹³⁶auxiliary = do; main verb word = brush.
¹³⁷does
¹³⁸did
^{139A}auxiliary = will; main verb word = pass.
^Bauxiliary = would; main verb word = pass.
¹⁴⁰must have been drinking
¹⁴¹Three

WHAT FOLLOWS THE VERB

¹No
²No
⁶Complete as is
⁷my leg, my arm, etc.
⁸Complete as is
⁹a job, a boy friend, etc.
¹⁰love, happiness, a car, etc.
¹¹Yes, they should.
¹²nouns
¹³Coal is fuel
¹⁴jury has reached verdict
¹⁵Jones acknowledged mistake
¹⁶Negotiations should begin

¹⁷people have smoked
¹⁸Collaborators will be executed
¹⁹California has weather
²⁰Max might have been taking train
²¹United States became nation
²²noun
²³(C)
²⁴Lombardi gave rookie encouragement
²⁵we are getting customers
²⁶keeper threw chimp banana
²⁷bum called girl creep

³⁴Jane and Jean

³⁵Bonnie and Clyde robbed men

³⁶Bonnie and Clyde robbed and killed men

³⁷Bonnie and Clyde robbed and killed men
and women

³⁸Charlie was waiting

³⁹Was Charlie waiting

⁴⁰was Charlie waiting

⁴¹encyclopedia contains

⁴²Does encyclopedia contain

⁴³Shut
⁴⁴Submit
⁴⁵Fly
⁴⁶Hit
⁴⁷Return
⁴⁹understood
⁵⁰You
⁵¹You

WORDS THAT CHANGE THE PICTURE

¹changes, modifies
⁷modifiers
⁸a
⁹b
¹⁰modifiers
²¹modifiers
²²The yellow, the seven
²³Any two strong young, this light
²⁴Our new, the American, a lengthy
³¹before
³²Yes
³³completer
³⁴green
³⁵tough
³⁸portrait
³⁹modifiers
⁴⁰Local, higher
⁴¹The heavy, massive urban
⁴²Your new, hideous
⁴³This revolutionary new, unsightly
⁴⁴Some little third-string, an additional six
⁴⁵Director; Shut; Door
⁴⁶quickly
⁴⁷thoroughly
⁴⁹changes, modifies
⁵⁰cleaned
⁵¹verb
⁵²Weary
⁵³His, ancient
⁵⁴Carefully
⁵⁵-ly
⁵⁶how
⁵⁷how
⁵⁸seldom
⁵⁹never

⁶⁰yesterday
⁶¹now
⁶²then
⁶³when
⁶⁴when
⁶⁵here
⁶⁶nearby
⁶⁷far
⁶⁸away
⁶⁹where
⁷⁰where
⁷¹angrily, there, yesterday
⁷²Angrily
⁷³There
⁷⁴Yesterday
⁷⁵Yes
⁷⁶lovingly
⁷⁷often
⁷⁸anywhere
⁷⁹often, lovingly, anywhere
⁸⁰It can be put at any of several places in a
sentence.
⁸¹Using the verb modifier *cautiously* as an
example, here are all the possibilities:
Holden crossed the street cautiously;
Holden cautiously crossed the street;
Cautiously, Holden crossed the street.

⁸⁹(Frequently) I feel (severe) pains (here.)

⁹⁰(Nowadays) (alert) police are (effectively)
preventing (violent) crimes.

⁹¹Watergate has (certainly) become famous
(worldwide) (lately.)

⁹²Mary is (really) (a) (grand) (old) gal.

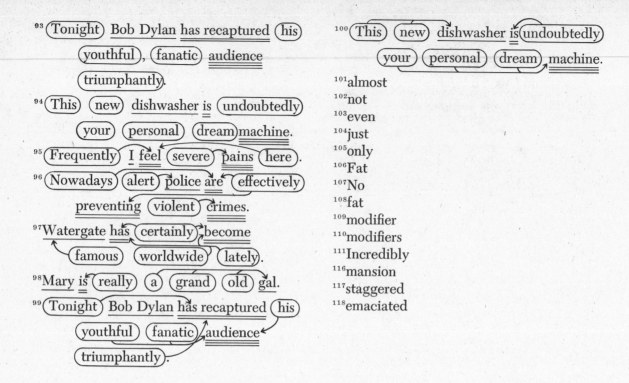

93 (Tonight) Bob Dylan has recaptured (his)
(youthful), (fanatic) audience
(triumphantly).

94 (This) (new) dishwasher is (undoubtedly)
(your) (personal) (dream) machine.

95 (Frequently) I feel (severe) pains (here).

96 (Nowadays) (alert) police are (effectively)
preventing (violent) crimes.

97 Watergate has (certainly) become
(famous) (worldwide) (lately).

98 Mary is (really) (a) (grand) (old) gal.

99 (Tonight) Bob Dylan has recaptured (his)
(youthful) (fanatic) audience
(triumphantly).

100 (This) (new) dishwasher is (undoubtedly)
(your) (personal) (dream) machine.

101 almost
102 not
103 even
104 just
105 only
106 Fat
107 No
108 fat
109 modifier
110 modifiers
111 Incredibly
116 mansion
117 staggered
118 emaciated

WORDS THAT HOLD EVERYTHING TOGETHER

1 and
2 and
3 link
5 nouns
6 verbs
7 modifiers
8 Yes
9 No
10 ham, eggs
11 washed, ironed
12 bores (and) annoys
13 you (and) friend
14 pass (or) quit
19 mayor (or) secretary
20 partner (or) I
21 (Either) partner (or) I
29 Of, with, in
30 blonde hair
31 the navy
32 with new Waxo
33 in a burlesque show
34 of the school
35 (1) to, (2) toward, (3) from, (4) over,
(5) above, (6) around, (7) past, (8)

by, (9) into, (10) behind, (11)
through, (12) off, (13) beneath, (14)
below, (15) under, (16) on, (17)
inside, (18) outside, (19) near, (20)
at, (21) up, (22) down

36 *between*
37 *among*
39 modifiers
40 No
41 On our new campus, in medical technology, to students, with fifteen credits,
of biology
42 We offer courses
43 We offer courses
46 44
48 Yes
49 No
50 No
51 before
52 after
53 during
54 until
55 since
56 for
57 without
58 despite

⁵⁹except
⁶⁰like
⁶¹against
⁶²instead of
⁶³in addition to
⁶⁴as well as
⁶⁵in front of
⁶⁶because of
⁶⁷out of
⁶⁸(After the storm) (with ice) Yes

⁶⁹(After the storm) (in the northeast end) (of the state) (during the first week) (of this month) No

⁷⁰(In the gloomiest corner) (of the musty old library) (behind a monstrous pile) (of books) No

NAIL-DOWN

¹Will light
²Noun
³modifier
⁴Verb
⁵Noun

⁶Modifier
¹⁰modifier
¹²modifier
¹⁴modifier
¹⁵verb

MODULE 8

COMBINING
IDEAS

Previous modules required: Basic Sentence Parts (7)

INTRODUCTION

Three people wanted to write the same information to a group of adults. This is how each wrote it:

SELECTION A

(1) Once there were many carousels in the United States. (2) Hundreds of towns and cities had them. (3) They delighted children. (4) Now there are fewer than 100 left. (5) The carousels are old and costly. (6) So amusement parks have been replacing them. (7) They use modern rides instead. (8) These rides are made of plastic and aluminum. (9) That makes them peppier and easier to maintain. (10) Meanwhile, the carousels are chopped up. (11) Their horses are turned into bar stools. (12) Their heads are cut from their bodies. (13) The carved wooden animals are sold to antique dealers.

SELECTION B

(1) Once there were many carousels in the United States, and (2) hundreds of towns and cities had them, and (3) they delighted children, but (4) now there are fewer than 100 left, and (5) they are old and costly, and so (6) amusement parks have been replacing them with (7) modern rides. (8) These rides are made of plastic and aluminum, and (9) that makes them peppier and easier to maintain, but meanwhile, (10) the carousels are chopped up and (11) their horses are turned into bar stools and (12) their heads are cut from their bodies, and (13) the carved wooden animals are sold to antique dealers.

SELECTION C

Although (3) they were once a children's delight in (2) hundreds of towns and cities, carousels (1) in the United States (4) now number fewer than 100. (6) Amusement parks have been replacing these (5) costly old merry-go-rounds with (7) modern (8) plastic and aluminum rides that (9) are both peppier and easier to maintain. (10) The carousels, meanwhile, are chopped up, (11) their horses turned into bar stools, (12) heads cut from bodies, and (13) carved wooden animals sold to antique dealers.

— A, B, and C adapted from Time *(November 19, 1973), p. 18*

Which one of these sounds as if it were written by a child? _____ Which sounds most as if it were written by an experienced adult writer? _____ Since they all contain the same ideas, the difference must be in the *way* each writer expressed those ideas. Unfortunately for writers A and B, even though they had the same ideas as writer C, most people doubtless would accept writer C's ideas simply because he sounded more intelligent from his writing. What is it in C's writing that makes it sound more adult, more intelligent? Look at the way each writer puts together the parts of his idea. Each of the three pieces contains thirteen thoughts (numbered). How many sentences does A use to present those thirteen thoughts? _____ How many does B use? _____ C? _____

The number of ideas he can combine into one sentence is one element that marks an experienced writer. Yet since both B and C have almost the same number of sentences, there must be at least one more element. What do you think C did that makes most readers prefer his writing to B's? Did C use fancier words? If you think so, list some of them:

_____ Look at something else. Writer A put a ⁷p_ _ _ _ _ _ between each two ideas. What word did B use eight times where A used periods?

_____ What other word did B use twice? _____ How has C connected his ideas? How many of B's eight *ands* does C keep in connecting the numbered

thoughts? _____ What words does C use instead—for example, between ideas

8 and 9? _____ Keep this word in mind as one alternative to *and*. To how many

words did C reduce thought 5? _____ (Do you know what kind of words these

are? _____) Thoughts 10 through 13 are still connected in basically the same way

in B and C, but which unneeded words has C dropped? _____ _____

_____ _____ _____ _____

_____

These are some of the ways an experienced writer avoids *choppy* writing, like A, where all the ideas are chopped like sausages into short pieces, and *stringy* writing, like B, where all the ideas are strung out in a row with *ands* and *buts* like shirts on a clothesline. Your writing will improve, then, when you use   ¹⁵☐ different,   ☐ the same   connectors throughout, and when you   ¹⁶☐ add fancy words,   ☐ cut unneeded words. In the economy modules you will discover how to cut unneeded words; in this module you will discover four different ways to connect ideas in a sentence—not just to make your writing *sound* smoother but to make your meaning clearer as well.

You may be able to combine ideas effectively right now. On your own paper, try improving this half-choppy, half-stringy paragraph:

SELECTION D

During the Second World War scientists turned away from using inorganic chemicals to kill insects. They turned to a new wonder world. It was the world of the carbon molecule. But a few of the old inorganic materials are still used. Chief of these inorganic materials is arsenic. It is still a basic ingredient in a variety of weed and insect killers. Arsenic is a highly poisonous mineral, and it is found widely with the ore of various metals, and it also occurs in very small amounts in volcanoes, and it is in the sea and in spring water too.

— *Adapted from Rachel Carson,* Silent Spring
(Boston: Houghton Mifflin, 1962), p. 17

How many sentences did you use? ¹⁷‡_____ How many *ands* and *buts*? ¹⁸‡_____
Rachel Carson's original version had three sentences containing three *ands*, no *buts*, and 67 words. (Your instructor may read it to you.) Remember that Miss Carson is an experienced

professional writer. If you came close to her writing, congratulations! In any event, now that you have stretched your mind a bit on the subject, you are ready to move ahead.

COMBINING WITH *AND* LINKS

Read these two sentences:

    a. Jack is majoring in math, and Jill is concentrating on history.
    b. Adolf Hitler was once a paperhanger, and he caused millions of deaths in World War II.

Which sentence sounds better to you? In which do the two ideas seem more to go together naturally with the *and* between them? That is, in which do the two ideas seem to be of equal

importance? ^{1} _____ If you answered correctly you have already discovered the proper use of *and:* to join two ideas that you feel are *equally* important. Is the fact that Hitler was once a paperhanger as important as his causing millions of deaths? That is why sentence b probably sounded wrong to you.

    There are other conditions attached to our use of *and.* In which of the following

sentences does *and* seem to be the sensible, natural link? ^{2} _____

    c. Basil showered gifts and affection on Shirley for a year, and she eventually married him.
    d. Basil showered gifts and affection on Shirley for a year, and she eventually married Harry.

You probably sensed that some other link would have fit better in d. If you picked sentence c you have discovered that *and* is used to join equal ideas on a one-plus-one basis, merely adding one fact to another related fact. This will become more clear to you as you learn the other links.

    The final condition for using *and* is fairly obvious. In which of the next two sentences

are the two ideas sensibly connected? ^{3} _____

    e. Orion is a brilliant constellation, and the ancient Greeks believed in many gods.
    f. Orion is a brilliant constellation, and the ancient Greeks looked forward to its appearance each year.

In sentence e, what relation was the writer trying to show between the brilliance of Orion and the belief of the Greeks in many gods? The *writer* may have seen a relation between them, but it certainly is not the one-plus-one relation that *and* indicates; this is why sentence e probably puzzled you, the *reader.* The two ideas we connect with *and* must logically belong together.

    Write two original sentences in which *and* appropriately connects two ideas [not just two words, like *Jack and Jill,* but two S V(C)(C)'s]:

_____

_____

_____

_____

THE OTHER AND-LINKS

In "Basic Sentence Parts" you learned several other *and*-type links (see page 184);

they are ⁶b____, o___, and y____. You may also have learned *nor*. Why do we need these different links? What is the difference between these sentences?

    g. I like Scotch, and Lorna likes rye.
    h. I like Scotch, but Lorna likes rye.

Which would more likely be an answer to "What do you two like to drink?" ⁷_____

Which would more likely be an answer to "Do you both drink the same thing?" ⁸_____
What relation between two equal ideas do you think *but* shows?

    ⁹☐ that the second idea is merely added to the first (one-plus-one)
      ☐ that the second idea is opposite to the first
      ☐ that the second idea is caused by the first

At the beginning of this section you met the sentence *Jack is majoring in math, and Jill is concentrating on history.* What happens to the meaning if we change the *and* to *but*?

    Jack is majoring in math, *but* Jill is concentrating on history.

You are now saying that what Jill did is the   ¹⁰☐ same as,   ☐ opposite of,   ☐ result of   what Jack did.

    But is the link used when we went to show the oppositeness of two equally important ideas. In each sentence below, decide whether *and* or *but* is the link that makes more sense. If you find any sentences where either makes equal sense (with different meanings, of course), write them both in, like this: *but/and.*

    ¹¹Roger studied all night for the psych test, _____ he flunked.

    ¹²Roger studied all night for the psych test, _____ he made an *A*.

    ¹³The English Department now has ten professors, _____ they expect to have twelve next year.

[14]The English Department needs three more instructors for next year, _____ they have been allotted money for only one.

Now, what link (besides *and* or *but*) makes sense in the blank in the following sentence?

[15]Dad will drive you to the station, ____ you can walk if you like.

The writer is stating a *choice* here. But what link makes better sense when the choice is a negative one?

[16]I will not pay for your college education, _____ will I let you live at home without a job.

Nor is the negative of *or*. And what link means the same as *but*?

[17]Roger studied all night for the psych test, _____ he flunked.

The five *and*-links—*and, but, or, nor, yet*—all behave alike: They join ideas to which we want to give equal stress. You may have noticed two other facts about them: (1) Their position is always [18]☐ in front of, ☐ between, ☐ after the two ideas they are connecting; (2) they normally have [19]☐ a comma before them, ☐ a comma after them, ☐ no comma near them when they connect two ideas—two S V(C)(C)s.

Here are five sentences summarizing what you have learned about *and*-links. Remember that they are used between ideas to which we attach *equal* importance:

I like Scotch, *and* Lorna likes Rye. [one-plus-one]
I like Scotch, *but* Lorna likes rye. [oppositeness]
Do you want some Scotch, *or* would you prefer rye? [choice]
I dislike Scotch, *nor* do I care for rye. [negative choice]
I dislike Scotch, *yet* I drink it to be sociable. [oppositeness]

There is a grammatical term you need to learn at this point. Any of the ideas we have joined with *and*-links could have made a sentence by itself, as

        S V   C
Sentence: I like Scotch.

        S   V   C
Sentence: Lorna likes rye.

But when we join them we cannot call each a *sentence* anymore, since each has become

part of a larger [20]s_____. The term for each of these joined ideas is a *clause*.

       clause   clause
      S V   C   S V   C
Sentence: I like Scotch,   and   Lorna likes rye.

The *and*-links join two [21]c_ _ _ _ _ _ _ of equal importance.

Underline each clause in this sentence:

[22]This summer I'm working for the Park Department, and in the fall I'm going to California.

Now you are ready for some practice on the five *and*-links. Combine the two sentences in each item with the *and*-link that seems best. Write your combined sentence in the long blank, and in the short blank write *one-plus-one, oppositeness, choice,* or *negative choice* to show your intention. Punctuate naturally.

[23]‡He looked dapper in his stylish suit. His graying hair was carefully groomed.

_____

_____

[24]‡He looked dapper in his stylish suit. His face was puffed, his eyes bloodshot.

_____

_____

[25]‡The math department makes its majors take three semesters of calculus. Most math students have room for only two in their programs.

_____

_____

[26]‡The State Department will not meet the kidnappers' ransom demands. It will make no attempt to storm the kidnappers' hideout. [You will need to switch two words and change one.]

_____

_____ will it _____ _____

[27]‡When I was a child I spoke as a child. Now that I am a man I speak as a man.

_____

_____

[28]‡American women began their struggle for equality over a century ago. They are still struggling today.

_____

_____

[29]‡The Japanese armada could have steamed north to intercept the main American fleet. It could have turned south to overtake the weaker American secondary force.

Write original sentences, joining two clauses with the link given. To be sure you have two complete clauses [S V(C)(C)s], underline the subject once and the verb twice in each clause. Punctuate naturally.

30‡[and] _____

_____

31‡[but] _____

_____

32‡[or] _____

_____

33‡[nor] _____

_____

34‡[yet] _____

Before we leave the *and*-links there is one more point to reinforce. Read this sentence:

> i.   Three city employees were indicted for embezzlement, and they were tried, and they have been convicted.

The sentence is grammatical; all the clauses have links (*ands*) between them. But is

it *good* writing, according to what you learned at the beginning of this module? _____
35

Why or why not? _____ Remember how childish
36
the paragraph of stringy sentences about the carousels sounded? How could sentence i be improved? In the following sections of this module you will discover several ways to improve it. (Here is one way: *Three city employees who were indicted and tried for embezzlement have been convicted.*) Experienced writers normally use no more than one *and*-link in one sentence to join clauses.

A NEW KIND OF LINK (*THEREFORE-LINKS*)

If our use of *and* is limited, what do we use instead? One of the beauties of the English language is that it gives us so many different ways to word an idea that we can always say exactly what we mean, and at the same time we can avoid putting our readers to sleep with a monotonous style.

For instance, besides the *and*-links there is a completely different set of links you can use for joining ideas. Many of them mean the same as some *and*-links; however, most of them give a different tone to your writing than the *and*-links. What kind of tone? You discover. Think of a word (besides an *and*-link) to join these clauses:

^{1*}Charles Wilcox was in a Chinese restaurant at the time of the murder; _____, he could not possibly have committed the crime.

If you have not thought of the one that fits, try again, with a hint:

²Every auto engine emits poisonous carbon monoxide; th_____e, no driver should ever run his motor in a closed garage.

Why is this link considered different in type from the *and*-links? You have probably noticed one reason already: what punctuation mark came before *therefore* in both sentences 1 and

³

2? _____ You will soon learn other reasons besides this punctuation difference.
    What other links work like *therefore*? There are many; we will call them *therefore*-links. Can you think of a fairly common one to fit this sentence? (We used it in the second paragraph of this section.)

^{4*}I am not a candidate for political office; _____, I will gladly accept a draft.

Again, with a hint:

⁵Congress is putting great pressure on the White House; h_____r, the President is determined to resist it.

⁶

Add this link to your list. It means the same as which two *and*-links? _____ _____
    Since many of the *therefore*-links are less common than the *and*-links, you may need some aid in discovering them. Try the sentences below; the hints should help you. (Some of these links contain more than one word.)

⁷It was snowing heavily; nev____t____l____, Archer sped recklessly along the twisting mountain road.

⁸Give me five dollars; ot____w____ I won't tell you her phone number.

⁹The Indians were frenziedly preparing for the attack; m____w____l____, back at the ranch, everyone slept peacefully.

¹⁰Norman, I'm too old for you; be_____s, I've known you for only two hours.

¹¹Your relatives are all crazy; f____ i__st_____, your cousin Warren is a motorcycle freak.

¹²In operas many heroines commit suicide; f____ ex_____, Tosca hurls herself from a prison wall.

[13]You might be throwing your money away on an investment like this; o__

t__e ot____ h_____, it could make you rich.

Nevertheless, otherwise, meanwhile, for instance, besides, for example, and *on the other hand* all behave the same as *therefore* and *however*. Here are sentences with more links of this type:

You have failed three major subjects; *moreover,* you have been brought home by the police three times this month.

You have failed three major subjects; *furthermore,* you have been brought home by the police three times this month.

(These two links mean about the same as what *and*-link? [14]_____ As what other *therefore*-link? [15]_____)

You discover these next links:

[16]Your disbursement is being terminated; in ot_____ w_____, I'm cutting off your allowance.

[17]The U.S. military forces were not prepared for Pearl Harbor; on the c_____y, they had been lulled into a false sense of security.

[18]First, you mix these roots and herbs in a cauldron of boiling blood; s_____, you add the wing of a bat; n___t, you stir in a cup of spider's webs; fi____ly, you throw in three chopped toadstools; th___ your magic potion is complete.

—— [19]Until shortly after World War II there were no blacks in organized professional baseball; li__w__e, there were no integrated army units until then.

[20]He didn't even stop the car; i_st____, he gunned the yellow Rolls Royce on into the night.

[21][Either of two links fits here.] The world's resources are distributed unevenly;

$\begin{Bmatrix} \text{t\_\_s} \\ \text{c\_ns\_qu\_\_\_ly,} \end{Bmatrix}$ some nations prosper amid the poverty of others.

What other *therefore*-link also fits sentence 21? [22]_____

Here is a summary of the *therefore*-links you have learned; those similar in meaning are grouped together:

Cause-effect	*Addition* (*one-plus-one*)	*Oppositeness*
therefore	furthermore	however
thus	moreover	nevertheless
consequently	besides	on the other hand
		on the contrary
		instead

Condition	*Example*	*Restatement*
otherwise	for instance	in other words
	for example	

Time sequence	*Similarity*
second, third, . . .	likewise
next	
finally	
then	
meanwhile	

There are still other *therefore*-links, but the ones you have learned are the most common. What should you know about using them? First of all, remember what you noticed about their punctuation. After the first clause, what mark normally appears?
[23]☐(,) ☐(;) ☐(:) ☐(.)

Do you know the difference between a comma (,) and a semicolon (;)? In which of the sentences below would you come to a nearly full stop between clauses? _____[24]_____ In which would you just pause a bit and go right on? _____[25]_____

    a. Wayne didn't buy a Chevvy, but he bought a Ford.
    b. Wayne didn't buy a Chevvy; he bought a Ford.

The comma (,) signals only a pause, a slowing down; the semicolon (;) signals a stop. (You will learn more about these marks in the module "Punctuation.") In sentences with *therefore*-links, most speakers come to a stop between the clauses. In fact, the semicolon (;) works so much like the more common stop mark, the period (.), that people often use a period before a *therefore*-link, making two separate sentences:

> In times of inflation people must spend more on necessities; therefore, sellers of luxury products suffer.
> In times of inflation people must spend more on necessities. Therefore, sellers of luxury products suffer.

Both sentences are grammatical; the semicolon, however, indicates a closer connection between the two ideas and may make your writing sound less choppy. By the way, is the *therefore*-link capitalized after a semicolon?

26

_____

You have probably also noticed a comma *after* the link, as in

I was most decidedly wrong; therefore, I humbly apologize to you all.

This comma is used often but not always.

Try combining the following sets of sentences with *therefore*-links.

27‡The rains are swelling the Susquehanna to flood stage.
State troopers have ordered evacuation of low-lying areas.

The r_____

_____; th_____, s_____

_____.

28‡In Shakespeare's play, Juliet is only thirteen.
The director searched for a teenage actress.

In _____

_____; _____, _____

_____

29‡The price of artichokes has risen sharply.
They are in short supply.

_____

_____; _____ _____.

30‡Adlai Stevenson was soundly defeated twice for the presidency.
Many scholars now regard him as one of America's great statesmen.

_____

_____

31‡Daisy thought she loved Gatsby.
She declared her love for Tom.

_____

_____

³²‡[Write item 27 again with a different *therefore*-link.]

_____

_____

³³‡[Write item 27 again with still another *therefore*-link.]

_____

_____

³⁴‡[Write item 28 again with another *therefore*-link.]

_____

_____

³⁵‡[Write item 28 again with another *therefore*-link.]

_____

_____

³⁶‡[Write item 29 again with another *therefore*-link.]

_____

_____

THREE MORE POINTS

Here are three more points about *therefore*-links. First, look at these sentences:

c. Linus is a fine scholar; however, Charlie always has trouble in school.
d. Linus is a fine scholar; Charlie, however, always has trouble in school.
e. Linus is a fine scholar; Charlie always has trouble in school, however.

What word from sentence c floats in sentences d and e to different positions in the second

clause? _____ 37 Does the floating link ever float back into the first clause? _____ 38
Some *therefore*-links, then, are floaters; we can put them at more than one place in the

second clause. But does the semicolon float with them? _____ 39 And can all
therefore-links float? Read this sentence:

Chauncey's father has a new Cadillac; he besides has two Mustangs.

Does the sentence sound sensible? _____ 40 You must use your ear to decide whether
each particular link sounds right when floated.

The second point concerns the strangest link word you have ever seen. In fact, you have *never* seen it, because it is not there. Meet the phantom link:

    f.   Don't ask me for favors; ask me for forgiveness.
    g.   The Russians insisted on a closed border; the Americans demanded an open one.

With the phantom link we join two clauses with no word at all, just a semicolon. But the semicolon *must* be there.

This way of linking can be very effective when we want to show oppositeness. We write two clauses similar in form but opposite in meaning; then we join them with the phantom link and let the oppositeness speak for itself, as in sentences f and g and in this famous one:

    Ask not what your country can do for you; ask what you can do for
        your country.

Try one. Join these two sentences with the phantom link:

    [41]The Republicans nominated Dewey.
    The Democrats stuck with Roosevelt.

Of course, before joining two sentences with the phantom link (or with any link, for that matter), be sure the two ideas *belong* together. What would you as a reader think of this?

    Chemistry is difficult for me; I have math on Saturdays.

The connection between these ideas certainly does not speak for itself. In fact, it is hard to see what the connection is. Either these two ideas do not belong in the same sentence at all, or the writer must supply words that show the connection, such as

    Chemistry is difficult for me; therefore I dropped it and am taking math on Saturdays.

    The final point about *therefore*-links concerns when to use them. Since many of them have nearly the same meaning as some of the *and*-links, you will often have to decide between the types. For instance, which of the following would you more probably say in a

[42‡]

romantic situation? _____

    h.   Betty darling, I love you madly, and I want to marry you.
    i.   Betty darling, I love you madly; consequently, I want to marry you.

Everyone but an overzealous English instructor would doubtless use the first version. On the other hand, which of the next two would you more likely write in a research paper or

[43]

report? _____

j. The Arab oil embargo of 1973 caused a widespread gasoline shortage in the United States, and so thousands of workers in automotive industries lost their jobs.

k. The Arab oil embargo of 1973 caused a widespread gasoline shortage in the United States; consequently, thousands of workers in automotive industries lost their jobs.

Many of the *therefore*-links are more suitable for formal situations; that is why you may need some practice in using them. Nevertheless, many others are as familiar on the lunchroom line as in the lecture hall, such as *besides, in other words, next, then, meanwhile, otherwise, instead, likewise, on the other hand.*

To conclude this section, choose ten of the *therefore*-links you have learned (including the phantom link), and on your own paper write an original sentence for each of those ten. Try floating the link in one or two sentences. If you did the box on page 213, try using a period instead of a semicolon once or twice. (A caution: Like many other words, some of these links have other uses in other situations you have not learned yet. Use these links only to link two clauses. You will be sure you have two clauses if you can underline two separate sets of subject and verb.)

Do this additional assignment if your instructor directs: Write a paragraph of nine to eleven sentences on a topic from the master list or one suggested or approved by your instructor. Do not use *and* more than three times or *but* more than twice. Try to use as many *therefore*-links as possible without sounding unnatural.

If your instructor directs, also do one of the following with either or both of the above assignments before submitting them to him:

A. Exchange papers with another student for mutual evaluation; then revise your own paper.

B. In a group of four or five, constructively discuss and evaluate the papers of all or several group members; then revise your own paper.

A KEY CONCEPT (SUBGROUPS)

Before we go further, you need to grasp a key concept in combining ideas. Up to now you have been combining ideas that were equal in importance. But what if you want to let your reader know that some parts of what you are saying are more important than others? Imagine a stage show in which all the secondary and bit players insisted on jamming the front of the stage and sharing the spotlight with the stars; the audience would have a hard time telling which performers were really the stars. The same would happen with sentences if we gave all ideas equal prominence. Since your childhood you have been separating main from secondary ideas in your speech; now you need to transfer all of that ability to your writing.

Let us look at one of the simplest ways to make some ideas secondary, or subordinate. Suppose you and your date went to a movie and afterward stopped off for a pizza. The next day, when recounting the evening's events to your roommate, you would probably first tell him something about the movie; after that, which of these would you more likely say?

☐ [1]The movie ended, and we went for a pizza.
☐ [2]After the movie we went for a pizza.

All movies end; your roommate knows that. What you really want to tell him is where you went afterward. Therefore you would naturally put the idea of the movie ending into a form that makes it secondary in the sentence. Instead of connecting it to the pizza idea with an *and,* which would show an equal, one-plus-one relation, you reduce it to just *After the movie.* You learned in "Basic Sentence Parts" (pages 186–189) that you should think of each *of-*group, like *after the movie* (or *of the plot* or *with Jeannette*), as being surrounded by a plastic bubble to show that it is a self-contained unit, acting as if it were a single word. For example, *After the movie* in sentence 2 is doing the same job as what single-word [3]

modifier in the sentence below? _____

Afterward we went for a pizza.

*Of-*groups are just the first of several kinds of groups you will soon meet, all of which reduce a whole idea to a secondary, or subordinate, role in the sentence. For this reason

let us call all such groups *subgroups. Of-*groups are the simplest kind of [4]s__ __g__ __ __ps. The concept of subgroups is so important that we will review *of-*groups before going on to the larger subgroups. In the following sentence there are six *of-*groups. Can you find them? Circle each one:

[5]Before the wedding a huge cake of five tiers, with a bride and groom at the top, was ordered from the bakery on Grand Avenue.

Next, in each sentence below, two or more unequal ideas have been connected illogically with *and-*links, as in sentence 1. Rewrite each sentence to make it more logical, like sentence 2, by reducing each idea to an *of-*group except the one you want to stress. Circle each *of-*group. The first item is done for you as an example.

As a reminder, here are nearly all the common *of-*links:

Place		*Time*	*Other*
to	through	before	of
toward	throughout	after	for
on	behind	during	with
upon	in front of	since	without
over	out (of)	until	because of
above	up		instead of
around	down		on account of
about	within		like
into	between		against
inside	among		except
outside	from		
below	past		
beneath	by		
under	at		
underneath	near		
across	beyond		

[6]‡There was a Hungarian restaurant, and James ate there.

James ate (at a *Hungarian restaurant*.)

[7]All the U.S. presidents have been Protestants, but one, John Kennedy, was not.

All _____

ex__ __ __ _____ .

[8]There was a graduation ceremony, and Professor Snuffwell went there, and he took his wife.

Professor _____ w_____ t__ the _____

_____ w__ __ __ h_____ .

Or

‡Professor _____ took _____

t__ _____ .

[9]‡My sister bought a house, and it had a gas station on one side and another gas station on the other side.

My _____ be__ __ __ __ __

two _____ .

[10]‡The hockey game was going on, and Dr. Browne received an emergency call, and the caller was old Mrs. Underweather.

D__ __ __ __ __ _____

_____ .

There is another important reason for knowing *of*-groups and other subgroups. *Of*-groups obviously have some meaning. But do they have enough meaning to be sentences by themselves? Are the *of*-groups below sentences? (Do they have subjects and verbs?)

11

_____

In the paper.
After my lung operation.

An *of*-group or any other subgroup can never be a sentence by itself. Subgroups play subordinate parts, not leading roles. Continuing with our analogy of the players on a stage, suppose the subordinate players step back out of the spotlight. Can we then tell who the leading players are? Of course—they are the ones left in the spotlight. Your ability to recognize subgroups in a sentence enables you to remove these subordinate players from the spotlight of the sentence; then the stars of the sentence—the subject and verb—are much easier to spot. Look at this sentence, in which the *of*-groups have been circled:

(At the end) (of the rainbow) a pot (of gold) waits (for you.)

What is the subject? _____ The verb? _____ How easy it is to spot them after you isolate all the subgroups inside their plastic bubbles! As you learned in "Basic Sentence Parts," neither the subject nor the verb is ever inside those plastic bubbles. Each subgroup is a little self-contained unit; nothing in it can break out of the bubble and be anything in the rest of the sentence outside the bubble. This is why recognizing *of*-groups and other subgroups will make it much easier for you to master sentence writing.

To conclude this section, write two original sentences containing a total of at least five *of*-groups. Circle each *of*-group; then underline the subject of each sentence once and the verb twice:

14‡

_____

_____
15‡

_____

_____

Show your work in this section to your instructor.

COMBINING UNEQUAL IDEAS (*WHO*-LINKS)

You have learned that the *and*- and *therefore*-links are used between two ideas (clauses) that you want to stress equally. But look again at a sentence you met earlier:

> Adolf Hitler was once a paperhanger, and he caused millions of deaths in World War II.

Would you as the writer really want to give equal emphasis to these two ideas—to say that you attached as much importance to Hitler's youthful occupation as to the millions of deaths he caused? Most likely you would not. Those two ideas are not related on a one-plus-one basis, as these would be:

> Adolf Hitler was once a paperhanger, and his henchman Joseph Goebbels was an unemployed journalist.

You can show the maturity of your thinking by combining two ideas in ways to indicate that you want to stress *one* idea over the other. Can you think of a way to stress the millions of deaths over the paperhanging? There are several ways, but we will concentrate on one for now.

The two basic ideas we are working with are

a. Adolf Hitler was once a paperhanger.
b. Adolf Hitler caused millions of deaths in World War II.

How can we show that we consider b more important than a? Suppose we were able to *hide* idea a *inside* b.

> Adolf Hitler ⟨Adolf Hitler was once a paperhanger⟩
> caused millions of deaths in World War II.

This gives us

> Adolf Hitler Adolf Hitler was once a paperhanger caused millions of deaths in World War II.
>
> *Or*
>
> Adolf Hitler, Adolf Hitler was once a paperhanger, caused millions of deaths in World War II.

Either way it sounds terrible—and ungrammatical. That may be what ancient man thought the first time he tried it. But suppose we invented a short word to replace the repeated noun (*Adolf Hitler*). That is just what someone did thousands of years ago—even before English was born. Can you think of such a word?

> [1]*Adolf Hitler, _ _ _ was once a paperhanger, caused millions of deaths in World War II.

Need another hint?

> [2]Adolf Hitler, w_ _ was once a paperhanger, caused millions of deaths in World War II.

Now you have it. This sentence clearly says what it intends to say. It *sub*merges, or *sub*ordinates, the paperhanger idea inside the main idea. It replaces the repeated *Adolf Hitler* with *who*. The idea we want to stress, the millions of deaths, stays in its original form; this way it keeps its importance.

What you are learning now is another kind of subgroup. Remember what subgroups are? Word groups that are [3]s_____ parts of the sentence. That is just what we have made of the paperhanger idea:

> Adolf Hitler, ⟨who was once a paperhanger,⟩ caused millions of deaths in World War II.

Just like *of*-groups, groups like *who was once a paperhanger* are subgroups; think of them too as being inside plastic bubbles. We will call such subgroups *who*-groups. Try one yourself; combine a and b below. In this and in following sentences, assume that you want to stress the idea marked *:

a. The Beatles came from England in the early 1960s.
b. The Beatles initiated a whole new era in American popular music.*

In the blank below, write b, the idea to be stressed, *outside* the bubble. This becomes the main idea (main clause) of your new sentence:

⁴The Beatles, (who c_____ ,)

i_____ .

Now write a, the unstressed idea, *inside* the bubble. This is your *who*-group.

When you have two facts about a person, then, and you want to stress one of them, you can reduce the other fact to a subgroup beginning with *who*. Try 5, 6, and 7 below. Remember that the idea you want to stress (*) goes *outside* the bubble and the unstressed idea is reduced to a subgroup *inside* the bubble.

Many Americans do not like to repaint their rooms every few years.
Many Americans are covering their walls with wood paneling.*

⁵Many _____ (who _____

_____) _____ .

Hester was a sinner in the eyes of the townspeople.
Hester was forced to wear a symbol of her sin all her life.*

⁶Hester, (who _____ ,)

_____ .

Clyde wanted to marry wealthy Sondra Finchley.
Clyde was determined to dispose of his current girl friend.*

⁷Clyde, who _____ ,

_____ .

In each sentence so far, we have told you which idea to stress. Suppose, though, that you want to stress the other idea. Can you? Surely, if it makes sense to do so. For example, in sentence 1, suppose you want to emphasize not the millions of deaths that Hitler caused but the fact that a man of such ruthless power began in such a harmless, powerless occupation. You start with the same two ideas:

Adolf Hitler was once a paperhanger.*
Adolf Hitler caused millions of deaths in World War II.

But now you reduce the *millions of deaths* idea to a *who*-group inside the *paperhanger* idea.

(Adolf Hitler caused millions of deaths in World War II)
Adolf Hitler _____↓_____
was once a paperhanger.

⁸Adolf Hitler, _ _ _ _ caused millions of deaths in World War II, was once a paperhanger.

Try another. Check which of these two ideas *you* want to stress:

Step 1:   *The Wizard of Oz,* $\overbrace{\text{I still watch}\ \cancel{\text{it}}\ \text{every year,}}^{\text{which}}$ is the best children's movie ever made.

[17]Step 2:   *The Wizard of Oz,* w_____,

is _____.

The Everglades harbors several vanishing wildlife species.*
A new law protects the Everglades.

[18]‡The Everglades, _____,

_____.

Before going on, we should note that *who* may appear in two other forms, *whose* and *whom.* *Whose* works this way:

Mark Twain's real name was Samuel Clemens.
Mark Twain took his pen name from the cry of riverboat navigators.*

[19]Mark Twain, whose real _____

_____, took _____

_____.

Try this one:

Martin Luther King's assassination shocked America.
Martin Luther King was a winner of the Nobel Prize.*

[20]Martin Luther King, whose _____

_____, _____

_____.

Whom does present some problems. When should you use *who* and when *whom*? We will discuss this complex problem in the "Noun and Verb Problems" module, but for now, here is a way you can often avoid it. If you cannot decide between *who* and *whom* in c, what word can you use in 21 to avoid the problem?

a.   I met a girl yesterday.
b.   The girl can get free tickets to the country music festival.*
c.   The girl (who, whom) I met yesterday can get free tickets to the country music festival.

[21]The girl t_ _ _ I met yesterday can get free tickets to the country music festival.

In fact, in many cases like this we can even leave out the *who*-link entirely:

The girl I met yesterday can get free tickets to the country music festival.

You will have a chance to practice this in the economy modules.

(Note: the *who*-group may come at the *end* of the sentence instead of the middle, as in

There was a strange taste in the lasagne (that Aunt Stella made yesterday).)

If you still feel unsure about where to put the stressed idea, do the items below. Remember that the idea you reduce to a *sub*group is the one you want to *sub*merge, to put inside the plastic bubble, to *sub*ordinate to the main clause. In the following sentences, check the idea that the writer is stressing:

a. The Treaty of 1783, which ended the Revolution, guaranteed America's independence.

The writer in a is stressing that   [22]☐ the treaty ended the Revolution,   ☐ the treaty guaranteed America's independence.

b. The Treaty of 1783, which guaranteed America's independence, ended the Revolution.

The writer in b is stressing that   [23]☐ the treaty ended the Revolution,   ☐ the treaty guaranteed America's independence.

Here is some practice. Combine each of the following sets of ideas into one sentence by reducing one of the ideas to a *who*-group. Put a check mark in the box next to the idea you intend to stress as your main clause. Circle your *who*-group with a plastic bubble. You may change, add, or omit words as necessary. Punctuate naturally:

☐ [24]‡The workers are demolishing the old warehouse.
☐ The workers are being paid overtime.

_____

_____

[25]‡[Combine the two sentences in item 24 again, this time stressing the other idea.]

_____

_____

☐ [26]‡This twilight world is neither at peace nor at war.
☐ This twilight world affords most Americans only anxiety.

☐ [27‡]Eldridge Cleaver served a term in Folsom Prison.
☐ Eldridge Cleaver vividly described the regimentation of a convict's life.

☐ [28‡]Many professors enjoy teaching evening students.
☐ Evening students often show great industry and seriousness of purpose.

☐ [29‡]I usually avoid eating eggs.
☐ Eggs have a high cholesterol level.

☐ [30‡]Some cars have been made since 1975.
☐ These cars are required to have emission controls.

☐ [31‡]The Library of Congress classification system is designed for certain libraries.
☐ These libraries contain extensive research material.

Do this only if you did the box on page 225.

☐ [32‡]James Cagney's "tough guy" movie roles made him famous.
☐ James Cagney was also an accomplished song-and-dance performer.

The next three items are more difficult; they require you to combine *three* ideas into one sentence, using *who*-groups. First combine two ideas that seem to fit together more naturally. Then work the third in. Circle each *who*-group:

[33]Miss Grunk has been teaching here for forty years.
Miss Grunk likes to teach only certain children.
These children never ask her questions.

Miss Grunk, who has _____ , likes

_____ children that _____.

34‡Campers once had to "rough it" with pup tents and sleeping bags.
   Campers today can live in air-conditioned trailers.
   These trailers are as comfortable as their living rooms back home.

Campers, w_____

_____

_____.

35‡Hank Aaron is quiet and unassuming.
   Hank Aaron broke the home-run record of Babe Ruth.
   Ruth was boisterous and loved publicity.

_____

_____

_____.

In the next three blanks, write three original sentences using *who*-groups. Circle each *who*-group:

36‡
_____

37‡
_____

38‡
_____

CHOOSING THE BEST LINK

So far you have practiced with each of these types of links:

Of-links	*And-links*	*Therefore-links*		*Who-links*
of	and	therefore	next	who (whom, whose)
with	but	however	finally	which
to	or	nevertheless	besides	that
in	nor	thus	moreover	
for	yet	then	furthermore	
by		second,	for instance	
on		third . . .	for example	
from			; [*phantom*]	
. . .			. . .	

Now it is time for situations where you must first choose which *type* of link is best. In the following items join all the ideas in the way you find most appropriate. Decide first whether one idea should be stressed over the other(s); then build from there. Remember what you have discovered about not repeating the same link in a sentence. Refer to the list above if you need help. For example:

> Dr. Farnsworth placed the X-rays against the light.
> The specialists searched the X-rays for dark spots.
> The dark spots would indicate diseased tissue.

We can combine these to make

> Dr. Farnsworth placed the X-rays against the light, *and* the specialists searched them for dark spots *that* would indicate diseased tissue.

> *Or*

> Dr. Farnsworth placed the X-rays against the light; *then* the specialists searched them for dark spots *which* would indicate diseased tissue.

There are still more possible combinations for these three ideas; likewise, there is more than one effective way to combine the ideas in most of the items below:

[39]Barbra Streisand gained fame as a singer.
Barbra Streisand has done many dramatic screen roles.

_____

_____

[40]Interstate 80 runs from New Jersey to San Francisco.
San Francisco was also the terminus of the old Lincoln Highway.

_____

_____

[41]‡Propane-gas stoves are the simplest camping stoves to operate.
Liquid-fuel stoves are more economical.

_____

_____

[42]‡The prohibition law of the 1920s was felt by many Americans to be unfair.
The prohibition law was disobeyed freely.

_____

_____

[43]‡Captain Ahab had lost a leg to Moby Dick.
Captain Ahab wanted revenge on Moby Dick.
Captain Ahab pursued Moby Dick halfway around the world.

_____

_____

_____

⁴⁴‡Patti had a strange roommate at college.
The roommate kept pet snakes.
Patti did not move to another dorm.

_____

⁴⁵‡Some Japanese went to live abroad.
These Japanese complained about high prices there.
Living costs abroad were actually lower than in Japan.

_____

⁴⁶‡Advanced courses are disasters for many science majors.
They must take these courses before they graduate.
These courses include Inorganic Chemistry, Microbiology, and Particle Physics.

_____

⁴⁷‡[From answers 39–42, pick one that you can write *another* way that would be as good as the version you wrote, or nearly so. Write this second version.]

_____

_____

⁴⁸‡[From answers 43–45, pick one and follow the instructions for 47.]

_____

_____

_____

The best demonstration of your ability to combine ideas will be a paragraph or so of your own writing. Before writing that, warm up with the second best demonstration: taking a weakly written paragraph and combining its ideas as best you can. On your own paper, rewrite the paragraph below. Remember what you have learned about variety; like a good baseball pitcher, vary your offerings: not all fastballs, not all curves.‡

SELECTION E

Fifty years ago the scientific world believed that Asia was the birthplace of man. Louis Leakey was a young adventurer. He wanted to hunt early human fossils in Africa. Scientists scoffed at him. For 35 years the scientific foundations gave him no money. He worked patiently alone in East Africa. His wife and son joined him. They struggled along on shoestring budgets. They spent much of their own money.

In 1959 the Leakeys finally found the nearly complete skull of an extinct form of man. The Leakey family has revolutionized our understanding of man's origin.

— *Adapted from* The New York Times Magazine
(March 3, 1974), p. 13

Now, on your own paper write a paragraph of ten to twelve sentences on a topic from the master list or one suggested or approved by your instructor. Combine ideas as best you can. Try not to use *and* or *but* more than five times altogether to join ideas. When finished, do whichever of these your instructor directs:

A.   Exchange papers with another student for mutual evaluation; then revise your own paper.

B.   In a group of four or five, constructively discuss and evaluate the papers of all or several group members; then revise your own paper.

C.   Submit the paper to your instructor.

COMBINING TO SHOW SPECIAL RELATIONS (*IF*-LINKS)

So far you have learned four ways of combining ideas in a sentence: with *of-, and-, therefore-,* or *who*-links. Are there still other ways? If there are, why do we need them? You can answer these questions yourself. Try to combine the two ideas below by using any kind of link you have learned so far:

a.   You can come with us on one condition.
b.   You must tell us all about Judy's new boy friend.

¹‡

_____

_____

Did you come up with something fairly presentable but a bit wordy, like

You can come with us on the condition that you tell us all about Judy's new boy friend

. . . or did you give up? In any case, there is another kind of link that gives us a much simpler and smoother way of combining ideas a and b. Can you discover it?

²‡You can come with us ___ ___ you tell us all about Judy's new boy friend.

Need a hint? What word begins these well-known sayings?

³___ ___ I had my way

___ ___ I were king

___ ___ wishes were horses

___ ___ I had the wings of an angel

Write the word in 2 if you have not already done so.

What does *if* do as a link? It shows that two ideas are related in a special way: One will happen only on the condition that the other happens. This and other special kinds of relations between ideas cannot be expressed smoothly (and sometimes cannot be expressed at all) with *of-*, *and-*, *therefore-*, or *who*-links. That is why the English language gives us another type of link—to show such special relations between ideas. There are over two dozen links that work like *if*; each of them shows a different special relation. You have, of course, been using many of them in your speaking since you were five years old.

Try *if* as a link in combining the two ideas in each item below, changing the wording where necessary:

I can have my car fixed on one condition.
My pay check must arrive Tuesday.

⁴I _____

if my _____.

The company will give the workers a raise on one condition.
The workers must promise to increase productivity.

⁵The com_____

___ the w_____.

Short hair may come back into style.
Then the barbers will be happy.

⁶The b_____ ___ ___ _____

_____

Charlie may call tonight.
Then I will go out with Charlie.

⁷

_____ ___ ___ _____

_____.

Each time you put *if* in front of one of the ideas in items 1 to 7, that idea clearly is no longer a separate sentence but only a part of the new combined sentence. We have, then, a new type of subgroup; we will call such subgroups *if*-groups and the links they begin with *if*-links. As you did with other subgroups, think of each *if*-group as being encased in a plastic bubble:

You can come with us (if you tell us all about Judy's new boy friend).
I will go out with Charlie (if he calls tonight).

(Do you remember what the main part of the sentence—the part *outside* the bubble—is

called? The ⁸m___ ___ c___ ___ ___e.) Circle each *if*-group in the sentences below:

⁹Jacob faced death at the hands of his brother Esau if Jacob came home.

[10]What would America be like today if the South had won the Civil War?

Write two original sentences, each containing an *if*-group. Circle the *if*-group:

[11‡]

_____

if _____ .

[12‡]

_____

_____

In any of the sentences you have written so far, were you tempted to *start* the sentence with *if*? If you were, your linguistic instincts are working well. Do sentences c and

[13]

d mean the same? _____

c. The barbers will be happy if short hair comes back into style.
d. If short hair comes back into style, the barbers will be happy.

Anytime we wish, we can take almost any *if*-group and shift it—the whole plastic bubble, including the *if*-link—to the beginning of the sentence. Try it:

I can have my car fixed (if my pay check arrives Tuesday.)

[14]If _____ ,

I _____ .

Go back to sentence 2 (page 231); shift the *if*-group to the beginning:

[15]

_____

_____

Below, rewrite sentences 5 and 7 (page 232) with the *if*-groups shifted to the beginning. Make any necessary changes in wording:

[16]

_____

_____

[17]

_____

_____

Now that you know *how* to shift *if*-groups, can you see *why* you might want to? One reason is to put a little variety in your writing. If you have several *if*-groups in a paragraph, your writing will sound more lively if you put some of them at the beginning of the sentence.

(A word on punctuation: you may have noticed from the answer pages that *if*-groups are sometimes set off with a comma and sometimes not. Did you notice a pattern? When the

if-group comes after the main clause, is it set off by a comma? [18] _____ When it comes

before the main clause, is it set off? [19] _____ This is the usual pattern. You will go into it more in the module "Punctuation.")

OTHER LINKS LIKE *IF*

What other links work like *if*? You can discover many of them by thinking of words (other than *and-*, *therefore-*, or *who*-links) that fit the blanks in the sentences below. (Some of these links contain more than one word. A few others you have met earlier as *of*-links also.)

[20]The first quarter of the game was nearly over w_ _ _ _ we arrived.

[21]The first quarter of the game was ending a_ _ we arrived.

[22]The first quarter of the game was nearly over b_ _ _ _ _ _ we arrived.

[23]We left the stadium a_ _ _ _ _ Army scored its fifth touchdown.

[24]We left the stadium a_ _ s_ _ _ _ a_ _ Army scored its fifth touchdown.

[25]Navy scored two field goals wh_ _ _ _ we were still stuck in traffic outside the stadium.

[26]We've seen the Army-Navy game every year s_ _ _ _ _ _ we moved to Philadelphia.

[27]We stayed at the stadium u_ _ _ _ _ the game became one-sided.

[28]We take my brother-in-law to a football game w_ _ _ _ _ _e_ _ _r we have an extra ticket.

Look at the nine new links you have just learned: *when, as, before, after, as soon as, while, since, until,* and *whenever.* Though their meanings vary, they all show that the two

ideas they join are related in what special way? By the [29]t_ _ _ _ _ when each happened. Since these new links work like *if*, we will classify them as *if*-links and we will classify the subgroups they introduce as *if*-groups. Do you remember all the *if*-links you have learned so far?

i___ ___   a___ ___ ___ ___   u___ ___ ___ ___

w___ ___ ___   a___ s___ ___ ___ a___   w___ ___ ___ ___ ___ ___ ___

a___   w___ ___ ___ ___ ___

b___ ___ ___ ___ ___   s___ ___ ___ ___

Can *if*-groups beginning with any of these ten *if*-links be shifted elsewhere in the sentence? Try rewriting sentences 31 and 32 with the *if*-group shifted to the beginning of the sentence. If you need help, do it like this: draw a plastic bubble around the whole *if*-group in sentence 31, including the *if*-link. In the blank below it, write everything in the bubble. Then write after it everything else from sentence 31. (Adjust punctuation and capitalization.) Do the same with sentence 32.

³¹The first quarter of the game was nearly over when we arrived.

_____

_____

³²We left the stadium as soon as Army scored its fifth touchdown.

_____

_____

Now practice what you have learned. Use a different one of the nine *if*-links of time to combine each of the following sets of ideas. Begin with the main clause, not the *if*-group, unless you are directed otherwise:

Carlos turned on the radio.
Carlos could find nothing but news.

³³Carlos could _____

_____ .

The judge gaveled the court to order.
At that time a shot rang through the crowded courtroom.

³⁴A shot _____

_____ .

The catalog requires students to take the literature survey first.
Then they can take advanced literature courses.

35

_____

_____

³⁶[Rewrite 34 with the *if*-group shifted to the beginning.]

In each of the following items, the two ideas have been combined weakly with an *and*-link. Improve each item by rewriting it, combining the ideas with an *if*-link instead. Change word order where necessary.

_____

_____

³⁷Ohio entered the Union in 1803, and from that time more presidents have been born there than in any other state.

_____

_____

³⁸The United States was scoring great diplomatic successes overseas, and at the same time it faced serious crises at home.

_____

_____

³⁹The bank opens at 9 A.M., and up to then I can't let you in.

_____

_____

Now write an original sentence for each link listed below. Circle each *if*-group. You should have a full main clause, which would make a sentence by itself, *outside* the circle.

^{40‡}[before] _____

_____

^{41‡}[since] _____

_____

^{42‡}[while] _____

_____

^{43‡}[when] _____

_____

^{44‡}[whenever] _____

_____

Do the following if your instructor directs: On your own paper, write a paragraph of seven to nine sentences telling of something humorous or odd that happened to you. Use at least four of the *if*-links you have learned so far. Circle each *if*-group. Do not use *and so* or *and then* at all.

SHOWING OTHER RELATIONS WITH *IF*-LINKS

Here is another group of *if*-links; they show a relation other than time. How many can you discover? Can you tell what relation they show?

[45]We were late b_ _ _ _ _ _ our car had broken down.

[46][This link is also an *if*-link of time.] We won't be able to go to the rock

concert Friday night, s_ _ _ _ _ it's completely sold out.

[47][This one is also an *of*-link.] I want you to be my wife, Letitia, f_ _ _ I'm madly in love with you.

[48]Craig canceled all his social engagements s_ t_ _ _ _ he could cram for his psych test.

[49]Craig canceled all his social engagements i_ or_ _ _ _ t_ _ _ _ he could cram for his psych test.

What do these five links—*because, since, for, so that,* and *in order that*—have in common? *Why* were we late? *Why* can we not go to the rock concert? *Why* do I want Letitia to be my wife? *Why* did Craig cancel his social engagements? *Because, since, for, so that* and

in order that are used when one of the two ideas we are joining tells the [50]re_ _ _n for the other idea. Each of the sentences below contains two ideas weakly connected, as inexperienced writers tend to write them. Combine the ideas more logically, using a different one of these five new links for each item:

[51]Othello thought Desdemona was unfaithful, and so he strangled her.

Othello s_____ b_ _ _ _ _ _

_____.

[52]The company has set high goals in its new sales campaign, and so it is offering big bonuses to its most successful salesmen.

The company is _____

_____.

[53]The engineers are still working on the design of the new jetliner, so the first planes will not be delivered for three more years.

The first _____

_____.

[54]Langdon wanted to feel important, and because of this he bought a big, flashy car.

_____ he could

_____ .

[55][Rewrite 51 with the *if*-group shifted to the beginning.]

_____

_____

You have now moved quite a distance toward clearer, more logical sentence construction. There are only a few more *if*-links you need to be familiar with to be able to express almost any kind of relation between two ideas in a sentence.

Remember what relation *if* itself shows? It indicates a *condition* under which something will be done. Can you think of a link that indicates an opposite kind of condition?

[56]I won't go with you u_ _ _ _ _ you pay for the tickets. [*not* until.]

There is a third *if*-link of condition; this one indicates that the condition does not matter.

[57]I'll go with you wh_ _ _ _ _ _ you pay for the tickets or not.

In earlier sections of this module you met the links *but* and *however*, which show oppositeness. Are there any *if*-links that show oppositeness? See if you can discover any:

[58]I can't go out with you Saturday night, a_ _ _ _ _ _gh I'd like to. [This one

also has a shortened form: [59]_ _ _ _ _gh.]

Here is a very formal one to indicate oppositeness:

[60]The metric system is based on multiples of ten, wh_ _ _ _a_ the English measuring system contains all sorts of odd numeration.

Two *if*-links—one just a variation of the other—indicate place. They are not hard to discover:

[61]Take me wh_ _ _ _ the action is.

[62]I will follow you wh_ _ _ _ _er you go.

And finally, one shows similarity:

[63]Charlie swings the bat a_ _ i_ it weighed a ton.

Although there are more *if*-links, you have learned the most important ones. Remember that most *if*-groups can be shifted to the beginning of the sentence. Remember that the *if*-group, like other subgroups, rides inside its plastic bubble; when you shift an *if*-group, the whole bubbleful moves as a unit, including the *if*-link. Rewrite sentence 56 with the *if*-group shifted to the beginning:

64

_____

_____

Now write an original sentence for each *if*-link given. Begin some with the main clause, others with the *if*-group, as you prefer—as long as each sounds right. Circle each *if*-group.

65‡[if] _____

_____

66‡[after] _____

_____

67‡[as] _____

_____

68‡[while] _____

_____

69‡[until] _____

_____

70‡[since (*time*)] _____

_____

71‡[since (*reason*)] _____

_____

72‡[because] _____

_____

73‡[so that] _____

_____

74‡[unless] _____

_____

75‡[whether] _____

_____

76‡[whereas] _____

_____

77‡[although] _____

_____

78‡[whenever] _____

_____

79‡[as if] _____

_____

One of the most common weaknesses of inexperienced writers is connecting idea after idea with *ands*, *and thens*, and *and sos*. Rewrite each sentence below, replacing as many *if*-links as you can with appropriate *if*-links:

80‡Some French grapes grow under ideal conditions, and so they produce the best wines.
Some French grapes produce _____

_____.

81‡Zack strolled into the party, and then he saw Sherri, and he had just broken up with her a week ago, and so he walked right out again. [Make two sentences if you have to.]

When _____

_____

_____

82‡In the ninth inning Blatz singled, and then Jones walked, and the opposing team's manager saw that his pitcher, Dogfish Fowler, was tired, and so he replaced him with Don Key. [Make two sentences if you have to.]

_____

_____.

_____

_____

Now it is time to combine your knowledge of *if*-groups with what you learned previously about *who*-groups and other ways of combining ideas. In items 83 through 92, combine the ideas given, using either *who*-groups or *if*-groups or both, as you judge best. Here is an example:

> *Original:* The president left. Then his press secretary made an announcement. This announcement said that the president's departure plans had been kept secret for security reasons.
> *Revised:* After the president left, his press secretary made an announcement that his departure had been kept secret for security reasons.

Let us first do one step at a time.

> Dr. Robert Blank was sentenced to three years in prison. He is famous for leukemia research. He misused medicaid funds.

First, combine two ideas:

83A‡Dr. _____, who is _____,

was _____.

Then add the third:

83B‡Dr. _____, who is _____,

was _____ b_ _ _ _ _ he___

_____.

Now go on to these items:

84‡Love is an active power. This power breaks through walls separating persons.

_____

_____

85‡The young lawyer lost the big Framton case. He did a very skillful job. This job attracted the attention of the governor.

Al_____

_____

86‡An English couple finished a hearty breakfast in Guernsey last month. Both of them went into comas. They had eaten fried mushrooms. The mushrooms were poisonous.

_____

[87‡]You may want to break your pattern of life. This pattern seems to be basically destructive and unfulfilling. To break it you need good professional help.

If _____

_____

_____

Next, rewrite the following paragraph on your own paper, combining ideas as you judge best.‡

> The governor attended Easter services with his family today, and he received applause and even an Easter egg from a largely friendly crowd of worshipers. He was recovering from a sprained ankle and so he had motored the short distance from his mansion to the Community Church. The Reverend John Paul Matthew gave the sermon. The sermon was a traditional Easter message of hope and renewal. Last Easter the Governor's three top aides had been indicted for embezzlement two days earlier, and he had had to sit through a lengthy sermon on corruption in government. This year his secretary had told Reverend Matthew that the governor would attend Easter services on one condition, and that condition was that the reverend must give a friendly sermon. The reverend wanted the governor to attend. He agreed to this demand.

Finally, on your own paper, write a paragraph of ten to twelve sentences explaining how and why you do something the way you do; for example, the way you dress, some task you perform on your job, your method of studying, your technique for getting a person of the opposite sex interested in you. Use as many *if*-groups and *who*-groups as you can without sounding unnatural. Avoid connecting ideas with *and* as much as possible, and do not connect ideas at all with *so, and so,* or *and then.*

REVIEW You should now be almost ready for the mastery test of your ability to write clear, logical sentences with the several types of links you have learned. First, study the summary chart and do the review items. If necessary, review any sections of the module you are unsure of.

SUMMARY CHART OF LINKS
(*Of*-links are listed on page 218)

Situation	And-links	Therefore-links	Who-links	If-links
Two facts about a person or thing; one-plus-one	and	besides moreover furthermore	who which	

Situation	And-links	Therefore-links	Who-links	If-links
Identification [which one]			who which that	
Oppositeness	but yet	however instead nevertheless on the other hand on the contrary ; [phantom]		although though whereas
Choice	or nor	otherwise		
Reason		therefore consequently thus		because since for so that in order that
Time		meanwhile then next second, third . . . finally		when(ever) while before after as as soon as since until
Condition		otherwise		if unless whether
Similarity		likewise		as if
Place				where(ver)
Example		for instance for example		
Restatement		in other words		

You will probably do better on the mastery test if you can recall easily all the links you have learned and their uses. This review will help you recall. You should be able to complete the blanks below from memory with almost complete accuracy before attempting the main test.

The *and*-links: [1]a___, b___, o__, n___, y___

The common *therefore*-links: [2]th_____e, t__s, c_____y;

h_____r, n_____s, o_ t___ o____ ____, o_

t__ c_____, i_____d; f_____m__, m_____r, b_____s; f__ i_____e, f__ ex_____; i_ o_____ w_____; l_____e; o_____e; s_____d, t_____, n_____, t__n, f_____y, m_____le

The *who*-links: [3]w___, w_____, _____

The common *if*-links: [4]i__, u_____s, w___t___r; w____n, w__n____r, w_____e, b_____e, a____r, a_, a s_____a_, s_____, u_____; a_____gh, _____gh, w_____a_; a_i__; w____e, w_____r

Finally, try these practice items: Rewrite the ideas in each item into one or two clear, logical sentences. Change the wording where necessary:

[5]The Statue of Liberty stands 305 feet high. It weighs 225 tons. It was given to the United States by the French people. They wanted to show their friendship with America.

The _____, which _____

and _____, was _____

_____, who [*or* because they] _____

_____.

[6]Our garden is small, and it is beautiful. We laid it out last year. At that time we looked around our tiny city yard, and we discovered many good locations, and in these locations we placed dozens of small plants.

Al_____ our _____, it _____.

When we _____, we looked _____

_____ and d_____

where we _____.

MASTERY TEST

Part I. For each item, combine the ideas given into one or two sentences. Change the wording where necessary. Many items can be done in more than one way:

¹‡Vast crowds of Hindu faithful bathe in the Ganges each spring. The crowds are celebrating the festival of Kumbha Mela. [One sentence]

_____

_____

²‡The city's unemployment figures for last year were among the lowest in the nation at 3.5 percent. The city's unemployment figures for blacks were twice as high as those for whites. [One sentence]

_____

_____

³‡Morton is an accountant for our firm. He always walks around in a certain way. He seems to be drugged. [One sentence]

_____

_____

⁴‡On the Connecticut coast of Long Island Sound there is a new house. This house is one of the few solar-heated homes in the world, and so crowds of people drive out to see it every Sunday. [One sentence]

_____

_____

⁵‡In the end ring of the circus a clown squirts water at another clown from a huge buttonhole flower. The first clown is dressed in pink and green pantaloons. At the same time ten elephants parade around the center ring. They can dance on their hind legs. [One sentence]

_____

_____

⁶‡The Pineapple Flywheel rock group may split up. They may not. In any case, I will always be a fan of theirs. [One sentence]

_____

_____

⁷‡He is ugly. He has bad manners. He makes me pay on all our dates. I love him. [One or two sentences]

_____

_____

[8]In football, team A kicks the ball to team B, and then team B has four chances to move the ball ten yards, and sometimes it does this, and then it has four more chances to move ten more yards. [One or two sentences]

_____

_____

_____

[9]Elimination of tuberculosis in this country is possible with present means. It will not happen except on one condition. This condition is that more short-term cures occur. [One sentence]

_____

_____

_____

[10]Ray Sanford's car was damaged in a collision. Ray was given a summons. This was on account of he did not have his license with him. He will appear in court next week. He must pay a $25 fine. He will have to go to jail in case he does not pay it. [One or two sentences]

_____

_____

_____

_____

_____

Part II. On your own paper write a paragraph of twelve to fifteen sentences on a topic from the master list or one your instructor suggests or approves. Show your mastery of the idea-combining techniques you have discovered.

ANSWERS

INTRODUCTION

[1]Most people would say A; some would say B.
[2]Most people would say C.
[3]Thirteen
[4]Two
[5]Three
[6]None
[7]period
[8]And
[9]But
[10]One
[11]That
[12]Two (*costly, old*)
[13]Modifiers
[14]And, are, and their, are, their, the, are
[15]different
[16]cut unneeded words

COMBINING WITH *AND*-LINKS

[3]Sentence a
[2]Sentence c
[3]Sentence f
[6]but, or, yet
[7]Sentence g
[8]Sentence h
[9]that the second idea is opposite to the first
[10]opposite of
[11]but
[12]and
[13]and/but
[14]but
[15]or
[16]nor
[17]yet
[18]between
[19]a comma before them
[20]sentence
[21]clauses
[22]This summer I'm working for the Park Department; in the fall I'm going to California
[35]No
[36]It is stringy; too many ideas are connected by *ands*.

A NEW KIND OF LINK

[2]therefore
[3]semicolon [;]
[5]however
[6]But, yet
[7]nevertheless
[8]otherwise
[9]meanwhile
[10]besides
[11]for instance
[12]for example
[13]on the other hand
[14]And
[15]Besides
[16]other words
[17]contrary
[18]second, next, finally, then
[19]likewise
[20]instead
[21]thus, consequently
[22]Therefore
[23];
[24]Sentence b
[25]Sentence a
[26]No
[37]However
[38]No
[39]No
[40]No
[41]The Republicans nominated Dewey; the Democrats stuck with Roosevelt.
[43]Most experienced writers would use k.

A KEY CONCEPT

[1-2]Almost everyone would say sentence 2.

[3]Afterward

[4]subgroups

[5]Before the wedding, of five tiers, with a bride and groom, at the top, from the bakery, on Grand Avenue

[7]All the U.S. presidents have been Protestants (except [one,] John Kennedy.)

[8]Professor Snuffwell went (to the graduation ceremony) (with his wife.)

[11]No

[12]Pot

[13]Waits

COMBINING UNEQUAL IDEAS

[2]who

[3]secondary (or subordinate)

[4]The Beatles, who came from England in the early 1960s, initiated a whole new era in American popular music.

[5]Many Americans who do not like to repaint their rooms every few years are covering their walls with wood paneling.

[6]Hester, who was a sinner in the eyes of the townspeople, was forced to wear a symbol of her sin all her life.

[7]Clyde, who wanted to marry wealthy Sondra Finchley, was determined to dispose of his current girl friend.

[8]who

[9][If you checked a] The mayor, who is running for reelection, is worried about the crime rate. [If you checked b] The mayor, who is worried about the crime rate, is running for reelection.

[11]Which

[10]The Sears Tower, which is in Chicago, is taller than New York's World Trade Center.

[12]Interest in the devil, which had declined greatly during the twentieth century, was revived by such books as *Rosemary's Baby* and *The Exorcist*.

[13]that

[14]Yes

[15]My jacket that has blue stripes is in the cleaners.

[16]switch

[17]*The Wizard of Oz,* which I still watch every year, is the best children's movie ever made.

[19]Mark Twain, whose real name was Samuel Clemens, took his pen name from the cry of riverboat navigators.

[20]Martin Luther King, whose assassination shocked America, was a winner of the Nobel Prize.

[21]that

[22]the treaty guaranteed America's independence.

[23]the treaty ended the Revolution

[33]Miss Grunk, (who has been teaching here for forty years,) likes to teach only children (that never ask her questions.)

[39]Barbra Streisand, who gained fame as a singer, has done many dramatic screen roles. *Or,* Barbra Streisand gained fame as a singer; nevertheless, she has done many dramatic screen roles. [Other possibilities]

[40]Interstate 80 runs from New Jersey to San Francisco, which was also the terminus of the old Lincoln Highway. *Or,* Interstate 80 runs from New Jersey to San Francisco; this city was also the terminus of the old Lincoln Highway. [Other possibilities]

COMBINING TO SHOW SPECIAL RELATIONS

³If

⁴I can have my car fixed if my pay check arrives Tuesday.

⁵The company will give the workers a raise if the workers [*or* they] promise to increase productivity.

⁶The barbers will be happy if short hair comes back into style.

⁷I will go out with Charlie if he calls tonight.

⁸main clause

⁹if Jacob came home

¹⁰if the South had won the Civil War

¹³Yes

¹⁴If my pay check arrives Tuesday, I can have my car fixed.

¹⁵If you tell us all about Judy's new boy friend, you can come with us.

¹⁶If the workers promise to increase productivity, the company will give them a raise.

¹⁷If Charlie calls tonight, I will go out with him.

¹⁸No

¹⁹Yes

²⁰when

²¹as

²²before

²³after

²⁴as soon as

²⁵while

²⁶since

²⁷until

²⁸whenever

²⁹time

³¹When we arrived, the first quarter of the game was nearly over.

³²As soon as Army scored its fifth touchdown, we left the stadium.

³³Carlos could find nothing but news when he turned on the radio.

³⁴A shot rang through the crowded courtroom [just] as the judge gaveled the court to order.

³⁵The catalog requires students to take the literature survey before they can take advanced literature courses.

³⁶[Just] As the judge gaveled the court to order, a shot rang through the crowded courtroom. [Other possibilities]

³⁷Since Ohio entered the Union in 1803, more presidents have been born there than in any other state. [Other possibilities]

³⁸The United States faced serious crises at home while it was scoring great diplomatic successes overseas [Other possibilities]

³⁹I can't let you in until [*or* before] the bank opens at 9 A.M. [Other possibilities]

⁴⁵because

⁴⁶since

⁴⁷for

⁴⁸so that

⁴⁹in order that

⁵⁰reason

⁵¹Othello strangled Desdemona because he thought she was unfaithful.

⁵²The company is offering big bonuses to its most successful salesmen, since [*or* for] it has set high goals in its new sales campaign.

⁵³The first new jetliners will not be delivered for three more years, for [*or* since] the engineers are still working on the design of the planes.

⁵⁴Langdon bought a big, flashy car so that [*or* in order that] he could feel important.

⁵⁵Because Othello thought Desdemona was unfaithful, he strangled her.

⁵⁶unless

⁵⁷whether

⁵⁸although

⁵⁹though

⁶⁰whereas

⁶¹where

⁶²wherever

⁶³as if

⁶⁴Unless you pay for the tickets, I won't go with you.

MODULE 9

ECONOMY AND VARIETY

<u>Previous modules required:</u> Basic Sentence Parts (7)—Combining Ideas (8)

Read the following two letters:

Letter A

35 Corona Drive
Smithfield, Idaho
October 5, 19___

Parts Manager
Coldpoint Appliances
Detroit, Michigan

Dear Sir:
Would you please ship to me at the address which I have written above two shelves for a Coldpoint refrigerator, of which the model number is 1969AX7. The shelves which I need are number 7760J shelves, which are listed at $5.98 each in your company's catalog for 1976. I have enclosed a check for $12.78, which includes tax and postage in order that you can ship the shelves by air parcel post, which is how I want them.

Very truly yours,

Letter B

35 Corona Drive
Smithfield, Idaho
October 5, 19___

Parts Manager
Coldpoint Appliances
Detroit, Michigan

Dear Sir:
Please ship by air parcel post two number 7760J shelves for Coldpoint refrigerator model 1969AX7, listed at $5.98 each in your 1976 catalog. Enclosed find a check for $12.78 to cover all costs, including tax and postage.

Very truly yours,

If you were the busy parts manager at Coldpoint, which of these letters would you
1‡
rather receive? _____ How many lines does the body of letter A take up ? _____
2‡
3‡
How many does the body of letter B? _____ Does letter B tell the parts manager
4
all he needs to know? _____ If you now wish to change your answer to the first question, do so.

Since twentieth-century living in most countries is faster paced that it was in past centuries, people today like their writing that way, too. How many old stories did you lose interest in in high school because they started too wordily? (Dickens was reportedly paid by the word!) Also, since teachers often ask for compositions of so many hundred *words*, you may have fallen into the habit of using as many words as possible to say something.

Our world no longer seems to provide the leisure a nineteenth-century reader had to read wordy books or articles. "Less is more" is today's guideline. If you recall "Clear Writing: The First Steps," you will grasp what this means: Too many words often muddle your meaning. Because it is less wordy, letter B above communicates its message to the parts manager more clearly than A. That is part of what "less is more" means: writing that is lean and tight like an athlete's muscles instead of flabby like a beer belly.

Look once more at letters A and B. Besides its length, is there something else that
5
annoys you about letter A? If so, what? _____
(Hint: Which five-letter link appears six times?) The writer of letter A could think of only one way to join most of his ideas; as a result the letter sounds monotonous to most readers, and the writer unfortunately may seem less intelligent than he really is. A writer who does

not know how to use all his options is like a baseball pitcher who can throw only a fast ball or a painter who has only one color. Good writers, like good pitchers or painters, vary what they offer for maximum effect. Economy and variety are two marks of the experienced writer.

In this module and in "Economy and Clarity" you will discover how to trim from your writing words, word groups, and even whole sentences that are merely deadwood, contributing nothing to your meaning and possibly even muddling it. In this module you will discover types of word groups that can replace wordier groups without changing or muddling your meaning—and at the same time enliven your writing with some variety. Some of this you have already learned in "Combining Ideas." Recall, for instance, how you reduced these two sentences to one:

> Campers today can live in air-conditioned trailers. These trailers are as comfortable as their living rooms back home.

These became

> Campers today can live in air-conditioned trailers which are as comfortable as their living rooms back home.

Can you find two words around the middle of the sentence which also can be dropped to

tighten the sentence without changing the meaning? _____ _____ [6]. If you answered correctly, you are already catching on.

TRIMMING AND-LINK SENTENCES

We will start with a simple form of trimming. Do you recall the and-links? (Perhaps you need a quick review: the and-links are [7] a _____, b _____, o ___, n _____,

and y ___.) Examine these and-link sentences:

a. Pat likes her Volkswagen, and Donna may buy one too.
b. Pat likes her Volkswagen, and she takes good care of it.

One of these sentences can be tightened by trimming one needless word. Which sentence?

_____ [8] Which word? _____ [9] What is the difference between these sentences that makes one trimmable and the other not? Underline the subject (the person doing something) in the first half of sentence a. Underline the subject in the second half. Do the same with sentence b. Looking at the words you underlined, can you see why

sentence b can be trimmed and not sentence a? [10] _____
In a sentence where two ideas are joined by an and-link, then, you can drop the subject of

the second half if it is the [11] s _____ _____ as the subject of the first half. Your reader understands that you are talking about the same person or thing:

> ⎧─── Not same person ───⎫
> a. *Pat* likes her Volkswagen, and *Donna* may buy one too.

Same person

b. *Pat* likes her Volkswagen, and ~~she~~ takes good care of it.
c. Pat likes her Volkswagen and takes good care of it.

Here is another example:

d. I wanted to go to Harvard, but I had to settle for Backwash U.
e. I wanted to go to Harvard but had to settle for Backwash U.

You try one. Which of the following sentences can be tightened by dropping the unneeded second subject? Write the trimmed sentence in the blank:

f. Chem and physics are hard for me, but they arouse my interest.
g. Chem and physics are hard for me, but sociology is easy.

[12]Chem and physics are hard for me _____

_____.

Do another:

You will work harder around here, or you will find another job.
You will work harder around here, or I will fire you.

[13]‡You will work harder around here _____

_____.

(Let us go back for a minute. Did you notice what else disappeared in sentences c and e when we dropped the second subject? Compare carefully b with c, and d with e.
[14]

_____ Did you catch on to this and do it yourself in sentences 12 and 13?)
    Trim each of the following sentences that can be trimmed. Write *different subjects* in the blank if the sentence cannot be trimmed. Adjust the punctuation:

[15]Leontyne Price made her Metropolitan Opera debut in the early 1960s, and she has been a star there ever since.

_____

_____

[16]College administrators claim that *As* and *Bs* are easier to earn now than they were twenty years ago, yet many students would disagree.

_____

_____

[17]‡Reggie drank a bit too much last night, and he had to call in sick this morning.

[18]‡Webster wrote the best-known American dictionary, and he wrote a famous spelling book as well.

Look again at sentence 18. What else besides the *he* and the comma can be cut, to trim the sentence still more? (Hint: What else besides the subject is the same in both halves of the sentence? Is Webster doing the same action in both halves?)

[19]

_____ Write sentence 18 in the trimmest form possible.

[20]

_____

_____

Trim this sentence as much as possible:

[21]George and Sally are going skiing this afternoon, and they are going dancing tonight.

_____

_____

Thus you can (and usually should) drop everything in the second half of an *and*-link sentence that needlessly repeats information from the first half.

Same persons, same verb

George and Sally are going skiing this afternoon, and ~~they are going~~ dancing tonight.

How far can you trim these sentences?

[22]Poe liked to write about persons buried alive, and he also liked to write about beautiful women dying.

_____

_____

[23]Summer temperatures reach 110 degrees in parts of the United

States, but they reach only around 80 degrees in the British Isles.

_____

_____

TRIMMING *IF*-GROUPS

Remember *if*-groups? (Perhaps you need a quick review: Some of the common *if*-links are [1]i___, w_____, w___l___, u___l, u_____s, a___, s_____, al_____.) Put a circle around the *if*-group in each of these sentences:

[2]Your money will earn 7.5 percent yearly if it is deposited in our special savings account.

[3]When you are finished, you may turn in your exam paper and leave.

Sentences 2 and 3, like the sentences in the previous section, have two parts; in 2 and 3 the two parts are an *if*-group and a main clause. In 2, underline the subject of the main part of the sentence (main clause); then underline the subject of the *if*-group. Do both subjects refer to the same thing? [4]_____ Try writing a trimmed version of sentence 2, dropping the second subject. (Notice that another word in the *if*-group must be cut along with the subject.)

[5]Your money will earn 7.5 percent yearly _____.

Let us examine how this sentence is trimmed:

Same thing

Your money will earn 7.5 percent yearly if ~~it is~~ deposited in our special savings account.

For the trimmed sentence to make sense, what other word did you have to drop besides *it*?

[6]_____ Now try trimming sentence 3:

[7]_____, you may turn in your exam paper and leave.

In sentences 2 and 3, then, we were able to drop the subject of the *if*-group if it was the same person or thing as the subject of the main clause. This kind of trimming is quite common, as in

If [it is] defective, this radio should be returned to the dealer within ten days.

When [they are] hungry, cats will howl for hours.

While [I am] living on campus, I eat at Hamilton Hall.

Mrs. Martin's children constantly annoy her until [they are] threatened with punishment.

In each of the following sentences, underline the subject of the *if*-group and the subject of the main clause. Then write a trimmed version of the sentence:

[8]When you are in Japan, you must drive on the left side of the road.

_____

_____

[9][‡]If I am nominated, I will not run.

_____

Here is a slightly tricky one. Remember that a *you* subject is often omitted in commands and requests, as in

[You] Shut the door.

(This is called "*you* understood." If this is unclear to you, review pages (170–171) of "Basic Sentence Parts.") Therefore, the sentence

a. When you are in Rome, do as the Romans do

is really

b. When you are in Rome, *you* do as the Romans do.

Keeping that in mind, trim sentence a:

[10]

_____

In sentences 8–10 you were told to underline the subjects first so you would remember that both subjects must be the [11]s_____ person or thing before you can trim one of them. But what about this sentence? Underline the two subjects:

When I am in bed with my wife, my boss always calls me up.

[12]

Are the two subjects the same here? _____ Then can we trim one subject?

13

_____ What would happen to the meaning of this sentence if we trimmed it? Try it—just for laughs:

14

_____

_____

Do you think this is what the writer meant? Ridiculous sentences like this often result if you drop one subject when the two subjects are *not* the same person or thing. In the following sentences, you must first decide whether you can trim without upsetting the meaning of the sentence. Underline the two subjects. If the sentence cannot be trimmed, write *different subjects* in the blank. If the sentence can be trimmed, do it:

[15]When you are delivering prescriptions to Mrs. Gilbert, you should not accept a check from her.

_____

_____

[16]While they were still in diapers, their father had the twins modeling for infants' wear ads.

_____

_____

[17‡](Do this only if you did the box on page 257.) Guard this post until you are relieved.

_____

_____

[18‡]Even while he was going through Hell, I feel Dante never lost his faith in God.

_____

_____

Incidentally, did we change any punctuation when we trimmed any of these *if*-groups?

19

_____

TRIMMING TO A NEW KIND OF GROUP (*ING*-GROUPS)

How good do you think you are now at spotting deadwood? Trim this sentence as you did the ones above:

¹While I was strolling along the shore, I spotted a strange-looking boat out in the fog.

_____

_____

After checking the answer, consider this: Is there still another word that can be dropped from the *if*-group without changing or muddling the meaning of the sentence? Try it:

²S_ _ _ _ _ _ _ _ _ _ _____ _____ _____, I spotted a strange-looking ship out in the fog.

How about this one?

When he was running for president in 1948, Harry Truman campaigned from the rear platform of a train.

³R_____ _____ _____

_____, Harry Truman campaigned from the rear platform of a train.

One more:

When he is driving long distances on freeways, my husband takes along a thermos of coffee to keep awake.

⁴

_____,

my husband takes along a thermos of coffee to keep awake.

Sometimes, then, the *if*-link itself can be dropped. How can you know when you can drop it? By your ear and common sense. Does the trimmed sentence sound right and mean what you want? If so, you are safe in dropping. Do the following. If you think the *if*-link cannot be dropped, just write *no* in the blank:

⁵While he was waiting for Bill in front of the liquor store, Jerry was arrested for loitering.

_____

_____

⁶As she was entering the antique shop, Pam met George leaving with a huge old clock under his arm.

_____

_____

⁷Since they were packing to leave for Charleston, they had no time to visit the McCalls.

_____

_____

[8]Unless you are bringing a guest, you do not have to pay.

By dropping needless parts of an *if*-group in these sentences you have actually discovered a different kind of subgroup. In sentences 1 through 7, look at the first word of your

trimmed version. In each case, which three letters does this word end with? [9]_____
Since these trimmed versions no longer have their *if*-links, they are no longer *if*-groups; and

since they all begin with a word ending in *-ing*, let us call them [10]-_____-groups and call

the words they begin with [11]-_____-links. Here are some other examples:

> [While he was] Seek*ing* a cure for arthritis, Dr. Fremd accidentally discovered bubble gum.

> [As he was] Try*ing* to fix the sail, Vinnie fell overboard.

> Vinnie fell overboard [as he was] try*ing* to fix the sail.

The *-ing*-group is one of the most useful subgroups in English. It is a workhorse that often does the job of a whole sentence in half as many words. Recall that *if*-groups themselves are reduced forms of sentences. Notice how the process of combining and trimming works:

> *Two sentences:* Vinnie was trying to fix the sail. Vinnie fell overboard.
> *Combined with if-group:* As he was trying to fix the sail, Vinnie fell overboard.
> *Trimmed to -ing-group:* Trying to fix the sail, Vinnie fell overboard.

Here are pairs of sentences. Combine each pair, using an *-ing*-group. You may do it by the two-step method shown just above or, if you are sharp enough, you may be able to skip the first step:

> The old man was fishing off Cuba. The old man caught the largest fish he had ever seen.
> [12]F____ ____ ____ ____ ____ _____ _____, the old man caught the largest fish he had ever seen.

> Senator Filch was trying to avoid prosecution. Senator Filch hired F. D. Bailbond, the famous lawyer.

> [13]_____, Senator Filch hired F. D. Bailbond, the famous lawyer.

> Hardwicke was attempting to score from third base. He was cut down at the plate.
> [14]_____, Hardwicke was cut down

at the plate. (Why did we have to change the *he* to *Hardwicke* in 14? [15]_____

_____)

In each of the following, two ideas have been combined weakly, with *and*-links. Combine the two ideas more logically and concisely, using an *-ing*-group:

[16]Hardwicke was attempting to score from third base, and he was cut down at the plate.

_____

_____

[17]The Human Rights Club was planning a campus demonstration, and they invited leaders of all other student organizations to a discussion of plans.

_____

_____

_____

If you had difficulty with any sentences in this section, try first circling the *-ing*-form in the original sentence and all the words that you think belong to its group—like this:

Hardwicke was (attempting to score from third base,) and he was cut down at the plate.

TRIMMING *WHO*-GROUPS TO *-ING*-GROUPS

-Ing-groups can be used to trim other groups besides *if*-groups. Remember *who*-groups? (Perhaps you need a quick review: The *who*-links are [18]w____, w_____, t_____.) Circle the *who*-group in the following sentence. Can you find two deadwood words in it? If so, cross them out:

[19]Students who are failing more than one major subject will be put on probation.

Try the following. If you are not very sure of how to do them, start by circling each *who*-group in the original sentence and underlining the *-ing*-word you find in it, as shown below:

[20]FM stations (that are playing rock music) have been attracting more sophisticated audiences in the past few years.

[21]The police will have fifty extra men on duty Saturday to control traffic that will be heading for the stadium.

_____

_____

Now, use -*ing*-groups to combine the following uncombined or weakly combined pairs of ideas:

The muscular dystrophy campaign is nearing its goal of $10 million. The campaign has been carried on mainly by college students.

(Try the two-step method. First combine the two ideas using a *who*-group, then trim the needless words from that *who*-group.)

[22]*Step 1:* The muscular dystrophy campaign, w_____ ___ n_____

_____, has been carried on mainly by college students.

[23]*Step 2:* The muscular dystrophy campaign, n_____ _____

_____, has been carried on mainly by college students.

The Marine Corps is trying to recruit more college graduates, and it has assigned twenty more recruiters to visit campuses across the nation.

[24]*Step 1:* The Marine Corps, w_____, has assigned twenty more recruiters to visit campuses across the nation.

[25‡]*Step 2:* The Marine Corps, _____, has assigned twenty more recruiters to visit campuses across the nation.

[26‡]Celeste is taking six math courses, and she finds little time for her social life.

Step 1: [Do step 1 mentally or on scrap paper.]

Step 2: _____

_____

Who-groups, then, like *if*-groups, can often be trimmed down to -*ing*-groups. Is any other trimming possible with *who*-groups? The following *who*-group contains no -*ing*-link. Is there still a way to trim it? What two words can be dropped?

Everett Willis, who is a well-known science-fiction writer, will speak in Baylor Hall next Friday.

27Everett Willis, __ _____-_____ _____-_____

_____, will speak in Baylor Hall next Friday.

You have been doing this kind of trimming automatically in your speaking since you were a small child, as in

Our new teacher, [who is] Miss Meehan, gave us all lollipops.

Trim these:

We visited Federal Hall, which is the site of Washington's First Inaugural Address.

28We visited Federal Hall, _____

_____.

29‡General Abrams, who was the only Army Chief of Staff to die in office, is buried at Arlington.

_____

_____

Combine the following sets of ideas. Use *who*-groups, trimmed wherever possible. If you need to use the two-step method, do the first step on scrap paper:

30Vicki is the new president of the Student Government. She defeated five male candidates for the position.

_____

31Parsonville is the county seat. It is the oldest town in the county.

_____

_____

32‡[Do sentence 3 another way, switching the positions of the two ideas.]

_____,

_____.

Along the way, have you noticed a clue to when you can trim and when you cannot? Skim back over all the trimmable sentences from 1 to 31; which was the only verb that was ever trimmed out? For example, which verb was trimmed out in sentence 20? _____

28? _____ 29? _____ Are all these parts of the same verb? _____

35

What is that verb? _____ (If you are unsure, review pages 162–163 of "Basic Sentence Parts.") If you spot a part of the verb *be* in an *if*-group or a *who*-group, you may well have a trimming opportunity. If no part of *be* is there, you normally cannot trim. For example, only one of these can be trimmed from its present form:

a. Uncle Jed, who is a millionaire oil-well owner, is illiterate.
b. Uncle Jed, who owns a million dollars worth of oil wells, is illiterate.

36

Which can be trimmed? _____

However, sentences that at first glance do not look trimmable can often, if you think a bit, be changed to trimmable form. For example, can

37

we trim any words from this sentence as it stands? _____

As I walked down the lane, I saw Jeff waiting for me.

But what if we change the form of *walked* to *was walking?*

As I *was walking* down the lane . . .

Can we now trim the sentence? If so, write the trimmed version:

38

_____

_____

With a little thought you can trim many sentences that do not contain a part of *be* or an *-ing*-word, by mentally changing them to such forms. Do this sentence:

As they conferred throughout the night, the Democratic leaders moved gradually closer to agreement on a candidate.

[39]*Step 1:* As they w_____ c_____ing throughout the night,

the Democratic leaders _____

_____ .

TRIMMING TO *EN*-GROUPS

If you did well in the last section, you should not have much trouble with this next type of group, which works much like the -*ing*-group. Notice both the similarity and the difference in these sentences:

a. When he *was taking* Blake into custody, the policeman advised him of his rights.
b. When he *was taken* into custody by the policeman, Blake was advised of his rights.

Trim a as you have learned to do:

[1]

_____ _____ _____ _____, the policeman advised him of his rights.

Can b be trimmed in a similar way? Try:

[2]T_____ _____ _____ _____ _____

_____, Blake was advised of his rights.

Do these others:

Lionel, who was driving Bonnie home every day, fell desperately in love with her.

[3]Lionel, _____,

_____.

Bonnie, who was driven home by Lionel every day, realized that Lionel was in love with her.

[4]Bonnie, _____en _____ by _____,

_____.

Notice how, though they are different in meaning, -*ing*-forms and -*en*-forms appear in the same position and can be trimmed in the same way:

~~When he was~~ taking . . .   Lionel, ~~who was~~ driving . . .
~~When he was~~ taken . . .   Bonnie, ~~who was~~ driven . . .

We will call this new kind of group an -*en*-group, and the word that begins it an -*en*-link. (*En*-links are the same as the -*en*-forms you learned in "Basic Sentence Parts.")

Remember what you learned in "Basic Sentence Parts" about how irregular the -*en*-form is? It includes such words as *delayed, sung, made, caught,* and *stuck.* If you have forgotten about such irregularities, it is very important that you review pages 160–162 of "Basic Sentence Parts" before continuing in this module.

Now try trimming these sentences as you did with -*ing*-groups:

The soldiers left their comrade, who had been frozen to death, in the snow.

⁵The soldiers left their comrade, _ _ _ _ _en _____, in the snow.

The Dolphins, who were beaten by the Vikings, lost their bid for a third straight title.

⁶The Dolphins, _____, lost

_____.

Because it was swollen from Ali's punches, Forman's eye began to bleed.

⁷

_____,

_____.

His letter was written in great haste, and so it contained several glaring errors.

⁸W_____, his _____

_____.

⁹‡Mary had been stung by a bee, and she was cursing the whole insect world.

_____

_____

¹⁰‡I am finished with my exile, and I am ready to return to my native land.

_____

In the following sentences the verb is not in its -*en*-form. You will have to think first of what its -*en*-form is and then of how to trim to an -*en*-group:

He wrote the letter in great haste, and so it contained several glaring errors. [For help, look back at sentence 8.]

¹¹W_ _ _ _ _en _____, his letter

_____.

Hartley drove his car into a fire hydrant, and it received an unexpected washing.

12‡D_____, Hartley's car

_____.

Now try writing your own sentences in the blanks below; use a total of at least three -ing-groups and three -en-groups. Circle each group:

13‡
_____

_____

14‡
_____

_____

15‡
_____

_____

16‡
_____

_____

17‡
_____

_____

18‡
_____

_____

One final caution on -ing- and -en-groups:

    c.   Going to Harvard, Chang was offered a good job.
    d.   Having gone to Harvard, Chang was offered a good job.

In which sentence was Chang being offered the job while still in Harvard?
19

_____ In the other sentence, when was he offered the job?
20

_____ We use an -ing-group for an action that is going on at the *same* time as the action in the main clause. We must use *having* with an -en-group for an action earlier than the action in the main clause, as in d, in which Chang first went to Harvard and only afterward was offered a job.

Combine these ideas, using *-ing-* or *-en-*groups:

As Gertrude was drinking the poisoned wine, she fell to the floor.
21
_____ing _____, G_____

_____.

Gertrude drank the poisoned wine. After that she fell to the floor.
22
_____ing _____k _____, _____

_____.

Can *who*-groups be trimmed to anything even smaller than *-ing-* or *-en-*groups? Trim this *who*-group:

[23]The car that was speeding could not elude Dick Tracy.

[24]

To how many words were you able to trim this *who*-group? _____ But does the trimmed sentence now sound like grammatical English? Where must we now shift this one remaining word to make the sentence sound right? Write the word in the blank where it sounds right. Leave the other blank empty:

[25]The _____ car _____ could not elude Dick Tracy.

Do the same with 26 and 27 as you did with 25:

The boy who was embarrassed blushed deeply.

[26]The _____ boy _____ blushed deeply.
Abbie and I found a place that serves a pizza which is fantastic.

[27]‡Abbie and I found a place that serves a _____ pizza _____.

Thus the ultimate to which we can trim a *who*-group is a single word; then it becomes just an ordinary noun modifier, and we shift it to the normal noun-modifier position: just

[28]b_____ the noun. Try it with these sentences. Rewrite each sentence, trimmed, in the blank:

[29]‡The couple who were childless would adopt only a child who was normal.

_____

_____

[30]‡The plastic compounds which are quick-drying usually consist of an adhesive which is mixed with wood powder.

PRACTICING COMBINING

You have discovered that the experienced writer combines ideas in a way that not only will (1) give the reader his exact meaning but also will (2) not waste words and (3) not sound monotonous. Using all the ways you have learned in this and previous modules, combine the following sets of ideas as best you can to achieve these three goals of effective writing. Each of these sets can be made into a single sentence—in fact, each item originally was a single sentence. If trying to build one sentence becomes too complicated, settle for two. Most important, be sure your version has all the same meaning as the original. The first item is done for you as an example:

Paula Brassard announced a new rule.
Paula did this when she was elected Student Senate president.
The new rule allows seniors to park in the new faculty lot.
The lot is being built behind Alumni Hall.

First, pick a sentence containing what seems to be the basic or most important idea. Then work in the essential parts of the other sentences. In this case the writer decided that *Paula Brassard announced a new rule* was the most important idea:

~~Paula did this~~ when ~~she was~~ elected Student Senate president,

Paula Brassard announced a new rule,

~~The new rule~~ [which] allows seniors to park in the new faculty lot,

~~The lot is~~ being built behind Alumni Hall.

> *When elected Student Senate president*, Paula Brassard announced a new rule *which allows seniors to park in the new faculty lot being built behind Alumni Hall.*

Notice that in combining the original four sentences into one we have (1) achieved the exact meaning by putting the main idea in the main clause and reducing the other ideas to subgroups (italicized) and (2) dropped nine words of deadwood. What about our third goal, variety—avoidance of monotony? We might have combined the original four ideas in other ways, such as

> Paula Brassard, *who had just been elected Student Senate president*, announced a new rule *which allows seniors to park in the new faculty lot which is being built behind Alumni Hall.*

But which version sounds better because of its variety, the first or the second? (If you are not sure, examine the first word of each italicized subgroup in both versions.) [31] _____
Now, combine the following:

[32]According to Patrick Howley, the course in sensitivity training is already filled.

Patrick Howley is dean of the School of Education.
The course is beginning next week.

According _____, d_____

_____, the course _____

b_____ing _____ is _____.

³³Two New Hampshire policemen saw a flying saucer.
It was hovering and pulsating above them.
They were astounded.

_____

_____

_____

³⁴‡Now on a separate paper, improve this paragraph by combining its ideas as best you can—into as few as six sentences, if you are astute enough:

SELECTION C

TV soap operas often have an emotional effect on their audience. This effect is unintended. Once a CBS soap-opera actress wanted to leave her show. She had played the same heroine for several years. The actress's name was Teal Ames. The show was "The Edge of Night." The producers knew they could not replace her face. Her face was beloved. So they decided to kill her character off. They wrote an episode in which the heroine was crushed to death. She was saving her daughter from the wheels of a truck. This truck was onrushing. While this episode was still on the air, CBS received hundreds of phone calls and telegrams. They were from viewers. The viewers were grieving. They objected to the heroine's death. CBS had to show Miss Ames alive again on the next day's program.

— *Adapted from* The National Enquirer
(October 22, 1974), p. 8

Let us pause here and review. So far we have learned to trim wordy sentences by

A. Dropping a needlessly repeated subject in an *and*-link sentence, as in

Pat likes her Volkswagen, and ~~she~~ takes good care of it.

B. Dropping unneeded parts of an *if*-group, as in
~~While I was~~ walking along the shore, I spotted a strange-looking boat in the fog.
~~After he was~~ defeated in his reelection bid, Senator Claghorn retired to his Georgia plantation.

(But remember—you can drop a subject only if both subjects are the same person or thing:

~~While~~ (I) ~~was~~ walking . . . , (I) spotted . . .
~~After~~ (he) ~~was~~ defeated . . . , (Senator Claghorn) retired . . .)

C. Dropping unneeded parts of a *who*-group, as in

Students ~~who are~~ failing more than one major subject will be put on probation.
Lois Lane, ~~who is~~ Superman's girl friend, despises Clark Kent.
The widow, ~~who was~~ disconsolate, contemplated suicide. (This becomes
The disconsolate widow contemplated suicide.)

For each item below, write an original sentence using the subgroup mentioned. Circle that group in the sentence:

35‡Beginning with an *-ing*-group:

_____

_____

36‡Beginning with an *-en*-group:

_____

_____

37‡Containing a trimmed *who*-group:

_____

_____

38‡Containing a trimmed *if*-group:

_____

_____

39‡Containing any two of the subgroups mentioned in 35–38:

_____

_____

40‡Write an original *and*-link sentence with the second clause trimmed:

_____

_____

Now take a paragraph (or several consecutive paragraphs) totaling about 150 words from a paper you wrote earlier in the semester. On a separate paper rewrite the paragraph(s), trimming all deadwood and combining ideas effectively. Use a total of at least five trimmed subgroups or clauses. Circle each trimmed group or clause. Change the wording of the original in any way you want without dropping or muddling any of its ideas. At the end of your revision, record the number of words in the original and the number in the revision. Then do whichever one of these your instructor directs:

A. Submit the original and the revision to your instructor.

B. Exchange papers with another student. Read her *revision first*. Comment on the paper as to where she might further improve her economy and variety. Then read her original to see whether she left out or changed any ideas. (Remember to praise what she did well.) Return papers. Revise your paper once more in the light of the other student's comments (if you agree with them). Submit this final revision to your instructor.

TWO LETTERS THAT CAN SAVE SEVERAL WORDS (*TO*-GROUPS)

Now you are going to meet another very common word-saving construction that you have been using since you were about four years old. Remember these *if*-links?

a. Rocco worked overtime *so that* he could pay his car loan.
b. Rocco worked overtime *in order that* he could pay his car loan.

Can you think of a single two-letter word that can replace four words in a or five in b?

[1]‡Rocco worked overtime ＿＿ pay his car loan.

In case the word is eluding you, here is another try:

Some planes from Europe still stop in Newfoundland *so that* they can refuel.

[2]Some planes from Europe still stop in Newfoundland ＿＿ refuel.

This economical little device, *to* plus any verb, has several valuable uses. Look:

The wisest thing would be *if you married her*.
The wisest thing would be *to marry her*.
Some freshmen report to the college in July *because they must make up deficiencies in math*.
Some freshmen report to the college in July *to make up deficiencies in math*.

Try these:

Some people will arrive at a sale hours before the doors open *in order that they can save a few cents on a shirt*.

[3]Some people will arrive at a sale hours before the doors open ＿＿＿＿＿＿＿＿＿

＿＿＿＿＿＿＿＿＿＿＿＿＿＿＿＿＿＿＿＿＿＿＿＿.

Paul Price bought a motorcycle *because he was concerned about saving gasoline*.

[4]Paul Price bought a motorcycle to s＿＿＿ ＿＿＿＿＿＿＿＿＿＿.
Since it is my desire that I put Esmerelda in the mood for love, I will invite her to my apartment for cocktails and a candlelight supper.

[5]‡To ＿＿＿＿＿＿＿＿＿＿＿＿＿＿＿, I ＿＿＿＿＿＿＿＿

＿＿＿＿＿＿＿＿＿＿＿＿＿＿＿＿＿＿＿＿＿＿＿＿.

It is time to name this type of subgroup. Let us call it a *to*-group and call the pair of words that begin it (such as *to put*) a *to*-link.* Here are other examples of *to*-groups:

Joe always drives under fifty *to avoid accidents.*
To ensure a gleaming, grime-free finish on your car, use Gleam-Cote wax every time.

OTHER USES OF *TO*-GROUPS

What else can *to*-groups do besides replace *if*-groups? Can you replace part of this next sentence with a *to*-group?

The architect's plan, which called for building high-rise dormitories, met with intense student opposition.

⁶The architect's plan, _____,
met with intense student opposition.

If that was difficult, try 7 below; then try 6 again.

The best place at which people should stay in Peoria is the Happyday Inn.

⁷The best place __ __ s_____ in Peoria is the Happyday Inn.

In both 6 and 7 you used *to*-groups to replace *who*-groups. Here are other examples of how *to*-groups can be used after a noun, in the same position as *who*-groups:

Fran's burning desire, *to become a teacher of the handicapped,* was finally realized.
Their attempt *to scale Mt. Slidewell* met with disaster.
The police did not appreciate Charlie's need *to express himself by breaking windows.*

Try combining these sets of ideas, using *to*-groups:

Filchney had a new scheme.
He would manufacture musical hula-hoops.
The scheme drove him bankrupt.

⁸Filchney's new scheme t__ m_____
drove him bankrupt.
The boys bought some beer. The beer was intended for drinking at the beach.

⁹‡The boys bought some beer _____ d_____.
¹⁰‡Dick Diver had an ambition. He would become a great psychiatrist. This ambition was thwarted by his involvement with money and drink.

---

* The word *to*, as you remember, can also be an *of*-link, as in *to class, to Boston.* In that case, it is followed by a noun. We will use the terms *to*-link and *to*-group only for *to* followed by a verb, as in *to speak, to consider, to strike.* *Of*-group: *I am going* to bed. *To*-group: *I am going* to cry.

Now write three original sentences, using a *to*-group in each. Circle each *to*-group. (Remember not to confuse *to*-groups with *of*-groups.)

11‡

_____

12‡

_____

_____

13‡

_____

_____

Your instructor may wish to check your work at this point.

SOMETHING-SUBSTITUTES

You have now discovered how to use nearly all the subgroups that will let you write logical sentences with economy and variety. There is just one more major use of subgroups to learn. Consider these sentences:

a. Franklin liked *something*.
b. *Something* made Pam happy.
c. *Something* is dangerous.

Of course we want to know what the *something* is in these sentences. It may be just a simple noun, such as

Franklin liked *people*.
Music made Pam happy.
Lye is dangerous.

But what if that something cannot be expressed in a single noun? Take this set of ideas, for instance:

Pam met all her old friends for the first time in three years at her class reunion. This made Pam happy.

Can you think of any one noun (plus modifiers, if you wish) that states all of what made

1‡

Pam happy? _____ Perhaps you thought of

The class reunion made Pam happy.

But even this fails to include everything that made Pam happy. Is there a way to include all this? Yes; you can use the last type of subgroup you learned in the previous section. Can you do it without a hint?

^{2‡}

_____

_____ made Pam happy.

If you had trouble, here is some help:

³T__ m_____ _____

for _____ at _____

made Pam happy.

Yes, that super-useful subgroup, the *to*-group, can also substitute for a noun, such as *reunion*—in other words, it can slide into the *something* position in many sentences:

Franklin liked *something*.
Franklin liked *people*.
Franklin liked *to meet people at parties*.
Something is dangerous.
Lye is dangerous.
To spill lye on one's skin is dangerous.

Notice how the *to*-group can give much more information than a single noun, and how it can give that information more briefly than a separate sentence would.
Complete the sentences below with *to*-groups of your own:

^{4‡}To _____ will only get you into trouble.

^{5‡}I definitely intend to _____.

^{6‡}Frank and Charlene never expected _____.

^{7‡}It is my sworn duty _____.

Now combine each of the following sets of ideas into a single smooth sentence, using a *to*-group:

Drs. Morton and Williams planned something.
They would investigate the mating habits of the manta ray.

⁸Drs. Morton and Williams planned _____ ____

_____ ___.

I desperately want something.
It is that I find the right man.

⁹

_____

I sometimes eat in a good Japanese restaurant.
This reminds me of my days in the Orient.

¹⁰T_____ reminds me of my days
in the Orient.

One thing is the best.
You should confess everything.

¹¹‡The b_____ is for you t__ _____.

Finally, write three original sentences using *to*-groups as noun substitutes (in the *something* position). Circle each *to*-group:

12‡

_____

_____

13‡

_____

_____

14‡

_____

_____

ANOTHER FAMILIAR GROUP AS A *SOMETHING*-SUBSTITUTE

To-groups, then, can be used as noun substitutes. There are two other subgroups, one of which you have already met in another use, that can also be used as noun substitutes. Recall sentence a:

a.   Franklin liked *something*.
d.   Franklin liked *to meet people at parties*.

Can you think of a slightly different way to write d—keeping the same idea but not using a *to*-group?

¹⁵Franklin liked _____ people at parties.

If you had difficulty with that one, here is b, with a hint:

b.   *Something* made Pam happy.

   To meet all her old friends for the first time in three years at her class reunion made Pam happy.

¹⁶M_ _ _ _ _ _ all _____

_____ made Pam happy.

Now do this, with no hint:

c. *Something* is dangerous.
To spill lye on one's skin is dangerous.

$\underline{\hspace{7cm}}$ is dangerous.
^{17}

Thus in most cases you can use either a *to*-group or an *-ing*-group as a noun substitute. Both use about the same number of words, but having a choice of two kinds of subgroups

lets you give some ^{18}v_____y to your sentences. Here are some other examples of *-ing*-groups as noun substitutes:

Something reminds me of my days in the Orient.
Eating in a good Japanese restaurant reminds me of my days in the Orient.
Something will enable you to graduate in January.
Taking eighteen credits this semester will enable you to graduate in January.
I could never adjust to *something*.
I could never adjust to *working nights*.
The biggest drawback of *something* is *something*.
The biggest drawback of *living in a remote area* is *not being able to reach a doctor quickly*.

Now complete the sentences below with *-ing*-groups of your own:

^{19‡}_____ing _____ will only get you into trouble.
^{20‡}Officers Greco and Thomson discovered the perpetrators' hideout by

$\underline{\hspace{14cm}}$.

^{21‡}The National Security Council, in its report to the president, advised

$\underline{\hspace{14cm}}$.

Combine each of the following sets of ideas into a single smooth sentence, using an *ing*-group:

Fred Astaire and Ginger Rogers became famous for something. They danced together in Hollywood musicals.

^{22}Fred Astaire and Ginger Rogers became famous for _____ing

t$\underline{\hspace{13cm}}$.

Something made Brick start drinking.
He learned that his wife thought him a homosexual.

$\underline{\hspace{12cm}}$
^{23}

made Brick start drinking.

Ellison tried everything to make Audrey go out with him.
He wrote her love letters.

He sent her flowers.
He even asked her friends to put in a good word for him.

[24] Ellison tried everything to make Audrey go out with him: _____ing

_____, _____ing _____, even ____ing

_____.

The thought of something would not let Reina accept Nick's offer of something.
She might be assaulted.
Nick wanted to drive her out to a little place he knew by the lake.

[25] The thought of her b____g _____ would not let Reina

accept Nick's offer of d_____g _____

_____.

Something did not stop Ramirez from something.
Ramirez was handicapped.
Ramirez obtained a degree in engineering.

[26] _____ did not stop Ramirez

from _____.

Finally, write three original sentences using *-ing*-groups as noun substitutes. Circle each *-ing*-group:

[27]

_____

[28]

_____

[29]

_____

_____

THE LAST KIND OF SUBGROUP

Now you have discovered how to use two kinds of subgroups as noun substitutes: *to*-groups and *-ing*-groups. Here is the third kind; it is a new kind of subgroup you have not met before. Examine these sentences:

What caused the explosion? I know.

Is there a way to put these ideas together economically, so that you do not have to both ask and answer your own question? Your obvious intention in these sentences is not to ask for information but to give information, to tell us that you know something. Let us start with that.

I know *something*.

All right, what do you know? Replace the noun *something* with the thing you know. Can you do it?

[30]‡I know _____.

Here is a hint in case you had trouble:

[31]I know w _ _ _ c_____.

Can you discover how to combine the following sets of ideas?

The president did not hear *something*. What did the ambassador say?

[32]The president did not hear w_____.
Holmes was thinking of *something*. What might all these clues mean?

[33]Holmes was thinking of _____.

You have not met the word *what* among any of the links you have learned so far. Here, then, is a new kind of link that introduces a new kind of subgroup. We will, naturally, call it a *what*-link and call the subgroups it introduces *what*-groups. Here are more examples of *what*-groups. Notice how each group substitutes in the *something* place—the position of a

[34]n _ _ _:

Something puzzled the professor.
What he saw in the microscope puzzled the professor.
I asked the old man *something*.
I asked the old man *what this strange place was called*.
Fix the car with *something*.
Fix the car with *whatever you have in the tool box*.

The last sentence introduces to you a new *what*-link: [35]w _ _ _ _ _ _ _. Combine these sets of ideas, using *what*-groups:

What time is it? I can't tell.

[36]I _____ w _ _ _ t_____.
Tell me something. What do you do in this place?

[37]T_____.
Something bothers me. It is anything you do.

[38]W _ _ _ _ _ _ _____ b_____.

Now try writing original *what*-groups to replace the noun *something* in these sentences:

Something made Ramsey shudder.

39‡W_____ made Ramsey shudder.

40‡Freda did not like something.

_____

41‡Gulliver discovered something.

_____

Are there other *what*-links besides *what* and *whatever?* Yes, nearly a dozen. See how many you can discover in the sentences below:

The researchers tried to discover *something.*

42‡The researchers tried to discover h___ ___ *cancer cells form.*

43‡The researchers tried to discover w___ ___ *cancer cells form.*
Which of these attachments should I use in sewing this dress? Use *something.*

44‡Which of these attachments should I use in sewing this dress? Use

w___ ___ ___ e___ ___ ___ *attachment you want to.*
Someone will pay for this!

45‡W___ ___ e___ ___ ___ *short-sheeted me* will pay for this!

The four new *what*-links you have just discovered are 46h___ ___, w___ ___, w___ ___ ___-

___ ___ ___, and w___ ___ ___ ___ ___. Try writing an original *what*-group for each of these four links:

47‡Reverend MacDonald wondered h___ ___ _____

_____.

48‡W___ ___ _____ remained a mystery.

49‡The freshman counselor told Julie she could take w_____

_____.

50‡Go to the game with w___ ___ ___ ___ ___ _____

_____.

The complete list of *what*-links also includes seven words borrowed from the lists of *who-*

links and *if*-links you learned in "Combining Ideas." It should not be hard for you to discover them.

The stewardess forgot something.

⁵¹‡The stewardess forgot *w* ___ *had asked for more coffee.*

⁵²‡The stewardess forgot *w* _____ *passenger had asked for more coffee.* The pilot requested *something.*

⁵³‡The pilot requested *t* ____ *the passengers stop dancing in the aisles.* The passengers wondered *something.*

⁵⁴‡The passengers wondered *w* ____ *the plane would land.*

⁵⁵‡The passengers wondered *w* _____ *the plane would be diverted to.*

⁵⁶‡The passengers wondered *w* _____*r the plane would land on time.*

⁵⁷‡The passengers wondered *i* __ *the pilot knew what he was doing.*

The seven borrowed *what*-links you have discovered in sentences 51–57 are ⁵⁸w ___,

w _____h, t _____, w _____, w _____e, w _____, i__. Try writing an original *what*-group for each of these seven links:

⁵⁹‡After two days of investigation, Chief Ironside discovered w ___ _____

_____.

⁶⁰‡Make up your mind about w _____ _____

_____.

⁶¹‡The dean announced t _____ _____.

⁶²‡Even though Clarissa is nineteen, her mother still tells her w _____

_____.

⁶³‡W _____ _____ is always a problem.

⁶⁴‡For the boss, it was a question of w _____ _____

_____.

⁶⁵‡Assemblyman Miller could not determine i __ _____

_____.

Write three original sentences containing *what*-groups. (You can be sure that what you write is a *what*-group if it fits where the word *something* or *someone* would go in the sentence.) Circle each *what*-group:

66‡

_____

_____

67‡

_____

_____

68‡

_____

_____

REVIEW

It is time for a review of all the ways you have discovered in this module to achieve economy and variety through combining ideas.

A. Dropping needlessly repetitious words in an *and*-link sentence when both subjects are the same:

George and Sally are going skiing this afternoon, and ~~they are going~~ dancing tonight.

B. Dropping needlessly repetitious words from an *if*-group when the subject is the same in the *if*-group and the main clause:

When ~~you are~~ finished, you may turn in your paper and leave.

C. Dropping the *if*-link also to form an *-ing-* or *-en*-group:

~~While I was~~ walking along the shore, I spotted a strange-looking ship in the fog. ~~Because it was~~ swollen from Ali's punches, Forman's eye began to bleed.

D. Dropping a *who*-link and the verb *be* (or a verb that can be changed to include *be*) in a *who*-group:

Students ~~who are~~ failing more than one major subject will be put on probation. Our new teacher, ~~who is~~ Miss Meehan, gave us all lollipops.

The car ~~which was~~ (speeding) could not elude Dick Tracy.

E. Using a *to*-group to replace certain *if*-groups or *who*-groups:

to build
The architect's plan, ~~which called for building~~ high-rise dormitories, met with intense student opposition.

F. Using *to*-groups, *-ing*-groups, or *what*-groups as noun substitutes:

Drs. Morton and Williams planned ~~something. They would~~ ^{to} investigate the mating habits of the manta ray.

~~Something~~ (made Brick start drinking.) ^{Learning} ~~He learned~~ that his wife thought him a homosexual.

Holmes was thinking of ~~something.~~ ^w What (might) all these clues mean?

All of what you learned in this module has been aimed at enlarging the number of ways you know to combine ideas in sentences for exactness of meaning, economy, variety, and smoothness. The mastery test has two parts: combining given sets of ideas into sentences, and—as usual—writing an original paragraph. You will need some pretest practice in how to combine and trim several ideas in one sentence.

Combine each of the following sets of ideas into a single smooth sentence with dead-wood trimmed; be sure to retain the full meaning of the original sentences. Use all the skills you have learned in this and previous modules, but use your general knowledge of English and your common sense as well. The first few are partly done to help you. (If after several tries you cannot put an item into one sentence, then settle for two.)

Arthur Walters defeated Charles Beauregard in the Louisiana election.
Walters was the Democratic nominee.
Beauregard was an independent challenger.
The defeat was decisive.
The election was for governor.

1‡*Step 1:* Arthur Walters, who was _____

defeated Charles Beauregard, who was _____

_____, in the Louisiana election, which was for _____.
The defeat was decisive.

2‡*Step 2:* Arthur Walters, the _____,

d _ _ _ _ _ _ _ _ ly defeated Charles Beauregard, an _____

_____, in the Louisiana election for _____.

The president was angered by the steel industry's huge price increase.
He signed the bill.
This bill ordered a steel price rollback.

3‡*Step 1:* The president, who _____

_____, signed _____ which o_____

_____.

4‡*Step 2:* The president, a _ _ _ _ _ ed _____

_____, signed _____ o __ __ __ __ ing

_____.

For the remaining sentences, do step 1 mentally or on scrap paper:

5‡The Senate approved a bill.
The bill is designed to stop all pollution of the waterways by 1985.
The bill is strict and far-reaching.
The vote was 86-0.

By a v_____, the Senate approved a

_____ bill d_____

_____.

6‡Professor Aristotle Archimedes has been named the winner of the Nobel Physics Prize.
He is a scientist. He was born in Greece.
He earned the prize for discovering something.
He can take photographs in three dimensions.

_____

_____

_____

7‡Odysseus and his men were held prisoner by the cyclops. The cyclops was a one-eyed giant.
Then they sharpened the end of a huge log.
They did this in order that they could put his eye out and then they could escape.

_____

_____

_____

_____

MASTERY TEST

Part I. Combine each of the following sets of ideas into one smooth sentence trimmed of deadwood. (Avoid the use of *and* wherever possible.) If you cannot do an item in one sentence, settle for two. Do not be afraid to change wording:

INTRODUCTION AND TRIMMING *AND*-LINK SENTENCES

[4]Yes. It contains the same information as letter A.

[5]The writer overuses the same structure. There are six subgroups beginning with *which*.

[6]Which are

[7]and, but, or, nor, yet.

[8]b

[9]She

[10]In sentence a, a different person is doing the action in each part: *Pat* is the subject of the first part; *Donna* the subject of the second.

[11]same

[12]Chem and physics are hard for me but arouse my interest.

[14]The comma

[15]Leontyne Price made her Metropolitan Opera debut in the early 1960s and has been a star there ever since.

[16]Different subjects (*administrators* and *students*)

[19]The verb *wrote* can be cut, since it is the same in each half of the sentence.

[20]Webster wrote the best-known American dictionary and a famous spelling book as well.

[21]George and Sally are going skiing this afternoon and dancing tonight.

[22]Poe liked to write about persons buried alive and beautiful women dying. (Note that the *also* is dropped, too.)

TRIMMING *IF*-GROUPS

[1]if, when, while, until, unless, as, since, although

[2]if it is deposited in our special account

[3]When you are finished

[4]The two subjects are *money* and *it*. Since the *it* refers to money, the two subjects do refer to the same thing.

[5]Your money will earn 7.5 percent yearly if deposited in our special savings account.

[6]Is

[7]When finished, you may turn in your paper and leave.

[8]Subjects: you, you. Sentence: When in Japan, you must drive on the left side of the road.

[10]Subjects: you, you. Sentence: When in Rome, do as the Romans do.

[11]same

[12]No. The subjects are *I, boss*.

[13]No

[14]When in bed with my wife, my boss always calls me up.

[15]Subjects: you, you. Sentence: When delivering prescriptions to Mrs. Gilbert, you should not accept a check from her.

[16]Different subjects: they (referring to the twins) and father.

[19]No

TRIMMING TO A NEW KIND OF GROUP

[1]While strolling along the shore, . . .

[2]Strolling along the shore, . . .

[3]Running for president in 1948, . . .

[4]Driving long distances on the freeways, . . .

[5]Waiting for Bill in front of the liquor store, . . .

[6]The *if*-link can be dropped; the answer sentence will not be given.

[7]The *if*-link can be dropped; the answer sentence will not be given.

[8]The *if*-link cannot be dropped. *Bringing a guest* would mean the opposite of *Unless (you are) bringing a guest.*

[9]*-Ing*

[10]*-ing-*

[11]*-ing-*

¹²Fishing off Cuba, . . .

¹³Trying to avoid prosecution, . . .

¹⁴Attempting to score from third base, . . .

¹⁵Otherwise the word *Hardwicke* would disappear from the sentence, and we would not know whom we were talking about.

¹⁶Same answer as sentence 14

¹⁷Planning a campus demonstration, the Human Rights Club invited . . .

¹⁸who, which, that

¹⁹(~~who are~~ failing more than one major subject.) Trimmed this becomes: Students failing more than one major subject will . . .

²⁰FM stations playing rock music have been . . .

²¹. . . to control traffic heading for the stadium.

²²which is nearing its goal of $10 million

²³nearing its goal of $10 million

²⁴which is trying to recruit more college graduates

²⁷a well-known science-fiction writer

²⁸the site of Washington's First Inaugural Address.

³⁰ *Step 1:* Vicki, who is the new president of the Student Government, defeated... *Step 2:* Vicki, the new president of the Student Government, defeated...

³¹(One possibility) *Step 1:* Parsonville, which is the county seat, is . . . *Step 2,* the final answer, will not be given.

³³Are, is, was

³⁴Yes

³⁵Be

³⁶a: Uncle Jed, a millionaire oil-well owner, . . .

³⁷No (there is no part of the verb *be* in the *if*-group)

³⁸Walking down the lane, I saw . . .

³⁹As they were conferring through the night, the Democratic leaders moved . . .

TRIMMING TO -*EN*-GROUPS

¹Taking Blake into custody, . . .

²Taken into custody by the policeman, Blake . . .

³Lionel, driving Bonnie home every day, had . . .

⁴Bonnie, driven home by Lionel every day, realized . . .

⁵The soldiers left their comrade, frozen to death, in the snow.

⁶The Dolphins, beaten by the Vikings, lost . . .

⁷Swollen from Ali's punches, Forman's . . .

⁸Written in great haste, his letter contained . . .

¹¹Written in great haste, his letter contained . . .

¹⁹Sentence c

²⁰After he graduated

²¹Drinking the poisoned wine, Gertrude . . .

²²Having drunk the poisoned wine, Gertrude . . .

²³The car ~~that was~~ speeding could not elude Dick Tracy.

²⁴One (*speeding*)

²⁵The speeding car could not elude Dick Tracy.

²⁶The embarrassed boy blushed deeply.

²⁸before

³¹Most people would pick the first. In the second all three subgroups are *who*-groups (who had just been elected student president; which allows seniors to park in the new faculty lot; which is being built behind Alumni Hall).

³²According to Patrick Howley, dean of the School of Education, the course in sensitivity training beginning next week is already filled.

³³Two astounded New Hampshire policemen saw a flying saucer hovering and pulsating above them. *Or* Two New Hampshire policemen, seeing a flying saucer hovering and pulsating above them, were astounded. (There are still other acceptable versions.)

TWO LETTERS THAT CAN SAVE SEVERAL WORDS

[2]to

[3]to save a few cents on a shirt.

[4]to save gasoline.

[6]to build high-rise dormitories

[7]to stay

[8]to manufacture musical hula-hoops

SOMETHING SUBSTITUTES

[3]To meet all her old friends for the first time in three years at her class reunion made Pam happy.

[8]to investigate the mating habits of the manta ray.

[9]I desperately want to find the right man.

[10]To eat [sometimes] in a good Japanese restaurant

[15]meeting

[16]Meeting all her old friends for the first time in three years at her class reunion made Pam happy.

[17]Spilling lye on one's skin is dangerous.

[18]variety

[22]dancing together in Hollywood musicals.

[23]Learning that his wife thought him a homosexual

[31]what caused the explosion.

[32]what the ambassador said.

[33]what all those clues might mean.

[34]noun

[35]whatever

[36]I can't tell what time it is.

[37]Tell me what you do in this place.

[38]Whatever you do bothers me.

[46]how, why, whichever, whoever

[58]who, which, that, when, where, whether, if

MODULE 10

ECONOMY AND CLARITY

Previous modules required: Clear Writing: The First Steps (2)*—Word Choice (5)*
—Vocabulary Skills (6)*—Basic Sentence Parts (7)*—Combining Ideas (8)*

INTRODUCTION

This module continues the central idea of "Economy and Variety": less is more. If you have not done that module, read its first pages now; then return to this page.

In 1974 the National Council of Teachers of English began a "Doublespeak Award"—really a booby prize for the most confusing public statements of the year. Let us look at one of them, a statement by a presidential spokesman, in response to a question that called for a *yes* or *no* answer:

> *I would feel that most of the conversations that took place in those areas of the White House that did have the recording system would, in almost their entirety, be in existence, but the special prosecutor, the court, and, I think, the American people are sufficiently familiar with the recording system to know where the recording devices existed and to know the situation in terms of the recording process, but I feel, although the process has not been undertaken yet in preparation of the material to abide by the court decision, really, what the answer to that question is.*

1‡

What did he say? _____
If you had trouble answering, so did everyone else. Why? Is there any word in that para-

2

graph whose meaning you are not fairly sure of? _____ Then why was the statement singled out for its lack of clarity? Because it actually says nothing. (Boiled down, it says "I feel . . . what the answer to that question is," but the speaker does not tell us the answer.) Yet because the spokesman used a flood of big, often vague words (*entirety, existence, situation, process,* etc.), many listeners undoubtedly *thought* they heard an answer, and a few may have felt that the speaker was very smart because he could speak so eloquently and that they were very stupid because they did not understand him. People such as government and business officials and educators have often been accused of deliberately using such language to sound very intelligent or informative while actually having nothing to say or even trying to conceal the truth. This language has been given such names as gobbledygook, bureaucratese, linguistic pollution, marshmallow prose, and unlanguage. Since we cannot understand it, it is poor English. Some students, however, try to write this way, thinking it is the "educated" way to write.

As you have seen if you have done the modules "Clear Writing: the First Steps," "Word Choice," and "Economy and Variety," a good writer speaks briefly and directly (though not childishly), using not necessarily the biggest but the most exact words that his readers will understand. Sir Winston Churchill was a government leader who might have been tempted to use bureaucratese, but he was also a Nobel Prize winner for the excellence of his historical writing. Listen to him:

> *The question which we must ask ourselves is not whether we like or do not like what is going on, but what we are going to do about it. In war it is not always possible to have everything go exactly as one likes. In working with allies it sometimes happens that they develop opinions of their own.*
> — A Churchill Reader *(Boston: Houghton Mifflin, 1954), p. 207*

3

What big, vague words do you find? _____ Is this passage clear and direct?

Most people would say *yes.* Yet Churchill does not resort to slang or to childish words and sentences to bring across his meaning. As he himself said elsewhere:

Short words are best and the old words when short are best of all.

In Parliament he constantly twitted the opposing party for using bureaucratese expressions like *The lower income group* for *the poor, arresting increases in personal income* for *freezing wages,* and *accommodation unit* for *home.* He deplored unlanguage like *It is also important to bear in mind the following considerations* . . . (Can you reduce this to two or three words?

Try it: _____) You may not win a Nobel Prize if you write as clearly as Churchill, but people will understand you. And that is the first goal of good writing.

THE BASIC RULE

You will find no grammatical concepts to master in this module. Only one rule prevails: common sense. Let us start by trying to make plain adult English out of most of the selection on page 292. First, can you think of words that will simplify and clarify "The process has not been undertaken yet in preparation of the

material"? Try: "We have not [1]st _ _ _ _ _ _ p _ _ _ _ _ _ ing the _ _ _ _ _ _ _ _ ." Next, try "the American people are sufficiently familiar with the recording system to know where the recording devices existed." Is the speaker saying the same thing twice here? What is the difference between "to be familiar with" and "to know"? Why not eliminate one of them? Try it: "the American people know

[2]wh _ _ _ _ the r _ _ _ _ _ _ _ _ _ d _ _ _ _ _ _ _ e _ _ _ _ _ _ _ ." Now we come to "know the situation in terms of the recording devices." What does this mean? Here we must guess at what the speaker meant; let us assume he meant something like "know how the recording devices worked." In fact, why not say just "recorders" instead of "recording devices"?

What about the beginning? Why "I *would* feel . . ."? Did he feel or not? Throw out the *would.* Try tackling "conversations that took place in those areas of the White House that did have the recording system." This can be reduced from seventeen to eleven or twelve words by merely dropping several deadwood words and changing one or two others. Can

you do it? "Conversations [3]i _ _____ _____ _____

W_____ H_____ th_____."
Finally, simplify "would, almost in their entirety, be in existence." This is a hard one. If you can boil these eight words down to three, without hints, you are approaching expert status

already: [4]"_____ _____ _____ "

Look at what you have done. Here is your rewritten version (with one or two more small changes):

I feel that most of the conversations in areas of the White House that had the recording system are nearly complete; but the special prosecutor, the court, and,

*I think, the American people, know where the recorders were and how they worked;
but although we have not yet started to prepare the material as the court ordered . . .*

Do you now understand better what the spokesman was (apparently) saying? Besides
making this passage clearer, what else have we done? There were 92 words in the same part
of the original. What portion do you think we cut in the revision?

[5]☐ 1/8   ☐ 1/5   ☐ 1/4   ☐ 3/8

It is only fair to this presidential spokesman to point out that he was speaking, not
writing; if he had been writing, of course, he would have gone over his statement and
improved it—but probably not as well as we did, for verbose (wordy) language is often
habitual with persons in such positions. For example, during the Watergate hearings, several
prominent men testifying kept saying ". . . at this point in time . . . ," apparently by habit,
even after the newspapers had made a joke out of it. (Which two words do you think are

[6]

deadwood in "at this point in time"? _____ _____ Some of your own
textbooks may be evidence that unlanguage comes in written as well as oral form.

The following sentences are from actual freshman papers. Try to determine what each
writer meant; then, if you can, write in the blank a clear version of the italicized sections:

[7]He was the lonely one and needed someone *to occupy this necessity.* _____

_____

[8]When I *make the distance between the speedway and me minimal . . .* _____

_____

[9]My room at home is my castle. My [A]*subjects are congruent with my decisions
pertaining to my domain* and [B]*corroborate me in extracting any undesirables.*

[9A]
_____

[9B]
_____

[10]Descending from the bus, a cluster of teenagers *advanced themselves into
their accommodation* for the next three days, known as Rocking Horse Ranch.

_____

You should not worry if you could not complete the blanks. Just the fact that you had trouble
shows that you have discovered the point of this section: Overwritten sentences, instead of
impressing the reader, merely confuse him.

IF YOU HAD TO PAY

A wise old teacher once said that the best way to teach
economy in writing would be to have students communicate entirely by telegram, where they would have
to pay for every word. If your writing tends to wordi-
ness, then, try imagining that you are being charged
a nickel a word. For instance, here are some student
sentences that contain several words of deadwood. The

parentheses contain the amount the students would have saved, at a nickel a word, if they had written the same idea in the fewest possible words. Rewrite each idea to come as close as you can to that maximum saving. You are free to change or rearrange words as necessary. The first sentence is done for you as an example:

> As a small child I was allowed outside to play only during the hours from eight A.M. to eleven in the morning and from four P.M. to six in the afternoon. [Save 45¢—nine words.]

> *As a small child I was allowed outside to play only from eight to eleven a.m. and four to six p.m.*

(Do you see why *during the hours* can be dropped? Do *eight to eleven A.M.* and *four to six P.M.* obviously refer to hours? _____ Why can *in the morning* and *in the evening* be dropped? _____)

[3]My mother always seemed to avoid the mention of years—in effect, her exact age. [Save 20¢—four words.] _____

[4]During the past four years I have spent most of my time in a dental office. That may sound strange at first, but I am a dental assistant, which is why I spend most of my time at the dentist's. [Save 60¢—twelve words.]

_____

_____

[5]Throughout my life I have not always felt this way about my mother. [Save 15¢—three words.]

_____

[6][The writer previously identified herself as female.] When I was a little girl of about nine years old, I would pretend that I was a prisoner in a big house. [Save 30¢—six words.]

_____

Do you know the name for this kind of deadwood—needless repetition of words or ideas?

It is [7]r __ d __ __ d __ __ cy. What are the rules for trimming redundancy and other deadwood from sentences? Remember that the only rule is common sense. Common sense says: Look for two words or groups that say the same thing, and drop one; drop words or groups that merely state the obvious; drop "filler" words and groups that actually say nothing; find single words that can replace windy word strings. Here are more examples:

> You will notice various types of tropical flowers such as jerbriers and anthuriums, ~~just to name a few.~~ [Is there any difference between *such as* and *to name a few?*]

> Whenever I moved, my muscles ached ~~with pain.~~ [What else could they ache with?]

My research paper included a bibliography ~~of my sources of information for this paper~~. [What does *bibliography* mean?]

, which
The produce and meat departments share the same corner, ~~This particular~~
enough
~~corner~~ is large, ~~there is sufficient space~~ for both departments' cases.

(Here is a hint for situations like the one in the last example. Notice that the first sentence ends with *corner* and the next sentence uses the same word near the beginning. When you see the same word at the end of one sentence and near the beginning of the next, you can often combine the sentences with a *who*-link, dropping two or three words of deadwood. Review pages 220–225 of "Combining Ideas" if you are unsure of how to do this.)

ignored.
, which he ~~paid no attention to.~~
It was a nightmare when he heard the noise, ~~He paid no attention to the noise.~~

Notice the two-step thinking above. First the writer changes the sentence with the redundant second *noise* to a *who*-group (*which he paid no attention to*); then he thinks of a single word to replace *paid no attention to*. As you see, a good recall vocabulary helps in trimming deadwood. Now you try your common sense on these:

⁸My eyes are less than perfect when it comes to my vision. [Cut half the

sentence.] _____
⁹There were indescribable noises made by the washing machine, which occurred because the machine was unbalanced. [Cut half the sentence down to a single modifier.]

_____

_____

¹⁰‡Upon her arrival, she was very happy to see that we had been able to carry on and do all the things she used to do, in her absence.

_____

¹¹‡To some people, facing responsibility is a very difficult thing for them to do.

_____

¹²‡Ever since I can remember, my parents have always stressed the point about my learning how to face up to responsibility. [Cut at three separate places.]

_____

_____

This last sentence calls our attention to some *little* words which can be as annoyingly unnecessary as longer words and groups. Examine the following expressions:

[13]face up to reality   [16]mop up the floor

[14]meet up with a mugger   [17]where it was at

[15]fill up the tub   [18]return back soon

Which one or two little words are deadwood in each item? Cross every one out. Note particularly that little intruder, *up;* it has crept into dozens of our expressions. Sometimes it is there for meaning, sometimes for emphasis; often, however, it is just deadwood, as in the expressions above. In the following, judge whether *up* is needed for meaning or just redundant. If the sentence means just what you want it to without *up,* then *up* is deadwood; cross it out:

[19]Give up, or die!   [22]Wrap up that package as a gift.

[20]Sit up; look alive!   [23]The flying saucer rose up into the sky.

[21]Lift up the lid.   [24]Can you add up these figures?

There are quite a few common expressions that most people fail to realize are deadwood. Find such an expression in each of the following sentences; cross it out, and in the margin write a briefer substitute if necessary:

[25]Because of the fact that he no longer loved Avis, Chig decided to break their engagement.

[26]It is time for each and every one of us to protest against rises in tuition.

[27]In this modern day and age, adults are entitled to sexual freedom.

[28]In my opinion, I think *The Godfather* was boring.

[29]‡I arrived at the bus stop panting, due to the fact that I was out of breath.

[30]‡At this point in time we cannot tell the direction our nation will take.

[31]‡I was faced with no other alternative but to leave school.

Notice particularly the expressions *because of the fact that* and *due to the fact that.* If there were such a word as *deadest,* it would describe them perfectly. What do they do (besides

take up space) that the single word [32]b _ _ _ _ _ _ does not do as well?

Let us examine other common cases of deadwood.

A.   Thousands of students have written papers that begin like this:

In the novel *The Grapes of Wrath* it shows the plight of the farmers . . .

[33]‡

What two two-letter words can be dropped? _____ _____ (Hint:

[34]

What does *it* stand for? _____ Does the word it stands for appear elsewhere in

[35]

the sentence? _____ Then something is being said twice.)

B.   What do you see double in the following sentence? Cross out what should not be there:

[36]‡Avis said that if Chig went to law school that she would return his ring.

(If you have trouble with this, just circle the *if*-group [*if Chig went to law school*] and you will easily see what must go.)

  C. Which two words in each of the following are redundant? Cross them out:

    [37]‡The flying saucer had flashing red lights and was bright green in color.
    [38]‡After giving up his diet, Carl went up to 235 pounds in weight.

(Can green be anything but a color? Can pounds be anything but weight? Then do we need the words after *green* and *pounds*?)

  D. Thousands of students have also written papers including statements like these:

    In this paper I am going to write about the three reasons why Chig left Avis. To start with, I feel the most important reason is . . .

This writer has wasted half his words. What did he *not* have to tell the reader? Write only the facts of the original statement; you should be able to do it in ten words:

    [39]C＿＿＿ l＿＿＿ A＿＿＿ for ＿＿＿＿＿ r＿＿＿＿＿＿s. The

    m＿＿＿ i＿＿＿＿＿＿＿＿＿ is . . .

(Did he have to say that he was writing a paper? That he was going to write about something? That he felt what he was saying? That the reason he started with was the one he was going to start with? There is no need to keep telling the reader that you are writing a paper, or that you *feel* this or *think* that. It is usually clear that the thoughts and opinions are yours.)

  E. What redundancy has crept into the following sentence? Cross it out:

    [40]I am referring to a friend with whom I work with.

(How did the writer come up with this? There are two ways to end the sentence: *a friend with whom I work*, or *a friend whom I work with*. The writer started one way, forgot, and finished the other way.)

  F. Drop two deadwood words while combining these two sentences into one smooth one. Use the blank below:

    [41]The bus turned over and landed in a snowbank. This was because it had hit an icy patch on the road.

    ＿＿＿＿＿＿＿＿＿＿＿＿＿＿＿＿＿＿＿＿＿＿＿＿＿＿＿

    ＿＿＿＿＿＿＿＿＿＿＿＿＿＿＿＿＿＿＿＿＿＿＿＿＿＿＿

(Be suspicious when you see a sentence beginning with *This was because, This happened because,* or similar words. Usually you can drop the words before *because* and join the sentence to the one before it, as you just did above.)

  Now see how well you can do with the items below. They contain all kinds of deadwood. Follow A or B, as your instructor directs.

A. Rewrite the sentences, changing and/or rearranging words as necessary to make the sentences as brief as you can. (Of course, do not change the *meaning*.)

B. Working in groups of two to four arranged by your instructor, follow the directions for A.

42‡Men and women in the United States are marrying younger. This seems to be occurring because of women's liberation.

_____

_____

43‡Some young men never meet up with the right girl.

_____

44‡The papers were marked "Top Secret." The phrase "Top Secret" indicates something which has an extraordinary amount of value.

_____

_____

45‡Primitive tribes often held fertility rites in the spring. This was due to the fact that they recognized spring as the time of rebirth and regeneration.

_____

_____

46‡Washington declined to run for a third term as president. He did this because he did not believe that one man should rule for too long a time.

_____

_____

47‡Joe returned the book back to the library by 2 P.M. yesterday afternoon due to the fact that he wanted to take out another book to read. This book was a biography telling the life story of General Patton.

_____

_____

_____

48‡At the time when I will obtain my diploma and graduate from Dingaling Junior College after two years, I will then transfer over to being a student at a four-year senior college. At that institution I will complete my education and obtain a full four-year B.A. degree.

_____

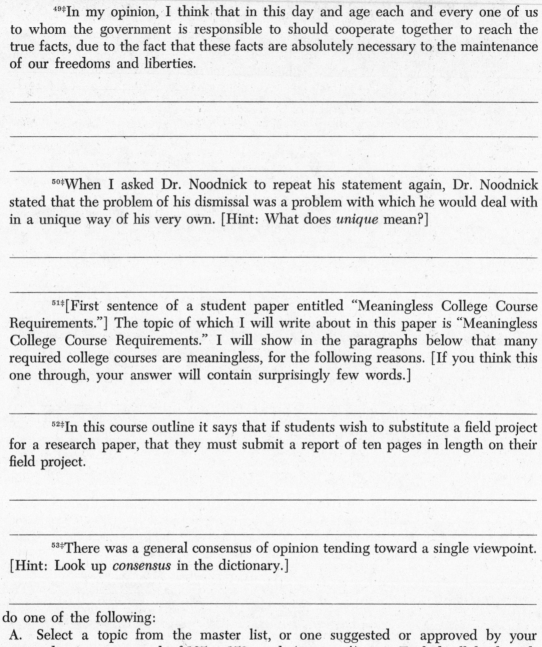

49‡In my opinion, I think that in this day and age each and every one of us to whom the government is responsible to should cooperate together to reach the true facts, due to the fact that these facts are absolutely necessary to the maintenance of our freedoms and liberties.

50‡When I asked Dr. Noodnick to repeat his statement again, Dr. Noodnick stated that the problem of his dismissal was a problem with which he would deal with in a unique way of his very own. [Hint: What does *unique* mean?]

51‡[First sentence of a student paper entitled "Meaningless College Course Requirements."] The topic of which I will write about in this paper is "Meaningless College Course Requirements." I will show in the paragraphs below that many required college courses are meaningless, for the following reasons. [If you think this one through, your answer will contain surprisingly few words.]

52‡In this course outline it says that if students wish to substitute a field project for a research paper, that they must submit a report of ten pages in length on their field project.

53‡There was a general consensus of opinion tending toward a single viewpoint. [Hint: Look up *consensus* in the dictionary.]

Now do one of the following:

A. Select a topic from the master list, or one suggested or approved by your instructor, and write a paragraph of 125 to 150 words (no more!) on it. Exclude all deadwood.

B. Rewrite a previous paper in which your instructor has found you guilty of much deadwood. Make it as concise as possible. (If you do not know what *concise* means, you can probably guess.)

When finished with A or B, do whichever of these your instructor directs:

C. Exchange papers with another student for mutual evaluation; then revise your own paper.

D. In a group of four or five, constructively discuss and evaluate the papers of all or several group members; then revise your own paper.

E. Submit the paper to your instructor.

FINDING THE ONE RIGHT WORD

So far you have learned to make your sentences briefer and clearer by:

   A.   Replacing long, abstract expressions with shorter, more exact words: *It has been brought to our consideration* becomes *We have learned.*

   B.   Dropping redundant words: *Repeat that again* becomes *Repeat that.*

Other kinds of deadwood can be similarly eliminated. Think about this sentence:

Readjusting my daily schedule was one of the most difficult things which I had to do.

How can we shorten this? Can you think of *one* word that means the same as a string of six words in the sentence? What do we call a thing which we have to do?

¹Readjusting my daily schedule was one of the most difficult _ _ _ s.

There is another word which might be even better: ²t_ _ _ _ s. If you have done "Word Choice" and "Vocabulary Skills," do you notice that we are actually just reviewing what you have learned in those modules? A strong recall vocabulary makes your writing not only exact but also concise.

Below is more practice. Do it individually or with a group, as your instructor directs. Again, there are no rules; just look for a string of words that can be replaced by one or two words. Some help is given in the first five sentences:

Of the two dresses I have decided that I like the red one better.

³Of the two dresses I find the red one pr_ _ _ _ _ able.

Now shorten this sentence still further:

⁴Of the two dresses I pr_ _ _ _ _ the red one.

(Notice that sometimes even the right word can appear in a lengthy form. *Prefer* is the right word, but the writer of the middle sentence above could not think of the right form and wrote *find preferable.* In the next few sentences you will find some other words in a lengthy form.)

Juliet and I must make a decision within a few hours on whether we should be united in holy wedlock.

⁵Juliet and I must _ _ _ _ _ _ _ within a few hours whether t_

m_ _ _ _ _ .

I have reached the conclusion that the men who fly our planes need further training in finding their way from one place to another.

⁶‡I have _ _ _ _ _ _ _ that our _ _ _ _ _ _ _ need further training in

n_ _ _ _ _ _ _ ing.

I saw my father stumble out of the bar and walk unsteadily down the alley, wavering from side to side.

⁷‡I saw my father stumble out of the bar and s_____ down the alley.
Only a small number of men survived the wreck.

⁸‡_____ men survived the wreck.
⁹‡I did not feel very well at all.

_____ _____ _____.

¹⁰‡The accident happened as I was getting close to the place where Route 27 crosses Pershing Boulevard.

_____

_____

¹¹Grubley swallowed his food very quickly and in very large mouthfuls.

_____

¹²‡Dr. Bonehenge performed an operation on Grubley to take out something which had gotten struck down in his throat.

_____

_____

_____

¹³‡Grubley did not pay attention to the instruction on the medicine bottle, which told him the amount of the medicine he was supposed to take.

_____

_____

SENDING IN A SUBSTITUTE

Can you find another kind of deadwood in this paragraph?

I will never forget Mr. Tilde, my instructor in Spanish. Mr. Tilde made Spanish a delight, because Mr. Tilde could teach Spanish better than anyone else. Mr. Tilde knew everything about Spanish, and Mr. Tilde made Spanish my favorite subject.

1

Which two nouns are used five times each? _____ _____ In "Basic Sentence Parts" you learned of a type of noun that can be substituted for other nouns to

avoid their repetition. Some of them are ²h__, s____, i__, y____, th____. (If you have forgotten, review page 149 of "Basic Sentence Parts.") Use words of this kind to improve the above paragraph:

³I will never forget Mr. Tilde, my instructor in Spanish. _____ made

Spanish a delight, because _____ could teach _____ better than anyone else. _____ knew everything about _____, and _____ made _____ my favorite subject.

Though they may not reduce the word count, these small substitute nouns reduce the bulk of a sentence and make it much less awkward and monotonous.

ONCE IS ENOUGH

So far we have focused on redundancy of words, mostly within a single sentence. Is there another kind of redundancy? Read this freshman paper, which you will see is excellent in vocabulary and grammar. How would you rate it on economy? Underline any redundancy you spot, and in the margin write the sentence number of the idea it needlessly repeats:‡

Why Are Americans Turning to Smaller Cars?

(1) The past few months have forced the automotive industry through profound changes that will affect the kinds of cars Americans drive. (2) Sales of compact and subcompact cars are surpassing those of large models for the first time in history. (3) The car of tomorrow will be smaller and more standardized.

(4) Many of today's new-car buyers are seriously considering the advantages of small cars and wondering whether they have been driving cars that are bigger than necessary.

(5) America's long romance with the automobile has ended. (6) Car owners have come to regard their automobiles as they would their appliances—they should quietly and efficiently do their job. (7) They no longer want a car that is a projection of their inner self and personality; they want performance. (8) This new attitude is fatal to the appeal of glamorous Lincoln Continentals and Cadillacs.

(9) The fuel crisis is the most popular explanation for the dismal sales trend of standard-size autos. (10) It is true that frustrating lines at gas stations and talk of $1-a-gallon gas have turned great numbers of motorists against the larger sized cars. (11) The driver waiting on a gas line with a Buick that gives him as little as ten miles per gallon is not so sure he would really rather have another Buick.

(12) The overall sluggishness of the economy is another cause of a purchasing slowdown, especially of more expensive, large-sized cars.

(13) The shift to functional small cars has been under way for years among affluent trend setters. (14) These people can afford to buy anything they want, and they are turning to the small car.

(15) The biggest thing that is killing the big car is uncertainty. (16) People are depressed over the Middle East crisis, inflation, gasoline shortages and, in general, bad news. (17) These problems cause uncertainty as to where we stand with respect to gasoline availability.

(18) Other factors that stimulate small car sales are that families are smaller, gas is costlier and parking spaces are scarcer. (19) It also is not stylish anymore to own a big car. (20) There is the realization that a certain proportion of people are doing something else, and usually we tend to go along with what is most popular.

(21) There are good reasons why a small car may be appealing. (22) For the

price of a standard-size car without any optional accessories, you can buy a small car with automatic transmission, air conditioning, radio, and other options. (23) Your insurance company may give you a small-car discount. (24) The little car is easier to handle in tight spaces. (25) Apart from initial cost, the other most attractive saving comes in lower fuel consumption and maintenance expenditures.

(26) With rising prices in almost every corner of our lives, it is no wonder we would turn to the most economical fare, and in the car industry, it is the compact car.

4‡

How many sentences needlessly repeat an idea of a previous sentence? _____ Let us see how well you did. What does sentence 4 tell us that we do not already know or can

5

assume from sentence 2? _____ Sentences 9 and 10 introduce the crisis in the

6

supply and price of gasoline. Which other three sentences repeat this idea? _____

_____ _____ What new information or food for thought do these

7

sentences add about the supply or price of gasoline? _____ In sentence 19, the writer talks about people buying small cars because it is the trend. In which two earlier

8

sentences has he said the same thing? _____ _____ There is still more redundancy in this student's paper. On a separate sheet, rewrite this paper to eliminate all possible redundancy. (Remember that reminding the reader of the central idea at the conclusion is a desirable practice, not redundancy.) Change wording as needed.‡ When finished, do whichever of these your instructor directs:

A. Exchange papers with another student for mutual evaluation; then revise your own paper.

B. In a group of four or five, constructively discuss and evaluate the papers of all or several group members; then revise your own paper.

C. Submit the paper to your instructor.

Here is part of another student paper. Combine what you learned earlier in this module about redundancy of words with what you have just learned about redundancy of ideas; rewrite the paper on a separate sheet, removing all deadwood. Here are some hints: How often does some form of the word *change* appear in the original? *Season?* After you read sentence 2, how much need is there for sentence 1? How much is sentence 3 telling us that we do not already know from sentence 2? In fact, how much is sentence 3 telling us that is not obviously true for everyone living in four-season areas? How can sentence 4 be reduced to thirteen or even eleven words? By examining the rest of the original equally closely, you should be able to write the whole selection with surprising compactness. When finished, follow the same directions as for the previous selection:‡

(1) I love the changing seasons. (2) I see myself reflected in the seasons and rejoice in their differences. (3) It seems my senses are affected and know each change. (4) The two seasons that are my favorite are spring and autumn, and each one brings different feelings.

(5) With spring's arrival, I open up my eyes and see a brand new day with

clear blue skies and a brightly shining sun. (6) The changing colors are a lovely thing to see in autumn. . . .

[Two paragraphs of description are omitted here. The paragraph below is the conclusion.]

(7) These two seasons affect me so differently, yet each one, in its own right, seems beautiful to me. (8) Yes, I love the changing seasons because they bring beauty and change to me. (9) I don't think I could ever change living in a four-season part of the country. (10) With each change of season, my senses are either depressed or elevated, but just the change makes my own life so interesting. (11) There is so much to look forward to in life, and each season change makes my life full of emotions that reflect upon my future growth.

At this point you may be ready to complain, "But if we cut so much out of our papers, we won't reach the 300 words the instructor said we had to have!" That would be true if the instructor meant *merely* words. What instructors mean when they require 300 words, however, is 300 words *worth of ideas.* (Most instructors also dislike pinpointing a word minimum; but if they do not, the first question from the class is usually, "How many words do you want?") Here is a little analogy. Going to the supermarket to buy supper, you may find two similar-looking packages of meat in adjoining trays. One says *Chopped Beef—99¢ a pound,* the other *Round Steak Chopped—$1.50 a pound.* Being a thrifty soul, you bring home the 99¢ meat, make it into patties, and put them into the frying pan. But when they are done you find they have shrunk to half their original size and are floating in a half-pound pool of fat. The next time you buy the $1.50 meat and find almost no shrinkage.

What instructors—and all alert readers—want is 300 words of solid meat—$1.50-a-pound ideas, with little or no fat. What students often give is 300-word papers with 150 words worth of ideas—99¢-a-pound papers, which shrink to half their size when the fat is removed, as you have seen in the two selections you just revised. The module "Paragraph Development" shows you how to fill your papers with meat. Here you have discovered how to remove the fat to see how much meat you really have.

HOW MUCH IS TOO MUCH?

By now you may be saying, "But I've seen many places in published modern writing—including this textbook—where the writers could have trimmed their wordage. Why didn't they?" The answer is in the definition of redundancy: *needless* repetition. The experienced writer knows when *not* to cut also. There are three reasons for sometimes using more than a telegraphic minimum of words. Can you discover the first reason from these sentences? Think carefully of what they mean.‡

a. While dressing in the men's locker room, his wife waited impatiently for him.
b. Elmore Hoskins said when he scored his 20,000th point he would retire.
c. Roscoe felt Marjorie's thighs were a bit too fat.
d. Harvard beat Yale worse than Princeton.
e. Suzuki's appetite is smaller than her sister.
f. The court ordered the black and white children to be bused to integrated schools.
g. Dr. von Stein favors voluntary sterilization as a means of reducing people with low IQs.
h. My great-grandfather fought with Grant against Lee and Jackson and McClellan and Sherman against Beauregard.

i. There was still some hope, for the survivors had little bread.
j. When Mickey's car hit the light pole, it was badly damaged.
k. Janet invited her brother and lover to her apartment.

Have you spotted any problems in meaning in any of these sentences? If so, what is causing them?

Perhaps these questions will aid you:‡

Sentence a: Why might a number of eyebrows be raised in the locker room?

Sentence b: Has Elmore scored his 20,000th point yet?

Sentence c: If you overheard only the first four words of this sentence, would you let Roscoe take your daughter Marjorie on her first date?

Sentence d: Harvard beat Yale in one game. Which team beat which in the other?

Sentence e: What two things are being compared? What two *should* be compared?

Sentence f: Have you ever seen striped children?

Sentence g: Does Dr. von Stein expect to compete with Weight Watchers?

Sentence h: Who fought with whom against whom?

Sentence i: Is the survivors' situation bad, good, or just confusing?

Sentence j: What was damaged?

Sentence k: Is Janet indulging in a little incest?

As you have probably discovered, the writers of these sentences were a little too eager to economize on words and, by overtrimming, made their sentences [9]unc _ _ _ _ _. That is the first reason for you not to trim with a heavy hand; you may be trimming live wood with the dead, cutting out words needed to make your meaning clear. Below, you will find the eleven sentences again, with blanks for the needed words. Write in what you think is needed for clarity:

[10]While _ _ _ _ _ dressing in the men's locker room, his wife waited impatiently for him.

[11]Elmore Hoskins said th _ _ when he scored his 20,000th point he would retire.

Or

[12]Elmore Hoskins said when he scored his 20,000th point _ _ _ _ he would retire.

[13]Roscoe felt _ _ _ _ _ Marjorie's thighs were too fat.

[14]Harvard beat Yale worse than th _ _ b _ _ _ _ Princeton.

Or

[15]Harvard beat Yale worse than Princeton d _ _ _.

¹⁶Suzuki's appetite is smaller than her sister_____.

¹⁷The court ordered the black and _____ white children to be bused to integrated schools.

¹⁸Dr. von Stein favors voluntary sterilization as a means of reducing _____

_____ _____ people with low IQs.

¹⁹My great-grandfather fought with Grant against Lee and Jackson and _____ McClellan and Sherman against Beauregard.

²⁰There was still some hope, for the survivors had _____ little bread.

²¹When Mickey's car hit the light pole, _____ _____ was badly damaged.

Or

²²When Mickey's car hit the light pole, _____ _____ was badly damaged.

²³Janet invited her brother and _____ lover to her apartment.

Often, then, we repeat *a, the, that,* an *of*-link, or whatever words we need to be clear, even if the result sounds slightly repetitious. Clarity comes first, always. In communication, the ton of ideas in your mind means nothing if only an ounce of them reaches your reader's mind clearly. Put yourself inside your reader's mind and try to blot out everything except what the reader will grasp from your written words alone. Will she find only the meaning you intended?

Clarity, therefore, is the first reason we do not always use the absolute minimum of words. What is the second? Turn back to page 304, to the student paper on the changing seasons. You found that some form of *change* appears nine times and *season(s)* eight times. Even though *change* is (as a noun) briefer than such words as *movement, alternation, difference, reversal,* or (as a verb) briefer than expressions like *become colder,* the writer might prefer to use some of these to avoid saying *change change, change. . . .* Likewise, he might substitute expressions like *time of year* for some of his *seasons.*

The final reason may be harder for you to see until you take more advanced English courses. It is called style. Perhaps an examination of Lincoln's famous Gettysburg Address will illustrate. Brief as it is, the address could have been made more concise if Lincoln had wished. Why did he not cut it further? Was he just adding fat to make a minute's worth of ideas last two minutes? On the right below is the Address as he gave it; on the left is what he might have written if economy had been his only concern:

Eight-seven years ago our fathers started this nation, conceived in Liberty and dedicated to equality for all men.

Four score and seven years ago our fathers brought forth on this continent, a new nation, conceived in Liberty, and dedicated to the proposition that all men are created equal.

Now we are in a great civil war; testing whether this nation or one like

Now we are engaged in a great civil war; testing whether that nation, or

it can last long. We have rightly come to a great battlefield of that war to dedicate part of it as a cemetery for those who died here to save the nation.

But, in a larger sense, we cannot dedicate, consecrate, or hallow this ground. The brave men who fought here have done this better than we can.

. . . we highly resolve that these deaths shall have been purposeful; this nation, under God, shall revive freedom; and government of, by, and for the people shall not die.

any nation so conceived and so dedicated, can long endure. We are met on a great battlefield of that war. We have come to dedicate a portion of that field as a final resting-place for those who here gave their lives that that nation might live. It is altogether fitting and proper that we should do this.

But, in a larger sense, we cannot dedicate—we cannot consecrate—we cannot hallow—this ground. The brave men, living and dead, who struggled here have consecrated it, far above our poor power to add or detract.

. . . we here highly resolve that these dead shall not have died in vain; that this nation, under God, shall have a new birth of freedom; and that government of the people, by the people, for the people, shall not perish from the earth.

Except for the last sentence, where need for clarity made Lincoln repeat the *thats*, the version on the left is just as clear as Lincoln's. Then why did Lincoln not write the version on the left? The answer involves elements such as tone (he wanted a solemn, almost religious tone to fit the occasion), emphasis, rhythm, and climax, which are beyond the range of this course. For now, just understand that there is a quality called style, which sometimes preempts economy. Perhaps as you read Lincoln's version you were able to sense the stronger effect its style makes it have on the reader.

Thus there are reasons for not carrying economy to an extreme—just as a good butcher leaves a *little* fat on your beef to make it juicy. The Gettysburg Address itself, by the way, beautifully illustrates in another way the virtue of brevity. The featured speaker at the dedication of the national cemetery at Gettysburg, a famous orator, spoke just before Lincoln—for two hours. No one remembers what he said. Lincoln spoke for two minutes and made history.

Economy is not the first goal of writers; it comes naturally from clear thinking, careful planning, alert proofreading, and choosing the right words. It is fitting that Lincoln is our last model in this module as Churchill was our first. Both men knew that exact, understandable words, not obscured by thickets of deadwood, say things best. Now you know it, too.

MASTERY TEST

Since there were no rules but common sense in this module, there is no pretest review. If you do feel you need a review, skim through the appropriate parts of the module again.

Part I. Rewrite each of the following to eliminate redundancy and other forms of deadwood:

¹‡I know a person who is very simple. Although this person is simple he sometimes acts like an Einstein. This person is not very old. One fault that is with this

person most of the time is daydreaming. He often daydreams at the job and throughout the rest of his daily routine. There is also a good side to this fault, which is that it gives this person a quality to invent and create new ideas which later on can be materialized.

2‡It was a small town called Caribou in the state of Colorado. Situated close to the Rocky Mountains, it seemed to be positioned exactly. A narrow winding road twisted around the mountain, leading to the town itself. It was elevated on top of a small ridge of the mountains. After reading a sign with information pertaining to this town, I realized that it had been a mining town many years ago in the past.

3‡Each and every week I have no other alternative but to face up to returning two dozen ginger ale bottles back to the store for the deposit. This is due to the fact that my bank account grows very small in size after my weekly parties every Sunday and I find myself in a financially embarrassed condition.

4‡After making the ground against the tree clear, I sat down with my back against the huge green pine tree. As I sat there I started to notice for the first time the simple things in nature which I had never really noticed before.

5‡As a final note at the conclusion of my paper I would like to say that I know mentally that students do better in a small college.

6‡Love has now become an artificial feeling. What do I mean when I say it has become an artificial feeling? Artificial is defined as something which is false and this is what I think love has grown into.

7‡The situation in regard to decisions on the possible expenditure of my monetary resources is such that any decision on such expenditure must be considered with extreme caution.

8‡The student government president said that throughout the semester that he had made an investigation of the error and it was partly the man who wrote the order and partly the man who sent it out.

Combine the sentences in each of the next two items below in the best way possible for clarity, smoothness, and economy. If you have done the "Economy and Variety" module, you should not find these items difficult.

9‡There are 600 tenants in Schwab House. Schwab House is located at 11 Riverside Drive. Three-fourths of the tenants have refused the owner's offer. He offered to sell them the building as a cooperative. His price was $19 million. This was $9.5 million more than its assessed valuation. The building has seventeen stories.

10‡It had already been determined that prices and wages would be limited. The limit on prices would be an average increase of 2.5 percent. The limit on wages would be an average increase of 5.5 percent. Despite all this, the decisions revealed a flexibility. These decisions were made in the first seven days of Phase Two. The flexibility added to the confusion.

Part II. Do A or B:

A. Write a paragraph of twelve to fifteen sentences on a topic from the master list or on one suggested or approved by your instructor. The paper should be free of all redundancy and other deadwood.

B. Rewrite a paper that has been found by your instructor to contain much redundancy or other deadwood. Eliminate these weaknesses.

ANSWERS

INTRODUCTION

[2]Most people would know all the words.
[3]Most people would find none.

[4]Remember that, *or* Remember these:, *or* Remember these points:

THE BASIC RULE

[1]started preparing, material
[2]where, recording devices existed (this can be even further tightened to: where the recorders were)
[3]Conversations in areas [*or* parts] of the White House that had the recording system
[4]are nearly complete
[5]3/8
[6]*Point in* or *in time* can be dropped without losing any meaning.

[7-10]Below are possible answers. Your own may differ:
[7]be with him *or* fill the void.
[8]approach the speedway *or* come close to the speedway.
[9A]family agree with my decisions about the room
[9B]help me in removing undesirables.
[10]walked toward their lodgings (*or* rooms *or* living quarters)

IF YOU HAD TO PAY

[1]Yes
[2]They mean the same as A.M. and P.M.
[3]My mother always seemed to avoid mention of her age.
[4]During the past four years I have spent most of my time in a dental office. That may sound strange at first, but I am a dental assistant. (The twelve words that were cut merely repeat the first sentence.)
[5]I have not always felt this way about my mother. (Does *throughout my life* mean the same as *always?*)
[6]When I was about nine, I would pretend [that] I was a prisoner in a big house. (Since we know the writer is a female, *I was a little girl* is not needed. What else could she have been at that age?)
[8]My eyes are less than perfect (*or* are imperfect).
[9]There were indescribable noises made by the unbalanced washing machine. *Even better:* The unbalanced washing machine made indescribable noises.

[13]face reality
[14]meet a mugger
[15]fill the tub
[16]mop the floor
[17]where it was
[18]return soon
[19]Leave as is; *give up* means *to surrender.*
[20]Leave as is; *sit up* means *sit erect.*
[21]Lift the lid.
[22]Wrap that package as a gift.
[23]The flying saucer rose into the sky.
[24]Can you add these figures?
[25]Cross out *of the fact that.*
[26]Cross out *and every one* or *each and.*
[27]Cross out *modern day and* or *modern . . . and age.*
[28]Cross out *In my opinion* or *I think.*
[32]because
[34]The novel
[35]Yes
[39]Chig left Avis for three reasons. (You figure out the rest.)
[40]Cross out either *with.*
[41]The bus turned over and landed in a snowbank because it had hit an icy patch on the road.

FINDING THE RIGHT WORD

[1]jobs
[2]tasks
[3]preferable
[4]prefer

[5]decide; to marry
[11]Grubley devoured (*or* gobbled *or* wolfed down) his food.

SENDING IN A SUBSTITUTE; ONCE IS ENOUGH; HOW MUCH IS TOO MUCH?

[1]Spanish, Mr. Tilde
[2]he, she, it, you, they (*or* them)
[3]He, he, it, He, it, he, it
[5]Nothing. If people are buying more small cars than big ones, they must have considered the advantages of small cars and wondered whether they were driving bigger cars than necessary.
[6]16, 17, 18
[7]Nothing. *Gasoline shortages, gasoline availability,* and *gas is costlier* add nothing to what earlier sentences told us.
[8]13, 14
[9]unclear
[10]he was (otherwise it sounds as if his wife was dressing in the men's locker, since *wife* is the subject of the main clause)

[11]that
[12]that (What is the difference in meaning between versions 11 and 12?)
[13]that (otherwise it sounds as if he was feeling Marjorie's thighs)
[14]they beat (Harvard beat Yale and Princeton)
[15]did (Harvard and Princeton beat Yale)
[16]sister's (appetite)
[17]the (two separate groups)
[18]the number of
[19]with
[20]a
[21]the car
[22]the pole
[23]her (two separate people)

MODULE 11

PUNCTUATION

Previous modules required: Basic Sentence Parts (7)—Combining Ideas (8)—Economy and Variety (9)*

At places marked † in the margin, it is required or suggested that matter in the text be read aloud to the students by the instructor or by someone in the class. For students working individually, the instructor may tape the readings or make other arrangements.

INTRODUCTION

The best way for you to begin this module is to turn back to the opening page of "Clear Writing: The First Steps" (page 8) and read or reread the little story about the czar's telegram. Exactly what was it that made the czar's message—*Pardon impossible to be executed*—unclear? If the general at the front could have heard the czar *speak* his message instead of just

seeing it in print, would he have made the same tragic error? Why not? _____

_____

In ancient days, when few people could write, those who could write just put one word after another on paper without any indication of where one thought ended and the next began—even though when they spoke, these same people undoubtedly stopped after every thought and frequently paused within a thought. When writing, they probably figured that the reader's instinct would lead him to understand what they meant. Fortunately, someone eventually thought of using dots as signals to the reader. These dots (their Latin name is *puncti*) were the beginning of our punctuation.

Some people have been gifted with an excellent ear for the rhythms and pace of the English language, without any need to study. It enables them in their writing to sense where they would stop or pause if speaking and to put punctuation marks at those places. How good is your punctuation sense? Read the paragraph below to yourself and with a *pencil* put in punctuation marks where you think they should go. (After you finish, change letters to capitals where needed.)‡

SELECTION A

Why do many people develop diabetes the answer is not known but doctors suspect a precipitating factor is necessary to trigger the disease such as obesity certain drugs some types of infections and even pregnancy insulin treatments give the diabetic a good chance that the disease will not shorten his life however despite the best intentions of doctors and patients some diabetics do develop serious complications one of them is eye trouble it may begin when a diabetic notices that things look cloudy not as sharp as they used to other times eye doctors spot this disease called diabetic retinopathy before much damage has been done either way until a few years ago they could do nothing to help diabetics preserve their sight except to prescribe new more powerful glasses now they can retard the disease itself

— Adapted from "Diabetes," Today's Health
(December, 1974), p. 27

† Now the preceding paragraph will be read to you aloud. Follow the paragraph again with your eyes and your pencil as you hear it. Add or cross out punctuation where your ear tells you to make a change. To give you time to work accurately, your instructor should read the selection at least twice. After you finish, continue below.

Was it easier to determine the punctuation from silently reading the selection or from hearing it? _____ This is your most important discovery in learning punctuation. Most punctuation marks we use are attempts to represent on paper the voice changes we would have used if we had been speaking instead of writing. In listening to selection A, you heard the speaker stop or pause, and raise or drop his voice at various places. What punctuation mark do you think represents a stop? Make that mark here:

_____ You probably know that we call this a [4]p_ _ _ _ _ _. What mark represents a pause? _____ We call this mark a [6]c_ _ _ _ _. These are the two fundamental punctuation marks. Of the two, which do you think is more important? If you have completed the modules "Basic Sentence Parts" and "Combining Ideas," you

know that it is the _____. This little dot signals the end of a [8]s _ _ t _ _ ce, our main unit of thought.

STOP MARKS

When we speak, we naturally stop when we reach the end of a sentence; not only that, but we do something else with our voices. Say the sentence below aloud several times, or have a friend say it to you:

Charlie failed math.

Along with stopping, what else does your voice do when it reaches the end of that sentence? Perhaps the following diagrams will help. The line represents the rising or falling (pitch) of your voice. Check the diagram that you think shows what happens to your voice at the end of a typical sentence. [9]Does it rise, stay the same, or drop?

a. ☐ Charlie failed math.
b. ☐ Charlie failed math.
c. ☐ Charlie failed math.

At the end of most sentences you drop your voice as you stop, to show that you have completed a thought. If English is your native language, you never even think of this in your speaking; you do it naturally. The following comparison may make this clearer to you if your ear has not detected it yet. Listen to the sentences below as someone in the class or you yourself say them aloud. Can you fill in one of the dotted lines

like this: ————

to show whether the speaker's voice rises, stays the same, or drops after the word *math* in each item?

† [10][Said by Charlie's friend, who does not believe he failed]

Charlie failed math?

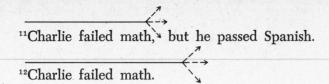

¹¹Charlie failed math, but he passed Spanish.

¹²Charlie failed math.

Do you see now how your voice normally both stops and drops at the end of sentences that are not questions? Recognizing this will help you greatly in determining where to put periods in your writing. But here is the bad news: Unfortunately, the ear alone is not a perfect guide to punctuation. One reason is that most people you hear are imperfect speakers; they may at times stop or pause at inappropriate places—for instance, to catch their breath or collect their thoughts. Another reason is that customs in speaking have changed faster than customs in writing. Once rules for punctuation were set down in books, over two centuries ago in England, it was hard to change them, even though some English speech patterns have changed with time and place. A third reason is that rules must simplify. The spoken language is far too flexible and complex for any set of rules to cover every possible situation. To put periods and other marks where they should be, then, most experienced writers rely not only on their ears but also on the principles of what makes a grammatical sentence, which you discovered in "Basic Sentence Parts." Knowing both (1) what makes a grammatical sentence and (2) how the voice changes will give you confidence in placing your marks.

(In most of the exercises in this module, you will find that a tape or cassette recorder is quite helpful. If you have none, perhaps the college library has one available. After you punctuate each exercise in this module, read the sentences into the recorder in the way you would naturally speak them; then as you listen to the playback, adjust the punctuation as your ear, governed by your common sense, tells you.)

¹³‡Here is some practice in using periods. In the following selection, put periods where you think they should be. (It is a good idea to do all exercises in this module in pencil, to make changes easy.) You may also insert any commas or other marks you think are needed, but do not worry about them now; concentrate on the periods. Change letters to capitals where needed. (Partial ‡)

SELECTION B

Since many persons have never seen a good marriage they borrow a concept of marriage from the highly romanticized fiction they read in such fiction the husband has a nice job as a junior executive in a large advertising company he comes home every night to a slender radiant wife awaiting him in the fifty-thousand-dollar home with Armstrong floors and sparkling windows candles are lit and the stereo is playing music to make love by the illusion begins to shatter however when the carpets are worn hand-me-downs from the in-laws and the stereo breaks down and the husband loses his job and stops saying "I love you" then the couple have nowhere else to turn they turn against each other

— *Adapted from Thomas A. Harris, M.D.,*
I'm OK—You're OK *(New York: Avon, 1969), p. 155*

If you are still having problems placing your periods, your instructor may refer you to "Basic Sentence Parts" or "Sentence Structure Problems."

ANO. U. OF THE PD.

You probably know that there is another use of the period, in abbreviations. This use does not represent a stopping or dropping of the voice at all; it is just a mechanical device (for readers only, not listeners) by which we show that certain letters stand for a whole word that we did not have the time or space—or ambition—to write out. *Ave., Inc., P.M., Calif., M.D.,* and *Mrs.* are common examples. (In some cases, people have even forgotten what the original words are. What does *P.M.* or *A.D.* actually stand for?) Most problems in abbreviations occur when the writer simply forgets the period. The best way to avoid such problems is to avoid most abbreviations. In fact, except for a very few standard ones, abbreviations in sentences are considered a discourtesy to the reader. In effect, you are saying to your reader, "I just didn't feel like bothering to write this word in full. You are not worth the effort." That may sound harsh, but it is the impression many readers receive from letters, reports, or papers containing abbreviations. Only the following are considered acceptable in sentences in formal writing:

> *Mr., Mrs., Ms., Dr., St.* (Saint) before a name only
> College degrees, such as *M.D., Ph.D.,* or titles, such as *Jr., Sr.*
> *A.M., P.M.* (or *a.m., p.m.*), *A.D., B.C.*
> Organizations that are well known by their initials, such as *FBI, IBM, TWA, VFW, NASA* (Today these are usually written without periods. Before you abbreviate such an organization, be sure all your readers know what its initials mean. Do you know what *NASA* stands for? It is best to write the organization's name in full the first time you mention it; after that you are free to use initials.)

There are special cases where other abbreviations are acceptable, as in footnotes or lists. But in your ordinary writing of sentences and paragraphs, a good rule of thumb on abbreviations is "If in doubt, write it out."

WHAT IS THE NEXT STOP MARK?

Is the period the only stop mark? You have seen hundreds of sentences in this book that end with a different mark; what is it? [14] _____ Of course. Why do we need question marks, though? How is the stop of a question mark different in sound from that of a period? Look again at the first and third versions of the sentence *Charlie failed math* on page 315. When we merely stated the fact, we said

Charlie failed math.

But when we found it hard to believe that he had failed, and asked if it were really true, we said

[15]Charlie failed math?

(Fill in the dotted line that shows the path the voice took.) We might also have asked the question this way:

[16]Did Charlie fail math?

(Fill in the right dotted line.) That is what the question mark does; it signals a stop at which a speaker usually raises rather than drops his voice. Read aloud or listen to these sentences. Fill in the line indicating the voice path:

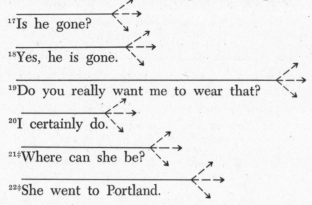

ⁱ⁷Is he gone?

¹⁸Yes, he is gone.

¹⁹Do you really want me to wear that?

²⁰I certainly do.

²¹‡Where can she be?

²²‡She went to Portland.

That is why we have question marks.* The biggest problem students have with them is simply forgetting to use them. Most writers have no trouble recognizing a question; the voice path, the meaning, or the form can indicate a question. Placing question marks is just a matter of careful proofreading.

> There is one fine point you should be aware of. *Do you know the time?* is obviously a question. But is the sentence below a question? If so, put a question mark after it; if not, put a period:
>
> ²³‡The old man asked me what time it was
>
> Is it actually asking a question or is it telling you that someone asked a question? _____ 24 If it is telling, not asking, should it have a question mark or a period? _____ 25 Here are other examples of sentences that may seem to be asking questions but are actually telling something about a question. Add the correct mark at the end of each:
>
> ²⁶I have no idea what his answer will be
> ²⁷Wendy refuses to ask Bill why he is staying away
> ²⁸The police are questioning everyone as to who the murderer is

Determine which stop mark belongs at the end of each of the following sentences, and put it there:

²⁹Why do so many people develop diabetes
³⁰Doctors now believe that diabetes can be retarded

---

* There are some questions that do not have a rising of the voice at the end; but for the sake of simplicity, it is the custom to end all written questions with a question mark.

³¹Is life so dear, or peace so sweet, as to be purchased at the price of chains and slavery

³²Nick kept asking me the time

³³The police kept demanding to know where I had the papers hidden

STILL ANOTHER STOP MARK!

There are two more important stop marks. What mark would you put after each of these? Write it in:

³⁴‡What a glorious day   Look out for that truck
Get that ball   How sweet it is
It's a touchdown   I'll kill that scum

What is this mark? It is the exclamation point! There is really only one principle to learn about using the exclamation point! How wonderfully simple this principle is! You should discover it easily! You probably know it already! Write what you think this paragraph is trying to show you about when to use and when not to use the exclamation point! _____
³⁵

_____ An exclamation point indicates that the sentence is to be read with strong or sudden feeling. (Here it is not a matter of raising or dropping the voice at the end of a sentence, but of increasing the force with which we say the sentence.) Which of the first seven sentences in this paragraph really expresses strong

³⁶‡   ³⁷‡

or sudden feeling? _____ Then which should have an exclamation point? _____
In the other sentences, exclamation points have been deliberately misused to help you discover that overuse of exclamation points defeats its own purpose: The one sentence in this paragraph that really is to be read with strong feeling, *How wonderfully simple it is!* is lost in the crowd of other exclamations and does not stand out as the writer wanted it to. Experienced writers save exclamation points for truly special occasions of strong emotion. And do you think a factual report, such as "The Causes of Hoof-and-Mouth Disease in
³⁸

Northern Mexico," should include emotional, exclamation-point ideas at all? _____
Be stingy with your exclamation points.

Which of the following sentences do you think need an exclamation mark? (One of them may or may not, depending on how you want it to be read.) Put the right stop mark at the end of each sentence:

³⁹Lincoln was shot in 1865

⁴⁰The president has just been shot

⁴¹What an exam Baxter gave

⁴²Professor Baxter administered the psychology exam

⁴³I've been accepted by Harvard Law School

A FOURTH STOP MARK; THIS IS THE LAST

Students often find the next stop mark the most puzzling; it is a period on top of a comma. Do you remember what it is called? A ⁴⁴s _ _ _ c _ _ _ n. What does it look like? ⁴⁵_____ Why do we need it anyway? In modern English speaking, is there really any detectable difference in sound between the following two sentences? Ask someone to read one of them to you without telling you which she is reading:

† a. Guerrillas last night infiltrated a border town and killed two residents; however, the local defense forces gunned down three of the attackers.
b. Guerrillas last night infiltrated a border town and killed two residents. However, the local defense forces gunned down three of the attackers.

Do you think there is any difference in sound between a and b? ^{46‡}_____ To the average listener, they sound the same. If there is no detectable difference in sound, then why bother using a semicolon? What could it possibly show the reader? Let us see. To the reader, what is the only *visible* difference between items a and b? In item a, both ideas

(both clauses) are in the ⁴⁷s_ _ _ sentence. That is the difference: The writer in item a wants to show the reader that the ideas in the two clauses are related closely enough to be in the same sentence. This most common use of the semicolon, with *therefore*-links, is treated fully in "Combining Ideas," pages 210–217; it need not be shown again here.

Can the semicolon also be interchanged with a comma? Not usually, for the semi-colon is much more a stop than a pause. But sometimes one of our sentences may become so crowded with commas that we need something else to show the most important dividing point of the sentence. In the following sentence, for example, is it clear at once where the first clause ends and the second begins?

⁴⁸Best-actor Academy Awards, those much-coveted statuettes, have been won by Gene Hackman, Ernest Borgnine, Cliff Robertson, and Broderick Crawford, and others little known at the time, and the supporting-actor awards, almost equally coveted, often have gone to even less-known figures, such as Jack Albertson, John Houseman, Ben Johnson, and George Chakiris.

With thirteen commas in the sentence, how can the writer show that one comma signals a more important pause than the others because it marks the main dividing point of the sentence, where the first clause ends and the second begins? With just commas, he cannot; therefore he escalates this main pause into a stop, using a semicolon. In the sentence above, change the comma to a semicolon at the point you think is the main dividing point of the sentence. Check the answer page.

Do not be afraid to use a semicolon. But if a doubtful case arises, ask yourself what you would put at that place if the English language had no such mark as a semicolon; then put your answer to that question in that place. For example, if there were no such mark as a semicolon, what would you put in the box in the following sentence? Put it there:

⁴⁹A new little Japanese car goes forty miles on a gallon of gas☐ American cars can not match that performance.

PRACTICING STOP MARKS

⁵⁰‡Here is a final practice on stop marks. Insert stop marks (and any other marks you wish) in the following paragraph. Change letters to capitals where necessary. Also correct any errors in abbreviation:

SELECTION C

What did Sherlock Holmes really look like the author of the Holmes stories Conan Doyle a dr. imagined him as a man with a thin hawklike nose and piercing eyes he was also so lean that he seemed taller than his actual six feet how amazingly different he looked to different illustrators one early drawing shows him with undertaker's side-whiskers and a magnifying glass as big as a sunflower another depicts him as a youth in a short coat and a high hat did you know that for years pictures of Holmes were based on the face of mister William Gillette who played Holmes on stage in the 1890s today most people think of the actor Basil Rathbone when they imagine Holmes we may well ask what the Holmes of the future will look like

— *Adapted from* The Sherlock Holmes Scrapbook,
ed. Peter Haining (New York: Clarkson N. Potter, 1974), pp. 33–35.

THE PAUSE MARK AND THE RULES

The punctuation mark that causes students most trouble is the pause mark, the comma (,). However, in the paragraph below you will make an important discovery that should remove a good part of your worries about commas. Put commas wherever you think they belong in the paragraph:

SELECTION D

(1) Late last night I was in my room listening to my stereo. (2) Suddenly I heard a scratching noise outside the window. (3) After a few minutes I heard it again. (4) I began to panic because I live in a high-crime area. (5) I turned off the light so that I could see outside better. (6) To my surprise there was nothing there except the empty driveway. (7) I tried to keep calm but I could not. (8) Not only my hands but my knees began to tremble. (9) Just then an announcer spoke on the stereo. (10) He apologized for technical difficulties which were causing odd background noises. (11) Then I realized that my strange noises were coming from the speakers on either side of the window.

1‡

How many commas did you use? _____ What is the right number? This is actually a trick assignment, since there is no right number. There is no place in the paragraph where you *must* put a comma but about twelve places where you *may*. Most likely the number of commas you used is somewhere between none and twelve. Check the answer page now to see where some writers would have put commas and others would not.[2]

Selection D shows that people who worry over every placement or nonplacement of a comma are often worrying needlessly. In the selection, whether or not you use a comma at any of those twelve places makes no difference whatever! The choice is yours, depending on whether you would want to pause at any of those places if you were speaking the words. You, not rules, control many of the pauses in your writing. Does this mean, though, that you have complete license to put or omit commas wherever you like? Your commas usually

must reflect actual [3]p _ _ _ _ s in sp _ _ _ ing. Obviously there are places where no one would pause, such as between the first two words of *Mary had a little lamb*. Likewise, there are places where every speaker would naturally pause, as in this sentence: *Billie Jean King, who has won tournaments in America, England and Australia, lives in California.* Insert a comma at each place where you would naturally pause in the following sentences:

[4]‡To be sure I used Arrid the salesman gave me a free sample.

[5]‡To be sure I used Arrid.

Can the pause possibly come at the same place in both sentences? _____[6] Sometimes you can give exactly the same words two vastly different meanings, depending on your pausing. Say the two sentences below:

Hank and Pat have some peanuts.
Hank and Pat, have some peanuts.

In which sentence is someone offering Hank and Pat some peanuts? _____[7] The

other sentence means merely that _____[8]_____.

Thus you have discovered two important points about commas: (1) that in more cases than you may realize, it makes no difference in meaning whether you use a comma or not; (2) that in many other cases, however, important differences in meaning depend on whether you use a comma or not.

In the next few sections you will learn the most common situations in which a clear reading and understanding of a sentence depend on the accurate placing of commas.

COMMAS WITH INTRODUCERS

Why does the presence or absence of commas change meaning? Do you recall the basic sentence pattern?

(If not, see page 169.) Write it: [1]___ ___(__)(__).
What, then, does a listener or reader expect usually to

follow the verb? A [2]c _ _ _ _ _ _ _ r. But suppose you wanted to combine the following two ideas, using the link *as*:

We were eating.

Giant flies and mosquitoes buzzed around our heads.

Start reading the result:

As we were eating giant flies and mosquitoes. . . .

Is the sentence really supposed to say that we were eating flies and mosquitoes? Of course not. The reader will soon realize that; he will back up and reread the sentence. But should he have to read any of your sentences twice to understand them? This diagram shows what happens:

If-group   *Main clause*

| As we were eating | giant flies and mosquitoes | buzzed around our heads. |

The reader cannot tell whether *flies and mosquitoes* is the end (completer) of the *if*-group or the beginning (subject) of the main clause. The solution to the problem is simple. Put it in below:

³As we were eating giant flies and mosquitoes buzzed around our heads.

This is the primary principle of all comma placing: Use a comma wherever it is needed for clarity. Put commas where you think they are needed in the following sentences:

⁴Because he wanted to hit Babe Ruth switched from pitching.

⁵Because he wanted to hit Babe Ruth the angry fan was arrested.

⁶When he came to Washington Lincoln faced an awesome burden.

⁷When he came to Washington asked what had hit him.

⁸Although Anthony had once hated life in Samoa he was now happy.

⁹[Punctuate this differently from item 8 to give it a different meaning.]
Although Anthony had once hated life in Samoa he was now happy.

Because of this possibility of misreading, it has become customary to put a comma after many kinds of word groups—especially *if*-groups, *-ing*-groups and *-en*-groups—coming before the main parts of the sentence. (Since such groups begin, or introduce, the sentence,

we call them ¹⁰in _ _ _ _ _ _ ers.) In each of the sentences below, put a comma where you think it is needed:

¹¹‡In surrendering the prisoners were promised a fair trial.

¹²‡In surrendering the prisoners the Vietnamese hoped to gain concessions from the enemy.

¹³‡Before burning down the house had stood for two hundred years.

¹⁴‡Before burning down the house the arsonist made sure no one was watching.

¹⁵‡Defeating Randolph Henry Houghton became the youngest senator in modern times.

¹⁶‡[Punctuate this differently from item 15 to give it a different meaning.]
Defeating Randolph Henry Houghton became the youngest senator in modern times.

When may the writer leave this comma out? Look back at selection D, on page 321. Reread sentences 1, 2, 3, 6, and 9. Circle the introducer in each of these sentences. From working on this selection, you already know that the writer may or may not put a comma after such introducers. (Check the answer page for selection D.) Why do you think he has

a choice with these? Because there is no danger of _____¹⁷.
Notice that they are also short—one to four words. What difference does long or short make? Say this sentence aloud:

¹⁸After trudging three miles through the snow lugging a five-gallon can to get gas for my car I found the gas station closed.

Find the subject and the verb. Now put one circle around the introducer(s). Would you put a comma at the end of the circle? If so, do it. This is the "take a breath" comma. Even though there is no danger of misreading the sentence, the introductory part is long enough that almost every experienced writer would feel a need to pause to indicate the end of the introducer and the beginning of the main parts of the sentence.

How long is long enough to require the comma? You be the judge. Here are five sentences. Determine where the introducer in each ends; then use your common sense to decide whether it is long enough to need a comma. (There may be some sentences where you may either use or omit the comma.)

¹⁹In the evening the scouts gathered around the campfire to sing and hear ghost stories.

²⁰Despite nearly four years of efforts to find the priceless fossil remains of Peking man the bones of that extinct race have not been found.

²¹Lately conditions have deteriorated to a crisis level.

²²For more than twenty years people throughout the country have been reporting unidentified flying objects to the government.

²³During the whole wretched ordeal of his trial Charles Darnay remained outwardly calm.

From checking the answers you can see that there is a large middle ground where it is completely up to you whether to use a comma or not. If you are in doubt, however, it is safer to use a comma.

COMMAS WITH INTERRUPTERS

Suppose you are writing a report on a movie you have recently seen. You found the plot weak; therefore you write

The plot is weak. The weakness in my opinion is that it is unbelievable.

But is your second sentence really saying what you mean? What is unbelievable according to the sentence? (Read just the second sentence aloud, without pausing.) What did you

intend the word *it* to stand for? [1]__ __ __ __ But instead what does *it* seem to stand for?

[2]__ __ __ __ __ __. Is there a way to correct this misreading? Suppose you remove *in my opinion*. You have

> The plot is weak. The weakness is that it is unbelievable.

[3]

Now does *it* clearly refer to plot? _____ But suppose you still feel that *in my opinion* should be in there. You need some way to show that *in my opinion* is not a necessary part of your sentence but a less important word group that interrupts the train of thought

of the sentence. How do you think we would indicate that in *speaking*? [4]_____

_____ Therefore in *writing* we can indicate

it by inserting [5]c__ __ __ __s. [6]Go back to the original sentence and do this to make it clear.

In my opinion is typical of many expressions we commonly use to interrupt the thought of a sentence. Can you identify these others?

> [7]You know, o__ c__ __ __ __ __e, what the consequences are.

> [8]The inspector, b__ t__ __ w__ __, may be coming around soon.

> [9]You are, t__ t__ __ __ t__ __ t__ __ __ __, a pain in the neck.

> [10]The Vietnam War lasted, as a m__ __ __ __ __r o__ f__ __ __, almost as long as the Trojan War.

> [11]Have you heard, in__ __d__ __ __ __ally, that Celeste and Babar are splitting up?

Since such expressions do interrupt the sentence, we naturally call them [12]in__ __ __ __-

__ __ __ __ers. Go back and read sentences 7 to 11 again, skipping the interrupters. Does

[13]

each sentence make sense without the interrupter? _____ Then are interrupters

[14]

needed in the sentence? _____ This is why they are set off, or isolated, from the rest of the sentence by commas—almost as if they were in parentheses. A speaker pauses before an interrupter to let his listener know an interrupter is coming, and he pauses again to let her know when the interrupter is over. He also usually drops his voice slightly when saying the interrupting words. Have someone read sentences 7 to 11 aloud; you will hear the pauses and perhaps hear the dropping of the voice too.

Here is an important point about interrupters. Is there anything wrong with the punctuation of these sentences?

¹⁵Jean's new boy friend, to tell the truth is ugly.

¹⁶Hattie McDaniel you may recall, was the first black to receive an Academy Award.

If you wanted to block out certain annoying noises (like the sound of your family fighting in the next room) while you were studying, would you use a single earmuff, covering only one ear? Not likely; it would let too much noise leak in. Only a complete pair of earmuffs would isolate you from all the outside noise. If you think of the commas around an interrupter as a pair of earmuffs which isolate it from the rest of the sentence, you will see at once what is wrong with sentences 15 and 16. You will see it also if you say the sentences aloud, exactly as they are printed. Insert accurate punctuation in both of these sentences now; then check the answer page.

Sentences 15 and 16 are examples of the most common of all punctuation errors: leaving out one of the commas around an interrupter. The earmuff comparison should help you remember that the commas around an interrupter are an unbreakable set; using a comma at only one end of an interrupter is, in fact, worse than using no commas at all.

What do you notice about interrupters from the following sentences?

a. Our new field house, by the way, is the largest in the Southwest.
b. By the way, our new field house is the largest in the Southwest.
c. Our new field house is the largest in the Southwest, by the way.

These sentences show that many interrupters can float to various places in the sentence, including the introducer position, as in sentence b. (Naturally, we do not use a comma at the very beginning or end of a sentence—before *By* in sentence b or after *way* in sentence c. This is the only case where the two-comma rule is overruled.)

Certain expressions may also have different meanings with or without commas. Notice these:

Standish is afraid, to tell the truth.
Standish is afraid to tell the truth.

You can tell, by the way, that he drinks.
You can tell by the way that he drinks.

Locate the interrupter(s) in each of the following sentences and punctuate each sentence. Some interrupters have not been mentioned so far; even so, you should not have much difficulty locating them:

¹⁷The governor has said that the prospects for mass transit aid frankly are poor.

¹⁸He may of course say what he wants to; I believe however that the aid will be granted.

¹⁹The governor knows in the first place that this is an election year; he knows moreover that he has millions in the state's rainy-day fund.

²⁰‡The governor will I am sure dramatically find the funds two days before election as usual.

²¹‡The governor you can bet will rescind the aid as soon as he is reelected; that is if he is reelected.

²²‡The voters may sad to to say fall for his trick. I promise in spite of the odds to expose such fraud.

A SPECIAL PROBLEM (RESTRICTIVE GROUPS)

What follows is the big curve ball of the pastime of punctuation—not an easy concept at all to grasp. Once you have grasped it, however, you will be able to handle hundreds of situations which may now be earning your papers a red-ink bath. Throughout this section, keep in mind that we are still dealing with interrupters; this means we will be

²³

using how many commas each time we meet an interrupter? _____ Do you recall that when you learned *who*-groups in "Combining Ideas," you were told that you would learn later how to punctuate them? You will learn now. Read the following sentence, in which your friend Shelly tells you about a strange building in town. (It will help if the sentences in this section are said aloud.)

d.   The building has ape footprints up the outside wall.

But if you want to see the footprints, does this sentence tell you which building, of all the

²⁴

buildings in town, to visit? _____ Suppose, however, Shelly knows that the building is at 350 Fifth Avenue. She puts this information into a *who*-group and says

e.   The building *which is located at 350 Fifth Avenue* has ape footprints up the outside wall.

Do you now know which one building, out of all the buildings in town, has the footprints?

²⁵

_____ Then is this *who*-group needed in the sentence to make clear which

²⁶

building in town the speaker is talking about? _____
Now suppose another friend, Ricki, tells you

f.   The Empire State Building has ape footprints up the outside wall.

Does this sentence tell you which building, out of all the buildings in town, has the foot-

²⁷

prints? _____ Now suppose Ricki wants to add a *who*-group telling the address of the building:

which is located at 350 Fifth Avenue

Do you already know, from sentence f, which building in town has the footprints?

²⁸

_____ Then do you need this *who*-group to tell you which building has the footprints? _____ Now—a group that is not needed is an [29] [30]in _ _ _ _ _ _ _ er

and must be isolated inside [31]c _ _ _ _ _ s. In which of the following two sentences, then,

is the *who*-group an interrupter? [32]_____ Put commas where they should be:

> [33]The building which is located at 350 Fifth Avenue has ape footprints up the outside wall.
> [34]The Empire State Building which is located at 350 Fifth Avenue has ape footprints up the outside wall.

Now you know why some *who*-groups and similar groups have commas and others do not. To know when to omit commas, we have to determine whether the *who-group* is needed to tell *which* person or thing we are talking about. Here is another example. Circle the *who*-group in sentences 35 and 37:

> [35]The girl who is wearing the red dress is looking for someone to buy her a drink.

Without the *who*-group, the sentence reads

> The girl is looking for someone to buy her a drink.

Is the *who*-group in 35 needed to tell us which girl (of all the girls at the party) wants the

drink? [36]_____

> [37]Sheila Levine, who is wearing the red dress, is looking for someone to buy her a drink.

Without the *who*-group, sentence 37 reads

> Sheila Levine is looking for someone to buy her a drink.

Is this *who*-group needed to tell us which girl wants the drink, or do we know already,

without the group? [38]_____ Then in which sentence is the *who*-group merely an

interrupter? [39]_____ That is why 37 has commas but 35 does not. Now you should be ready to try one. Circle the *who*-group in each of the next two sentences; for each sentence, determine whether the *who*-group is needed to tell which one of Bogart's movies is Jason's favorite. Then put in whatever commas may be needed. (If you find this difficult, try writing each sentence without the *who*-group, on scrap paper. You should see the difference.)

> [40]The movie which contains the song "As Time Goes By" is Jason's favorite Bogart film.
> [41]*Casablanca* which contains the song "As Time Goes By" is Jason's favorite Bogart film.

Try a few more. Add commas where needed:

⁴²The Sailors and the Bruins who finished first and second qualified for the playoffs.

⁴³The teams who finished first and second qualified for the playoffs.

⁴⁴The actor who played Humpty Dumpty in *Through the Looking Glass* brought out fully the character's arrogance.

⁴⁵W. C. Fields who played Humpty Dumpty in *Through the Looking Glass* brought out fully the character's arrogance.

Why are these commas so important? See whether you can spot the difference in meaning between these two sentences (both are correctly punctuated):

⁴⁶‡The freshmen who have been scheduled for Saturday classes are planning a protest.
⁴⁷‡The freshmen, who have been scheduled for Saturday classes, are planning a protest.

Circle the *who*-group in 46 or 47 that is punctuated as an interrupter. Since an interrupter is not needed in a sentence, reread the sentence in which you drew the circle, but do not read inside the circle. Which sentence, 46 or 47, tells you that *all* the freshmen will protest?
⁴⁸

_____ Which tells you that only *certain* freshmen (the ones with Saturday classes)
⁴⁹

will protest? _____ Whether commas were used or not, then, affected the meaning of these sentences. You, the writer, control the meaning of such sentences by using or not using commas. *Who*-groups that are needed to tell *which one(s)*   ⁵⁰□ do,   □ do not take commas. *Who*-groups that are not needed but are merely interrupters   ⁵¹□ do, □ do not   take commas.

Now try some on your own. Punctuate each sentence below to give it the meaning mentioned in the brackets. You will either insert a set of commas or leave the sentence alone:

⁵²Japanese who drink too much hot tea have high rates of stomach cancer.
[You want to tell *which* Japanese have high stomach cancer rates—the hot-tea drinkers.]

⁵³Japanese who drink too much hot tea have high rates of stomach cancer.
[You want to say that *all* Japanese have high stomach cancer rates.]

⁵⁴‡The express bus which operates via the turnpike does not run on weekends.
[You want to say that there is only one express bus.]

⁵⁵‡The express bus which operates via the turnpike does not run on weekends.
[You want to tell which one of several express buses does not run on weekends.]

Next, write sentences of your own. Change sentence b of each pair below into a *who*-group and insert it into sentence a at the place marked *. Punctuate the resulting sentence. The first item is done for you as an example:

  a. All the workers * are being paid overtime.
  b. They are demolishing the old warehouse.

Answer: *The workers, who are demolishing the old warehouse, are being paid overtime.*

  a. Some people * make me furious.
  b. These people call up at all hours of the night.

⁵⁶People _____ make

_____ .

  a. Some of the workers * are being paid overtime.
  b. These workers are demolishing the old warehouse.

⁵⁷‡The w __ __ __ __ __ s _____

_____ a __ __ b __ __ __ g p _____ .

  a. My boy friend loves all rock groups * .
  b. They are ear-shattering.

⁵⁸‡My boy friend l_____ which

a __ __ _____ .

  a. My boy friend loves some rock groups * .
  b. He loves the ear-shattering ones.

⁵⁹‡My _____ which _____

_____ .

If you did "Economy and Variety" you learned of trimmed *who*-groups, such as the ones in the following sentences:

  My husband, ~~who is~~ an army captain, will retire next year.
  Rocky Marciano, ~~who was~~ the heavyweight champion, retired undefeated.
  Finley, ~~who was~~ rounding third base, did not see the catch.
  The man ~~who was~~ rounding third base did not see the catch.
  Have you read the shocking story of Jean Valjean, ~~who was~~ imprisoned nineteen years for stealing a loaf of bread?
  Have you read the shocking story of the man ~~who was~~ imprisoned nineteen years for stealing a loaf of bread?

Since these groups, as you can see, are trimmed forms of *who*-groups, they are punctuated the same as regular *who*-groups.

Punctuate the following. (The first two contain hints.)

⁶⁰On her deathbed she made him pledge to marry Elizabeth Lavenza who was a fair-haired orphan. [Is there a need to tell which Elizabeth Lavenza?]

⁶¹Ralph Ellison's first novel which was *Invisible Man* tells of a young black man who is trying to find his identity. [Is there a need to tell which first novel?]

⁶²The Kentucky Colonels beaten by the Utah Stars on a questionable play filed a protest with the league's new president Harwood Dribble.

⁶³‡Ann Landers writing in the Baltimore *Sun* told her women readers to avoid men running away from unhappy marriages.

⁶⁴‡In 1930 Frank Whittle a young Royal Air Force officer obtained the first patent for an airplane engine operated by jet power.

It may help you to know that *who*-groups beginning with *that* always tell which person or thing. Therefore would they ever take commas? _____ ⁶⁵ Here are some examples (correctly punctuated):

Animals that hibernate in winter eat heavily in the fall.
Dictionaries that have confusing pronunciation keys do not help me much.

The same is true of groups in which you can substitute or add *that*:

that
Cars which guzzle gasoline are losing popularity.
that
Years ago, men seldom made passes at girls who wore glasses.
that are
Girls ∧ wearing glasses today can be especially attractive.

Here is your final practice on interrupters. Insert all needed commas, but no unneeded ones, in the following sentences:

⁶⁶‡The kind of summer rain that muddies the water usually improves catfishing.

⁶⁷‡The hen clucked a warning to her ten remaining chicks who scattered in search of cover.

⁶⁸‡A recent automotive invention is the Wankel engine which uses a rotary motion.

[69]‡Secretariat the first Triple-Crown winner in a quarter-century has been retired to his owner's largest stud farm situated in the bluegrass country of Kentucky.

[70]‡Policemen who drink on duty are a menace to the community.

For 71 to 75, combine a and b into one sentence by changing b into a *who*-group (or any kind of trimmed *who*-group) and inserting it into a at the place marked *. Change wording if needed. (See page 330 for an example.)

    a.   Some women * need psychiatric help.
    b.   These women set out to wreck happy marriages.

[71]‡Women _____

_____ .

    a.   All Christian clergymen * proclaim the message of the Bible.
    b.   These clergymen may be either ministers or priests.

[72]‡Christian _____

_____ .

    a.   Fairweather College's registration procedures * take ten hours to complete.
    b.   The registration procedures are needlessly complicated.

[73]‡ _____

_____

    a.   Our conversation was cut short by a message from the king *.
    b.   He summoned us to his chamber.

[74]‡ _____

_____

(Insert b at * and c at **.)

    a.   An expert * testified that the bullet was from Capone's gun ** .
    b.   The expert had been sent by the FBI.
    c.   The gun had been recovered from the river.

[75]‡ _____

_____

_____

OTHER USES—
AND NONUSES—
OF THE COMMA

SERIES

One of the first uses of commas you learned in elementary school concerned sentences like the one below. Punctuate it as you think it should be punctuated:

[1]Our new film course examines the movies of Bogart Cagney Gable Garbo and Hepburn.

This use of the comma, with items in a list or series, causes few problems. One is whether to put a comma before the final *and*. What should you write?

> . . . Gable, Garbo and Hepburn
> *or*
> . . . Gable, Garbo, and Hepburn.

Really, in a series like this it makes no difference, because the writer's meaning is clear either way. But what about series like the following?

> This year's models come in pink, beige, blue and white, red and gold.

Does the writer mean that we can buy a two-tone model in red and gold, or that we can buy either a red model or a gold model? [2]_____ Suppose he means separate red models and gold models. What can he do to the sentence to make this clear? You do it now.[3] But suppose he means the two-tone. Then *red and gold* is a single last item. What word should he add before *red and gold?* [4]A____. Write the sentence as it would be then, with all needed commas:

[5]

_____

_____

Remember that the speaker uses pauses where needed in a series to avoid confusion. You as a writer use commas for the same reason.

A series of longer items baffles some students. From the following sentence, copy in the blanks below the three items in a series (the three things Fanshawe remembered):

> Fanshawe now remembered where he had eaten where he had left his hat and cane and when he had paid his check and left.

[6]Fanshawe now remembered

w._____

w._____

and w._____

Do you think you need a comma for clarity after the next-to-last item? _____
Now go back and punctuate the original sentence.[8]

The only other reminder you need in this section can be shown by the sentences below. Circle any unneeded commas you find in them:

[9]The West Indies consists of islands such as, St. Thomas, St. Croix, St. Maarten, Martinique and Barbados.
[10]The gorgeous reds, oranges, golds and purples, of the sunset thrilled the young lovers.

Since speakers do not usually pause before the first item in a series, or after the last item,

[11]

should there be a comma at either place? _____
Punctuate these sentences:

[12]Interstate Highway 95 runs through Virginia North and South Carolina Georgia and Florida.

[13]The Virginia State University basketball team played Maryland West Virginia William and Mary and Washington and Lee.

[14‡]In the past few years this country has lost a sense of why it was founded what its values are and where it is going.

[15‡]Professor Howard assigned texts by Schafter and Schnifter Warren Webber and Partridge and Plink. [Punctuate this any way that makes sense.]

An interior decorator was hired to re-do a house. Below is a list of the color combinations he found in the rooms:

pink and gold   purple and white
red   white
orange and brown   fuschia

Write an original sentence telling the decorator's feeling on seeing these colors. List all the colors in a series in your sentence:

[16‡]

_____

_____

_____

_____

A COMMA TO DROP

This section is mostly a review of what you learned in parts of "Combining Ideas" and "Economy and Variety." You may want to reread pages 208 and 253–255 before continuing here.

Do you remember how we punctuated two clauses joined by an *and*-link? Punctuate these sentences:

[17]William <u>was born</u> two years after their marriage and <u>Annie</u> <u>arrived</u> two years later.

[18]<u>Paul</u> <u>grew</u> stronger over the years but <u>he</u> <u>remained</u> pale and quiet.

Notice that in each sentence above there is a [19]s ___ j _____ and a v ____ on either side of the *and*. Now examine the sentences below. How are they different from 17 and 18?

[20]

(Look at the underlined parts.) _____. Punctuate them as you learned in "Economy and Variety," page 000:

[21]‡<u>Paul</u> <u>grew</u> stronger over the years but <u>remained</u> pale and quiet.

[22]‡<u>William</u> <u>became</u> a shorthand clerk and <u>Annie</u> a housemaid.

The comma, then, is used in only one of the following situations. Put a comma in the little box before the only *and* that needs a comma:

[23]*Situation A:* | SUBJECT + VERB |☐ *and*-link | SUBJECT + VERB |

Situation B: | SUBJECT + VERB |☐ *and*-link | VERB |

Situation C: | SUBJECT + VERB |☐ *and*-link | SUBJECT |

But remember that the need for clarity outweighs all other rules. For example, even though the following sentence does not have a second subject + verb, do you think it would be wise to put a comma after the middle *and,* to make the sentence clear? If so, do it:

[24]Frank has gone out with Charlotte and Shirley and Marvin with Maebelle and Rosita.

SOME, ADVICE, ON, GOING, "COMMA-HAPPY"

Quite a few students say that an elementary or high school teacher told them always to put a comma before *and*. As you have just seen, this is not so. These students are probably recalling a hazy or partial version of what their teacher actually said. What you have learned here is what experienced writers do.

The whole problem of unneeded commas remains a major one for many people, however. Sometimes students go "comma-happy" after a lesson on commas and start thinking they see comma situations almost everywhere, as a boy walking back to his tent after hearing a campfire ghost story imagines a ghost behind every tree. A good guideline is not to use a comma unless your common sense or what you have learned can give you a definite reason to use one.

There is no set of rules for all the places *not* to put commas, any more than there is a set of rules for how to sink instead of swim. What you will meet ahead is a set of examples and cautions drawn from common student mistakes. In the following sentences, students have put commas where no speaker would naturally pause:

Long classroom <u>discussions</u>, <u>put</u> me to sleep. [Comma between the subject and verb. Why?]

The professor said, that he could tell the state I was born in from my speech. [Comma before a *what*-group. Is there a rule that says to do this? If you never put a comma before any use of *that*, you will be right 99 percent of the time.]

The copyright date, of *The Great Gatsby*, can be found on the card, in the card catalogue. [Commas around *of*-groups. Have you learned that you should do this? *Of*-groups, except for introducers and interrupters, are not isolated with commas.]

Although, she was only sixteen, we married and, we soon had a beautiful child. [Commas come often before *and*-links and occasionally before *if*-links, but they never come *after* either kind of link. In this sentence, only the comma after *sixteen* belongs.]

In each of the following sentences, circle any commas you think should not be there. Some do belong:

²⁵The rule, in this school, is that no one, is served a second bowl, of porridge.

²⁶Bernard Houndstooth, writes of the violent, lustful, exciting, world of the 1970s.

²⁷The availability of abortion has, always, existed to the woman who could pay a qualified doctor, to have one performed.

²⁸‡If, he really meant, what he said, he too, would have volunteered.

²⁹‡Often, American Literature II is offered in the day session, and, also, in the evening.

³⁰‡Emerson said, that we should hitch our wagon, to a star.

MINOR USES OF COMMAS

There are some minor uses of commas that you may be unsure about. The following are normally treated like interrupters:

A. The year in a date.

December 7, 1941, is a day that will live in infamy. [But when only a month and year are mentioned, commas are unneeded: *December 1941 was a fateful month in U.S. history.*]

B. The state or country in an address.

Boston, Massachusetts, was named after Boston, England.

C. Titles after a name, such as M.D., Ph.D., D.D. (Doctor of Divinity), Jr., Sr. (Senior).

Travis Waters, Jr., entered the office of Martin Mola, D.D.S.

D.   The name of a person we are talking directly to.

   Pat, put out the garbage tonight. [Notice the difference in meaning from *Pat put out the garbage tonight*.]
   I asked you, Pat, to put out the garbage.

E.   Often, expressions beginning with *not, particularly, especially, namely, except, according to*.

   The Mets, not the Dodgers, played Oakland in the 1973 World Series.
   I come to bury Caesar, not to praise him.
   The Falcons are a strong team this year, particularly on defense.
   Smoking, especially near the gasoline pumps, is dangerous here.

Punctuate the following:

   [31]Richard you should read the biography of Martin Luther King Jr. D.D. particularly if you are thinking of becoming a minister.

   [32]The payment of welfare is the result not the cause of poverty according to most sociologists.

   [33]Smoking in public buildings except in outhouses and the mayor's office is prohibited according to an ordinance of Gopher Gulch Wyoming passed on July 4 1873.

FINAL POINTS

   Before you do the final exercises on commas, remember that, except for cases where meaning is at stake, you as the writer often have an open choice between using or not using a comma. Among its other effects, your heavy or light use of commas will determine the speed with which your paper will be read. Will fewer commas make your paper read faster or slower? [34]_____ This is why newspaper writers tend to use as few commas as possible; they know people want the news fast. On the other hand, writers of advertising copy use much punctuation (see page 399) because they want people to linger on their ad as long as possible.
   But there is one caution you should note. What is wrong with the following?

   Yesterday horses and buggies crossed Midtown in fifteen minutes. Today, cars take half an hour because of congestion.

Do these two sentences begin in a similar way? [35]_____ But does the writer punctuate them similarly? [36]_____ Should he? [37]_____ Punctuate the same way in similar situations. Do not have a flood of commas in one sentence and a drought in the next similar sentence. Be consistent.

PRACTICE ON STOP MARKS AND COMMAS

The items below contain nearly all the pause-mark and stop-mark situations you have learned about in this module. Insert only needed punctuation:

38‡Jack Benny who spent over sixty years in show business often made jokes about Waukegan Illinois the town of his birth

39‡Although he rose to fame and wealth as a musician and singer Louis Armstrong still lived in his old neighborhood a middle-class New York City area called Corona

40‡After they finished fighting the Indians led all their surviving horses which were exhausted to a nearby waterhole

41‡Preston your story sounds too much like an excuse and I don't like it I'm telling you right now that I'll mop up the floor with you if I find out it's a lie

42‡Why was Dr. Bledsoe fired he was the only one not afraid to speak his mind according to the college paper what a shame

43‡My favorite stories to tell the truth are the old Biblical ones such as Adam and Eve Noah's Ark David and Goliath and Samson and Delilah not the trashy stories presented nowadays on television

From your papers that have been evaluated by your instructor, choose five sentences in which he has indicated punctuation errors but has not indicated the corrections. In the blanks marked A below, write these five sentences as you originally wrote them. In the blanks marked B, rewrite the sentences, punctuated as they should be:

44A‡

_____

_____

44B‡

_____

_____

45A‡

_____

_____

45B‡

_____

_____

46A‡

_____

_____

_____

_____

_____

_____

_____

_____

_____

_____

_____

_____

_____

_____

_____

_____

OTHER PUNCTUATION MARKS

There are eight other punctuation problems we will treat very briefly.

A. *The colon* (:) is not at all like the semi-colon (;). The colon generally introduces a list—even a one-item list. It means *and here they are* or *and here it is:*

To make pizza, you need the following ingredients: pizza dough, mozzarella and parmesan cheeses, olive oil, tomato sauce, and oregano.

I have only one thing to say to you, Marvin: you're fired.

Some people enter a church only three times in their lives: when they are hatched, matched, and dispatched.

Mentally substitute the words *and here they are* or *and here it is* where you intend to use a colon. Use the colon only if those words make sense there, as in the following:

Logical: There are six states in New England [and here they are]: Connecticut, Rhode Island, Massachusetts, Vermont, New Hampshire, and Maine.

Illogical: The six states in New England are [and here they are]: ... [Does this sound like sensible English?]

B. *The dash* (—). This is very different from the hyphen (-) as in *vice-president*. The hyphen joins; the dash separates. You may have noticed how the dash has been used occasionally in this book—to indicate a long pause. Often—as right here—dashes are used in pairs for a sharp interruption of the sentence. The best advice is to forget about the dash until you reach more advanced English work. Master the comma first.

C. *Parentheses* (( )). Like a pair of commas or a pair of dashes, parentheses are used for interruptions in the sentence. Parentheses indicate that the material inside them is much less important than the material outside. Before you use parentheses, ask yourself how important the words going inside them are. If they are fairly important, why not use a pair of commas instead? If the words are very unimportant, why not leave them out altogether? It is not a bad idea to forget about parentheses entirely, except for (1) birth and death dates, as in the example below, and (2) specialized uses in research papers, which you will meet in more advanced English work:

Adam Bede was written by George Eliot (1819–1880).

If you do use parentheses, remember the earmuff comparison you learned for commas with interrupters. Parentheses too are like earmuffs; they work only in pairs. Every set of parentheses you open you must close. Avoid this:

George Eliot (who was really a woman wrote *Adam Bede*.

D. *Brackets* ([ ]). These are different from parentheses. Forget about them until you study research paper documentation.

E. *Quotation marks* (" "). These, as you probably know, go around someone's exact words:

In 1933 Roosevelt said, "The only thing we have to fear is fear itself."

But would you use quotation marks in the sentence below? (Does the sentence still give

Roosevelt's *exact* words?) _____

In 1933 Roosevelt said that the only thing America had to fear was fear itself.

It is so important to have only the speaker's exact words inside the quotation marks that even if we just want to say two words like *she said* in the middle, we have to close the quotation for these two words and then reopen it—like this:

"The only thing we have to fear," said Roosevelt in 1933, "is fear itself."

But you do not have to use a new set of quotation marks for each sentence of a quotation, as long as the quotation is not broken by a *she said* or other words the speaker did not say:

> *Confusing:* Jennifer asked, "Why should we go to your apartment?" "Can't we hold hands here at the lounge?"
> *Clear:* Jennifer asked, "Why should we go to your apartment? Can't we hold hands here at the lounge?"

As with parentheses, the most common student mistake with quotation marks is forgetting to close what has been opened. The earmuff principle applies here too:

> *Illogical:* Roosevelt said, "The only thing we have to fear is fear itself.
> *Logical:* Roosevelt said, "The only thing we have to fear is fear itself."

You have probably noticed that we often use commas with quotation marks. Words like *she said,* when they interrupt a quotation, are isolated in commas just like any other interrupter:

> "Roberta," asked Clyde, "would you like to go rowing?"

If the *she said* comes at the end of a quoted sentence, we must use a period, question mark, or exclamation mark instead of a comma:

> "Let's go rowing, Roberta," said Clyde. "The fresh air will do you good." [Clyde's words were two sentences: "Let's go rowing, Roberta. The fresh air will do you good."]

Notice that the comma is used almost any time we open or close a quotation:

> Clyde said, "Roberta, would you like to go rowing?"
> "I'd love to. You're so considerate," answered Roberta.

(By the way, notice that periods and commas go *inside* closing quotation marks.)

That is all this book will attempt to explain about punctuating quotations. If the need arises, your instructor can explain other, less common situations.

F. *Italics* (slanted print, *like this*). We use these for words we want to give unusual emphasis to:

> I didn't say I don't want to go out with you. I said I don't want to go out with you *only.*

Naturally, if we do this too often, it will lose its effect. Once or twice in a full-length paper is usually enough; do not italicize for emphasis at all if you do not have to. Italics are also used for foreign words and for words referred to as words:

> Before we started eating, our host wished us *bon appetit.*
> *Culpable* comes from the Latin word *culpa,* meaning blame or fault.

G. *Punctuating titles.*

> Joe read Hamlet and Macbeth.
> Joe read Antony and Cleopatra.

How many plays did Joe read in the first sentence? How many in the second sentence? Without some punctuation, we cannot tell. By custom, we use italics for the title of a written work big enough to fill a book by itself:

> I read *Love Story* and *A Farewell to Arms.*

But we use quotation marks for the title of a written work small enough to be put with other works in a book or magazine:

> I read "The Killers" in *Great American Short Stories*.
> I read "Is the U.S. Ready If Switzerland Attacks?" in *Reader's Digest*.

One caution: Look at the title of this book as it is written on the title page. Is it in italics or quotation marks? Is there a need for either? As you saw in the *Hamlet* and *Macbeth* and the *Antony and Cleopatra* sentences, titles are punctuated to distinguish them from the surrounding words, thus avoiding confusion. But if a title is written alone on the cover or title page of a book, or at the top of a student's paper, there are no surrounding words; thus we use no punctuation. Which of these three, then, is the logical way for you to write a title at the top of your paper or on a title page?   2☐ "Revisiting Lake Squmpagook"   ☐ *Revisiting Lake Squmpagook*   ☐ Revisiting Lake Squmpagook

H. *Two punctuation marks together*. Since it is impossible to stop twice at the same time, we never use two stop marks together:

Illogical: You sold the cow for a handful of beans?!
You sold the cow for a handful of beans?!!
You sold the cow for a handful of beans???
Logical: You sold the cow for a handful of beans?
You sold the cow for a handful of beans!
Illogical: He asked, "Where the hell were you?".
Did he say, "Where the hell were you?"?
Logical: He asked, "Where the hell were you?"
Did he say, "Where the hell were you?"

And since it is impossible to pause and stop at the same time, we never use a pause and a stop mark together:

Illogical: When he said, "Where the hell were you?," I punched him in the nose.
Logical: When he said, "Where the hell were you?" I punched him in the nose.

Do this practice on the eight problems you have just learned to solve:

3Did Humphrey Bogart ever actually say that famous line Play it again Sam

4No what he actually said was just the following Play it

5When I first read Hansel and Gretel in Beloved Fairy Tales I was rooting for the witch. What brats those kids are I said to my mom

6‡American jazz was so popular that even the French called such music le jazz hot. The expression The Jazz Age was coined by F. Scott Fitzgerald 1896–1940

⁷‡Leo when are we ever going on vacation asked Mrs Tolstoy. You promised me we'd go right after you finished dashing off your latest little novel War and Peace

A word before you leave this section: This book has not attempted to teach you how to cope with every punctuation situation. No book really can, because language is too flexible. Rules are a crutch. Extensive reading is the only sure way to master punctuation. And if you see professional writers who seem to violate most of the "rules" yet still win fame and praise, remember that they are masters who are not ignorant of the rules but know them so well that they can go beyond them with confidence. You may too, some day.

CAPITALS AND NUMBERS

CAPITALS

Capitalization is not hard if you concentrate on a few basic ideas. Almost everyone knows that capitals are used at the beginning of sentences (including quoted sentences) and for the noun *I* at all times:

Ryder moaned, "Where am I? Who hit me?"

Let us move on from there.

A. Capitalize the name or official title of a *particular* person or thing, including a particular place, organization, date or historical event (the underlined words below); but do not capitalize ordinary nouns (the unmarked nouns below). For example, *John Henry* is the name of a particular person; *man* is just an ordinary noun. (There are many men but only one John Henry.) Here are other examples:

J. Worthington Foulfellow
Houston, Texas
that great big city in that great big state
the Houston Astros
Houston's baseball team
the Brooklyn Bridge
the bridge to Brooklyn
Great Britain
the British Empire
the British government
the Presbyterian Church
the church on the corner
Tuesday, January 9
a day in winter
English 320: The Modern American
    Novel
an English course in the modern
    American novel

Bruce Wayne Junior High School
my junior high school diploma
Washboard State University
a state university
the South in the Civil War
the south side of the house
a war of many nations
General Electric, Inc.
the electric company
Major R. W. Lopez
a major in the army
R. W. Lopez, the major on duty
the Chevrolet Nova
my Chevrolet sedan
the Democratic Party
a democratic form of government

B. In titles of written works or works of art or music, capitalize all words except *a(n)*, *the, of*-links, or *and*-links inside the title:

A Farewell to Arms
The Last of the Mohicans
The Cloister and the Hearth

Aristotle Contemplating the Bust of
    Homer
The Merry Wives of Windsor

C.   In some cases it makes no difference whether you capitalize or not, as long as you do it the same way every time:

Consistent: The Pope arrived at 9 A.M. and left at 11 P.M.
Consistent: The Pope arrived at 9 a.m. and left at 11 p.m.
Inconsistent: The Pope arrived at 9 A.M. and left at 11 p.m.
Consistent: The President and the Vice-President of our country attended the ceremony.
Consistent: The president and the vice-president of our country attended the ceremony.
Inconsistent: The President and the vice-president of our country attended the ceremony.

D.   Do not capitalize unless you can think of a reason. The underlined letters were mistakenly capitalized by the students who wrote the following sentences, which are correct here:

I was thankful that I still had my grandfather.
The author feels that modern man is suffering from schizophrenia.
Matt's father wanted him to be a doctor or a dentist.
The eighth grade went on a field trip to the zoo.
My involvement with group therapy influenced my life style.

E.   Do not capitalize a word for emphasis; if you feel you must show emphasis some way, use italics:

Not customary: He couldn't have meant he would NEVER return.
Customary: He couldn't have meant he would *never* return.

NUMBERS

Students are often puzzled by whether they should write numbers in their sentences in words or figures. Obviously we do not write all numbers out in words. There is no rigid rule in this matter except one—write out numbers from one to nine:

Do you want one lump of sugar or two?

Many people also write out other numbers that take only one or two words, as well as large round numbers that may be confusing in figures:

Adults between seventeen and forty are the heaviest smokers.
At the last meeting seventy-five members walked out.
Many stars are more than twenty-three trillion miles away. [Clearer than 23,000,000,000,000.]

Whatever you do, be consistent. Which of these sentences is not consistent in its use of numbers?

[1] ☐ The *Times* contained 60 pages yesterday and eighty today.
☐ The *Times* contained 60 pages yesterday and 80 today.
☐ The *Times* contained sixty pages yesterday and eighty today.

Thus we do not mix the two forms in the same list or series, even if it contains numbers from one to nine:

Inconsistent: Ahab Jones caught varying numbers of fish each day this week: 35, nine, 22, seven, 13.

Consistent: Ahab Jones caught varying numbers of fish each day this week: 35, 9, 22, 7, 13.

In fact, in addresses, dates, statistics, or number lists of any kind, we nearly always use figures.

In the sentences below, capitalize where there is a reason to and change figures to words where necessary. Add needed punctuation also:

[2] i have heard that students need only a 60 high school average and 350 on their college board scores to be admitted to blytheville college in sudstown.

[3] physicians dentists professors and clergymen of christian and non-christian faiths gathered at st paul's church and other churches in the city at 9 A M to demand the release of 7 political prisoners including an 80-year-old grandfather all of whom had all been held for 102 days by the commandant of the secret police.

[4] for whom the bell tolls a story of the spanish civil war is the first novel assigned in our literature course and stopping by the woods on a snowy evening is the first poem.

REVIEW In this module you have discovered the chief ways we use pause and stop marks to make our writing clear by indicating how it would be spoken. You also have had a quick survey of less common problems. Here is a short review before your mastery test:

[1]*The four stop marks are _____, _____, _____,

and _____.

[2]*Which diagram shows what our voices normally do at the end of sentences that are not questions?

[3]*Put a circle around the box of the diagram above that shows what our voices do at the end of most questions.

⁴‡We use a semicolon (;) instead of a period when we want to show that the ideas on either side of the stop mark are

☐ closely related,   ☐ unimportant,   ☐ not closely related.

⁵‡We regularly use semicolons with what kind of links? _____-links.

⁶‡We use the exclamation point (!)   ☐ as frequently as possible,   ☐ as rarely as possible,   ☐ any time we care to; it makes no difference how often we use it.

⁷‡☐ All,   ☐ Most,   ☐ Few   pauses in our speech are represented by commas in our writing.

⁸‡The first principle of using commas is to use one whenever our sentence

would be _____ if we did not.

⁹‡Whether an introductory expression is followed by a comma depends largely

on how _____ it is.

¹⁰‡An interrupter is   ☐ needed,   ☐ not needed   in its sentence.

¹¹‡The earmuff principle means that _____

_____.

¹²‡Interrupters need   ☐ no,   ☐ one,   ☐ two   commas.

¹³‡*Who*-groups and similar word groups that tell which person or thing ☐ always,   ☐ never,   ☐ may or may not   take commas.

¹⁴‡In a series we must use a comma before the *and* when _____

_____. Otherwise we may omit it.

¹⁵‡In general, to avoid unneeded commas, we should not use a comma in our

writing unless _____ or _____

_____ tells us we should.

¹⁶‡Although each writer has in many situations a choice of whether to use commas or not, he must be c__ns_____t every time the same type of situation occurs.

¹⁷‡Which of these marks should be used as little as possible by less experienced writers?   ☐ —   ☐ ( )   ☐ italics   ☐ all of these   ☐ none of these

¹⁸‡A colon (:) means *a____h_____t_____a____* or *a____h_____i__i__*.

¹⁹‡We include inside quotation marks only   ☐ the exact words that someone said,   ☐ expressions like *he said* or *asked Jeff,*   ☐ a restating of what someone said, in our own words, after *that* (such as *Jill said that her horse was tired*).

²⁰‡Which two punctuation marks can be used together?   ☐ ?,   ☐ ,? ☐ ?!   ☐ ,!   ☐ all of these   ☐ none of these

²¹‡Check the set of words below in which some words (besides the first word) take capitals:

☐ The entrance to the college library is on the south side of the campus.
☐ The north had a strong president in the civil war.

^{22‡}In sentences, we normally write in words the numbers _____
_____.

^{23‡}In addresses, dates, number lists, or statistics we ☐ almost always, ☐ almost never, ☐ may or may not write numbers in words.

^{24‡}Professional writers ☐ always adhere strictly to the rules, ☐ sometimes go beyond the rules, ☐ disregard the rules.

If you were able to answer a large majority of the questions above without looking back into the module (or if you had to look back but you now understand the answer), you are ready for the mastery test.

MASTERY TEST

Part I. The following sentences are taken directly or adapted from freshman papers. Each originally contained at least one error in punctuation, capitalization, or writing numbers. They are given here without any capitalization, with no punctuation except some periods, and with all numbers in figures. In the blank below each, write the sentence as it should be. This includes changing figures to words and periods to question marks or exclamation points, if you think they should be changed. Underline any word you want to italicize. In any case where two meanings are possible, choose either, but make that clearly the only meaning. (A final reminder: Avoid going "comma-happy.")

^{1‡}Many times in the past 15 years i have been asked by administrators of government agencies whether i possessed college skills.

_____

_____

^{2‡}I have a bit of a hearing problem and when someone mumbles or speaks low it's hard to understand or even hear him especially in a crowd.

_____

_____

^{3‡}First mr goldstein I would like to tell you that I am delighted to have you as the prof. in our anthropology course.

_____

_____

^{4‡}Another reason i am returning to school is the g i bill which helps me financially and gives me i feel a chance to further my education.

_____

_____

_____

[5]‡What a youth i've had. do you believe i'm only 20 and i've been to 3 continents including s. america.

---

[6]‡Shortly after we ate gaylord showed me his apartment particularly his fisher stereo set which he insisted no one could play 45 r.p.m. records on only albums.

---

[7]‡I on the other hand do not feel i have succeeded in knowing the other things that I can accomplish such as the following being a mother to 4 children holding a part time job tending a disabled husband and going to carswell college.

---

[8]‡When I read all 423 pages of b f skinner's latest book beyond freedom and dignity i said to my psychology teacher sigmund pavlov ph d do you honestly think sir that his ideas are valid.

---

[9]‡Fitzgerald wrote of the mad impetuous desperate youth of the years after world war I. Here was a new generation he said grown up to find all gods dead all wars fought all faiths in men shaken.

---

[10]‡Blacks who make up 11 percent of the u.s. population have an unemployment rate of over 35 percent in some regions according to the federal bureau of labor statistics.

Part II. Do A or B, as your instructor directs:

A. Write a twelve-to-fifteen-sentence paragraph about a memorable place that you have visited.

B. Rewrite one of your earlier papers in which your instructor has found quite a few punctuation errors (which he did not correct for you). Show your instructor the paper you wish to rewrite, for his approval.

Part III. (Optional) Write, from dictation, a paragraph that will be read to you by your instructor.

INTRODUCTION AND STOP MARKS

[1]Because the general would have heard him pause after *Pardon*

[2]For most people, it is easier from hearing it.

[3](.)

[4]period

[5](,)

[6]comma

[7]period

[8]sentence

[9]c

10 ⟶ (rising arrow)

11 ⟶ (level arrow)

12 ⟶ (falling arrow)

[13][Brackets around a punctuation mark mean that you may either use it or omit it.] Since many persons have never seen a good marriage, they borrow a concept of marriage from the highly romanticized fiction they read. In such fiction [,] the husband has a nice job as a junior executive in a large advertising company. He comes home every night to a slender, radiant wife awaiting him in the fifty-thousand-dollar home with Armstrong floors and sparkling windows. (You do the rest.)

[14]question mark (?)

15 ⟶ (rising arrow)

16 ⟶ (rising arrow)

17 ⟶ (rising arrow)

18 ⟶ (falling arrow)

19 ⟶ (falling arrow)

20 ⟶ (falling arrow)

[24]It is telling. (It tells that the old man asked me a certain question.)

[25]Period

[26-28]None should have question marks. (The first sentence tells that you have no idea about something. The second tells that Wendy is refusing to ask Bill something. The third tells that the police are questioning everybody as to something.)

[29]question mark (?)

[30]period (.)

[31]question mark (?)

[32]period (.)

[33]period (.) (You are expected to know this only if you did items 23–28 in the box.)

[35]Do not overuse the exclamation point.

[38]It should not.

[39]period (.)

[40]exclamation point (!)

[41]exclamation point (!)

[42]period (.)

[43]Either a period (.) or an exclamation point (!). (If you expected to be admitted to Harvard, you probably would not be excited, and your sentence would have a period. If you had been waiting anxiously for acceptance, you would probably express strong feeling, and your sentence would have an exclamation point.)

[44]semicolon

[45](;)

[47]same

[48]The semicolon follows *at the time.*

[49]A period (.), because the sentence has two ideas (main clauses) with no link between them.

THE PAUSE MARK AND THE RULES

[2]Late last night [,] I was in my room [,] listening to my stereo. Suddenly [,] I heard a scratching noise outside the window. After a few minutes [,] I heard it again. I began to panic [,] because I live in a high-crime area. I turned off the light [,] so that I could see outside better. To my surprise [,] there was nothing there except the empty driveway. I tried to keep calm [,] but I could not. Not only my hands but my knees began to tremble.

Just then [,] an announcer spoke on the stereo. He apologized for technical difficulties [,] which were causing odd background noises. Then [,] I realized that my strange noises were coming from the speakers [,] on either side of the window. (Hardly

anyone would use all twelve of these commas.)

³pauses, speaking
⁶No
⁷The second
⁸Hank and Pat are in possession of some peanuts.

COMMAS WITH INTRODUCERS

¹S V(C)(C)
²completer
³As we were eating, giant flies and mosquitoes buzzed around our heads.
⁴Because he wanted to hit, Babe Ruth switched from pitching.
⁵Because he wanted to hit Babe Ruth, the angry fan was arrested.
⁶When he came to Washington, Lincoln faced an awesome burden.
⁷When he came to, Washington asked what had hit him.
⁸Although Anthony had once hated life in Samoa, he was now happy.
⁹Although Anthony had once hated life, in Samoa he was now happy.
(If you had answer 9 for 8 and vice versa, you are also correct.)
¹⁰introducers
¹⁷misreading the sentence
¹⁸After trudging three miles through the snow lugging a five-gallon can to get gas for my car, I found the gas station closed.

¹⁹The introducer is *In the evening;* most people would feel no need for a comma after it, since it is short and there is no possible confusion of meaning.
²⁰The introducer is *Despite nearly four years of efforts to find the priceless fossil remains of Peking man;* probably everyone would put a comma after it because it is quite long.
²¹The introducer is *Lately;* since it is short and there is no possible confusion of meaning, most people would use no comma.
²²The introducer is *For more than twenty years;* since it is of middle length, probably just as many people would use a comma as would not.
²³The introducer is *During the whole wretched ordeal of his trial;* since it is fairly long, most people would put a comma after it.

COMMAS WITH INTERRUPTERS

¹Plot
²Opinion
³Yes
⁴By pausing before and after *in my opinion* (and perhaps also lowering the voice)
⁵commas
⁶The plot is weak. The weakness, in my opinion, is that it is unbelievable.
⁷of course
⁸by the way
⁹to tell the truth
¹⁰matter of fact
¹¹incidentally

¹²interrupters
¹³Yes
¹⁴No
¹⁵Jean's new boy friend, to tell the truth, . . .
¹⁶Hattie McDaniel, you may recall, . . .
¹⁷The governor has said that prospects for mass transit aid, frankly, are poor.
¹⁸He may, of course, say what he wants to; I believe, however, that . . .
¹⁹The governor knows, in the first place, that this is an election year; he knows, moreover, that . . .
²³Two

²⁴No

²⁵Yes—the one at 350 Fifth Avenue

²⁶Yes

²⁷Yes

²⁸Yes

²⁹No

³⁰interrupter

³¹commas

³²34

³³Sentence 33 takes no commas.

³⁴The Empire State Building, which is located at 350 Fifth Avenue, has . . .

³⁵who is wearing a red dress

³⁶Yes; without the *who*-group the sentence could refer to any girl at the party.

³⁷who is wearing a red dress

³⁸We know without the *who*-group; the girl is Sheila Levine.

³⁹Sentence 37

⁴⁰No commas; *who*-group: which contains the song "As Time Goes By"—needed to tell us which of all Bogart's films is Jason's favorite.

⁴¹*Casablanca*, which contains the song "As Time Goes By," is . . .

⁴², ⁴³*who*-group: who finished first and second. Sentence 42 has already told us which ones (of all the teams) were invited; therefore the *who*-group is not needed to tell which ones, and it takes commas. The opposite is true for 43.

⁴⁴No commas; *who*-group: who played Humpty Dumpty in *Through the Looking Glass*.

⁴⁵Same *who*-group as sentence 44; use commas.

⁴⁸47

⁴⁹46

⁵⁰do not

⁵¹do

⁵²No commas; the *who*-group is needed to tell which Japanese.

⁵³Japanese, who drink too much hot tea, have . . .

⁵⁶People who call up at all hours of the night make me furious.

⁶⁰. . . Elizabeth Lavenza, a fair-haired orphan.

⁶¹Ralph Ellison's first novel, *Invisible Man*, tells of a young black man trying to find his identity.

⁶²The Kentucky Colonels, [who were] beaten by the Utah Stars on a questionable play, filed a protest with the league's new president, [who is] Harwood Dribble.

⁶⁵No

OTHER USES—AND NONUSES—OF COMMAS

¹Our new film course examines the movies of Bogart, Cagney, Gable, Garbo [,] and Hepburn.

²We cannot tell; the punctuation leaves the meaning unclear. In fact, there is a third possible meaning. Can you find it?

³This year's models come in pink, beige, blue and white, red, and gold.

⁴And

⁵This year's models come in pink, beige, blue and white, and red and gold.

⁶where he had eaten
where he had left his cane
when he had paid his check and left

⁸Fanshawe now remembered where he had eaten, where he had left his hat and came, and when he had paid his check and left.

⁹. . . islands such as ⊙ St. Thomas, . . .

¹⁰. . . purples⊙ of the sunset . . .

¹¹No

¹²Interstate Highway 95 runs through Virginia, North and South Carolina, Georgia [,] and Florida.

¹³The Virginia State University basketball team played Maryland, West Virginia, William and Mary, and Washington and Lee.

¹⁷William was born two years after their marriage, and Annie arrived two years later.

¹⁸Paul grew stronger over the years, but he remained pale and quiet.

[19]subject, verb

[20]The ones below do not have both a subject and a verb after the *and*

[23]Situation A only

[24]Frank has gone out with Charlotte and Shirley, and Marvin with Maebelle and Rosita.

[25]All commas should be circled.

[26]Bernard Houndstooth Ⓐ writes of the violent, lustful, exciting Ⓐ world of the 1970s.

[27]All commas should be circled.

[31]Richard, you should read the biography of

Martin Luther King, Jr., D.D., particularly if you are thinking of becoming a minister.

[32]The payment of welfare is the result, not the cause, of poverty, according to most sociologists.

[34]Faster

[35]Yes

[36]No. *Today* is followed by a comma; *Yesterday* is not. Either both should have commas or neither.

[37]Yes

OTHER PUNCTUATION MARKS

[1]No

[2]Revisiting Lake Squmpagook—choice 3

[3]Did Humphrey Bogart ever actually say that famous line, "Play it again, Sam"?

[4]No, what he actually said was just the following: "Play it."

[5]When I first read "Hansel and Gretel" in *Beloved Fairy Tales,* I was rooting for the witch. "What brats those kids are!" I said to my mom.

CAPITALS AND NUMBERS

[1]Choice 1—*60* and *eighty*

[2]I have heard that students need only a 60 high school average and 350 on their college board [or College Board] scores to be admitted to Blytheville College in Sudstown. (Both numbers are in figures for consistency.)

[3]Physicians, dentists, professors [,] and clergymen of Christian and non-Christian faiths gathered at St. Paul's Church and other churches in the city at 9 A.M. [or a.m.] to demand the release of seven political prisoners, in-

cluding an eighty-year-old [or 80-year-old] grandfather, all of whom had been held for 102 days by the commandant of the secret police [or Secret Police, if that is the group's official title].

[4]*For Whom the Bell Tolls,* a story of the Spanish Civil War, is the first novel assigned in our literature course, [or ;] and "Stopping by the Woods on a Snowy Evening" is the first poem. (The poem is not a book-length work.)

MODULE 12

NOUN AND VERB PROBLEMS

Previous modules required: Basic Sentence Parts (7) (for "Noun and Verb Endings," "Time in Verbs," and "Subject and Completer Forms"); Basic Sentence Parts (7)—Combining Ideas (8)—Economy and Variety (9)* (for "Agreement" and "Clear Reference")

INTRODUCTION

Since nouns and verbs, the meat and potatoes of our writing, are the two most frequently used kinds of words, it is not surprising that their use causes quite a few problems. In this module you will discover how to overcome several of the most common of those problems. Before you go ahead, you must be certain of some basic facts about nouns and verbs that you learned in "Basic Sentence Parts." In the sentences below, underline each noun once (including substitute nouns such as *I, he, who, someone*), and underline each verb twice. There is a total of 25 nouns and verb words:

¹‡Books on grammar usually confuse me.

²‡Life is dear, and peace is sweet, but we should not buy them at the price of chains and slavery.

³‡The forecast for the next three days indicates heavy rain over the metropolitan area. It will turn to snow in the mountains.

Your instructor will check your answers or supply you with them. If you did not have 20 of the 25 right, review carefully the noun and verb sections of "Basic Sentence Parts" before going on.

NOUN AND VERB ENDINGS

THE TWO BASIC ENDINGS

Say these sentences aloud, or have some one say them to you:

a. Carla walked to the bus stop.
b. Carla walk to the bus stop.

Did you detect any difference in the sound of the second word in item a and the second word in item b? Most people do not, because the *-ed* of *walked* becomes lost in the *t-* of *to*. Because of this, people who have experienced most of their English through hearing rather than reading may not realize that an *-ed* is needed there when they write the standard dialect of English. Sentence b is not standard-dialect English. The same problem occurs to a lesser extent with the *-s* ending of some nouns and verbs and with the *-ing* ending of verbs.

In "Basic Sentence Parts" you learned that we say *a clerk▨* but *two clerk⃞s*; thus
⁴‡
when a noun names *more than one* person or thing, we add an _____ to that noun. You also learned that we say *He smoke⃞s* but *They smoke▨*; thus when a verb tells what
⁵‡
one person or thing is doing at the present time, we usually add an _____ to that verb. (*The present time* means not just *right now* but also *regularly, over a period of time.* The clerk is smoking not just right at this moment; he smokes regularly.) Notice the pattern:

The clerk▨ smoke⃞s.
The clerk⃞s smoke▨.
Our ceiling▨ leak⃞s.

Our ceiling[s] leak[ ].
A telephone[ ] ring[s].
Telephone[s] ring[ ].

You try some. In each box below, put either an *s* or nothing:

[6]A single star[ ] shine[ ].
[7]All the star[ ] shine[ ].
[8]That perfume[ ] attract[ ] me.
[9]Those perfume[ ] attract[ ] me.
[10]Diane, a sophomore[ ], work[ ] in the library.
[11]Diane and Dawn, two sophomore[ ], work[ ] in the library.
[12]The U.S. Constitution[ ] prohibit[ ] discrimination.
[13]All the state constitution[ ] prohibit[ ] discrimination.
[14]The birth-control pill[ ] cause[ ] some side effects. [One pill]
[15]Birth-control pill[ ] cause[ ] some side effects. [More than one pill]

Now let us look at the most troublesome ending, the *-ed*. In "Basic Sentence Parts" you learned that we say *Today we play[ ]* but *Yesterday we play[ed]*; thus when a verb tells that something happened in the past, we usually add an _____ to it. Notice the pattern:

Today we play[ ] volleyball.
Last spring we play[ed] field hockey.
Now they want[ ] shorter hours.
A week ago they want[ed] higher pay.
This year Sue and Chuck live[ ] on campus.
Last year Sue and Chuck liv[ed] at home.

Try these. In each box below, put either *ed* or nothing:

[17]Each January we open[ ] negotiations.
[18]Yesterday we open[ ] negotiations.
[19]Right now you wish[ ] you were in Paris.
[20]Last month you wish[ ] you were in Hawaii.
[21]In the 1970s housewives watch[ ] soap operas on television.
[22]In the 1940s housewives listen[ ] to soap operas on radio.
[23]I think the profs in the math department always talk[ ] too much in class.
[24]In my last math course the prof talk[ ] too much in class.
[25]Whenever I can, I visit[ ] Yoyo, who is in the alcoholic ward.
[26]When Yoyo was in the alcoholic ward, I visit[ ] him often.

Here are four sentences to show you how both the *-s* and *-ed* endings work:

One thing, present: My current Shakespeare course concern[s] the tragedies.

More than one thing, present: My current Shakespeare courses concern[ ] the comedies and the tragedies.

One thing, past: My previous Shakespeare course concern[ed] the histories.

More than one thing, past: My previous Shakespeare courses concern[ed] the histories and the poems.

Now try this practice, which combines the two endings you have learned so far. In each box, put *s, ed,* or nothing. (For words that already end in *-e,* just add *d* instead of *ed.*)

²⁷Stan and I travel☐ to Fort Lauderdale every Easter.

²⁸Stan and I travel☐ to Fort Lauderdale last Easter.

²⁹Whenever I purchase☐ new clothes, I can't help spending too much.

³⁰Whenever Sally purchase☐ new clothes, she spend☐ too much.

³¹When I had a job, I purchase☐ new clothes every month.

³²The first manned moon flight orbit☐ the moon and return☐ to earth.

(Watch your spelling in this next item.)

³³I start☐ college years ago and then drop☐ out, but now I attend☐ County College full-time.

³⁴People say☐ that accident☐ happen☐ only to those who are careless; but even though I am extremely careful, last week an accident happen☐ to me.

³⁵Now do this practice, which includes all you have learned in this section. (Partial ‡)

SELECTION A

All that day, so long ago on the island, I remain☐ by my corn patch to be sure all the bird☐ stay☐ away. Hundred☐ of those bird☐ perch☐ in the branch☐ of all the tree☐ around me. As the sun went down, they wait☐ until I start☐ to walk away; then they swoop☐ down and peck☐ at the corn☐ until I fire☐ my gun at them and kill☐ three of them. This was what I had wish☐ for; I strung the dead bird☐ up as we regularly string☐ up robber☐ in England for all to see, after the hangman do☐ his work. Such a sight always discourages robber☐, who see what happen☐ to criminal☐ that are caught. Back on the island, the same occurred with the birds. They abandon☐ that part☐ of the island once they had glimpse☐ their three dead comrade☐, and I never again worr☐ about scavenger☐ as long as my three scarecrow☐ hung there.

— Adapted from Daniel Defoe, Robinson Crusoe

OTHER VERB ENDINGS

You recall from "Basic Sentence Parts" that verbs have four forms:

Present form	Past form	-Ing-form	-En-form
walk(s)	walked	walking	walked
break(s)	broke	breaking	broken

In the last few pages we have had been working with the first two of these forms. Now let us look at the last two. In "Basic Sentence Parts" you learned the answer to these questions: Is the *-ing-* or the *-en*-form a full verb by itself? In the standard dialect of English, do we write either *I breaking the record* or *I broken the record?* What is the answer to both

³⁶

questions? _____ What else do those two verb forms need in order to be full verbs? Add it:

³⁷I _____ breaking the record. I _____ broken the record.

-Ing- and *-en-*forms need some form of the verbs ³⁸b __ or h _____. Do these:

³⁹With today's victory the Italian bobsled team h_____ beaten the East Germans.

⁴⁰Yesterday the score w_____ tied until the Germans went ahead at the last minute.

⁴¹For tomorrow's race, the Italians _____ planning a new strategy to beat

the German team, which they _____ never defeated.

⁴²The Italians should win unless it ___ snowing heavily during the race.

Some people put in the *be* or *have* but forget the *-ing-* or *-en-*form ending. They write

The Italian bobsled team has *tie* the East Germans.
The Italians are *plan* a new strategy to beat the German team, which they have never *defeat*.

Sentences written this way are not standard English. To write these sentences, as standard English requires, you need (1) a form of *have* or *be* in front of the main verb word, and (2) the *-ing-* or *-en-*form ending on that main verb word. Try these:

⁴³Within the last five minutes the captain of the Italian team h_____ announc[___]

that they a_____ withdraw[___] from the race, because the frame of their bobsled

_____ crack[___]. ⁴⁴The East Germans _____ now rejoic[___], since

the Italian withdrawal means that the Germans _____ captur[___] the

championship. ⁴⁵Such an easy victory _____ never happen[___] in the history of Olympic bobsledding.

The only other ending that students tend to forget is the *'s*, as in *Belle is Janie's cousin* and *The plane's pilot radioed that his navigator's instruments were malfunctioning.* This ending is treated in detail in the module "Spelling," pages 462–468. Study them if you need to.

MASTERY TEST

Part I. Eliminate all errors in endings in the paragraph below.‡ No boxes are provided this time. If you make no more than two or three mistakes, you are well on your way to overcoming the ending problem. Write additions or changes above the line, like this:

The bird͜s͜ are . . .

The Hawks ͜have won͜ just ͜win͜.

It was a dismal sight. The ship front end sticking fast in the reefs. Its stern was jam between two rock, and it side were crush to pieces from the surf. Its mast broken off. On the deck a dog wag his tail as if he saying hello to me. Suddenly he jump off the ship and paddle to me. I pulled him into my boat, where he cry and whimper from hunger. Seeing an animal suffer always make me sad. A man I know in London gave half his week wages to feed dog and cat that were starve. I brought this dog back to the island and care for him until he running around healthy again.

— Freely adapted from Daniel Defoe, Robinson Crusoe

Part II. Write a paragraph of nine to eleven sentences on any suitable topic from the master list; or, if your instructor directs, rewrite a paragraph in which he found a number of missing endings.

TIME IN VERBS

Before we go further into this module, you need to understand an important term used with verbs. In "Basic Sentence Parts" you learned four forms that verbs have:

Present form	Past form	-Ing-form	-En-form*
break(s)	broke	breaking	broken
walk(s)	walked	walking	walked
prepare(s)	prepared	preparing	prepared
go(es)	went	going	gone
will	would	[no form]	[no form]

You learned that the present form is used with something that is happening now or happens regularly, and that the past form is used with something that happened before now. Do you recall from your previous schooling the name for the various times as expressed in verbs?

It is [1]t__ns__. We say that the verb in *Joan prepares her mother's breakfast* is in the present tense, and the verb in *Joan prepared her mother's breakfast* is in the past tense.

Since there are three possible times—present, past, and future—we have a third tense to express the future. You probably know that it is made by adding the auxiliary *will* (or sometimes *shall*) to the present form: *Joan will prepare her mother's breakfast.* Thus from the two forms, the present form and the past form, we make three tenses: the present tense

---

* Recall that the *-en* ending is often disguised as *-n, -e, -ed, -t, -k,* or other letters.

[*break(s)*, *walk(s)*, . . .], the past tense [*broke, walked, . . .*] and the future tense [*will break, will walk, . . .*].

It may surprise you to learn that although there are only three possible times—present, past, and future—English has six tenses. The three extra tenses involve *combinations* of times. For example, how do we tell of something that began in the past and is continuing in the present? We combine the present and past, like this:

Old <u>John</u> <u>has</u> <u>gone</u> to the park daily since 1907.

John started going there in the past, and he is still going there in the present. Notice which forms we use to make this tense—the present form of *have*, and the *-en*-form of the main verb (in this case, *go*) to indicate the past:

Present form	Past form	-Ing-form	-En-form
(have (has))	had	having	had
go(es)	went	going	(gone)

John (has) (gone)

How would you say that you started smoking cigarettes in 1972 and still smoke them?

[2]I h___ ___ed cigarettes since 1972.

Since this tense combines the present and the past, let us call it the *present/past tense*. If this fourth tense, the *present/past*, combines the present and the past, you can probably guess that the fifth tense combines the [3]p___ and the past (we call it the *past/past*), and the sixth tense combines the [4]f___ and the past (we call it the *future/past*). Why do we need a past/past tense? We need it to tell of something that happened further back in the past than something else. What forms do you think we combine?

Present form	Past form	-Ing-form	-En-form
have (has)	(had)	having	had
go(es)	went	going	(gone)

When I arrived, Ellen (had) (gone.)

Both Ellen's going and my arriving happened in the past, but Ellen's going happened further back in the past than my arriving. How would you say that you started college at a certain time but your brother graduated before that time?

[5]My brother h___ g___ from Panhandle State when I started there.

The sixth tense, the future/past, is not very common. It tells that at a certain time in the future, something will be past:

By 1984 <u>Sandra</u> <u>will have completed</u> her Ph.D.

Here is a summary of the tenses:

Present: I go (He goes)	*Present/Past:* I have gone
Past: I went	*Past/Past:* I had gone
Future: I will go	*Future/Past:* I will have gone

(There is also another way to say each tense: *I am going, I was going, I will be going, I have been going,* etc.)

CHANGING TENSES IN MIDSTREAM

A student wrote this as part of his report on a novel:

SELECTION B

> *When the book opens, Nick comes to New York and rents a house on Long Island. He found he was living next to the mansion of the mysterious Gatsby. Shortly afterward Nick receives an invitation to a party at Gatsby's, where everyone tried to guess who Gatsby really is. When Nick asked a man in a pink suit if he knew what this Gatsby did, the man replies, "I'm Gatsby."*

6‡

What, if anything, did you find inconsistent in selection B? _____

_____ (Hint: Is the student telling the plot as something that is happening now, or as something that happened in the past?) Return to the selection and circle every verb you find that is in the present tense (telling the action as if it were happening now). Put a box around every verb you find that is in the past tense (telling the action as if it happened some time ago). How many circles do you have? _____ How many

boxes? _____

    As you now know, this student bounces back and forth between present and past in relating the story. Why? The actual events he tells do not alternate between present and past. For a writer to switch between present and past without a reason is inconsistent and illogical; it signals his reader that he is not thinking clearly about what he is doing. This mistake occurs most frequently when a student writes about the events in a book or a play.

    Which tense should you use, present or past, in discussing a plot? You may use either—as long as you stay in that tense. It is just as logical to say *Nick comes to Long Island and rents a house* as it is to say *Nick came to Long Island and rented a house.* What is illogical is *Nick comes to Long Island and rented a house,* or *Nick came to Long Island and rents a house.*

    As a practice, rewrite selection B entirely in whatever tense seems more natural to you; use your own paper.‡ (Develop the habit of discussing all books in the same tense. It is also a good idea to write *present* or *past* at the top of your scrap paper to remind yourself of the tense you are working in.)

    There are two points you should know on choosing tenses when there are two verbs in a sentence. Here is the first. Put two lines under each verb in these sentences:

     9If I go into nursing, I often will work nights.

    10If I went into nursing, I often would work nights.

Look back at the list of forms on page 360. *Will* is which form, present or past? _____

Would is which form, present or past? _____ Returning to this section, examine sentences 9 and 10 again. In 9, *go* and *will* are ¹³☐ both present forms, ☐ both past forms, ☐ one present and one past. In 10, *went* and *would* are ¹⁴☐ both present forms, ☐ both past forms, ☐ one present and one past. When using *will* or *would*, then, we must be consistent: either present forms in both parts of the sentence (as in sentence 9) or past forms in both parts (as in sentence 10)—never a mixture. Here is another example:

If you ⌐are⌐ elected mayor, what ⌐will⌐ you do about housing?

If you ⌐were⌐ elected mayor, what ⌐would⌐ you do about housing?

There is one more point about *will* and *would*. In 9, 10, or the sentences above, is

will or would ever used more than once? _____ Sentences like *If I would be elected mayor, I would improve housing* are illogical; *will* or *would* belongs in the main part of the sentence only.

What is true for *will* and *would* is also true for *can* (present) and *could* (past):

If I ⌐qualify⌐ for the loan, we ⌐can⌐ buy the car.

If I ⌐qualified⌐ for the loan, we ⌐could⌐ buy the car.

Fill in the blanks in the following sentences with *will*, *would*, *can*, or *could*:

¹⁶If I finish work early, we _____ go to the Jolly Tinker Pub tonight.

¹⁷If I finished work early, we _____ go to the Jolly Tinker Pub tonight.

¹⁸"If you w_____ the only girl in the world

And I _____ the only boy, . . .

I _____ say such wonderful things to you;

There _____ be such wonderful things to do. . ."

¹⁹ᵗIf Dr. Zilch ask_____ all multiple-choice questions on the final, I

_____ get an A.

²⁰ᵗ[Do this one another way.] If Dr. Zilch ask_____ all multiple-choice

questions on the final, I _____ get an A.

The second point on tenses concerns the use of the present/past and past/past tenses—the ones that use *have* (*has*) and *had*. Examine these two sentences:

a. Old John went to the park daily for fifty years.
b. Old John has gone to the park daily for fifty years.

In which sentence, a or b, is John no longer going to the park? _____ [21] In which

is he still going? [22] _____ This is the basic difference between the past tense and the present/past tense. As their names indicate, the past tense tells of something that happened entirely in the past (as in sentence a), whereas the present/past tells of something that began in the past but is still happening (as in sentence b). Whenever you use the present form *have* (*has*), you should be telling of happenings that touch the present time. Fill in the blanks in the following sentences so that 23 tells of something that happened entirely in the past and 24 tells of something that started in the past and is still happening. (Use the verb *go*.)

[23]Alec _____ out with Tess for three months.

[24]Alec _____ out with Tess for three months.

Write two original sentences. In 25 tell of something that happened entirely in the past; in 26 tell of something that started in the past and is still happening:

25‡

_____

_____

26‡

_____

_____

Let us look at one more situation. Examine these sentences:

c. When Robert arrived, Maria left.
d. When Robert arrived, Maria had left.

In which sentence, c or d, did Maria leave at the same time as Robert arrived? _____ [27]

[28] In which did she leave before he arrived? _____ This is the basic difference between the past tense and the past/past tense. As its name indicates, the past/past tense tells of something that happened further back in the past than something else (as in sentence d). Notice that the more recent action (*arrived* in d) is in the ordinary past tense.

Fill in the blanks in the following sentences so that 29 tells of two events that happened at the same time and 30 tells of an event that happened further back in time than another event. (Use the verb *faint*.)

²⁹At the time Rottensky aimed his gun at him, Kojak _____.

³⁰At the time Rottensky aimed his gun at him, Kojak _____.

Write two original sentences; in 31 tell of two events that happened at the same time; in 32 tell of one event that happened before the other, using the past/past tense.

31‡

_____

_____

32‡

_____

_____

_____

MASTERY TEST

Part I. Rewrite the paragraph below on your own paper, eliminating all tense errors.‡ (Suggestion: Use the tense of the first verb as your basic tense.)

Love Story *began as Oliver, a wealthy Harvard athlete, meets Jenny, a poor Radcliffe girl. They became lovers when they went out together several times. But complications arose when Oliver's father threatens to disinherit him if he married Jenny. "If you marry her, I would cut you off without a cent," he roared. Defiant, Oliver told Jenny he will marry her even if he was penniless. Her father is different. "Dad lived in an old house in Providence for forty years," Jenny told Oliver. "Let's visit him there." After Jenny's father approved, they married and are happy until the doctor tells Oliver that Jenny contracted leukemia. At the end she dies in Oliver's arms.*

Part II. Write a paragraph of nine to eleven sentences telling the plot of a short story or a movie (one with a simple plot) that you are familiar with.

AGREEMENT

Read this sentence:

a. When students makes mistakes in agreement, the cause are usually that the subject and the verb is separated and each error become hard to see.

All the mistakes in the sentence above were actually made by freshmen (though not all in one sentence). How could someone write such obvious errors? Look:

b. When students in a freshman class in English makes mistakes in agreement, the cause of most of the errors are usually that the subject and the verb, which constitute the heart of the sentence, is separated, and each error caused by this distance between the two words become hard to see.

Sentence b is identical with sentence a except that several subgroups have been added. Are the mistakes as obvious in sentence b as they were in sentence a? _____ Now circle the added subgroups in sentence b. Do the mistakes become obvious again?[2]

In "Basic Sentence Parts" (pages 152–153) and earlier in this module (pages 356–357) you learned that we put an -s on the verb when only one person or thing (other than *I* or *you*) is the subject (as in *The new car perform⌐s⌐ smoothly*); we say *I, you, we, they, the dogs, the cars, . . . perform▨*, but *he, she, it, the dog, the car, . . . perform⌐s⌐*.

To use the verb form that in standard English belongs with its subject—to say *I perform*, not *I performs*—is called *agreement*. Readers may interpret lapses of agreement as lapses of clear thinking. As you saw in sentences a and b, agreement—or lack of it—becomes harder to spot as subgroups come between the subject and verb, pushing them further apart.

If you do not feel confident about identifying subgroups, especially *of*-groups, review "Basic Sentence Parts," "Combining Ideas," and "Economy and Variety." In the following sentences, circle all *of*-groups; then see if you find any agreement errors. The verb must agree with the subject, not with some word in an *of*-group. Change either the subject or th verb. (Cross out unneeded letters or words completely, or add needed ones this way:

My car run⌄*on kerosene.*) [with small *s* above the ⌄]

[3]The deep blue of the waters seem to reflect the sky.

[4]Traffic in the islands of the Caribbean flow at a snail's pace.

[5]The survival chances of all those prisoners in the Nazi camps was extremely s m.

[6]Though the turbulence still persist, the effects of the oil crisis is decreasing.

[7‡]Nixon's and Kennedy's career in Congress were started in 1946. [How many car rs?]

[‡]Photographs of Kennedy in front of a cheering multitude was common.

Not only *of*-groups but also larger groups, such as *who*-groups, *if*-groups, and *-ing*-groups, can come between your subject and your verb, making it hard for you to see that they should agree. In the following sentences, circle all subgroups; then correct any agreement errors:

[9]Many things that Joe Rabble preached was true, but his way of solving problems were too violent.

[10‡]All these things, along with the special love and attention that my daughter needs, has taught me the value of caring.

In the following sentences, add an *s* or *es* in every box that you think needs it; leave the other boxes empty. Circling the subgroups should help you:

¹¹The current power of American labor unions cause☐ nonunionized workers difficulty; the ability of these workers to bargain for wages lack☐ strength.

¹²Elton John, after two appearances at Carnegie Hall during next week, travel☐ to Boston; there his fans, who number nearly a million, plan to greet him with a parade.

¹³‡In New York, music lovers of all ages boast☐ of Lincoln Center. Here the nation's best performances of opera reach☐ the stage.

¹⁴‡The advantages of living in a housing project clearly outweigh☐ the disadvantages.

¹⁵‡Faulkner's source of materials for his works consist☐ of family records and county journals.

¹⁶‡The gerbil and the parrot stay☐ at Aunt Mary's while we are on vacation.

Underline the subject in 16. Is it one thing or two? ¹⁷_____ Two subjects joined by *and* are usually treated as more than one thing: *Ruby and Earl are being married*.

Sometimes, though, two objects are so closely associated that we think of them as one: *Ham and eggs is the most popular American breakfast*. If in doubt, consider two subjects joined by *and* as more than one thing. Continue below:

¹⁸The physics department and the math department plan☐ a joint major.

Here is a special case in which two steps are required:

At the party Darlene met two boys who was/were in her brother's fraternity.

Should we say *was* or *were*? Circle the *who*-group. A *who*-link (*who*, *which*, or *that*) always stands for some earlier noun in the sentence. Mentally substitute that noun for the *who*-link and you will know which verb to use. Which noun does *who* stand for in the sentence above?

¹⁹_____ was/were in her brother's fraternity.

The answer should be easy to see now. ²⁰Cross out the wrong verb in the sentence. Now try these next two; cross out the wrong verb in each:

²¹I will always remember all the wonderful (friends) that has/have visited me in my illness.

²²‡Hemingway's style was free from flowery and poetic passages which was/were characteristic of earlier writers.

Write two original sentences in the present tense, in which at least one subgroup comes between the subject and the verb:

There is one more special case: when the subject comes after the verb. Sometimes instead of saying a sentence like *A tavern is in the town,* we change the word order and say *There is a tavern in the town.* What is the subject now? It is still *tavern* because that is the thing we are telling about. (*There* is just a "nothing word," a throw-in.) But what if the town has two

taverns? Then we must say *There* [25]a____ *two taverns in the town.* Do these:

[26]There _____ too many rules in English grammar.

[27]At the dean's open house last week there _____ over a hundred students.

ANOTHER KIND OF AGREEMENT

There is another kind of agreement. Two of the sentences below have it; one lacks it:

c. A jail was intended as a place of rehabilitation, but they became places of punishment.
d. Jails were intended as places of rehabilitation, but they became places of punishment.
e. A jail was intended as a place of rehabilitation, but it became a place of punishment.

[28]

Which sentence seems to have an illogical lack of agreement? _____ Circle the words that you think are out of agreement with the rest of the sentence.[29‡] The writer of sentence c started talking about *a jail* (one typical jail—one thing), but later in the sentence he uses *they* to refer to *jail.* But does *they* mean one thing or more than one thing?

[30]

_____ This writer, then, has illogically used a word that means more than one thing to stand for one thing. You have now discovered that agreement does not concern just the subject and verb; it covers the whole sentence—and even following sentences—demanding that all words that stand for a noun agree with that noun.

Do you recall from your previous schooling the term that means *referring to one*

person or thing? [31]S___g_____r. And the term that means *referring to more than one*

person or thing? [32]P___r_l.

The words in this column stand for one person or thing; they are singular	The words in this column stand for more than one person or thing; they are plural
I, my, mine, me, myself	we, our, ours, us, ourselves
he, his, him, himself	they, their, theirs, them, themselves
she, her, hers, herself	
it, its, itself	
each, every, one, oneself	ones
everyone, anyone, someone, no one	
everybody, anybody, somebody, nobody	
everything, anything, something, nothing	
this, that (as in *that man*)	these, those

You may be surprised to find words like *everyone* and *everybody* in the singular column, [33]

but do we say *Everyone are ready* and *Everybody are ready?* _____ *Everyone* and *everybody* mean every single person. All the words ending with *-one*, *-body*, or *-thing* are singular. Notice also that (except for *no one*) every word in both columns is one word: *himself*, not *him self; themselves*, not *them selves; anybody*, not *any body*. One more point: [34]

Are there any such words as *hisself, his self, theirself* or *their self* in either column? _____ These words do not exist in standard English.

There is a name for most of the words in both columns above. In "Basic Sentence Parts" you learned that this type of word substitutes for another noun, as, for example, *he* for *Roger*, or *them* for *typewriters*. The Latin syllable *pro-* means (among other things) *for* or *in place of;* therefore the natural name for a noun used in place of another noun is

[35]‡ _____ noun.‡ *It, he, me, someone, themselves,* and other such nouns are called pronouns.

As you have already discovered, a pronoun must agree with the noun it stands for. In each of the following sentences, draw a line from each circled word to the noun it stands for and circle that noun. If the two circled words do not agree (if they are not

(singular) (singular) or (plural) (plural)), cross out one of them and change it to agree with the other. The first item is done for you as an example:

In the London subway, (a rider) pays according to the distance (they) travel. *he* *s*

(Since *a rider* is singular and *they* plural, the writer changed *they* to *he*. Notice that the writer then had to add an *s* to *travel* to make it agree with *he*. No nonagreeing nouns or verbs must remain.)

[36][Change this a different way from the sentence above, keeping *they* but changing the word *they* stands for—the word you will circle.] In the London subway, a rider pays according to the distance (they) travel.

[37]We teach every woman that there is nothing (they) cannot do as well as a man.

[38]‡If a stranger tried to talk to her, she would just look at (them) and smile, even though she understood what (they) were saying.

[39‡]Someone said to me yesterday that women cannot play men's basketball. (They) really made me angry by saying that.

If you often slip by using *they* or *their* when referring to a singular noun, blame the English language, not yourself. English lacks a singular pronoun that means *he or she,* and rather than resort to that awkward expression, as in

Everyone in the stands rose to his or her feet as Gehrig stepped onto the field

most people tend to resort to the pronouns that do combine masculine and feminine: *they, them,* or *their*. Also, with the rise of the women's movement, many women dislike using *he, his,* or *him* for a mixed group, as in

Everyone in the stands rose to his feet as Gehrig stepped onto the field.

Moreover, strict adherence to agreement can sometimes sound confusing or downright silly, as in

Men, when the general enters the barracks, everyone take off his hat.

40

(Whose hat might the men take off? _____) Using *they, them,* and *their* to refer to singular pronouns that obviously stand for more than one person or thing, such as *everyone* and *everybody,* is generally considered acceptable in informal English today, as in

Everyone in the stands rose to their feet as Gehrig stepped onto the field.

Almost everyone speaks this way. In more formal English too, this *everyone-their* custom is gradually gaining in acceptance, but many teachers, writers, and editors still regard it as an error except in instances like the general's-hat sentence above. Follow the guidance of your instructor as to how strictly you should observe agreement in situations like *everyone-their* in your papers. When you are clearly referring to one person, however, agreement must prevail, as in

If a stranger tried to talk to her, she would just look at him [*not* them].

One very good way to avoid the problem is to write the sentence in a completely different way, such as

All the (people) in the stands rose to (their) feet when Gehrig stepped onto the field.

If (strangers) tried to talk to her, she would just look at (them.)

Are words such as *more, most, all, none,* and *some* singular or plural? Examine these sentences:

All (of) the money was gone.
All (of) the gold pieces were gone.

41

In the first sentence, is *all* singular or plural? _____ In the second sentence?
_____ How did you know? _____
The five words listed above can be either singular or plural, depending on the person or thing they refer to. (This is the only time words in an *of*-group affect the agreement of words outside the *of*-group.) Try these sentences; cross out the wrong verb:

⁴⁴Most of the treasure was/were gone.
⁴⁵Some of the cars on this lot is/are lemons.
⁴⁶All the beauty has/have vanished.

Rewrite each sentence below with all logical agreement. Assume that the sentences are formal English. In one or two items you will have to decide whether common sense should overrule grammatical logic:

⁴⁷‡The management now turned to its last resort; they asked the federal government for help with their financial problems.

_____

_____

⁴⁸‡A person can understand themself only in relation to the world around them.

_____

_____

⁴⁹‡Each student brought their own beer with them.

_____

_____

⁵⁰‡Everyone in the stadium were cheering and waving his or her hat after Dempsey kicked the field goal.

_____

_____

⁵¹‡Most of the executives of U.S. Frisbee, Inc., feel that the company should stop its policy of firing their employees as they approach retirement.

_____

_____

_____

⁵²‡When the teacher told her to, every girl in the class took her books off her desk.

_____

_____

I, YOU, AND A PERSON

There is one more kind of agreement, which you may already have learned about in the module "Word Choice" (pages 92–94). It concerns an illogical *I-you* shift, as in

(I) like swimming because it develops (your) muscles.

Does it make sense for *me* to like swimming because it develops *your* muscles? Besides the *I-you* shift, beware of the *a person-you* shift or the *a person-I-you* shift as in

When (a person) first passes through the great gold gates of Bellywhop U.,

(you) feel a thrill of expectation. (I) found the thrill soon leaves, however, when

(you) have to visit the bursar's office.

When you are referring to yourself, use *I*. When you are referring to your reader, use *you*. When you are referring to any person or a typical person, use *a person, a visitor, a student, a freshman,* etc.

Rewrite the example above from the point of view of *I* or of *a freshman*:

53

_____

_____

_____

_____

_____

MASTERY TEST

From your papers evaluated by your instructor, find five sentences where he indicated lack of agreement (but did not correct it.) In the blanks marked A below, write the original versions as they appeared in your papers. (If one agreement error involves two sentences, you will have to copy both.) Then in the blanks marked B, write clear, grammatical versions of those sentences:

1A‡

_____

_____

1B‡

_____

_____

2A‡
_____

_____

2B‡
_____

_____

3A‡
_____

_____

3B‡
_____

_____

4A‡
_____

_____

4B‡
_____

_____

5A‡
_____

_____

5B‡
_____

_____

CLEAR REFERENCE

a. Wilbur saw the dean as he was riding by in his new car.

1‡

Who was riding in the car? _____ Whatever your answer is, are you certain it is not the other person? You have learned in other modules that being clear is the most important requirement in writing. For clarity, you need to be sure that every *he, it, they,* or other such pronoun you use stands for one noun only. How can you tell? Circle the two nouns before *he* in sentence a. The way the sentence is written, is there

2

any way you can tell which of those two nouns *he* stands for? _____ Can you think of two ways to make this sentence clear? (Before you start, decide which person you

4

want to put in the car.) The first way is to change the word ³__ __ to _____.

5

Write sentence a clarified this way: _____

_____ The second way is less simple, but it may give you a better-sounding sentence. This way is to reorganize the sentence. For example, the original sentence a puts both nouns, *Wilbur* and *dean*, before *he,* so that *he* can refer to either. Why not reorganize the sentence so that only one noun comes before *he? As he was*

riding by in his new car is an ⁶_____-group. Can such a group be moved elsewhere in the
  ⁷
sentence? _____ Below is sentence a with the *if*-group moved to the front. Fill in the blanks, using *he* or *him* in one blank and the two names in the others:

⁸As _____ was riding by in his new car, _____ saw

_____.

Now do it so that the other person is in the car:

⁹As _____ was riding by in his new car, _____ saw

_____.

We call the problem in sentence a a *vague reference,* and the solution, as in sentences 8 and 9, *clear reference.* You have just discovered that we can solve this problem by (1) replacing the vague pronoun with a noun or (2) reorganizing the sentence so that the pronoun clearly can stand for only one noun.

Do whatever you must to each item below so that it clearly has only one meaning. (You decide which of its possible meanings to give it.) Write the clarified sentence in the blank:

¹⁰When the (Dodgers) beat the (Giants) on the last day, *they* ended the season in third place. [Who ended in third place?]

_____

_____

¹¹(Taylor) told (Arroyo) that *he* hadn't had much spirit in the last game. [Who hadn't had much spirit?]

_____

¹²When Schultz presented his highly negative criticism of the novel *Catch-22,* the professor said he thought *it* was well written. [What was well written—Schultz's criticism or *Catch-22?*]

_____

¹³‡Considering all the muggers the campus security guards have just missed catching lately, you'd think they'd change their tactics.

_____

_____

[14]‡Sue Smith told Greta Grabo that she was sure she had seen her boy friend going into a motel with Toodles La Fleur. [This one has several possibilities.]

_____

_____

Remember that *who, which,* and *that* lead a double life—they are pronouns as well as links. They too must refer to only one noun. Can you handle this sentence?

[15]‡(Paul Phootlight,) the son of (Phil Phootlight,) *who* starred in *The Destiny of Fate,* never wanted to be an actor. [Who starred in *The Destiny of Fate,* Paul or Phil?]

_____

_____

To avoid vague reference, place a *who*-link right after the noun it stands for and be sure there is no other nearby noun it might also refer to. For example, examine this sentence:

(Laddie), the son of (Lassie), *who* does Woofo dogfood commercials, has the mange.

Who does the commercials? There are two possibilities:

[16](Laddie), *who* d ___ ___ ___ W_____

and is th_____, has the mange.

[17](Lassie), *who* d_____, has a son,

Laddie, who h_____.

If you had trouble with sentence 15, go back now and try it again.[18] Then continue below:

[19]‡The door leading to the stage, which had been riddled with bullets, was spattered with blood.

_____

_____

[20]‡The amendment to the Taft-Hartley Act, which had been the subject of heated debate, passed in a close vote.

_____

_____

Can you see any vague reference in the next sentence? Can you draw an arrow from the circled pronoun to the noun it stands for?

b. Luckily my family had gone to the dining car before (they) started serving lunch at 11:30.

21

What does *they* actually stand for? _____ Sentence b shows one of the most common forms of vague reference—a *they, it, this,* or *which* that does not refer to any previously mentioned person or thing at all. In our informal conversation we often make statements like sentence b, but in our writing we need greater clarity, since our readers are not present and cannot ask us what we meant. How can we easily clarify sentence b?

22

By substituting the words _____ for _____. Rewrite sentence b clarified:

23

_____

_____

Try this:

In England they drive on the left side of the road.

24

They really stands for _____. Rewrite the sentence, clarified:

25

_____

(If your sentence sounds redundant, try again below, starting with *The English:*

26

_____)

The same problem can arise with *it:*

In the *Times* it says that the Urban Development Corporation has agreed to build the Hostos housing project.

What does *it* stand for? The *Times?* Then the writer is saying *In the* Times *the* Times *says.* . . . This problem has an easy solution:

²⁷T _ _ *T* _ _ _ _ _ s _ _ _ _ _____

_____.

Rewrite this sentence:

²⁸‡In the minutes of the last meeting it erroneously stated that I was absent.

Do you find anything odd about the next sentence?

> Eleanor and Amory often strolled for hours across the meadows in the moonlight, which made them tired.

[29]Circle the noun that *which* seems to be referring to. But is this what made them tired? Is there actually any noun in the sentence telling what made them tired—a noun that could substitute for *which*? [30]_____ The writer has used *which* to refer to the whole idea of strolling for hours across the meadows in the moonlight—with confusing results, as you have discovered. The writer's best way out of this problem is to reorganize the whole sentence. Try it, starting as indicated:

> [31]Strolling often _____
>
> made _____ ___ ___ ___ ed.

A similar problem can happen with *this*. Is *this* singular or plural? [32]_____ Then is there anything unclear or illogical about the following item?

> Neil arrived early at the party. He drank four martinis on an empty stomach, ate a whole bowl of potato chips with sour-cream dip, smoked three cigars, devoured a buffet plateful of lasagne, swedish meatballs, and creamed onions, and topped it off with ice cream drowned in green crème de menthe. This made him feel nauseous.

What does *this* stand for? [33]_____ Was it just the crème de menthe that made Neil nauseous; was it the ice cream with the crème de menthe; or was it everything? You can make this item clear by just changing the second sentence. If it was everything that made him sick, what can you say? [34]*A___ th___ ___ made him nauseous.*

If it was only the crème de menthe, what can you say? [35]*Th___ l___t i___m made him nauseous.* If it was the ice cream with the crème de menthe, what can you say? [36‡]

_____ Clarify the following:

> [37]Almost all of these cellar rooms were wet and damp, causing many illnesses, and they died of tuberculosis, just what they had fled Ireland to avoid.

_____

_____

_____

[38]In *Sports Illustrated* it says that Muhammed Ali is going to retire because they are taking too much tax out of his fight earnings to make it worthwhile.

_____

_____

_____

[39‡]Across the shimmering river lay the dandelion-flecked meadow; beyond rose the jagged granite mountain with a barely visible herd of mountain goats clinging to a seemingly inaccessible ledge. This filled me with awe.

_____

_____

_____

[40‡]Dr. Frankenstein had seemed very hesitant when he prescribed the purple medicine, which made Igor wonder how sane he was.

_____

_____

Write two original sentences of at least twelve words each. Use *which, it, this,* and *they* at least once each in the total of two sentences:

41‡

_____

_____

42‡

_____

_____

_____

_____

MASTERY TEST

Take five instances of unclear references indicated by your instructor on your own papers (but not corrected). In the blanks marked A below, write the original versions as they appeared in your papers. (If one reference error involves two sentences, you will have to copy both.) Then in the blanks marked B, write clear versions of those sentences:

1A‡
_____

_____

1B‡
_____

_____

2A‡
_____

_____

2B‡
_____

_____

3A‡
_____

_____

3B‡
_____

_____

4A‡
_____

_____

4B‡
_____

_____

5A‡
_____

_____

5B‡
_____

_____

SUBJECT AND COMPLETER FORMS

This section concerns problems in when to use *I* or *me*, *he* or *him*, *she* or *her*, *we* or *us*, and *they* or *them*. First of all, let us divide these pronouns into two columns indicating the two sets we have to choose between. Below are two sentences. Try saying each of the above pronouns in the blank in sentence 1; then try each in the blank in sentence 2. In column 1 write the five pronouns that sound right in sentence 1; in column 2 write the five pronouns that sound right in sentence 2. (For now, leave the parentheses empty.)

^{1‡} _____ will meet Charlie.

^{2‡}Charlie will meet _____.

‡Column 1 (_____)   *‡Column 2* (_____)

_____   _____

_____   _____

_____   _____

_____   _____

(_____)   (_____)

As a good linguistic scholar should, you have classified the pronouns. All the words in column 1 are used in situations like the one in sentence 1. What is that situation? Let us

see. Write the basic sentence pattern: ³__ __(__)(__). The blank in sentence 1 occupies

which of the four positions of the sentence pattern? The position of the ⁴___ ___ ___ ___ ___.

Then the pronouns in column 1 must be for the ⁵s___j___ ___ ___s of sentences. Write *Subject forms* in the parentheses at the head of column 1. The blank in sentence 2 occupies

which position in the sentence pattern? The position of the ⁶___ ___ ___ ___ ___ ___ ___ ___(s).

Then the pronouns in column 2 must be for the ⁷c___p___ ___ ___ ___ ___s of sentences. Write *Completer forms* in the parentheses at the head of column 2. Thus we have

Subject forms			*Completer forms*	
I				me
he				him
she	will meet Charlie	Charlie will meet		her
we				us
they				them

(Before going on, be sure your answers in columns 1 and 2 match the forms in the brackets just above.)

Most of the time we use the right forms naturally. But problems do arise in writing when we cannot easily see whether we are dealing with a subject or with a completer—most commonly when an *and* is involved. Nobody but Tarzan ever says *Me will go* or *Him will go*, but you may often hear *Charlie and me will go*, or even *Him and me will go*. There is a very simple way to discover whether you have the right form. *Charlie and me will go* is really a combined form of [8]C_____ *will go* and _____ *will go*. Does any word now sound wrong to you? If so, cross it out and write what sounds right. That is really all there is to problems with *I/me, he/him*, etc., in *and*-sentences. Just say the sentence, leaving out *and* and the word after it: *Him ~~and me~~ will go*. Then reverse the process, leaving out *and* and the word before it: *~~Him and~~ me will go*. If either subject (*him* or *me* in this case) does not sound right, replace it with a pronoun that does—one of the subject forms: *He will go; I will go; He and I will go*. You try it; cross out any ungrammatical pronoun below and write above it the pronoun that sounds right:

[9]Fran and them should be back soon.

[10]She and us saw the accident.

[11]The policeman questioned she and us.

Are the pronouns in sentence 11 in the subject position or the completer position? [12]_____ Then they should be in the [13]_____ form. The same procedure we used at the beginning of the sentence will also work at the end. Try each pronoun separately: *The policeman questioned she. The policeman questioned us.* Which one sounds wrong? Trust your own thinking here; rely on sound plus your knowledge of subject forms and completer forms. Many people mistakenly think that combinations like *him and me* or *them and us*, because they are ungrammatical in the subject position, are always ungrammatical. But the separation test (*The policeman questioned him; The policeman questioned me*) shows that these forms are right as completers. Is this next sentence right? If not, cross out any ungrammatical pronoun and write in the grammatical one:

[14‡]Harry and he took Pat and her.

Besides the subject position and the completer position, there is one more place where some people tend to use ungrammatical pronouns: *Henry and he went (with Pat and she/her.)*

[15‡]

Do you recognize the circled group? It is an ___ ___-group. Apply the separation test to this *of*-group. Which forms sound natural in it, the subject forms or the completer forms—*with Pat, with she* or *with Pat, with her?* [16]_____ In an *of*-group, then, use the completer forms: *Pop is furious at him and her. It is a do-or-die struggle between them and us.*

Put a grammatical pronoun in each blank below:

¹⁷I had to shoot; it was a choice of _____ or _____.

¹⁸_____ and _____ have made an agreement with

_____ and _____.

^{19‡}Just between you and _____, Caspar is not the slightest bit con-

cerned about either _____ or _____.

(*Between you and I, for you and I,* and *with you and I* are favorite expressions of some
people who are trying a little too hard to be "correct." Are these expressions grammatical?
²⁰_____. What should each *I* be? ²¹_____)

^{22‡}_____ and our allies fought _____ and their cohorts

for the peace and happiness of you and _____.

There are two points that need mentioning before this module ends. One concerns
that infamous pair, *who* and *whom.* A growing number of scholars and editors are pro-
claiming "the doom of *whom*"—the fact that in general speech, even among many educated
persons, *whom* is no longer used, except directly after an *of*-link, as in *to whom* or *for whom.*
These scholars and editors are willing to accept *who* in all other situations where *whom*
technically should be used. Many others, however, believe that *whom* should still be used
the way it has been in the past. Follow your instructor's guidance in this matter. If your
instructor says to follow the traditional use of *whom,* do the box below:

> Turn back to your list of subject forms and completer forms on
> page 380 and add *who* in the parentheses at the bottom of the subject
> column and *whom* in the completer column. Thus, use *who* in subject situa-
> tions and *whom* in completer situations and in *of*-groups. Another way to
> think of these two words is to use *who* wherever you would use *he,* and use
> *whom* wherever you would use *him*:
>
> a. <u>Who</u> helped Oswald assassinate Kennedy?
> b. (<u>He</u> helped Oswald assassinate Kennedy.)
> c. <u>Whom</u> did Oswald know in Dallas?
>
> To see why *whom* is used, switch sentence c back to its natural order:
> *Oswald did know <u>whom</u> in Dallas?* Now you should be able to see how
> *whom* is used where *him* can be used:
>
> d. (Oswald did know <u>him</u> in Dallas.)
> e. With <u>whom</u> did Oswald communicate in Dallas?
> f. (Oswald did communicate with <u>him</u> in Dallas.)

The grammatical use of *whom* is not easy. Try these. Add *m* where you think it necessary:

²³Who☐ knew his whereabouts that day?
²⁴Who☐ were the police questioning about the shooting?
²⁵‡(The police were questioning who☐ about the shooting?)
²⁶To who☐ was he going?

A case similar to *who/whom* is the question of which form to use after a *being*-verb (see pages 156, 162 of "Basic Sentence Parts"). Grammar books point out that a *being*-verb (such as *be, appear, seem, become*) is like an equals sign; what comes before it equals what comes after it: *God is love* (God = love). *This flower is a begonia* (flower = begonia). Therefore, say the books, we should use the same form (the subject form) after a *being*-verb as we do before it. (*I am he. It is they. The guilty ones are we.*) Others argue that since few people actually say *It's I* or *That was he*, we should not concern ourselves about forms but say what sounds natural. The general thinking is that in informal English, "Do what comes naturally," but in formal English, follow the before = after principle. Again, do as your instructor advises in this matter. Do the box below only if he tells you to do it:

Insert in the blanks a pronoun in the form your instructor has advised you to use. (Assume the sentences are formal English.)

²⁷‡It is not _____ but _____ who must bear
the brunt of war, if it comes.
²⁸‡The murderer, Mr. Holmes, was undoubtedly _____.
²⁹‡When the envelopes are opened, I am sure the award winner

will be _____.

MASTERY TEST

Take five instances of ungrammatical or inappropriate use of pronouns indicated by your instructor on your papers (but not corrected). In the blanks marked A below, write the original versions as they appeared in your papers. In the blanks marked B, write grammatical versions of these sentences.

1A‡

_____

_____

1B‡

_____

_____

_____

_____

_____

_____

_____

_____

_____

_____

_____

_____

_____

_____

_____

_____

_____

_____

FULL MODULE MASTERY TEST

Part I. The following paragraphs contain quite a few instances of most of the problems you have studied in this module. On your own paper, rewrite the paragraphs clearly and grammatically.‡ Sometimes, to determine the right form to use, you will have to look back into an earlier sentence. Assume that you are writing formal English.

When a camper goes to a store to pick out a tent, it must be a reliable one. They often try to sell you inferior merchandise, but if a camper know what they are looking for, they will find a good bargain. This happen quite often. Everyone who buy tents from salesmen know that they can be gyps. A girl I know, preparing for her first camping trip, bought one that leaked, and when she brought it back the salesman says, "Honey, they never leak." She reply, "Oh, yeah?" and goes outside and fills a bucket with water. She re-entered the store, threw the tent over his head and empties it on top of the tent, which made the salesman so wet and so furious that he swung at her. However, by this time she already left the store, and she never went back there since then.

  There is different kinds of tents everyone who go camping should know about. The cabin tent, related to the wall tent, which was developed by the army, is the most roomy. Everyone in a cabin tent has room to stand up when dressing themself. All the height in cabin tents are provided by the vertical sides and steeply pitched roof. One of the lightest tents is the pup tent, which has no floor. The salesman told my brother that he could pitch one in three minutes. Just between you and I, if people would shop more carefully for camping tents, they will enjoy it more. It is not I alone whom feel that way; my brothers and me, and thousands of other campers, share that opinion.

Part II. Write a paragraph of eleven to thirteen sentences on a topic from the master list or on one suggested or approved by your instructor.

INTRODUCTION AND NOUN AND VERB ENDINGS

[6]star shine [s]
[7]star [s] shine
[8]perfume attract [s]
[9]perfume [s] attract
[10]sophomore, work [s]
[11]sophomore [s], work
[12]Constitution prohibit [s]
[13]constitution [s] prohibit
[14]pill cause [s]
[15]pill [s] cause
[16]-ed
[17]open
[18]open [ed]
[19]wish
[20]wish [ed]
[21]watch
[22]listen [ed]
[23]talk
[24]talk [ed]
[25]visit
[26]visit [ed]
[27]travel

[28]traveled
[29]purchase
[30]purchases, spends
[31]purchased
[32]orbited, returned
[33]started, dropped, attend
[34]say, accidents happen, happened
[35]remained, birds, stayed; Hundreds, birds, perched, branches, trees; waited, started, swooped, pecked, corn, fired, killed (You do the rest.)
[36]No (to both questions)
[37]am [or was], have
[38]be or have
[39]has
[40]was
[41]are, have
[42]is
[43]has announced . . . are withdrawing . . . has cracked
[44]are now rejoicing . . . have captured
[45]has never happened

TIME IN VERBS

[1]tense
[2]have smoked
[3]past
[4]future
[5]had graduated
[7]Not counting the sentence in quotation marks, you should have six, for *opens, comes, rents, receives, is, replies.*
[8]You should have six, for *found, was living, tried, asked, knew, did.*
[9]go, will work
[10]went, would work
[11]Present
[12]Past

[13]both present forms
[14]both past forms
[15]No
[16]will or can
[17]would or could
[18]were, was (or were), would or could, would or could
[21]a
[22]b
[23]went
[24]has gone
[27]c
[28]d
[29]fainted
[30]had fainted

AGREEMENT

[1]To most people, they would not be.
[2](in a freshman class), (in English), (of most), (of the errors), (which constitute the heart of the sentence), (caused by this distance between two words)
[3]The deep blue (of the waters) seems . . .

[4]Traffic (in the islands) (of the Caribbean) flows . . .

[5]The survival chances (of all those prisoners) (in the Nazi camps) were . . .

[6]Though the turbulence still persists, the effects (of the oil crisis) are decreasing.

[9]Many things (that Joe Rabble preached) were true, but his way (of solving problems) was too violent.

[11]The current power (of American labor unions) cause[s] . . .; these workers' ability (to bargain for wages) lack[s] strength.

[12]Elton John, (after two appearances) (at Carnegie Hall) (during next week), travels[s] (to Boston); there his fans, (who number nearly a million), plan . . .

[17]gerbil *and* parrot; two things
[18]The physics department and the math department [*two things*] plan🔲 . . .
[19]boys

[20]At the party Darlene met two boys who were in her brother's fraternity.
[21]. . . friends that have . . .
[25]are
[26]are
[27]were
[28]c
[30]More than one thing
[31]Singular
[32]Plural
[33]No
[34]No
[36]In the London subway, (riders) pay according to the distance (they) travel.
[37]We teach every (woman) that there is nothing (she) cannot do as well as a man.
[40]The general's
[41]Singular
[42]Plural
[43]It depends on what the word *all* refers to.
[44]*Was* is the verb, since *most* refers to *treasure.*
[45]*Are* is the verb, since *some* refers to *cars.*
[46]*Has* is the verb, since *all* refers to *beauty.*
[53]When I first passed through the great gold gate of Bellywhop U., I felt . . . (You do the rest.) *Or,* When a freshman passes through the great gold gate of Bellywhop U., he feels . . . (You do the rest.)

CLEAR REFERENCE

[2]No (the two nouns are *Wilbur* and *dean*)
[3]he
[4]Wilbur *or* the dean (whichever you wish to put in the car)
[5]Wilbur saw the Dean as Wilbur was riding . . . *Or,* Wilbur saw the dean as the dean was riding . . .
[6]*if*
[7]Yes (See "Combining Ideas," page 233.)
[8]As Wilbur was riding by in his new car, he saw the dean. *Or,* As he was riding by in his new car, Wilbur saw the dean. (If you want the dean in the car, see below.)
[9]As the dean was riding by in his new car, he saw Wilbur. *Or,* As he was riding by in his new car, the dean saw Wilbur.
[10]*One possibility:* When they beat the Giants on the last day, the Dodgers ended the season in third place.
[11]*One possibility:* Taylor felt that Arroyo hadn't had much spirit in the last game [,] and told him so. *Another possibility:* Taylor told Arroyo, "You didn't have much spirit in the last game."
[12]*One possibility:* When Schultz presented his highly negative criticism of *Catch-*

22, the professor said his paper was well-written.

[16]Laddie, who does Woofo dogfood commercials and is the son of Lassie, has the mange.

[17]Lassie, who does Woofo dogfood commercials, has a son, Laddie, who has the mange.

[18]*One possibility:* Phil Phootlight, who starred in *The Destiny of Fate* and is the father of Paul Phootlight, never . . .

[21]The waiters

[22]the waiters, *for* they

[23]Luckily my family had gone to the dining car before the waiters started serving lunch at 11:30.

[24]the English

[25]In England the English drive . . .

[26]The English drive . . .

[27]The *Times* says . . .

[29]Moonlight (since that is the nearest noun)

[30]No

[31]Strolling often for hours across the meadows in the moonlight made Amory and Eleanor tired.

[32]Singular

[33]We cannot be sure.

[34]All these . . .

[35]This last item . . .

[37]Almost all of these cellar rooms were wet and damp, causing many illnesses, and the immigrants [the victims, *etc.*] died of tuberculosis, just what they . . .

[38]*Sports Illustrated* says that Muhammed Ali is going to retire because the government is taking too much tax out of his fight earnings to make boxing worthwhile.

SUBJECT AND COMPLETER FORMS

[3]S V(C)(C)

[4]subject (S)

[5]subjects

[6]completer(s)

[7]completers

[8]Charlie will go, me will go.

[9]Fran and they (Fran should be back soon. They should be back soon.)

[10]She and we

[11]her and us

[12]Completer (The <u>policeman</u> <u>questioned</u> her and <u>us</u>.)

[13]completer

[16]*With Pat, with her* should sound more natural.

[17]him or me, *or* them or us [or any other completer forms]

[18]*He and I* [or any other subject forms] have made an agreement with *her and them* [or any other completer forms]

[20]No, since they are subject forms in *of-* groups.

[21]Me

[23]*Who* knew his whereabouts? (*He* knew his whereabouts.)

[24]Whom

[26]whom

MODULE 13

SENTENCE STRUCTURE PROBLEMS

Previous modules required: Basic Sentence Parts (7)—Combining Ideas (8)—Economy and Variety (9)

INTRODUCTION

There is nothing new to learn in the first two sections of this module; they merely go more carefully through areas of sentence writing where you may still be having trouble and provide more practice in those areas.

First, let us review quickly what you have discovered in "Basic Sentence Parts," "Combining Ideas," and "Economy and Variety."

¹‡Write the basic sentence pattern: _____ _____ _____ _____

²‡Circle the *of*-groups in this sentence: Since his marriage to Nancy, Fred has gained twenty pounds from her cooking of Italian and German food.

³‡In the above sentence, underline the subject once, every word in the verb twice, and any completers three times.

⁴‡Circle the *who*-groups (including trimmed ones) and *if*-groups in this sentence: When Congress reconvenes in January, Senator Breithart, an Arizona Democrat, will filibuster unless the Senate passes the clean air bill that he introduced.

⁵‡Circle all *-ing*-groups and *-en*-groups in this sentence: Discouraged by the condition of her elbow broken in a fall last winter, Billie Jean, desiring a return to competition, tried visiting a chiropractor.

⁶‡Circle all *to*-groups and *what*-groups in this sentence: Whoever complains to the manager is told to leave the store; he can buy elsewhere what he wants.

⁷‡All the groups mentioned in 2, 4, 5, and 6 are called _____ groups.

⁸‡Write a sentence containing two clauses joined by an *and*-link:

_____

_____

⁹‡Write a sentence containing two clauses joined by a *therefore*-link:

_____

_____

¹⁰‡Can the subject or the verb of a sentence ever be a word inside a subgroup?

_____ Can a subgroup by itself ever be a sentence? _____

Your instructor will mark this test or provide you with the answers; he will then tell you whether to go ahead.

PIECES OF SENTENCES

In "Basic Sentence Parts" (pages 167–169) you discovered this basic sentence pattern: S V(C)(C). This pattern, you may recall, is just another way of writing our description of a sentence: a string of words telling that some person or thing was doing, having, or being something. Of the four parts in this pattern, which ones are necessary to make a sentence? Does this make a sentence: S (C)(C)? _____(1)_____ Does this: V (C)(C)? _____(2)_____ Does this: (C)(C)? _____(3)_____ Does this: S V? _____(4)_____

In the blank after each item, write S if it has just a subject part, V if it has just a verb part, and S V if it has both:

(5)The sportswoman of the year. _____

(6)Received a solid gold trophy. _____

(7)The sportswoman received a trophy. _____

Which of the three is the only sentence? _____(8)_____ If what you write between an opening capital letter and a period does not have both an S and a V, a subject and a verb, it is only a piece of a sentence. Items 5 and 6 are only pieces of sentences. Another word for *piece* is (9)fr___m___t. This is the word instructors usually use for pieces of students' sentences written as if they were full sentences—beginning with a capital and ending with a period. Items 5 and 6 are fragments. The appearance of several fragments in one paper signals your reader that you need to sharpen your basic knowledge of what makes a sentence.

Would you write the string of words below as a sentence—beginning with a capital and ending with a period?

he with the ever man

Hardly anyone would. It is obviously not a sentence. But what about this next one?

a woman of great dedication to her race

Is this a sentence? Before you write your answer, circle any *of*-groups you find. Remember that the circle is a plastic bubble, isolating everything inside it. Once again—can the subject or the verb of a sentence ever be a word inside the plastic bubble of a subgroup? _____(10)_____ Now—is the second string above a sentence? _____(11)_____ Is this next string of words a sentence? (Before you answer, circle any kind of subgroups you find in it: *of*-groups, *if*-groups, *who*-groups, etc.) _____(12)_____

a woman who has aided countless poverty victims

In each of the following strings of words, first circle any kinds of subgroups that you find; then decide whether the string is a sentence. Write *sentence* or *not sentence* in the blank at the right of each item. (‡Answers to the circling are given, but not to the blanks.)

[13]a woman to remember for many years _____

[14]because she has aided countless poverty victims _____

[15]suffering from inadequate food, clothing, and shelter _____

[16]victims who have almost lost the will to live _____
[17]a woman of great distinction to her race because she has aided countless poverty victims who have almost lost the will to live _____
[18]a woman to remember for many years, who has aided countless poverty victims suffering from inadequate food, clothing, and shelter _____

In which items from 13 to 18 were both a subject and a verb left *outside* the plastic bubbles after you circled all the subgroups? [19]_____ Then which items are sentences?

[20]_____

REPAIRING FRAGMENTS: I

Have you discovered the simple secret of avoiding fragments? It is this: A subgroup cannot be a sentence. In fact, a subgroup cannot even have inside it the main subject or verb of a sentence. Thus by isolating all the subgroups in circles, you will quickly see whether you have a sentence. This is one reason it is so important to be able to spot subgroups. Most fragments consist of one or more subgroups, with no subject and verb *outside* the subgroups.

Try your new knowledge now, with no aids at all. Circle all the subgroups in the items below. Then decide whether each item is a sentence or not; write *sentence* or *not sentence* in the blank at the right:

[21]‡telephone and telegraph service at the flick of your fingers _____

[22]‡a very powerful story that really puts its message across _____

[23]‡after seven years our day in court finally came _____

[24]‡then we saw it _____
[25]‡her mother a maid in a rich man's house, and her father a seaman on an oil tanker _____

Spotting fragments in your writing as you proofread is, of course, only part of the job; the more important part is rewriting to make full sentences. There are several ways to do this. The first is easy to discover; if you were to find that your newly bought stereo set lacked an essential part—say the needle—what would you do? Put one in, of course. We do the same with fragments; we supply the missing parts. Below are the three fragments from the last exercise, with a blank for you to supply the missing parts. It should not be hard for you to determine the kinds of words that must go in each blank. Supply any word or words of those kinds that make sense:

²⁶_____ telephone or telegraph service at the flick of your fingers.

Or

²⁷Telephone and telegraph service _____ at the flick of your fingers.

²⁸_____ a very powerful story that really puts its message across.

²⁹Her mother _____ a maid in a rich man's house, and her father

_____ a seaman on an oil tanker.

To check yourself, circle each subgroup again; then underline the subject once and the verb twice in each sentence. (Sentence 29 has two clauses.)³⁰

REPAIRING FRAGMENTS: II

To understand the second way to repair fragments, recall that subgroups begin with links: *of*-links, *who*-links, *if*-links, *-ing*-links, *-en*-links, *to*-links, or *what*-links. The job of

a link is, of course, to ³¹l __ __ k. But notice what the writer has done in item a below:

a. I decided to return to college this semester. After I had been away since 1959.

The writer thought these should be two separate sentences. But is the second really a sentence? The link *after* tells you that the second "sentence" is really only a ³²s __ __ -

g __ __ __ p:

I decided to return to college this semester. (After I had been away since 1959.)

What do you think we should do with this subgroup? (Hint: What are links for?)
³³
_____ Write item a as it should have been
³⁴
written: _____

People often make the mistake that the writer of item a did: They write a subgroup as if it were a separate sentence, instead of linking it with the sentence it belongs to. Remember: *A subgroup by itself is a fragment.* Link every such subgroup to the sentence it belongs to. Try it with the items below. Rewrite each as it should be, in the blank:

³⁵My little girl became a special kind of joy. Although I had really wanted a son.

_____

_____

[36]I could read this fear in the faces of the people. Waiting nervously for the next bomb to go off.

_____

_____

[37]I occupied my mind with memories. Of our Christmas together, our summer vacations, and our hunting trips.

_____

_____

[38‡]We decided to sue the owners of the apartment house. To make them pay for the injuries that their negligence had caused.

_____

_____

Remember, though, that some subgroups can also come at the beginning of the sentence they belong to:

After I had been away since 1959, I decided to return to college.

Here is another important reason for avoiding fragments. Suppose you see that you have written something like this:

b.   She lived with him for five years. Because he remained quiet and mild-mannered. She finally decided to leave him.

In b circle the subgroup that is a fragment.[39] Do you think it belongs to the sentence *before*
[40‡]
it or to the sentence *after* it? _____ In this kind of case the subgroup can make sense with either sentence. The writer must join the subgroup to whichever sentence will convey his meaning better. Rewrite b, joining the fragment to the first sentence:

[41]

_____

_____

Rewrite it once more, joining the fragment to the second sentence instead:
[42]

_____

_____

Notice that the first rewriting gives a much different meaning from the second. In the first
[43]
rewriting, what did she do because he remained quiet and mild-mannered? _____

_____ In the second rewriting, what did she do because he remained quiet

and mild-mannered? _____ Thus one major
reason for avoiding fragments is that they can muddle your meaning.

REPAIRING FRAGMENTS: III

So far you have discovered two ways to correct fragments. Here is a third way, which
is best for some fragments. Is the second "sentence" in item c actually a fragment?
^{45‡}

_____

    c. I decided to return to college this semester. The reason being the higher pay of
        college graduates.

Remember what you learned in "Basic Sentence Parts" about the *-ing-* and *-en*-forms of
verbs. In the standard dialect of English, can the *-ing-* or *-en*-form be a full verb by itself
^{46}

(as in items d and e)? _____

    d. Jerry walking across the campus.
    e. Dad taken my car away.

(If you need refreshing on this matter, see pages 158–164 of "Basic Sentence Parts.") You
learned that these forms are only *parts* of verbs. *Jerry walking across the campus, Dad
taken my car away*, and *The reason being the higher pay of college graduates*, then, are
fragments because they have only parts of verbs, not full verbs. Therefore the way to make

them sentences is to give them a ^{47}f_____ v_____. You can do this by just adding an
auxiliary before the *-ing* or *-en* form:

    ^{48}Jerry w_____ walking across the campus.

    ^{49}Dad h_____ taken my car away.

But sometimes it is better to change the verb to the present or past form, which needs no
auxiliary. Try to do it with the two fragments:

    ^{50}Jerry _____ed across the campus.

    ^{51}Dad t_____k my car away.

This way is sometimes better with fragments containing *being*, such as item c. Here is
item c again. Rewrite it, changing *being* to the present or past form of *be:*

    ^{52}I decided to return to college this semester. The reason _____
the higher pay obtainable by college graduates.

Try the following. Rewrite the second part of each, making it a sentence:

[53]Regina decided to take a cab home from the party. Her boyfriend Roy being too interested in another girl.

_____

_____

[54]A new television policewoman drama received bad reviews. The heroine looking too old for the part.

_____

_____

You may need this reminder about fragments involving subgroups. Remember how we often trim *who*-groups, as in

My sister, ~~who is~~ a medical technologist, eloped with a veterinarian

and

The vet ~~that~~ she married specializes in tropical birds.

When trimmed, subgroups may not be so easy to recognize. Is the following a sentence or a fragment? Before answering, circle any subgroups you can find, including trimmed ones:

[55]‡The room they reserved for the wedding.

At first glance you may see *they reserved* and conclude that 55 is a sentence because it has

a subject and verb. But can the word *that* fit in front of *they reserved?* [56]_____
Then *they reserved for the wedding* is really trimmed from *that they reserved for the wedding,* a subgroup. Circling it, we have

The room (~~that~~ they reserved for the wedding.)

Is 55 a sentence? [57]_____ One of the next two items is a sentence; the other is a

fragment. Which is the sentence? [58]_____

    f.   Two men I knew well from our days in the army.
    g.   Two men I knew well stayed in the army.

Here is a final caution, about two links that may lead you into fragments: *such as* and *for example.* Is the second part of either of the following items a sentence?

[59]Some of our presidents lived until nearly ninety. Such as Hoover and Truman.

Is the second part a sentence? _____

[60]Some of our presidents were not college graduates. For example, Lincoln and

Truman. *Is the second part a sentence?* _____

By now you should be able to quickly spot the absence of a subject and a verb, but you would be surprised at how often people mistakenly write just a list beginning with *such as* or *for example* as if it were a sentence. Never begin a sentence with *such as*. Link it to the previous sentence, as in

Some of our presidents lived until nearly ninety, such as Hoover and Truman. (*Even better:* Some of our presidents, such as Hoover and Truman, lived until nearly ninety.)

Never begin a sentence with *for example* either, unless you follow it with a full clause, as in

Some of our presidents never went to college. For example, <u>Lincoln</u> <u>taught</u> himself law, and <u>Truman</u> <u>went</u> into the clothing business.

Now you should be ready for the mastery test on avoiding fragments.

MASTERY TEST

Part I. In each blank below, write a sentence that is not a question, beginning with the word(s) given:

[1]‡When _____

_____

[2]‡Because _____

_____

[3]‡A man who _____

_____

[4]‡Knowing _____

_____

[5]‡To pay for _____

_____

(Before going on, check yourself on the items above by circling all subgroups.) Next, rewrite the following items, repairing all fragments:

[6]‡A woman of great distinction to her race because she has aided countless poverty victims who have almost lost the will to live.

_____

[7‡]An office where people all hurriedly moved about, performing their daily tasks.

_____

_____

[8‡]As I look back, I realize that growing up in Rockaway was a very rare experience. The hot, sunny summer days when we walked down to the seashore, the cool nights when we sat on our porches enjoying the breeze.

_____

_____

_____

_____

[9‡]Many critics speak of Hawthorne's concern with original sin in his characters. The one trait which blinds them to reality.

_____

_____

[10‡]When I arrive at Lake Squigi, certain urges grow within me. To go places out of sight or sound of anyone else. To feel free and be my own self.

_____

_____

_____

From your own writing for this course, find five fragments indicated by your instructor but not previously corrected. In blanks 11A to 15A, copy each just as you originally wrote it. Then in blanks 11B to 15B, write each as it should be written. (To do this you may have to include the sentence that originally came before or after some of the fragments.)

11A‡
_____
11B‡
_____

_____
12A‡
_____

12B‡

_____

_____

13A‡

_____

13B‡

_____

_____

14A‡

_____

14B‡

_____

_____

15A‡

_____

15B‡

_____

_____

Part II. Write a paragraph of nine to eleven sentences on one of the topics from the master list or on a topic suggested or approved by your instructor. Be sure it contains no fragments.

> Before you leave this section, you should be aware of the deliberate fragment. Look at this newspaper ad:
>
> > *Come fly with Tasmanian Airlines. To the South Pacific. To the Orient. For fun. For excitement. For the sheer joy of it. Take off in a Tasmanian superjet and begin the greatest adventure of your life. You'll enjoy 22 glorious days. And 21 enchanting nights.*
>
> You probably spotted several fragments right away. Does this mean the ad writer flunked freshman English? Of course not. The ad man is deliberately violating normal sentence structure, putting stops where pauses should be, to slow you down so you will spend more time with the ad. You should be aware that this is a specialized use of the language. Do not imitate it unless you are hired by an advertising agency.
>
> Writers of stories may also use deliberate fragments, usually to represent the fragmentary thoughts in a character's mind, such as
>
> > *I'm almost there. Only a mile now. Can see the cabin lights. Snow getting deeper. Got to make it!*
>
> Whether you should try to use such fragments in this course depends on your experience, your ability, and most of all the type of paper you are

writing. Follow your instructor's advice on whether to attempt deliberate fragments.

There is one more kind of acceptable fragment. Here is an example:

"Why did you chop her to bits with the axe?" "Because I loved her."

It would be redundant for the person answering to have to say *I chopped her to bits with the axe because I loved her.* As long as it is clear that the writer is answering a question, readers will accept fragments like *Because I loved her.*

SENTENCES THAT FORGET TO STOP

Remember the old saying, "A chain is only as strong as its weakest link"? A chain where one link was missing completely would obviously be of no use at all. Read these two sentences:

Nicole is a bright child.

She learns very fast.

One student put these two ideas together like this:

a.   Nicole is a bright child she learns very fast.

In "Combining Ideas" and "Economy and Variety" you learned several kinds of links you could use to join two ideas in one sentence. What is the link in item a, the combined "sentence"? _____ If there is no link, then has this writer really joined his ideas at all? _____ And if they are not joined, should they be in the same sentence? _____ Why? Because most speakers would naturally come to a stop between these two ideas.

Nicole is a bright child she learns very fast is what most instructors call a *run-together** —two sentences put between an opening capital letter and a closing period, without any link, as if they were one sentence. A run-together, with its ideas unlinked, is like the chain with a link missing; no one will accomplish much with it. In fact, such a chain is really no longer one complete chain but two smaller ones. What do you think is the very *simplest* way—without adding any words—to correct a run-together such as item a?

Nicole is a bright child she learns very fast.

The simplest way is to settle for two small chains—in other words, to break the run-together

---

* Some texts and instructors use the term *run-on* instead. *Comma splice* and *comma fault* and *fused sentences* are other names for some run-togethers.

into two ⁴s__p____ate s____t____ces. It is not often the best way, but sometimes it will do in a pinch. Break item a into its two separate sentences:

⁵N_____. S_____.

Do the same with the following. If you cannot sense where the break should be, find and underline the two sets of subject and verb:

⁶Mr. Van Tassel had invited Brom Bones he came on his horse, Daredevil.

_____

_____

⁷The music began Ichabod danced with Katrina.

_____

⁸Ichabod joined a group of older folks for stories about local ghosts the story about the headless horseman terrified him most.

_____

_____

(Did you find the last one harder than the others? Short run-togethers are usually easy to spot; it is longer ones that give students trouble.)

We could correct all run-togethers by simply breaking them in two, but as you can imagine, our writing would be terribly choppy if we did. What other way is there? If our chain had a link missing, what could we do to repair it instead of settling for two small

chains? ⁹_____

This is the much more common way. Why? Not merely to avoid choppy sentences, but for a more important reason, which you discovered in "Combining Ideas." If you do not recall how we clarify meaning by combining ideas, do this box:

What does this sentence mean?

b. Diane married Ben Marshall joined the army.

Confusing? Certainly. But what happens when a link is added?

Diane married Ben, *and* Marshall joined the army.
Diane married Ben, *but* Marshall joined the army.
Marshall joined the army *after* Diane married Ben.
Diane married Ben; *therefore* Marshall joined the army.

Item b has no clear meaning. Each different link inserted gives the sentence one clear meaning. The link shows the exact relation the writer intends between the two ideas.

To eliminate run-togethers from your writing, you must know your links. This is so important that below is repeated a section of the practice test you did in "Combining Ideas." Do it again before you go further; you need 85 percent to 90 percent success on this to be able to beat the run-together problem. Follow your instructors directions on scoring it.

Fill in the blanks:

[10‡]The *and*-links: a ____, b ____, o __, n ____, y ____

[11‡]The common *therefore*-links: th _____ e, t ____ s,

c _____ y; h _____ r, n _____ s,

o __ t __ o _____ _____, o __ t __ c _____,

i _____ d; f _____ m ____, m _____ r,

b _____ s; f __ i _____ e, f __ ex _____;

i __ o ____ w ____; l _____ e; o _____ e;

s ____ d, t ____, n ____, t __ n, f _____ y,

m _____ le; and the phantom link, ____ alone

[12‡]The *who*-links: w ____, w _____, _____

[13‡]The common *if*-links: i __, u _____ s, w __ t __ r; w __ n,

w __ n ____ r, w ____ e, b _____ e, a ____ r, a __,

a __ s ____ a __, s _____, u _____; a _____ gh, _____ gh,

w _____ a __; a __ i __; w ____ e, w _____ r; b _____ e,

f ____, s __ t ____, i __ o _____ t ____

REPAIRING RUN-TOGETHERS WITH *AND-* AND *THEREFORE*-LINKS

The first and simplest type of link you learned is the [14‡]_____-link. Correct the following run-togethers by supplying *and*-links:

[15]Nicole is a bright child she learns fast.

[16]Nicole is a bright child her school grades are low.

_____

[17]The party broke up at one in the morning Ichabod lingered for a few final words with Katrina.

_____

_____

Just as we would have choppy writing if we broke every one of our run-togethers into two separate sentences, so we would have stringy writing if we relied constantly on *and*-links. We need to know how to use other links. Probably the most important type of link in correcting run-togethers (and the one most errors are made with) is the *therefore*-link. Before practicing with it, however, you need to master the most important point on run-togethers. Answer this question: Is the comma (,) a link? (Was it, by itself, anywhere on our lists of links?) _____[18]_____ Thus is the following a logically joined sentence or a run-together? _____[19]_____

Nicole is a bright child, she learns very fast.

Probably most of the run-togethers your instructor has found in your papers are of this type, where the writer mistakenly tries to link two ideas with only a comma. Why does a comma not do the job? Why is it not a link? Remember that a comma means merely a [20]p_ _ _ _, not a s_ _ _. When there is no link word, something stronger than just a pause is needed to signal where the first clause ends and the second begins. Thus a comma alone is not strong enough to be a link. What mark is strong enough? What is the mark that comes before every *therefore*-link? (See pages 211–216 of "Combining Ideas" if you are unsure.) _____[21]_____ And what is the phantom link you learned with *therefore*-links? _____[22]_____ In the three blanks below, rewrite the given sentence three times, each time using a different *therefore*-link that makes sense. Use the phantom link in the third rewriting:

[23]Nicole is a bright child, she learns very fast.

_____

_____

_____

Inserting a *therefore*-link is one of the most effective ways to correct a run-together; in fact, the phantom link (; alone) will provide an instant remedy for most run-togethers. (Of course, like any single device, it should not be used too often.) Here are some run-togethers taken from freshman papers. Rewrite them, using *therefore*-links; use the phantom link at least twice:

24His stories paralleled his own life, he wrote mainly of the romantic rather than the physical.

_____

_____

25Faulkner deals with red men, white men, black men alike, his general theme is the destruction of the wilderness.

_____

_____

26‡My kingdom is very serene, even on the most hectic occasions it is isolated from reality.

_____

_____

27‡I was unable to control my emotions at this time, immediately I began to cry hysterically.

_____

_____

28‡He found me and asked me to come out, his voice did not sound as angry as I thought it would.

_____

_____

Once again: Which punctuation mark normally comes before every *therefore*-link?
29

_____ Then is anything wrong with the items below? If so, add directly to the sentences what should be there. Circle what you add:

30‡The ticket agent had sold 81 tickets to boarding passengers, however there were only 11 empty seats on the entire train.

31‡He did not believe man's destiny was determined by forces beyond his control, on the contrary he believed that man's greatest enemy was himself.

32‡The girl was born with her skull slightly cracked, therefore the doctor said her growth would be retarded.

³³‡Sheer exhaustion had caught up with me, thus I had no trouble falling asleep.

³⁴‡During the past five years there have been many significant changes in juvenile court laws, for example, in certain states where bail was not given, it now must be.

³⁵‡I thought it was the end of the world, however, it turned out to be just a temporary setback.

REPAIRING RUN-TOGETHERS WITH *IF-* AND *WHO*-LINKS

So far you have learned two major ways of eliminating run-togethers. The first is to break the run-together into separate sentences, as in

Nicole is a bright child. She learns very fast.

The second way is to add an *and*-link or a *therefore*-link, as in

Nicole is a bright child, *and* she learns very fast.
Nicole is a bright child; [*therefore*] she learns very fast.

Are there other ways? Yes, since there are other types of links, such as *if*-links and *who*-links. We could, for example, take this run-together,

The <u>music</u> <u>began</u>, <u>Ichabod</u> <u>danced</u> with Katrina.

and write it with an *and*-link or a *therefore*-link:

The <u>music</u> <u>began</u>, and <u>Ichabod</u> <u>danced</u> with Katrina.
The <u>music</u> <u>began</u>; therefore <u>Ichabod</u> <u>danced</u> with Katrina.

But what other kind of link might do even better here? Are the two ideas in the sentence related by time—or by cause-effect, or by both? This suggests what kind of link? An

³⁶
_____-link. Try it:

³⁷Ichabod danced with Katrina _____ the music began.
Or
³⁸_____ the music began, Ichabod danced with Katrina.

Here is another:

Ichabod had heard too many ghost stories, he started homeward quivering with fright.
³⁹Ichabod started homeward quivering with fright[,] _____ he had heard too many ghost stories.
Or
⁴⁰_____ Ichabod had heard too many ghost stories, he started homeward quivering with fright.

Do the blanks at the beginning of 38 and 40 confuse you? If so, do this box:

Remember that *if*-groups can shift to the beginning of the sentence. If you circle the *if*-groups in 37, 38, 39, and 40, you should see the *if*-group shift clearly. The important point is that 38 is exactly the same sentence as 37, and 40 is exactly the same sentence as 39; the link in 38 and 40 is still doing its job even though not in its usual position. Sentences 38 and 40 are grammatical sentences, not run-togethers.

Try the following. Rewrite each item in the blank below it, using an *if*-link. In at least one of the items, put the *if*-group at the beginning of the sentence:

⁴¹All I had with me was three dollars, I had left my wallet home.

_____

_____

⁴²The waitress called the manager over, I became thoroughly embarrassed.

_____

_____

Why not try *who*-links for the following? The first is done for you as an example:

who

Mr. Van Tassel had invited Brom Bones, ~~he~~ had come on his horse, Daredevil.

⁴³The waitress handed me the check, it came to four dollars and some cents.

_____

_____

⁴⁴Stella gave me three rolls of her bingo pennies, they were the last of her money.

_____

_____

You now know how to avoid run-togethers. Much of what you have done in this section is a review of "Combining Ideas"; as you do these sentences, more and more of what you learned there should come back to you.

There is one final pitfall to be pointed out. The sentence below illustrates it:

c. The restaurant check almost made me faint, because I had left my wallet home, I couldn't pay for the meal.

Is item c a run-together? _____ Why? There are three ideas in item c. What

link joins the first and second ideas? _____ But what link joins the second and

third ideas? _____ Do you see what happened when a student wrote this? She
started writing sentence d, which has an *if*-group linked by *because* to the main clause:

> d. The restaurant check almost made me faint, (*because* I had left my wallet home.)

Then she must have grown forgetful and started writing sentence e, using the same *if*-group:

> e. (*Because* I had left my wallet home,) I couldn't pay for the meal.

Can one subgroup be linked to two different main clauses at once? _____ In the
chain below, if you have one link to add, you can make it join sections A and B, or B and C;
but you cannot make it do both at once:

To avoid problems like this, circle any subgroups you suspect of leading a double life—
of trying to belong to two main clauses at once. For instance, go back to item c and circle
the *if*-group. Which main clause do you want to join it to, the one before it or the one

after it? _____ Draw an arrow from the circled *if*-group to the main clause you
decided to join it to. Now combine that clause and the *if*-group into one sentence and write
that sentence:

_____

_____

That is all we can put in one sentence, because there is no other link in item c.

But then what do we do with this remaining clause—the one your arrow did *not*
point to? Since it is linked to nothing, we chop it off and make it a separate sentence. Below,
write item c (all of it) as you think it should be written. (There are two possible answers.)

_____

_____

_____

Here are two more of the same kind:

[52]Those of us who owned cars ignored the rule, because we were seniors, we never worried about campus regulations.

_____

_____

_____

[53‡]It was a cloudy, sultry afternoon when we sighted our first school of whales, the cry of "Lower the boats" rang throughout the ship.

_____

_____

_____

Before moving on to the mastery test, do this practice. Most of the following are run-togethers; one or two may be correct sentences. Decide which are the run-togethers and rewrite each correctly in the blank below it. Do nothing with any sentence already correct. For the longer ones it will help if you circle the *who*-groups and *if*-groups and draw an arrow to the main clause each is linked to. Try not to correct all the run-togethers the same way:

[54]One of the experimental groups of rats grew bigger and healthier these were called the aristocrat rats.

_____

_____ (Partial ‡)

[55]During the mating dance the female rat would normally come out of her burrow, however, the males stopped dancing as the population increased.

_____

_____

_____

_____ (Partial ‡)

[56]Now the country was in trouble, and nothing really could be done, the Jews wanted to be reunited with relatives who had come here earlier.

_____

_____

_____ (Partial ‡)

[57‡]The Irish immigrants did not go into farming here for fear of the blight coming to America; however, the Germans did go into farming, they had no fear of the blight.

_____

_____

_____

[58‡]With the passage of the British "Poor Law" in 1847, Irish landlords who owned ten acres of land were disqualified from poor relief.

_____

_____

For 59 and 60, combine the sentences given into one sentence, using links to avoid run-togethers:

[59]Reverend Dimmesdale became overworked in performing his duties. He was sent to Dr. Chillingworth. The doctor determined to know all about him before trying to heal him.

_____

_____

_____

[60‡]Magua discovered Duncan and Alice together.
He was about to order them tortured.
Hawkeye suddenly appeared.
He overpowered Magua.
He rescued Duncan and Alice.

_____

_____

_____

_____

For 61 and 62, find in your own writing for this course two run-togethers indicated by your instructor and not previously corrected. In blanks 61A and 62A, copy each just as you originally wrote it. Then in blanks 61B and 62B, rewrite each run-together as it should be written:

61A‡

_____

_____

61B‡

_____

_____

_____

62A‡

_____

_____

62B‡

_____

_____

_____

You should now be ready for the mastery test.

MASTERY TEST

Part 1. For items 1, 2, and 3, find in your own writing for this course three run-togethers indicated by your instructor and not previously corrected. In blanks 1A, 2A, and 3A, copy each just as you originally wrote it. Then in blanks 1B, 2B, and 3B, rewrite each run-together as it should be written:

1A‡

_____

_____

1B‡

_____

_____

2A‡

_____

_____

2B‡

_____

_____

_____

_____

_____

_____

_____

For each item from 4 through 10, combine the sentences given into one or two sentences, avoiding run-togethers:

⁴‡Clyde Griffiths had parents without the strength or wisdom to bring up their family properly. Clyde grew ashamed of his parents, his clothes, and his ugly surroundings.

_____

_____

_____

⁵‡Clyde grew older. He dreamed of a life of wealth and elegance. He spent most of his meager earnings on clothes and luxuries for himself. He contributed little to his parents.

_____

_____

_____

⁶‡Clyde managed to impress his wealthy uncle. The uncle owned a factory. He gave Clyde a job. This increased Clyde's desire to climb socially.

_____

_____

_____

⁷‡One night Clyde's uncle invited him to a dinner. There he saw wealthy, beautiful Sondra Finchley. She filled his thoughts for days afterward. He became determined to have her.

_____

_____

_____

^{8‡}Clyde still desired Sondra. She was too far above his social position. He met Roberta. She was a factory girl. She loved him. She became pregnant by him.

_____

_____

_____

^{9‡}One day Sondra accidentally met Clyde. She liked him. She agreed to marry him. This made Clyde see his dreams of wealth and social status coming true.

_____

_____

_____

^{10‡}Roberta told Clyde to marry her or she would reveal to everybody what he had done to her. Clyde saw his dream of marrying Sondra in ruins. He remembered a newspaper article about a girl who had drowned in a rowboat accident. He invited Roberta to go rowing.

_____

_____

_____

Part II. On your own paper, write a paragraph of nine to eleven sentences on one of the topics from the master list or on a topic suggested or approved by your instructor. Be sure it contains no run-togethers.

PARALLEL STRUCTURE

Read these two sentences only once:

a. The chief ordered Smart to go to the vault, he should bring out all the secret papers, and the plans for the transistorized hula-hoop were to be given to him.

b. The chief ordered Smart to go to the vault, bring out all the secret papers, and give him the plans for the transistorized hula-hoop.

^{1‡}

Which of the versions above is clearer to you, the first or the second? _____
Now read these:

c. ... government of the people, that the people run themselves, and the people benefiting by it, shall not perish from the earth.

d.   . . . government of the people, by the people, and for the people shall not perish from the earth.

Which version is clearer, the first or the second? _____ [2‡] Was your answer the same in blanks 1 and 2? _____ [3] Can you see why the second version of each is clearer? Look:

First versions	*Second versions*
A. go to the vault	A. *go* to the vault
B. he should bring out all the secret papers	B. *bring* out all the secret papers
C. the plans for the transistorized hula-hoop should be given to him	C. *give* him the plans for the transistorized hula-hoop

A. of the people	A. *of* the people
B. that the people run themselves	B. *by* the people
C. the people benefiting from it	C. *for* the people

In each sentence, the writer had several items of the same kind. In sentences a and b, the chief ordered Smart to do three tasks; in sentences c and d, Abraham Lincoln spoke of three qualities of government. How good a linguistic scientist are you? Can you now state the best way for writing clearly items of the same kind? "Items of the same kind are most clear when they are written in the [4]s __ __ __ f __ __ m."

What you have just discovered is one of the strongest devices we have for clear writing. It is called *parallel structure*. This simply means that for clarity, items of the same kind should be written in the same form. Thus, in the second version of each sentence, parts A, B and C are best written in the same form: three verbs (*go, bring,* and *give*) for sentence b, and three *of*-groups for sentence d. Using parallel structure often gives students trouble, yet it will not be hard if you are fairly good at identifying different types of words and subgroups or if, as some people are, you are blessed with a natural sense of what is parallel.

Here are more examples of parallel structure. Show how well you understand what it is by numbering and underlining the parallel items. The first sentence is done for you as an example:

(1)
But in a larger sense we cannot dedicate,

(2)   (3)
we cannot consecrate,   we cannot hallow this ground.

[5]Studies serve for delight, for ornament, and for ability.

[6‡]Spending a day at the race track and an evening in a cocktail lounge is my idea of recreation.

(Be careful on item 6; where does the first parallel item begin? Underline only the words that are part of each parallel item. For example, is *spending* part of one of the items?

Should it be underlined? _____[7]_____ To help yourself see which words belong to the parallel items and which do not, try listing the items in a column on scrap paper, like this:

a day at the race track
an evening in a cocktail lounge)

[8]‡My fellow Americans, I present to you tonight a man who holds the common people in his heart, who loves this great country of ours, who has always been a fighter for the little guy, and who will on election day attain the highest office in the land.

[9]‡A business letter should be accurate, brief, and courteous.

[10]I knew what I was supposed to do, but not when I was expected to do it or how I could accomplish it.

What is the smallest number of parallel items you found in the sentences above? _____[11]_____ You have been writing parallel structure since you wrote your first sentence about Jack and Jill, or Dick and Jane. When you first learned of *and*-links in "Basic Sentence Parts," you were also learning parallel structure. You learned that you can link two [12]n _ _ _ s, like *ham* and *eggs;* two [13]v _ _ _ s, like *rise* and *shine;* or two [14]m _ _ _ _ _ _ _ _ s, like *high* and *dry*. In fact, you can link two (or three, or more) of almost anything, including main clauses and all kinds of subgroups. There is only one kind of item you cannot logically link to others. What kind? Read the following two sentences to find out. Below each, list the three items that follow the verb:

[15]‡<u>Rico</u> <u>is</u> intelligent, handsome, and has no wife.

(1) _____

(2) _____

(3) _____

[16]‡<u>Rico's pastimes</u> <u>are</u> swimming in the winter, hunt alligators in Florida, and to ascend in balloons.

(1) _____

(2) _____

(3) _____

Now examine the items in each list. In sentence 15, which item is not made up of the same kind of words as the others? [17]_____ In sentence 16, is the second item in the same form as the first? [18]_____ Is the third item in the same form as either the first or the second? [19]_____

In our informal English we are not all able to think ahead fast enough to put a set of items into the same form—into parallel structure. However, in our formal English, we do have the time, and our readers expect us to take the care. (To most readers, parallel structure shows a careful, logical mind at work. To these readers, an erratic, nonparallel arrangement of items of the same kind signals a lack of clear, logical thinking in the writer's mind; it is often just a short step from there to the reader's losing confidence in the writer's intelligence.) In formal English, then, we can link two or more of almost any kind of words or groups as long as all the words or groups are of the *same* kind. Let us look more closely at the listed items in sentences 15 and 16:

Rico is
- (1) intelligent, ————→ (1) modifier
- (2) handsome, ————→ (2) modifier
and
- (3) has no wife. ————→ (3) verb (+ completer)

How can we rewrite sentence 15 in parallel structure? If most of the listed items are modifiers, then the easiest way would be to make all the items [20]m__ __ __ __,__ __ __s, if possible. Can you think of a modifier which means the same as *has no wife?* [21]S__ __ __ __e (*or* un__ __ __ __ __ed). Now write the sentence in parallel structure:

[22]Rico is
- (1) _____, ————→ (1) modifier
- (2) _____, ————→ (2) modifier
and
- (3) _____. ————→ (3) modifier

Let us focus on sentence 16:

Rico's pastimes are
- (1) swimming in the winter, ——→ (1) *-ing*-group
- (2) hunt alligators in Florida, ——→ (2) verb (+ completer)
and
- (3) to ascend in balloons. ——→ (3) *to*-group

How can we rewrite this in parallel structure? Here the writer has used *three* different structures. Can we choose any one of the three and change the others to that form? Yes, providing we make one check first. Would each item on the list sound grammatical if it were the *only* item on the list? Check the one below that sounds *un*grammatical:

[23]☐ (1) Rico's pastime is swimming in the winter.
☐ (2) Rico's pastime is hunt alligators in Florida.
☐ (3) Rico's pastime is to ascend in balloons.

You now know that you should stay away from the structure in item (2) (verb + completer) when rewriting. That leaves you with a choice between making all three items -ing-groups or making them all to-groups. Try it each way:

²⁴Rico's pastimes are

(1)   swimming in the winter,   (1)   -ing-group

(2) _____ alligators in Florida,   (2)   -ing-group

and (3) _____ .   (3)   -ing-group

²⁵Rico's pastimes are

(1) _____ in the winter,   (1)   to-group

(2) _____ ,   (2)   to-group

and (3)   to ascend in balloons.   (3)   to-group

When you list your items in a column, it is much easier to see whether your structure is parallel.

Here are some sentences with incomplete sets of items. Make up items to complete the sets, and write them in parallel structure in the blanks. To help you, columns are provided for listing some of the parallel items:

²⁶When I think of Maine I picture tall pines, _____ ,

_____ , and _____ .

... I picture

(1)   tall pines,

(2) _____ ,

(3) _____ ,

and (4) _____ .

²⁷When I think of California I picture the Pacific surf crashing against wooded

cliffs, girls sunbathing on sunny beaches, _____ ing

_____ , and _____ .

... I picture

(1)   Pacific surf crashing against wooded cliffs,

(2)   girls sunbathing on sunny beaches,

(3) _____ ing _____ ____ ,

and (4) _____ .

[28]With the rise in prices and _____, people are forced to spend more on _____ and less on

_____.

[29]‡Our college is located amid rolling hills, has _____,

_____, and _____.

(Be careful of this one. With what kind of word do the first two items begin?

[30] _____ Then with what kind of word must the last two items begin?

[31] _____ Fill in the second column below *before* the first.)

[32]Our college
(1) is located amid rolling hills | (1) verb (+ ...)
(2) has _____, | (2) verb (+ ...)
(3) _____, | (3) _____
and (4) _____. | (4) _____

There is another way to approach sentence 29. Let us suppose your answer was

(2) has beautiful buildings,
(3) has excellent recreational facilities,
and (4) has a 400-seat beer hall.

You are perfectly clear and perfectly grammatical. But perhaps you feel that you have repeated *has* too much. Is there any way to stay clear and logical yet drop a *has* or two? How about thinking in terms of *two* sets of parallel items like this?

[33]Our college
(1) is located amid rolling hills
and (2) has
(1) beautiful buildings,
(2) _____[,]
and (3) _____

If this confuses you, forget it; stay with the original version.

[34]This semester I resolve to study harder, _____,

and _____ .

(Here again you have two possible arrangements:)

[35‡] . . . I resolve ⎡ (1) to study harder,

　　　　　　　　　⎢ (2) to _____ ,

　　　　and　　　 ⎣ (3) to _____ .

[36‡] . . . I resolve to ⎡ (1) study harder,

　　　　　　　　　　　⎢ (2) _____ ,

　　　　　　and　　　 ⎣ (3) _____ .

This is a good place to pause and examine a very common writing mistake. Suppose you had written

　　e.　This semester I resolve to study harder, watch less TV, and to drink less beer.

[37]

Under which of the two arrangements above, 35 or 36, does sentence e fall? _____
Do you see the problem? Sentence e uses the *to* with item (1), drops it with item (2), then uses it again with item (3). This fits neither arrangement 35 nor arrangement 36. It is not parallel and therefore not logical. It is safer, and usually clearer, to repeat the link at the beginning of each subgroup in a list. For example, sentence 25 says *to swim, to hunt,* and *to ascend.* Let us return to the exercise:

　　[38]I know *not only* what you said *but also* _____ .
　　　I know not only ⎡ (1)　what you said

　　　but also　　　 ⎣ (2)　_____ .

With two-part links, like *both . . . and, either . . . or,* and especially *not only . . . but also,* it is very easy to slip out of parallel structure. What comes after the second part should be in the same form as what comes after the first part. Writing the two items in a column is the best way to be sure your items are parallel. For example, what is wrong here?

　　f.　I not only know what you said but also did.
　　　I not only ⎡ (1)　know what you said

　　　but also　 ⎣ (2)　did

The secret in using two-part links is to be sure the two parts of the link come right before the brackets when you write your items in a column. In sentence f, when *not only* and *but also* are put right before the brackets, it is easy to see that the items in the brackets
[39]☐ are,　　☐ are not　　parallel.

²⁑O'Neill made the audience aware both of the conscious and the subconscious.

both {(1) _____

and {(2) _____

[Write the whole sentence.] _____

_____

³⁑Jenny's role involved much suffering, such as not being able to have children, she knew her husband hated his father, the cancer that rendered her helpless, and then to die.
[Make your own list.]

[Write the whole sentence.] _____

_____

_____

Part II. Answer 4 to 8 in a single sentence each. Adjust wording as needed to achieve parallel structure:

⁴⁑Tell four things you do not know.

_____

_____

_____

_____

⁵⁑Compare three things you like to do.

I like _____ better than _____

_____ or _____ .

⁶⁑Tell any three actions you performed in a row today.

Today I _____,

_____,

and _____.

[7‡]Here are four causes of the War of 2002. Write a sentence listing them all.
(1)   European nations starving for caviar
(2)   the Antarctican army occupied Tasmania
(3)   Lapland, desirous of its independence
(4)   the cessation of jumping-bean exports by Mexico

_____

_____

_____

_____

[8‡]Here are three qualities of Elizabeth. Fit them into the sentence below. You may either use the blank after *Elizabeth* or leave it empty.
(1)   a beautiful person
(2)   vivacious
(3)   there is a seductive look in her eyes

Elizabeth _____ not only _____

but also _____

and _____.

Part III. A freshman made a list of what he did not like about his college. He had so much trouble putting the items into a short paragraph that he gave up. Below are his notes. Write his paragraph for him, using not more than four sentences.‡ Use parallel structure wherever it should be used:

"What I Dislike at Dillydell College," by Warren Wimple
   1.   tuition too high (not too serious—Dad's paying)
   2.   there is no social life
   3.   to reach town you have to hitchhike
   4.   waking up in the icy dorms
   5.   dull faculty
   6.   the food is never varied
   7.   I can't take the courses I want
   8.   girls of low desirability (dislike this most of all)
   9.   how much work the professors want
  10.   isolated area

ANSWERS

PIECES OF SENTENCES

[1]No
[2]No
[3]No
[4]Yes
[5]S
[6]V
[7]S V
[8]Item 7
[9]fragment
[10]No
[11]No (a woman (of great dedication) (to her race))
[12]No (a woman (who has aided countless poverty victims))
[13]a woman (to remember for many years)
(Groups inside other groups do not need a separate circle in this exercise.)
[14](because she has aided countless poverty victims)
[15](suffering from inadequate food, clothing and shelter)
[16]victims (who have almost lost the will to live)
[17]a woman (of great distinction) (to her race) (because she has aided countless poverty victims) (who have almost lost their will to live)
[18]a woman (to remember for many years), (who has aided countless poverty victims) (suffering from inadequate food, clothing, and shelter)
[19]There should have been none.
[20]None
[26]There is, You have, etc.
[27]are available, are yours, etc.
[28]It was, This is, *Love Story* is, I read, etc.

[29]is, was, *or* had been [for each blank]
[30]*Sentence 26:* you have, etc.
Sentence 27: service is, etc.
Sentence 28: It was, etc.
Sentence 29: mother was *and* father was, etc.
[31]link
[32]subgroup
[33]Link the subgroup to the sentence.
[34]I decided to return to college this semester, after I had been away since 1959.
[35]My little girl became a special kind of joy, although I had really wanted a son.
[36]I could read this fear in the faces of the people [,] waiting nervously for the next bomb to go off.
[37]I occupied my mind with memories of our Christmas together, our summer vacations, and our hunting trips.
[39](Because he remained quiet and mild-mannered)
[41]She lived with him for five years because he remained quiet and mild-mannered. She finally decided to leave him.
[42]She lived with him for five years. Because he remained quiet and mild-mannered, she finally decided to leave him.
[43]She lived with him.
[44]She decided to leave him.
[46]No
[47]full verb
[48]was
[49]has *or* had
[50]walked
[51]took
[52]is *or* was
[53]Regina decided to take a cab home from the party. Her boyfriend Roy was too interested in another girl.
[54]A new television policewoman drama received bad reviews. The heroine looked too old for the part.

[56]Yes
[57]No
[58]Item g ([*That*] *I knew well* is a subgroup)
[59]No
[60]No

SENTENCES THAT FORGET TO STOP

[1]There is no link.
[2]No
[3]No
[4]separate sentences
[5]Nicole is a bright child. She learns very fast.
[6]Mr. van Tassel had invited Brom Bones. He came on his horse, Daredevil.
[7]The music began. Ichabod danced with Katrina.
[8]Ichabod joined a group of older folks for stories about local ghosts the story about the headless horseman terrified him most. (The subjects and verbs in this item have been underlined for you. Write the answer sentence on your own.)
[9]Put a link in.
[15]Nicole is a bright child, and she learns very fast.
[16]Nicole is a bright child, but [*or* yet] her school grades are low.
[17]The party broke up at one in the morning, and [*or* but *or* yet] Ichabod lingered for a few final words with Katrina.
[18]No
[19]A run-together
[20]pause, stop
[21]Semicolon (;)
[22]Semicolon (;) alone
[23]Nicole is a bright child; therefore she learns very fast. Nicole is a bright child; thus she learns very fast [Other possibilities]. Nicole is a bright child; she learns very fast.
[24]His stories paralleled his own life; thus [therefore, etc.] he wrote mainly of the romantic rather than the physical.
[25]Faulkner deals with red men, black men, white men alike; his general theme is the destruction of the wilderness. [Other possibilities]
[29]Semicolon (;)
[36]*if*
[37]when *or* as
[38]When *or* As
[39]because *or* since
[40]Because *or* Since
[41]All I had with me was three dollars, since I had left my wallet home. [Other possibilities]
[42]When the waitress called the manager over, I became thoroughly embarrassed. [Other possibilities]
[43]The waitress handed me the check, which came to four dollars and some cents.
[44]Stella gave me three rolls of her bingo pennies, which were the last of her money.
[45]Yes
[46]Because
[47]There is none.
[48]No
[50]The restaurant check almost made me faint, because I had left my wallet home. *Or,* Because I had left my wallet home, I couldn't pay for the meal.
[51]The restaurant check almost made me faint[,] because I had left my wallet home. I couldn't pay for the meal. *Or,* The restaurant check almost made me faint. Because I had left my wallet home, I couldn't pay for the meal.
[52]*One possibility:* Those of us who owned cars ignored the rule because we were seniors. We never worried about campus regulations.
[54]Subjects and verbs: one grew, these were called
[55]Subjects and verbs: rat would come, males stopped, population increased
[56]Verbs: was, could be done, wanted, had come

[59] When Reverend Dimmesdale became over-worked in performing his duties, he was sent to Dr. Chillingworth, who determined to know all about him before trying to heal him. [Other possibilities]

PARALLEL STRUCTURE

[3] Most people would agree that both second versions (b and d) are clearer.

[4] same form

[5] (1) for delight, (2) for ornament, (3) for ability

[7] No

[10] (1) what I was supposed to do, (2) when I was expected to do it, (3) how I could accomplish it

[11] Two (in sentence 6)

[12] nouns

[13] verbs

[14] modifiers

[17] The third item: *has no wife* (verb + completer; the first two are modifiers)

[18] No. The first item is an *-ing*-group; the second is not.

[19] No. It is a *to*-group; the first and second items are not.

[20] modifiers

[21] Single (*or* unmarried)

[22] intelligent, handsome, single

[23] (2)

[24] (1) swimming in the winter, (2) hunting alligators in Florida, (3) ascending in balloons

[25] (1) to swim in the winter, (2) to hunt alligators in Florida, (3) to ascend in balloons

[26] *Sample answer:* (1) icy lakes, (2) rocky shores, (3) old country stores, (4) pine-covered mountains

[27] *Sample answer:* (3) movie stars signing autographs, (4) cable cars clanging up San Francisco's hills

[28] *Sample answer:* the drop in employment, necessities, luxuries.

[30] Verb (is, has)

[31] Verb

[32] *Sample answers:* (2) has beautiful buildings, (3) owns an adjacent golf course (verb + . . .), (4) enrolls 5,000 freshmen a year (verb + . . .)

[33] *Sample answers:* (2) excellent recreational facilities, (3) a 400-seat beer hall

[34] *Sample answers:* drink less, give up smoking

[37] Neither

[38] what you did [Other possibilities]

[39] are not

[41] *Sample answer:* believing

[42] *Sample answer:* to believe

[43] *Sample answer:* living as a coward

[44] *A three-dollar admission charge;* the other items all concern the content of the movie

[45] *Red-haired* is a physical trait; all the other items are character traits. Tartan's red hair has no connection with his private life.

MODULE **14**

SPELLING

Previous modules required: for "Homonyms," "Apostrophes," and "Other Problem
Words"; Basic Sentence Parts (7); for "Apostrophes" (in contractions): Word
Choice (5)*; for all other sections: none

INTRODUCTION

Their is nothing more obvius in your writting then a speling error. Your avaridge reader may overlook a fragmant or redundencey in your pargraphs, but you're mispelled words jump rite off the paper and hit him bitween the eyes; wrightly or rongley, his oppinion of your abbility and intelegence is effected.

The paragraph above should prove its own point. What did you think as you began to notice misspellings? What would your reader think of a paper of yours that had a dozen misspellings? A half-dozen? Two? Misspelling is the gravy stain of writing; it has the same effect on your reader as a large gravy stain right down the front of your best suit or dress would have on a person you were introduced to—especially when you were hoping to make the best possible impression on him. Far more college or job application letters than you may realize have gone to the "reject" file because personnel officers judged the applicants as careless from their misspellings.

"I've always been a poor speller; I can't do anything about it" is a frequent student lament.* One advantage you have in and after college, however, is that you will do most of your writing where you have access to a dictionary—at home, in the library, in your office; some instructors may also allow you to use a dictionary when writing in class.

This module will not give you lists of hundreds of words to memorize; instead, it will let you discover a few basic principles (or is it *principals?*) to help you eliminate the most common types of mistakes.

First, as a brief warm-up, look back at the opening paragraph of this module and see how many misspellings you can find in it. There are twenty. Without resorting to a dictionary or other aid, see how many you can spot and respell correctly. Use the blanks below:

[1](1) _____   (11) _____

(2) _____   (12) _____

(3) _____   (13) _____

(4) _____   (14) _____

(5) _____   (15) _____

(6) _____   (16) _____

(7) _____   (17) _____

(8) _____   (18) _____

(9) _____   (19) _____

(10) _____   (20) _____

Score: _____ right

---

* Some famous people have been poor spellers. F. Scott Fitzgerald, the author of *The Great Gatsby,* was a notoriously bad speller; for example, until the end of his life he wrote the name of his close friend Hemingway with two *m*'s.

Since no two people have identical spelling problems, you need to keep a list of the words you yourself misspell. The space below is for such a list. On it, put every word your instructor marks as misspelled on your papers and every error on any spelling quizzes he may give. Of course, check the dictionary to be sure you put only correct spellings on your list. It is a good idea to underline the part of the word you misspelled. For homonyms there is

a separate section of the list. (Remember what *homo-* means? ²S___ ___ ___; *nym* means name. Homonyms are two or more words that sound the same but are spelled differently, such as *to, too,* and *two.*) To master a homonym you need to write each of its forms and a short sentence using each correctly. Underline the one form you actually misused. You may need your instructor's help in checking these for accuracy.

Personal Spelling List
A.   Misspelled words from your own papers:

(1) _____	(17) _____
(2) _____	(18) _____
(3) _____	(19) _____
(4) _____	(20) _____
(5) _____	(21) _____
(6) _____	(22) _____
(7) _____	(23) _____
(8) _____	(24) _____
(9) _____	(25) _____
(10) _____	(26) _____
(11) _____	(27) _____
(12) _____	(28) _____
(13) _____	(29) _____
(14) _____	(30) _____
(15) _____	(31) _____
(16) _____	(32) _____

(Use your own paper for any additional words.)

B.   Sets of homonyms you wrongly used (leave blanks 1, 2, and 3 for any triple homonyms, such as *there/their/they're;* use your own paper if you run out of space):

Homonym sets	Sentences using each homonym of sets

(1) a. _____ _____

   b. _____ _____

   c. _____ _____

(2) a. _____ _____

   b. _____ _____

   c. _____ _____

(3) a. _____ _____

   b. _____ _____

   c. _____ _____

(4) a. _____ _____

   b. _____ _____

(5) a. _____ _____

   b. _____ _____

(6) a. _____ _____

   b. _____ _____

(7) a. _____ _____

   b. _____ _____

(8) a. _____ _____

   b. _____ _____

(9) a. _____ _____

   b. _____ _____

(10) a. _____ _____

   b. _____ _____

Your instructor may give you one or two short individual quizzes on your personal list during the course. A word of advice: Do not avoid using a word in your writing because you are afraid of misspelling it or because you want to keep your spelling list short. Most instructors would rather see you use the best words you know, even if you misspelled some, than hand in a paper filled with perfectly spelled weak or inaccurate words. Besides, you are in the course to learn, and you cannot improve your spelling by ducking the very words you need most to learn.

PROBLEMS SOLVED BY SOUND

Spelling problems are of two kinds: those that your ear can help you solve, and those that it cannot. Let us work on the ear-related problems first. Examine the words below. Listen to your instructor say each, or perhaps a tape will be available. You should be able to find every misspelling just by listening carefully— more than once if possible—to each sound or syllable. †

If you are alert for extra or missing sounds in the spelled word, you may be surprised at how well you do. One word in each pair is misspelled. Write that word correctly in the blank: (As an aid, the words have been broken into syllables. A *syllable* is a single sound. Some words, such as *foot* and *ball,* have only one sound [one syllable]; others, such as *football,* have two sounds; still others, such as *sportsmanship, stadium,* and *quarterback,* can have three or more syllables.)

[3]fam il i ar ⎱
sim il i ar ⎰ _____

ath e lete ⎱
cath o lic ⎰ _____

ac cid ent ly ⎱
mech an ic al ly ⎰ _____

li bra ry ⎱
Feb u ary ⎰ _____

col lege ⎱
priv lege ⎰ _____

min i a ture ⎱
temp a ture ⎰ _____

en vi ron ment ⎱
gov er ment ⎰ _____

qual i ty ⎱
quan i ty ⎰ _____

lav a to ry ⎱
lab a to ry ⎰ _____

e quipt ment ⎱
bank rupt cy ⎰ _____

You can solve some problems, then, by sounding out words carefully or (for long-range progress) by listening closely to accomplished speakers, such as most radio and television newscasters. Not all sound-related spelling problems are that easy, however. The solution to most involves understanding two basic ideas, both of which you first learned in elementary school. We will review them here because of their importance.

First, do you recall the two kinds of letters in the alphabet? Here are the letters of the first kind: *a, e, i, o, u* (and sometimes *y*). All the other letters are of the other kind. Why do these five or six letters form a special kind? The answer is another question: Have

---

† At places marked † in the margin, it is required or suggested that matter in the text be read aloud to the students by the instructor. For students working individually, the instructor may tape the readings or make other arrangements.

you ever seen an English word—or even a syllable of a word—without an *a, e, i, o, u,* or *y* in it? Can you possibly pronounce this: *phldlph?* But adding some of those six special letters, we have *Philadelphia.* The six special letters are the ones that really carry the sounds of

our words. Do you remember the name for these six letters? ⁴V _ _ _ _ _ s. These letters behave quite differently from all the other letters; understanding vowels is the key to solving

most spelling problems. Write the six English vowels: ⁵_ _ _ _ _ _ (_) Do you recall the name for all the other letters of the alphabet—the ones that are not vowels?

⁶C _ ns _ _ _ _ _ ts. Thus all letters are either ⁷‡v _ _ _ _ s or c _ _ _ _ _ _ _ _ _ s. The second basic idea concerns the different vowel sounds. Though nearly every consonant has only one sound, every vowel has at least two sounds. Say these two words:

> hop   hope

⁸
Is the sound of *o* different in each word? _____ In which word does your voice
⁹
hold the sound of *o* longer? _____ The sound of *o* in *hope* is called the *long* sound of *o,* and the sound in *hop* is called the *short* sound. Dictionaries use marks over vowels to show their length; the usual marks are a straight line for the long vowel (hōpe) and a curved line for the short vowel (hŏp).

What do the long and the short sounds of the other vowels sound like? Think of the way each vowel is pronounced in the alphabet. Take, for example, *hat* and *hate.* In which
¹⁰
of these words do we give *a* the same sound as when we say it in the alphabet? _____
Say the alphabet aloud, listening carefully to the way you pronounce *e, i, o,* and *u.* In which column below are the underlined vowels pronounced the same as they are in the alphabet? Circle that column:

> ¹¹met   meter
> kit   kite
> dot   dote
> jut   jute

¹²
Do you think each underlined vowel in the column you circled is short or long? _____
It is the *long* sound of a vowel that is the same as the sound of that vowel in the alphabet. Put the long (–) or short (˘) vowel mark over the first vowel of each word in the two columns above.¹³ Then do the same with each word below. (‡ last three columns)

> ¹⁴hat   ice   bite   skinny   ape
> hate   stick   cute   lice   apple
> pet   home   gable   mender   local
> Pete   cure   gabble   medium   locking
> gate   cub   stony   Lynn   hamburger
> let   bit   stopper   lying   spicy
>   cut   union

If you did poorly on those words, restudy this section and try again or ask your instructor for help. To see the reasons behind much of the apparent wildness of English spelling, you must be able to tell short vowel sounds from long ones.

THE LONG AND SHORT OF IT

Why does *written* have two *t*s but *writing* only one? Why do *conferring* and *referring* have double *r*s but *offering* and *conference* only single *r*s? It is problems like these that have made grown men cry over English spelling. In these next sections, however, you will see that what seems to be inconsistency is only the simple short-long vowel difference in action.

Now you are going to be a linguistic scientist. Why is the vowel pronounced long in some words and short in others? Here are some of the words you have met in the previous section, rearranged in short-vowel and long-vowel columns:

	Short		*Long*
	ă p p l e		ā p e
l ĕ t		m ē d i u m
s k ĭ n n y		l ī c e
l ŏ c k i n g		l ō c a l
c ŭ b		c ū r e

Do the *other* letters in the words cause these vowels to be short or long? Look at the *first* slot (box) after each short and long vowel above. This first letter is *always* a [15]☐ vowel, ☐ consonant.   Now look at the *second* slot in each word. Do you see a difference there between the first and the second column?

In the short-vowel column, this second slot   [16]☐ always,   ☐ never   contains a vowel.
In the long-vowel column, this second slot   [17]☐ always,   ☐ never   contains a vowel.

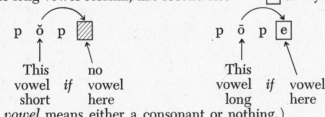

This   no
vowel *if* vowel
short   here

This   vowel
vowel *if* vowel
long   here

(*No vowel* means either a consonant or nothing.)

Now you know the secret: Usually, to determine whether a vowel is long or short, we jump over the consonant in the first following slot and examine the second slot.

(Let us call this second slot after a short or long vowel the *one-jump-over* slot, since we jump over one letter to reach it.)

Practice this one-jump-over principle on the words below, some of which you are probably not familiar with. Examine the slots following each underlined vowel and decide whether that vowel should be pronounced long or short. Then mark each underlined vowel with the long or the short mark (partial ‡):

[18] g l u t ▨   i c o n   g r a p h i c‡

r i m e   w h i n i n g   p o m a n d e r‡

f l u m e   p e t r i f y‡   p o m a n d e r‡

w r i t ▨   p e n a l‡   i c t h y o l o g y‡

If you had ten or more right, you have now mastered the most important concept in all English spelling. Why is it so important? Because so many of the seemingly haphazard English spelling changes are made simply to keep long vowels long and short vowels short.

THE LONG VOWEL AND THE FINAL *E*

Let us apply your new knowledge to two of the most common English spelling problems. First of all, do you see why thousands of English words end with a silent *e*? Without that *e, kite* would be *kit, spite* would be *spit, rate* would be *rat,* and so forth. Now quite a few misspellings occur when we need to add an ending such as *-ing, -ed, -er,* or *-able* to a silent-*e* word. When we do this, is the *e* still needed to keep the previous vowel

[19]

long? For example, do we write *hopeing?* _____ Why not? Because even without the *e* the letter in the one-jump-over slot is a   [20]☐ vowel,   ☐ consonant. Since *-ing, -ed, -able* and other such endings bring their own vowels with them for the one-jump-over slot, we drop the original final *e*.

h ō p i n g   w r ī t i n g

You try some. Below, add the ending indicated for each word. Spell the resulting word in the blank (partial ‡):

[21] slide + ing = _____   shake + able = _____ ‡

fame + ous = _____   hope + ed = _____ ‡

write + er = _____   cute + est = _____ ‡

rake + ing = _____   advise + able = _____ ‡

investigate + or = _____   rope + ing = _____ ‡

But suppose we want to add an ending such as *-ful, -ness, -ment, -hood,* or *-ly?*

[22]

Do these bring their own vowels with them for the one-jump-over slot? _____ If we drop the *e* of the root word, we will have words like

h ō p f u l   s t a t m e n t   l o n l y

Will that destroy the long-vowel sound of the root word? _____ But if we keep the original *e*, giving us

h o p⟨e⟩f u l   s t a t⟨e⟩m e n t   l o n⟨e⟩l y

will that preserve the long-vowel sound of the root word? _____ Then that is what we do: when the ending to be added does not bring its own vowel with it, we keep the *e* of the root word. Try these (partial ‡):

[25]home + ly = _____   state + hood = _____ ‡

spade + ful = _____   polite + ness = _____ ‡

sincere + ly = _____   safe + ty = _____ ‡

Now do this mixed set (‡ last two columns):

[26]dine + ing = _____	create + ive = _____	state + ly = _____
spite + ing = _____	sure + ly = _____	love + able = _____
spite + ful = _____	advise + ment = _____	shine + ing = _____
home + less = _____	persevere + ance = _____	desire + ous = _____
home + er = _____	state + ing = _____	white + ness = _____
		use + ful = _____

Now you have it. When adding an ending, drop the final silent *e* of the root word if the *e* is no longer needed to keep the previous vowel sound long; keep the *e* if it is needed.

THE SHORT VOWEL AND DOUBLING

Solving the next spelling problem also depends on understanding the long-short vowel difference. First, recall that a vowel is normally long if a jump over the following consonant lands us on a vowel, as in

r ă p⟨e⟩

Recall also that a vowel is normally short if a jump over the following consonant lands us on something that is not a vowel—either nothing or a consonant, as in

r ă p⟨▨⟩   r ă p⟨t⟩u r e

Suppose we want to add an ending such as *-ing* or *-er* to the short-vowel words below. What problem arises?

Does *rap* + *ing* become *raping?* But then what is *rape* + *ing?*
Does *hop* + *ing* become *hoping?* But then what is *hope* + *ing?*
Does *bar* + *ing* become *baring?* But then what is *bare* + *ing?*
Does *wag* + *ing* become *waging?* But then what is *wage* + *ing?*

What has happened here? If we add the *-ing* directly to a short-vowel word such as *rap* above, what kind of letter falls into the one-jump-over slot that must not contain a vowel

(e.g. rap⟨i⟩ng)? A _____²⁷. When the reader sees the vowel in that slot, he pronounces the previous vowel long. (For example, he says *rāping.* This can be embarrassing if you want to say that you were *rap* + *ing* at someone's door.) Thus, if we want to add *-ing* to *rap*, we must move the vowel out of that one-jump-over slot to keep the *a* short. How? We cannot have a blank space:

r ă p ▨ i n g

The only other thing to put in that slot is a _____²⁸. And the only consonant that will not garble the word is _____²⁹. Thus we solve the problem by writing

r ă p p i n g

Now the *a* stays short and the word is not confused with *raping.*

You have just discovered why so many final consonants are doubled before *-ing* and other endings that bring their own vowel, such as *-ed, -er, -able, -ous, -ance, -ive.* Here is some practice in adding such endings (Partial ‡):

³⁰bit + en =   b ĭ t □ e n   big + est = _____‡

stop + ed = s t ŏ p □ e d   blot + er = _____‡

slap + ing = _____   shop + ing = _____‡

bat + er = _____   swim + ing = _____‡

If you feel confident about spelling such words, let us move on. Do you think we

double in words like *grand* + *est* and *flirt* + *ing?* _____³¹ Why not? What is already in the one-jump-over slot?

g r ă n d   f l ĭ r t

Since there is a consonant there already, there is no need to double. Try these: *sink* + *ing* =

_____³²; *plant* + *er* = _____³³ And what about *cup* + *ful, sad* + *ness* and *man* + *ly?* Is there any need to double in these three words to avoid a vowel in the one-

jump-over slot (c ŭ p f u l)?³⁴ _____ Write the three words, with the endings added: _____ _____ _____ Next, try this mixed set. The one-jump-over principle will work for you every time (Partial ‡):

[36]red + est = _____   ship + ment = _____ ‡

stack + ed = _____   slop + y [*Does* y *have a vowel sound*

fat + er = _____   *here?*] = _____ ‡

ship + ing = _____ ‡   cramp + ed = _____ ‡

You have now mastered the basic part of what is called the doubling principle. (You will meet the more complicated part later.) Although the doubling principle is not easy, it is worth the effort of learning because it applies in hundreds of common cases and has hardly any exceptions.

The next step is to combine what you have just learned with what you previously learned about final-*e* words. Use the one-jump-over principle; it will rarely fail you. Circle the word in column A or B that each word on the left was made from (Partial ‡):

	A	*B*
[37]sloping	slop	slope
wading	wad	wade
cuter‡	cut	cute
stripped	strip	stripe
shamful‡	sham	shame
hatful‡	hat	hate
staring‡	star*	stare
diner‡	din	dine
planed‡	plan	plane
riddable‡	rid	ride

Spell these:

[38‡]run + er = _____   farce + ical = _____

wrap + ed = _____   nine + ty = _____

camp + er = _____   sense + ible = _____

scrap + ing = _____   immediate + ly = _____

love + ly = _____   safe + ly = _____

---

* Consider the *ah* sound of *a*, as in *star* and *start*, as a short vowel.

write + ing = _____   move + able** = _____

[*Do you see now why the -en part
of* write (written) *has two* ts?
Notice the change in the sound of i
from wrīte *to* wrĭtten.]

sting + er = _____

spine + al = _____

come + ing* = _____   mop + able = _____

man + hood = _____   pore + ous = _____

man + ish = _____   shame + less = _____

Remember the one-jump-over principle: From a vowel, take a one-letter jump over the following consonant. If you land on another vowel, then the original vowel normally is long, as in

s p ō k e

If you land on anything else (a consonant or nothing), the original vowel is normally short, as in

t ĕ n d   t ĕ n

(One final caution: In this section, all the vowel sounds we worked with had only one letter. A vowel sound can have two letters, as in *train, read, noun*. Since a two-letter vowel usually has some kind of long sound, there is no need to double after such a vowel. Thus we write *training* and *reading*, not *trainning* and *readding*.)

DOUBLING IN LONGER WORDS

We now have to deal with some of the thornier parts of the doubling principle. Did you notice that all the short-vowel words in the last section had only one syllable? Do words of two or more syllables, such as *confer* or *benefit*, behave the same way? Let us see. In this section you will have to use your ear sharply. To start with, examine the five words below. Apply the one-jump-over principle to the *final* vowel in each. Is each of these final vowels

39

short? _____

refer   confer   defer   offer   prefer

Then according to what you learned in the last section, each word should double its final *r* before an ending like *-ing* or *-ed*. But one of these five words does not double the *r*. Can you

---

* For uniformity, it is customary to drop *all* final silent *es* before a vowel, even when the sound of the previous vowel is not fully long, as in such words as *come/coming, love/loving, festive/festival*.

** *Moveable, saleable, useable,* and *mileage,* even though the *e* is not needed, are also accepted spellings. *Mileage,* in fact, is more common.

tell which? _____ More important, can you see or hear *why* it does not double?

_____ To discover why, say each word aloud distinctly, noticing which syllable you naturally stress. (Better, listen to your instructor say † the words.) Here are the words broken into syllables. In each word, circle the syllable you stress—the one you say with more force. Every word of two or more syllables has one such syllable. We call it the accented syllable.

⁴²re fer   con fer   de fer   of fer   pre fer

Check your answers.

One way of determining the accented syllable is to say the word more than once, each time putting the accent on a different syllable. For example, say aloud every word below; then circle the correct version of each word:

⁴³RE fer   DE fer   OF fer   BEN e fit   CON fer ence
re FER   de FER   of FER   ben E fit   con FER ence
                                  ben e FIT   con fer ENCE

Which word in 42 above is accented on a different syllable from the others? _____

On which syllable is its accent? _____ If this is the word you said does not double its *r* before endings like *-ing*, you were right:

re FER [r]ing   de FER [r]ing   pre FER [r]ing
con FER [r]ing   OF fer [⁄]ing

When a word has two or more syllables, then, we follow the same doubling principle as with one-syllable words, but *only* if the accent is on the *last* syllable of the original word. *Offering* does not double its *r* because the accent in *offer* is not on the last syllable. Here is some practice. Help is provided with the first five items:

⁴⁶in FER + ed = _____   ex CEL + ing = _____

oc CUR + ed = _____   QUAR rel + ing = _____

HAP pen + ed = _____

From here on, first determine the accented syllable yourself and circle it before answering. The first four words have been divided into syllables as a help (Partial ‡):

⁴⁷sig nal + ing = _____   o mit + ed = _____

o pen + er = _____   recur + ing = _____ ‡

but ter + ed = _____   rebel + ion = _____ ‡

develop + er = _____ ‡   commit + ed = _____ ‡

† If you can hear which syllable in the original word is accented, the words you meet here should give you little trouble. The practice below mixes what you have learned here with what you learned earlier. Remember to check first whether you have a short-vowel or long-vowel situation; if it is a short-vowel situation and the root word has two or more syllables, circle the accented syllable:

[48‡]tap + ing = _____   allot + ment = _____

tape + ing = _____   admit + ance = _____

shop + er = _____   pain + ful = _____

trim + able = _____   rebel + ious = _____

prove + able = _____   begin + ing = _____

loom + ed = _____   approve + al = _____

sincere + ly = _____   adapt + able = _____

debate + able = _____   occur + ence = _____

regret + able = _____   benefit + ed = _____

allot + ing = _____   woman + ish = _____

If you had seventeen or more right above, you are ready to attack the toughest part of the doubling principle; do the following box. If you had fewer than seventeen right, follow your instructor's directions.

Earlier in this module the question was asked: Why does *conferring* have two *r*s but *conference* only one *r*? You may hear the answer if you say the two words aloud. You already know that the root word is pronounced *con FER*. But which pronunciation of the two words below is correct? Circle the correct version of each:

[49]CON fer ring   CON fer ence
con FER ring   con FER ence

[50]

What has happened to the accent in *conference*? It has _____

_____. The jump of the accent back from *FER* in

the root word *con FER* to *CON* in *CON fer ence* explains why the doubling principle does not apply and *conference* has only one *r*. Notice, however, that in *con FER ring* and *con FER red,* the accent stays on *FER*, and the doubling principle applies.

Try the following. (Be careful; the accent may not always jump back before *-ence*.) (Partial ‡):

[51]pre FER + ing = _____   refer + ing = _____ ‡

PREF er + ence = _____   refer + ence = _____ ‡

in fer + ing = _____   occur + ing = _____ ‡

in fer + ence = _____   occur + ence = _____ ‡

re cur + ing = _____ ‡

re cur + ence = _____ ‡

Did you discover that the accent jumps back in some *-ence* words but not in others?

The jumping accent makes mastery of the doubling principle a bit more challenging, but if you have carefully followed each step in these sections, you should be able to handle doubling and final *e* problems with confidence. And one of the best points about these principles is that they have very few exceptions.

RELIEVING A PIECE OF SPELLING GRIEF (IE)

Ie? Ei? How can we tell which to use? Unfortunately, no matter how we approach this problem, there are many exceptions. Let us try this fairly uncomplicated approach.

First, sharpen your ear to the normal sound of both *ie* and *ei* in English. Take *believe* as an example. What is the sound of *ie* in this word? Is it the same as if we spelled this

[52]

word *beleeve?* _____ The normal sound of *ie*, then, is *ee* (like the long *e* in *Pēte*). What about *ei?* Does the *ei* in *receive* also have the long *e* sound? (Would we say it the

[53]

same if we spelled it *receeve?*) _____ The normal sound of both *ie* and *ei*, then, is *ee*.

Now, as a linguistic scientist, examine the following words, all of which are correctly spelled and contain either *ie* or *ei*. Find the answer to these two questions: Which is the *more* common spelling, *ie* or *ei?* What similarity do you find in all the words spelled the *less* common way? (Answer below the list.)

chief	relieve	piece	grievance
belief	ceiling	achieve	frontier
receive	field	conceited	deceive

The *more* common spelling is _____. Now circle all the words with the *less* common spelling.[55] What similarity do you find just before the *ei* in the four words

[56]

you circled? _____ From your investigation,

[57]

then, can you form a principle? Try it: In an *ie/ei* choice, choose _____, except

[58]

after the letter _____. Or, if you remember the old grammar-school rhyme: [59]Put _____

before _____ except after _____. Next, use your discovery to spell these words (Partial ‡):

[60]br __ __ f   rec __ __ ve   conc __ __ ve‡

n __ __ ce   perc __ __ ve   rec __ __ pt‡

s __ __ ge   y __ __ ld‡   hyg __ __ ne‡

pr __ __ st   f __ __ nd‡   f __ __ rce‡

Remember that in all the words we have discussed so far the *ie* or *ei* has had the *ee* (long *e*) sound. Now let us look at some other words:

neighbor	foreign	height
weigh	freight	veil

Do these words have the long *e* sound? If they do, they would sound the same if you wrote them with *ee* instead of *ei*. Do *neeghbor, weegh, foreegn, freeght, heeght,* and *veel* sound

[61]

right to you? Then do the words listed have the *ee* sound? _____ Then what else can we conclude? That when words do not have the *ee* sound, we use   [62]☐ *ie,*   ☐ *ei.*
Spell these words, without looking back (Partial ‡):

[63]fr __ __ ght‡   for __ __ gn‡   v __ __ n‡

n __ __ ghbor‡   forf __ __ t   r __ __ gn‡

w __ __ gh‡   r __ __ n   th __ __ r‡

h __ __ ght‡   sl __ __ gh   counterf __ __ t‡

v __ __ l‡

You have now mastered the basic *ie/ei* principles. Here they are in brief:
(1)   Normal (*ee*) sound: Use *ie* (except after *c*).
(2)   Other than *ee* sound: Use *ei*.

You will see that some seeming exceptions actually follow the principles if you realize that *either, neither,* and *leisure* are pronounced *EYEther, NEYEther,* and *LEZZure* by the British (who are responsible for most of our spelling). Thus they follow principle (2) above, for words not having the *ee* sound. Without looking back, spell these:

[64]‡___ther, n___ther, l___sure.

There are still some important exceptions, but you will meet them in a later section.

SOFT AND HARD

Early in this module you learned that most consonants have only one sound. But does *c* have the same sound in both *cell* and *call?* If we respelled the first word *sell* and the second word *kall,* would they sound the same as the original words? _[65]_____ Thus *c* can have the sound of either *s* or *k*. By looking at the letter following each *c* in the lists below, try to determine when *c* sounds like *s* and when it sounds like *k:*

cent	cat
cider	cover
cycle	crow
citizen	clown
cemetery	cut
cylinder	collect
cereal	cave

In the first column, *c* is always followed by one of three letters: [66]__, __, or __. In the second column, does any of these letters follow *c?* _[67]_____ You have discovered another principle of English sounds: when *c* is directly followed by *e, i,* or *y,* it takes the sound of *s*—which we call the *soft* sound of *c*. When *c* is directly followed by anything else, it takes the sound of *k*—which we call the *hard* sound of *c*.* Notice the two patterns in these words:

cigar	cable
cyanide	criteria
central	claustrophobia
reception	criticism
license	incarcerate

---

* The combination *ch* as in *church* or *charade* gives other sounds of *c*, which we are not considering here.

Is there any other letter that has both a soft and a hard sound? Examine these words:

giant	gate
gin	gone
gentle	gun
gym	grow
germ	glow
gyroscope	ghost

In each word of the first column, *g* has the same sound as which other letter? _____68
(Hint: think of a boy's name pronounced the same as a word in the first column.) Do the
69
words in the second column begin with this same sound? _____ Thus *g* also has
two sounds: a soft sound, the same as *j*, as in the first-column words above; and a hard
sound, as in the second-column words. According to the words above, is *g* soft in front of
70
the same letters that make *c* soft? _____ You have discovered that *c* and *g* are
normally soft before *e*, *i*, and *y*, and hard elsewhere. In the words below, circle every *g* that
is soft; do nothing with any *g* that is hard (some words have two *g*s) (Partial ‡):

[71]gigantic	gelatin	regurgitate‡	dirigible‡
gregarious	gyp	gorgeous‡	legal‡
religious	tangent	conglomerate‡	legislate‡

Why is this soft-hard distinction important? Notice what happens when we try to add certain
endings to such words as *force, service, manage,* and *courage.* You have learned that we
normally drop the final *e* before endings such as *-able* or *-ous.* But that gives us *forcable,
servicable, managable,* and *couragous* (FORK *able,* SER *vik able,* MAN *a ga ble,* and
cour AGG ous). Since that is not how these words are pronounced, we must make whatever
spelling changes are needed to keep the soft sound. There are two ways this is done:
   A.   Which ending, *-able* or *-ible,* must be used in the words below to keep the soft
sound of *c* or *g* (Partial ‡)?

[72]forc__ble	invinc__ble	neglig__ble‡
reduc__ble	leg__ble‡	irasc__ble‡
elig__ble	tang__ble‡	incorrig__ble‡

The words above, then, use an ending beginning with a vowel that will give a soft sound.
   B.   Which letter must be kept in the blanks below to keep the soft sound of *c* or *g*
(Partial ‡)?

[73]servic__able	notic__able	pronounc__able‡	advantag__ous‡
manag__able	replac__able	courag__ous‡	gorg__ous‡
chang__able	trac__able‡	outrag__ous‡	

The words above, then, keep their final *e* so the sound of *c* or *g* will remain soft.

> Here is another situation where your knowledge of the soft-hard principle will help you. With words ending in *c*, such as *picnic* or *panic*, what do we do to keep the hard sound when we have to add *-ing* or *-ed*? Since we want the sound of *k*, we add the only consonant that can solve the problem, *k: picnicking, panicked, trafficking.*

One final note: There are a good number of exceptions in which *g* still takes the hard sound in front of *e* or *i*, such as *get, girl, begin, gill;* but most of these are so common that they are rarely misspelled.

You should now be able to spell all the following words without looking back. Either one, two, or no letters may go in each blank:

[74]gig_____antic   tang_____ble   notic_____ble   invinc_____ble

elig_____ble   courag_____ous   chang_____ble   picnic_____ing

manag_____ble   advantag_____ous

PROBLEMS NOT SOLVED BY SOUND

We are now largely finished with spellings that can be determined by our ears. We must look for other ways to solve the remaining spelling problems. In the sections that follow you will find quite a few lists of words. You are not expected to memorize them; rather, you should look over each list slowly and thoroughly to absorb a picture of the words into your mind, so that if you ever misspell that word at some future time, your mind will say "That looks wrong." Of course, this is an imperfect way to learn hundreds of words; the best way to register the correct form of each word in your mind is to read, read, read.

THE "UH" VOWEL

Say the words below aloud or listen to them. In ordinary speech, how differently is the underlined vowel pronounced in each: *CAL en d**a**r   B**A** ker   MO t**o**r   POR t**e**r*
[1]
*COUN sel **o**r   BUR s**a**r   e LIX **i**r?* _____
Each of these vowels is an   [2] ☐ accented,   ☐ unaccented   syllable.

You have now discovered one of the chief horrors of English spelling: that most

unaccented vowels sound the [3]s_____. *A, e, i, o,* or *u,* (and at times *y*), in unaccented syllables, all tend to come out sounding something like a soft *uh.** The two spellings listed in the dictionary for *advis**o**r/advis**e**r,* the two words *curr**e**nt/curr**a**nt,* and the common confusion of *_a_ffect/_e_ffect* and *_a_ccept/_e_xcept* all show that the underlined vowels of each pair of words are pronounced the same by most people. This sameness of sound, as you may

---

* Some dictionaries represent this sound by an upside-down *e*, like this: ə (called a *schwa*).

PROBLEMS NOT SOLVED BY SOUND

PROBLEMS NOT SOLVED BY SOUND   445

imagine, causes countless spelling problems. In most cases there is no easy solution; many of these spelling differences trace all the way back to Latin, where the sounds were different.

Here are some aids to remembering, however. Let us first take words that end in the unaccented vowel plus *r*. Since the large majority of such words end in *-er*, you need to remember only the words that end differently. These are nearly all the common *-ar* words:

angular	cedar	grammar	polar	solar
beggar	cellar	hangar	popular	stellar
binocular	circular	liar	radar	sugar
bursar	collar	lunar	regular	vehicular
calendar	dollar	perpendicular	similar	vulgar

There are many more *-or* words, but some of them fall into patterns which you can easily remember. For example, what syllable comes before *-or* in each of these words? [4]Allig____or, educ____or, radi____or, regul____or, indic____or. When the next-to-last syllable is *-at-*, then, you can be almost certain that the ending is *-or*. Spell the following words:

[5]creat____   dictat____   speculat____   orat____

investigat____   equat____   generat____   narrat____

aviat____   simulat____   spectat____   demonstrat____

escalat____   senat____   moderat____   imitat____

legislat____   liberat____   operat____

These are other common *-or* words:

actor	director	investor	reflector
aggressor	doctor	major	scissor
author	emperor	mayor	sculptor
censor	error	minor [Opposite	sponsor
conductor	factor	of *major*]	tailor
connector	governor	possessor	traitor
corridor	horror	professor	tutor
counselor	juror	projector	visitor
		prosecutor	

Hardly any words end with unaccented *ir*, *ur*, or *yr*. The only common ones are *murmur*, *sulfur*, and *martyr*. Remember: Any other word of this type you meet probably ends in *er*.

Spell these words without looking back:

[6]‡mak____   escalat____   lawy____   sug____

lun____   profess____   doct____   legislat____

of housing the_____, officials in the Kremlin believe that the_____ policy benefits both those who leave Russia and the_____ countrymen who stay the_____.

C. *Woman/women.* It is amazing how both men and women students will write sentences like *I met a women.* Would they write *I met a men?* You will avoid this mistake if you just remember these:

wo | man | wo | men |

One person is a *man* or a *woman;* two or more persons are *men* or *women.* If you mentally drop the *wo-,* you will easily see whether you have the word for one person. Try these:

[14]She was a wo_____ of rare charm and grace.

[15]So was her mother. They were both unforgettable wo_____.

D. *Where/were.* Like *here* and *there, where* (WAYR) refers to a place. Again, remember the saying [here], t[here], and everyw[here]. *Were* (WUR) is the past form of *are,* as in

We *were* caught in the raid.

Do these sentences (Partial ‡):

[16]W_____re w_____re you when the lights went out? W_____ you w_____ you should have been? Why w_____ren't you the_____?

E. *Alright/all right.* This is the easiest of all. There is just no such spelling as *alright* in formal English. You mean *all right.* Try this:

[17]‡If it's a_____ right with you, I'll tell Charlie everything's a_____right now.

F. *Principal/principle.* If you learned *The principal is your pal* in elementary school, forget it; it is a misleading half-truth. Just remember:

princip | le |
ru | le |

A *principle* is a rule, or guiding idea, as in

The Ten Commandments are *principles* (rules) of behavior toward God and other people.
The Pythagorean theorem is a *principle* (rule) of mathematics.

Anything else is *principal,* as in not only

> The *principal* is your pal

but also

> The *principal* cause of her death was old age.
> Some rich people live on the interest of their bank accounts and never have to touch the *principal.*
> The *principal* export of Ireland, it is said, has been its people.

18

What does *principal* seem to mean? _____ Try these (Partial ‡):

[19]The princip____s of good business demand that we invest the princip____ portion of our funds in the Swiss Merchant Marine Company. If the dividends are good, we can leave the princip____ untouched, and spend the princip____ part of our retirement years in wealth. It is a firm princip____ of mine always to provide for the future.

G. *Then/than.* Careful pronunciation may prevent you from confusing these two. T ⟦hen⟧ rhymes with w ⟦hen⟧, and both *when* and *then* concern time: *When did you do it? I did it then. Than* rhymes with *Fran;* it is used when we compare, and follows soon after a word ending in *-er* or the word *more,* as in

> Nan had a better time *than* Fran.
> You are even more beautiful *than* I dreamed.

Try these (Partial ‡):

[20]When I saw Sue's tan, I was th__n convinced that she had a better tan th__n Fran, whose tan was th__n fading, since she had been home from Florida longer th__n Sue.

H. *Lead/led.* This is hard. The *lead* we are talking about rhymes with *head.* It means the metal. Think of this sentence: L ⟦ead⟧ *in the h* ⟦ead⟧ *makes one d* ⟦ead⟧. For anything else pronounced the same way, write *led,* as in J ⟦ed⟧ *l* ⟦ed⟧ *old N* ⟦ed⟧ *to b* ⟦ed⟧. Do these (Partial ‡):

[21]The police found Bronsky dead in bed from l____d poisoning. A hunch l____d Detective Tracy to suspect foul play. He arrested Klonsky for killing Bronsky with l____d. The police l____d Klonsky away to jail.

I.   *Lose/loose.* This is not hard. *Loose* rhymes with *goose;* remember the expression *loose as a goose. Lose* is the troublesome one; people often think—with good logic—that it should have two *o*s; actually, it rhymes with *whose.* Remember the sentence *It's whose turn to lose?* Test your ability on these (Partial ‡):

[22]Fidgwick, who is usually l____se and relaxed in chess games, somehow

became nervous and began to l____se his concentration. He could not l____se his

feeling of tension; the more he tried to l____sen up, the more tense he became. He

knew he would l____se the game.

J.   *Affect/effect.* Since the first syllable of both these words is unaccented, most people pronounce both words the same: *uh FECT.* Therefore you will have to use your knowledge of grammar to untangle the two. Is *affect* (as in *The rain may affect the rhubarb*) a noun or a verb? [23] _____ Is *effect* (as in *The oil price rise had a disastrous effect on the economy*) a noun or a verb? [24] _____ (If you have trouble telling nouns from verbs, see pages 147–152 of "Basic Sentence Parts.") Remember the word *VANE:* [V] erb- [A] ffect; [N] oun- [E] ffect. Now do these (Partial ‡):

[25]The first ___ffect of Jane's moving to her own apartment was that she felt a

great sense of freedom. But soon her new responsibilities ___ffected her. One such

___ffect was that housework cut into her free time. After a while, loneliness began to

___ffect her also.*

K.   *Past/passed.* Here again both words are pronounced the same, and since they are similar in meaning, we again have to rely on grammar to see the difference. The *-ed* on

the end of *passed* tells us it is a [26]v__ __b; it tells what some person or thing did. It means *went by, went through, put through,* or *sent:*

On the way to Denver we *passed* [went by] fourteen Howard Johnson motels.
Julius *passed* [went through] chemistry on the fourth try.
The Senate *passed* [put through] a bill to increase foreign aid.
Kilgore *passed* [sent] the news on to his relatives.

Use *past* for anything else:

Uncle Eben always talks about the *past.* [Noun]
Uncle Eben always talks about *past* times. [Modifier]
Ursula is afraid to walk *past* the men's dorm at night. [*Of*-link]

---

* There is another use of *effect,* but since it is not common it will not be mentioned here, to avoid confusion.

Try these (Partial ‡):

[27]As Fred and I strolled across the campus in the moonlight, we pas_____

Hondo Hall, where I had taken my first archeology course. I pas_____ that course

with an A+, because it dealt with the pas_____, which I love to learn about. As we

walked pas_____ that building, my thoughts went back to my pas_____ love affair

with the archeology teacher. It hadn't lasted long, because the administration soon

pas_____ a rule that faculty could not date students.

L.   *Accept/except*. These are two more words that most people pronounce the same or nearly so. Just remember:

|ex| cept
|ex| cluding

Except means *excluding;* for anything else, use *accept*.* Try these (Partial ‡):

[28]I am sending party invitations to everyone _____cept Hugo. I hope every-

one else will _____cept the invitation. I will not have Hugo at the party because I

cannot _____cept his terrible behavior. At the last party he pinched every female

there _____cept my grandmother, and he was headed in her direction when I threw
him out.

THE CHAMELEON PRINCIPLE

Have you ever seen a chameleon (ka MEEL yon)? It is a little lizardlike animal that can change its appearance to match its surroundings. If put on a leaf, it turns green; if put amid rocks, it turns the gray or brown of the rocks. There is a chameleon in spelling too. It is the little syllable *ad-* (which comes from Latin, usually meaning *to, toward, near,* or *greatly*) when added at the beginning of a word root, as in *addict.* But something odd happens to *ad-* when it is put in front of words or roots beginning with a letter other than *d.* Watch:

ad + claim = not *adclaim* but *acclaim*
ad + fair = not *adfair* but *affair*
ad + prove = not *adprove* but *approve*
ad + sure = not *adsure* but *assure*
ad + tune = not *adtune* but *attune*

Like the chameleon, the *d* of *ad-* usually [29]ch _____ s its a _____ance in front of a root beginning with a letter other than *d.* Thus, in front of a root beginning with *c,*

---

* There is another use of *except,* but since it is not common it will not be mentioned here, to avoid confusion.

such as -cess-, the d of ad- changes to c to match the c of -cess-, and we have access. Before -locate, ad- becomes al-, and we have allocate. Likewise, we have announce (ad + nounce), arrest (ad + rest), and over a hundred other words, many of which are common spelling problems. (This chameleon change occurs to make the word easier to say; announce, for instance, is easier to say than adnounce.)

Now that you understand why these words have double letters where the first two syllables meet, you should be able to spell such words as the following (Partial ‡):

[30]ad + celerate = _____   ad + prehend = _____

ad + cent = _____   ad + cursed = _____ ‡

ad + cept = _____   ad + fect = _____ ‡

ad + cident = _____   ad + fluent = _____ ‡

ad + commodate = _____   ad + gression = _____ ‡

ad + lure = _____   ad + rive = _____ ‡

ad + nul = _____   ad + semble = _____ ‡

ad + pear = _____   ad + sociate = _____ ‡

ad + petite = _____   ad + tempt = _____ ‡

ad + lot [meaning to give out in por-   ad + tract = _____ ‡
tions; do not confuse with a lot, mean-

ing many] = _____

By the way, since the combinations aqq- and akk- do not exist in English, ad- becomes ac- instead of aq- or ak- before a q or k, so that we have not aqquaint (or aquaint) but acquaint, and not akknowledge (or aknowledge) but acknowledge. Other words like this are acquiesce, acquire, and acquit. (The only common English words that begin with aq- are words having to do with water [Latin aqua], such as aquamarine, aquarium, aquatic, aqueduct.)

Is ad- our only chameleon prefix? A few others also change to agree with some following letters: in- (meaning either not or in) becomes il-, as in

illegal   illegitimate   illiterate   illuminate
illegible   illicit   illogical

In- becomes im-, as in

immaculate   immeasurable   immense   immoderate
immature   immediate   immigrant

In- becomes *ir-*, as in

irrational	irrelevant*	irresistible
irredeemable	irreligious	irresponsible
irregular	irreparable	irreversible

Con- (meaning *with* or *together*) becomes *col-*, as in

collaborate	collateral	college
collapse	colleague	collide
collate	collect	colloquial

Con- becomes *com-*, as in

command	commercial	communicate
commemorate	commission	commute
commend	committee	

Sub- (meaning *under*) becomes *suc-*, *suf-* or *sug-*, as in

succeed	suffer	suffocate
success	sufficient	suggest
succumb	suffix	

Remember the chameleon principle. It explains why there are double letters where the prefix meets the root in hundreds of words.

Here is more practice on the chameleon principle. Put the right letter in the blank; if no letter should go there, leave the blank empty. Do the last column only if you did the box on page 453.

[31‡]i___legal   co___lapse   a___quire

i___legible   co___memorate   a___quit

i___mature   co___mission   a___knowledge

i___relevant   co___munist   a___quarium

THE DO-NOTHING RULE

This is the easiest part of the module; it tells you to do nothing. Try to spell the following:

[32‡]dis + ability = _____   mis + state + ment = _____

dis + solve = _____   legal + ly = _____

---

* Avoid spelling this word inside out, as *irrevelant*. It is *ir* + *relevant* (*related*).

dis + satisfied = _____   equip + ment = _____

dis + appear = _____   comical + ly = _____

un + natural = _____   im + mediate + ly = _____

un + natural + ly = _____   dis + appoint = _____

re + commend = _____   un + necessary = _____

mis + spell = _____   re + collect = _____

inter + rupt = _____   de + scription = _____

pro + fessional + ly = _____   suc + cess + ful + ly = _____

inter + related = _____

In how many of the words above did you add a letter when combining the given parts to
spell the whole word? _____33‡_____ In how many did you drop a letter? _____34‡

If you dropped or added anything, why did you? _____35‡_____
The answer to these questions is that no letters should have been dropped or added in any
of the words above, simply because there is no reason to do so. Notice that wherever you
were asked to add an ending, that ending began with a   36☐ vowel,   ☐ consonant.
You are right to conclude that endings beginning with a consonant normally require no
change in the root word at all. Thus *comical* + *ly* = *comical|ly.* (Remember that you are
adding the *-ly* to *comical,* not to *comic.*)

What about prefixes? Except for the chameleon cases you learned in the previous
section, there is no change in either the prefix or the root word when they meet. This
explains why *dis|appoint* and *dis|appear* have one *s* but *dis|satisfied* and *dis|solve* have two *ss.*

In general, think this way: Unless you recognize a situation (such as final *e* or
doubling) where you must drop or add or change a letter, leave the prefix, root, and ending
alone when they meet.

As a final check, go back over the words at the beginning to be sure you have put
their parts together with no letters dropped or added.

WHAT TO TRY WITH Y

The first part of this section will tell you to do exactly the same as the last section
did—nothing. Examine the words in list A below. Obviously they all end in *y.* But what
other similarity can you notice about their endings? (Comparing lists A and B should help
you.)

List A

alley	monkey	delay	donkey
buy	portray	annoy	attorney
key	chimney		

The letter before *y* in all the words of list A is a _____. Go back to the list and add an *s* to each of these words. You have already learned half of this section's work! When we wish to add an ending—any ending—to a word that ends in *y*, we just add it— provided the letter before *y* is a vowel. We do not double, drop, or change any letters. Thus,

    annoy + ed = annoyed
    portray + al = portrayal
    buy + er = buyer

Do these (Partial ‡):

[38]donkey + s = _____   buy + ing = _____ ‡

portray + ing = _____   employ + er = _____ ‡

annoy + ance = _____   journey + ed = _____ ‡

That, of course, was easy. But what happens if the letter before *y* is not a vowel? Pick the five words from list B that you are most sure you can spell correctly when you add the ending in parentheses; then spell those five in the blanks below the list:

List B

[39]fly (+ es)   marry (+ age)   happy (+ ness)
cry (+ ed)   tragedy (+ es)   magnify (+ cation)
try (+ es)   busy (+ ness)   reality (+ es)
carry (+ er)   hurry (+ ed)   liberty (+ es)

_____   _____   _____

_____   _____

Check your answers. What do we do, then, when we want to add an ending to a word that

[40]

ends in *y* but has a consonant before the *y?* We change the _____ to _____. That is all there is to it. Without looking again at the answer page, write in the spaces below the remaining seven words from the list above, adding the ending in parentheses to each:

[39]
_____   _____   _____

_____   _____   _____

_____

To sum up: When adding an ending to a word that ends in a vowel + *y* (*-ay, -ey, -oy, -uy*), change nothing; when adding an ending to a word that ends in a consonant + *y* (such as *-cy, -ly, -ry, -ty*), change the *y* to *i*.

Combine each word with its ending (Partial ‡):

[41]angry + ly = _____   valley + s = _____

relay + s = _____   authority + es = _____ ‡

enemy + es = _____   ready + ness = _____ ‡

carry + age = _____   decay + ing = _____ ‡

horrify + ed = _____   satisfy + ed = _____ ‡

lonely + ness = _____   chimney + s = _____ ‡

lively + hood = _____   library + es = _____ ‡

x-ray + ed = _____   Thursday + s = _____ ‡

A final note: You undoubtedly realize that these do not look right: *satisfiing, hurriing, criing*. Do not change a *y* to *i* if *ii* will result. Leave the *y* alone. A double *i* is not natural to English.* (Do not just drop the *y* and write *satisfing, hurring,* or *cring,* either.) Thus,

    cry + ing = crying
    try + ing = trying
    hurry + ing = hurrying

Do these (Partial ‡):

[42]carry + ing = _____   horrify + ing = _____ ‡

hurry + ing = _____   satisfy + ing = _____ ‡

magnify + ing = _____

-ANCE/-ENCE AND -ABLE/-IBLE

One of the real monsters of spelling is *-ance/-ence*. Again, Latin is to blame for the problem. You cannot tell from a word's sound which of these endings to use. Back on page 447 you learned one way to determine the spelling of some of these words: by finding another form of the word where the doubtful vowel fell in an accented syllable, as in *influ<u>e</u>ntial/influ<u>e</u>nce*. Unfortunately, there is no other principle to help you; memory is the only way. Here are some of the most troublesome *-ance* words. (If a word ends in *-<u>a</u>nce*, its other forms, as you might expect, will end in *-<u>a</u>nt* and/or *-<u>a</u>ncy*.)

acquaintance	defendant	[extravag<u>a</u>nza]	inheritance
applicant	dominant	guidance	lieutenant
[applic<u>a</u>tion]	[domin<u>a</u>tion]	ignorance	maintenance
appearance	entrance	[ignor<u>a</u>mus]	malignant
assistance	extravagant	importance	migrant

* It exists in only two common words, *skiing* and *taxiing*. The roots of both words are foreign.

[migration]	perseverance	relevant	significance
occupant	pleasant	remembrance	[signification]
[occupation]	redundant	sergeant	

Here are some of the most troublesome -ence words. (If a word ends in -ence, its other forms will end in -ent and/or -ency.)

audience	current*	independence	presence
affluence	correspondence	intelligence	prominent
apparent	difference	interference	reference
coherence	[differential]	occurrence	repellent
coincidence	efficient	opponent	residence
[coincidental]	equivalent	patience	[residential]
conference	excellence	permanent	sentence
confidence	existence	persistence	superintendent
[confidential]	[existential]	preference	tendency
convenience	experience	[preferential]	violence

See how many of the following words you can spell without looking back at the lists:

[43]‡appear__nce   inherit__nce   relev__nt

exist__nce   independ__nt   perman__nt

oppon__nt   correspond__nce   occurr__nce

resid__nt   superintend__nt   excell__nce

ignor__nce   repell__nt   guid__nce

malign__nt   pleas__nt

lieuten__nt   defend__nt

A monster almost as frightening as -ance/-ence is -ible/-able. However, as you have seen on pages 447 and 457, we can solve the problem in some words by finding another form of the word where the doubtful vowel falls in an accented syllable. Try to fill in the blanks in the list below (Partial ‡):

[44]alteration/alter__ble   communication/communic__ble‡

restoration/restor__ble   irrigation/irrig__ble‡

demonstration/demonstr__ble   inflation/inflat__ble‡

duration/dur__ble‡

---

* There is also a fruit named a currant, but you will probably rarely use this word.

Now here is another list. What can you discover from it (Partial ‡)?

[45]repress<u>io</u>n/repress__ble   conversion/convert__ble‡

impress<u>io</u>n/impress__ble   immersion/immers__ble‡

comprehens<u>io</u>n/comprehens__ble   division/divis__ble‡

From this list you have discovered that words with another form ending in *-sion* will often

end in [46]__ble.

Thus we can often make the *-able/-ible* choice by thinking whether the word also has an *-ation* or a *-sion* form: *-ation* = *-able; -sion* = *-ible.* Try these (Partial ‡):

[47]install__ble (installation)   impress__ble‡

reform__ble (reformation)   inflat__ble‡

revers__ble (reversion)   convert__ble‡

permiss__ble (permission)‡   admiss__ble‡

tax__ble   communic__ble‡

What about all the other words that do not end in *-ation* or *-sion?* Here you must either rely on memory, use the dictionary, or play the percentages.* *-Able* is far more common than *-ible*, especially in everyday words. Thus if you become familiar with the following *-ible* words, you will be fairly safe using *-able* in all other cases:

accessible	digestible	irresistible	responsible
audible	edible	perceptible	sensible
compatible	flexible	plausible	susceptible
corruptible	imcompatible	possible	visible

Spell these words without looking back at the lists:

[48]‡impress__ble   lov__ble   ed__ble   perish__ble

imposs__ble   advis__ble   intoler__ble   access__ble

dur__ble   inelig__ble   consider__ble   indispens__ble

sens__ble   plaus__ble   imcomprehens__ble   leg__ble

imcompat__ble   admir__ble   comfort__ble   invis__ble

vis__ble   not__ble   divis__ble   flex__ble

---

* You learned another way of determining some *-ible* words in the "Soft and Hard" section.

TWO MARKS THAT AFFECT SPELLING

Consider this sentence:

a. Barney is an old car collector.

Is Barney an old collector of cars or a collector of old cars—or is it impossible to tell from this sentence? _____ One tiny addition will clarify that sentence:

b. Barney is an old-car collector.
c. Barney is an old car-collector.

In which sentence is Barney a collector of old cars? _____ In which is he an old collector of cars? _____ The little mark (-), called a hyphen (HY fen) marries two words; it shows that they are to be considered as one. As you have just seen, it is often used to avoid a confusion of meanings. The following types of words are also customarily spelled with hyphens:

A. Titles beginning with *vice-:* vice-president, vice-admiral, vice-principal.

B. Words beginning with *ex-* when it means *former:* ex-wife, ex-president, ex-champion.

C. Also, uncommon or made-up words beginning with these prefixes:

pro-: pro-American, pro-abortion, pro-labor
anti-: anti-American, anti-abortion, anti-labor
non-: non-partisan, non-participant, non-involvement
self-: self-regulating, self-sealing, self-supporting
re- [especially to clarify pronunciation or distinguish a word from other words]: re-enter, re-examine, re-establish, re-lay [to lay again (*I have to re-lay these floor tiles*), as opposed to *relay,* to pass on (*I have to relay this message*)]

D. Two-word numbers between 21 and 99, and fractions: twenty-one; thirty-nine; sixty-six; one-half; three-eighths. (But notice that the words hundred, thousand, and million do not take hyphens before or after: two hundred twenty-one; five thousand sixty-six; three million five hundred sixty-nine thousand seven hundred eighty-two. The module "Punctuation," page 344, tells more about writing numbers.)

E. In general, any expression we want the reader to consider as one word:

I have *first-hand* information about the *last-minute* changes in the *cost-of-living* index.

Part-time employees are the first to be fired and the last to be rehired, according to the latest *labor-management* agreement.

Farley's future *mother-in-law* saw him at the *drive-in* smooching with a girl who was definitely not his *bride-to-be.*

Over-fed fifteen-year-old girls often go on a *three-week* crash diet, which they think will be a *cure-all* for the problem caused by their *ill-controlled* appetite for *fifty-cent* shakes at *fast-food* establishments.

Two cautions: (1) Do not go hyphen-happy, putting hyphens almost everywhere. Use them only for clarity or in customary situations. Extensive reading will make you familiar with what those situations are. (2) Do not confuse the hyphen (-) with the dash (—). The hyphen is the same length as one letter of handwriting or typing; its job is to join two words. The dash is about the same length as two letters; its job is just the opposite—to separate two words. (See "Punctuation," page 340.)

F.   Of course, the hyphen is also used when a word cannot fit at the end of a line and must be continued on the next line, like this:

> *Four score and seven years ago, our fath-*
> *ers brought forth upon this conti-*
> *nent a new nation, . . .*

Two points to remember in this use of the hyphen are (1) to break a word only at the end of a syllable: *fath-er*, not *fat-her; conti-nent*, not *co-ntinent* or *contine-nt* (one syllable words, no matter how long, cannot be broken: *through*, not *thr-ough*); (2) to put the hyphen only at the end of a line, never at the beginning of the next line:

conti-	*not*	conti
nent		-nent

⁴Do the following practice on hyphens. Put a hyphen wherever you think one should be. Your common sense will help you. (Partial ‡)

SELECTION A

> *My father in law re established his whole life in his twenty years of retire ment from his job as vice president of the Franklin National Bank. He had been in charge of thirty eight of the bank's one hundred twenty five branches. Under the bank's thirty year old age retirement plan, he made a pre retirement con tribution of five per cent of his salary, which the bank matched on a one for one basis. Since most of the money was invested in tax exempt bonds, he now lives com fortably in a first class retirement home on two thirds of his final salary, with few worries about cost of living problems. In fact, he is enjoying an out of wedlock rela tionship with a cute little eighty year old widow.*

THE APOSTROPHE

The most demonic of spelling demons is not a word at all—not even a letter. It is the little mark (') that has been called "a comma that got up in the world": the apostrophe (a POSS tro fee). Some people use it in words that should not have it; others put it in the wrong place in words; but by far most mistakes are made by people who just forget to use it at all in a word that needs it. There are only two situations where it is commonly used.* The first, which you will meet in more detail on pages 87–90 of "Word Choice," needs only a brief mention here:

are not ———→ aren't	there is ——→ there's
did not ———→ didn't	it is ——→ it's

---

* There is a third, uncommon use, but to avoid confusion it will not be mentioned here.

you are ——————→ you're   they are —→they're
Germany is ——→ Germany's   writer is —→writer's

Do you remember what the forms with the apostrophe are called? [5]C＿＿nt＿＿＿＿＿tions. [6]Put apostrophes where needed in the following paragraph:

SELECTION B

> *Were sure youll love the expanded first-class service on our Guano Airlines superjets. Youre in for a big surprise. Theres an entirely new cabin decor, and our hostesses will provide your every comfort: Theyre ready with drinks, steaks, magazines, and pillows. Well make you say, "Heres an airline Ill fly again; its Guano for me!" Guanos the one for you.*

If you are not sure whether a certain word above should take an apostrophe, think of whether the word can be written as two words and make sense. For example, can the first word, *we re*, be written as *we are*, and does *we are* make sense in that place? Then *we re* is a contraction for *we are* and should be written *we're*.

Let us turn to the second use of the apostrophe. When Charlie has a problem, which do we say?

[7] ☐ It is Charlie problem
    ☐ It is Charlie's problem
    ☐ It is Charlies' problem

Look at the answer page. If you knew the right answer, your problem with apostrophes is probably not serious. You know the words that need them; you just forget to use them. If you are fairly sure you know which kind of word takes an apostrophe, skip the box below. However, if you checked the first or third choice above (or if you only *guessed* at the second) you need to do this box:

When we say *It is Charlie's problem,* we are saying that the problem

[8]b＿＿l＿＿＿gs to Charlie. In this section, then, you will learn how to write words of belonging. Examine the sentence about Charlie. Something *belongs* to Charlie; in this case it is a problem, but it can be a car, an aunt, a headache, his hair, his income tax return, his thoughts—any noun that *can* belong to him. How do you know when you have a belonging situation?

Charlie and *problem* are both what kinds of words? [9]N＿＿＿＿＿s. When you see two nouns right near each other, then, ask yourself, "Does [the second noun] belong to [the first noun]?" For instance, "Does *the problem* belong to *Charlie*?" If the answer is yes, you have a belonging situation, and you put an apostrophe and an *s* on *Charlie*. Here is another example. Suppose you find yourself writing

---

Tomorrow is Hattie birthday.

You see the two nouns, *Hattie* and *birthday*, right near each other; therefore you ask "Does the birthday belong to Hattie?" Does it? _____ [10]

Then do we have a belonging situation? _____ Then what do [11] we add to which word? _____. Write the sentence as it should be: [12]

_____ [13]

Now you should be able to do these:

[14]It is Charlie☐ car.
[15]It is Charlie☐ hair.
[16]‡It is Charlie☐ gray hair.
[17]‡It is young Charlie☐ income tax return.
[18]‡It is my younger brother☐ income tax return.
[19]‡It is the government☐ money.
[20]‡It is the tax agent☐ expert opinion.

That is the basic way to show belonging. Now do some without the aid of the boxes. Write in whatever is missing (Partial‡):

[21]The other driver fault   Centerville tax rate‡
The men room   Centerville property
Our children welfare   tax rate‡
     Centerville exorbitant
        property tax rate‡

Here are typical situations of belonging. Put apostrophes where they are needed (Partial‡):

[22]The captains bed   The books ending‡   The Presidents private,

The drivers seat   Englands first queen‡   carpeted helicopter‡

The mayors friend   Malcolm Xs dramatic   Chinas changing foreign

           autobiography‡   policy‡

The states new tax-deferred retirement plan‡

The following sentences each contain one or more situations of belonging. Insert apostrophes:

[23]Catfish Hunters fast ball is livelier than any other in the league.

[24]The professors lecture concerned Shakespeares use of blank verse.

²⁵On the secretarys desk was the financial aid directors report.

²⁶‡Unemployment insurance means that a persons income is sustained by the issuance of money to him.

²⁷‡The storys climax occurs when Dirty Dans gun misfires after the heros horse has stumbled in the middle of the towns main street, leaving the hero helpless at the feet of the villains gang.

In the five sentences above, you met over a dozen words ending in -s. Do all of them show

²⁸
belonging? _____ You may already realize that not every word that ends in -s takes an apostrophe, because not every such word shows belonging. For example, if your name were Agnes Jones, would you sign it *Agne's Jone's?* Of course not. Avoid tossing an apostrophe before every final -s you see. There are three kinds of words that end in -s even when there is no belonging. The first kind, of course, is words that just happen to end in -s, such as *helpless, gas, basis, chassis.* How many apostrophes should the following

²⁹
sentence have? _____

His distress on seeing the mess on the bus was the basis of the crisis.

The second kind is the simple plural of a noun—a word that refers to more than one of a thing. (See pages 356, 368 of "Noun and Verb Problems" for a full explanation of plurals.) Compare these sentences:

a.   That sophomore failed one health course.
b.   Those sophomores failed two health courses.

The only difference between the sentences a and b above is that a different number of people

³⁰
are failing a different number of courses. Is there any belonging situation in a?_____
³¹
Then is there any belonging situation in b? _____ Should any word in b take an
³²
apostrophe? _____ How many apostrophes should the following sentence have?
³³
_____

The retinas in the eyes are subject to several kinds of diseases and injuries.

The third kind is the -s ending we put on verbs. Compare these sentences:

The children play until noon and then eat.
Each child plays until noon and then eats.

³⁴   ³⁵
Can we say that something belongs to *plays?* _____ To *eats?* _____

Are any apostrophes needed? _____ The five sentences you did on pages 463–464 contain several such verbs. If you put an apostrophe in any verb, you may want to review pages 150–153 of "Basic Sentence Parts" to reinforce your ability to recognize verbs.

[37]Here is a real test of your apostrophe ability; it includes both words of belonging and other words ending in -s that do not show belonging. Put apostrophes only where they are needed. (Partial ‡)

SELECTION C

A high school athletes fondest dreams concern athletic scholarships to colleges. If a schools basketball star averages twenty points a game or makes an all-star team, that boys phone rings constantly and his mailmans bag is stuffed with offers from colleges. But very often the young players hopes are falsely aroused by offers of financial aid that turns out to be no better than a nonathletes aid. A recruiters description of a tree-shaded campus overflowing with lively, eager girls can stimulate a city youths imagination to the point where no reality can match what his minds eye envisions. This young mans disappointment is all the keener when he learns that the colleges aid offer is too low for his dreams fulfillment.

When, and why, does the apostrophe sometimes come after the -s? First of all, it comes after the -s much less frequently than before it. (Thus, if you must guess, you will be right more often if you put the apostrophe before the -s.) To discover how to place it with certainty, however, answer the questions on the right below:

[38‡]That girl's room (The room belongs to _____.)

[39‡]The girls' dormitory (The dormitory belongs to _____.)

In 38, the room belongs to a *girl*, which does not end in -s; therefore, as you know, we add the -s, like this: *girl's*. But what about 39? The room belongs to *girls*, which already ends in an -s. What do we do? Since there is no need to add an -s, we add just an apostrophe in the original sentence: *girls'*. Here are more examples:

[40]Muhammed Ali's strategy (The strategy belongs to _____.)

[41]The Boston Celtics' strategy (The strategy belongs to _____.)

[42]One twin's trust fund (The fund belongs to _____.)

[43]The twins' trust fund (The fund belongs to _____.)

[44]a state's government (The government belongs to _____.)

[45]the fifty states' government (The government belongs to _____

_____.)

In 41, 43, and 45, something belongs to persons or things already ending in -*s*. There is no need to add another -*s*; we add just an apostrophe to that word in the original sentence.*

Try one. Where does the apostrophe go in the following sentence?

The quintuplets mother was near exhaustion.

Say to yourself, "The mother belongs to _____[46]."

Does the last word you put in the blank end in -*s*? _____[47]
[48]Now put the apostrophe in the sentence, and check the answer page. Put any needed apostrophes in these:

[49]The American Secretary of State attended a meeting with

five European nations ministers. (The ministers belong to

_____[50].)

[51]‡A dozen houses electricity was cut off by the storm. (The electricity

belongs to _____[52].)

[53]‡A three years delay is expected in completing the bridge. (The

delay belongs to (lasts) _____[54]‡.)

[55]‡All the students grades on Professor Higgins exam were *C* or lower.

[56]‡It took Fran five nights work as a ladies room attendant to earn

bus fare home.

There is one more point about apostrophes, which may be difficult because it seems to contradict what you have learned so far. Remember these seven words—*ours, yours, his, hers, its, theirs, whose?* It may surprise you to learn that even though these words show belonging, none of them ever takes an apostrophe! Fix them firmly in your mind. How

many apostrophes should the following item have? _____[57]

Whose fault was it? It was not his or hers, or mine or theirs; it was yours.

---

* This way of determining the place of the apostrophe and the addition of -*s* does have a few exceptions, but to avoid confusion we will leave them to a more advanced course.

You are probably saying, "But I know I've seen *it's* and *who's* countless times!" You have. But are these the same words as *its* and *whose?* Look:

The dog wagged its stubby tail.
It's clear that you don't love me.

58

We have met *it's* earlier in this section, as a contraction of _____. To determine whether to use *its* or *it's* in any sentence, just mentally substitute *it is*. If *it is* makes sense, then you need the contraction ⁵⁹☐ its, ☐ it's. Anywhere else, use *its*. Try it. Put any needed apostrophes in this sentence:

⁶⁰Its [It is?] plain to see that the government has abandoned its [it is?]

responsibility to its [it is?] youth.

The same holds true for *whose* and *who's,* and for those other troublesome sets, *your/you're* and *their/they're/there*. Use the form with the apostrophe only if the full form—*who is* (or *who has*), *you are, they are*—makes sense in the sentence. ⁶¹Do the following, crossing out the word(s) not wanted at each choice (partial ‡):

SELECTION D

Your/You're first downhill run on skis will be something you'll never forget. Its/It's frightening to be pulled higher and higher up the mountain in the chair lift. Everyone whose/who's ever skied has felt the same. You'll find that its/it's almost impossible to get off the lift without falling when your/you're a novice. At the top of the slope you'll check to see that each of your/you're boots fits tightly in its/it's binding and that your/you're skis have their/they're/there runaway straps looped around your/you're legs. When you start down the hill you'll be afraid of running into other skiers, but usually their/they're/there aware that your/you're a beginner, and its/it's likely their/they're/there going to keep away. When you finally reach bottom, you'll look back up and say "Whose/Who's going to believe I skied all the way from up their/they're/there?"

⁶²‡On your own paper, write original sentences using each of the following words. Underline each in its sentence. You may use two or more in one sentence:

your	they're	whose	you're	their
its	it's	who's	there	

⁶³‡Now you are ready for a final practice on all uses of the apostrophe. Put all needed apostrophes—and no unneeded ones—into the selection below, and where two forms of a word are given, cross out the wrong one. (To give you practice with contractions, this selection is deliberately less formal than customary.)

SELECTION E

When the legislatures of the fifty states discuss bills for womens rights, their/they're/there invariably influenced by each legislators sex. Since many states legislatures contain no women representatives, its almost impossible for women to influence the lawmakers votes. The men of one states assembly, whose/who's treatment of their/they're/there only two women colleagues was so rude that the ladies walked out in protest, voted a years postponement of one bill on womens rights and six months postponement on another. This countrys females still face a hard fight to secure all the rights that should be theirs/their's.

From your own writing, find five sentences in which your instructor has indicated mistakes in apostrophes (but has not corrected them). In each A blank below, copy one of those sentences just as you wrote it. (If the sentence is a long one, copy just the part with the error.) In each B blank, rewrite the words in A as they should be:

64A‡
_____

64B‡
_____

65A‡
_____

65B‡
_____

66A‡
_____

66B‡
_____

67A‡
_____

67B‡
_____

68A‡
_____

68B‡
_____

EXCEPTIONS AND OTHER PROBLEM WORDS

As you have known since elementary school, every English spelling rule has its exceptions. Some rules have few; others have many. Below are the most important exceptions to the principles you have learned in this module.

A. *The final e principle:* Recall that we keep the final *e* in such words as *statement* and *lonely*, where we still need the *e* to keep the previous vowel long. Exceptions are *truly* and *argument*. By the way, there are two words you can never misspell, because they are right either with or without the *e: judg(e)ment* and *acknowledg(e)ment*.

B. *The doubling principle:* Recall that we double the final consonant to keep the single vowel before it short, if that syllable is accented, as in *stopped* and *referred*. The word *equipped* follows the doubling principle even though *ui* is not a single vowel.

C. *The* ie *principle:* Recall that in words with an *ee* sound, we put *i* before *e* except after *c*, as in *believe, chief, receive.* Exceptions are *seize, weird, financier,* and *species.*

D. *The chameleon principle:* Recall that the last letter of *ad-, in-,* and *con-* usually changes to match the following letter, giving us a double letter, as in *accommodate, immersion,* and *collect.* However, there are two other prefixes, *ab-* and *a-,* which have different meanings from *ad-.* They cause no change in the root word, and therefore words beginning with *ab-* (except *abbreviate* and *abbey*) do not double the *b.* Thus:

abandon	abide	abortion	abroad
abdicate	ablaze	abrasive	absent
abduct	abolish	abridge	abuse

These other words also do not double their second letter:

across	aloft
agree	apartment
aground	inoculate

E. *The final* y *principle:* Recall that final *y* after a consonant changes to *i* before an added ending, as in *fly/flies, battery/batteries;* but *y* after a vowel does not change, as in *betray/betrays* and *monkey/monkeys.* Exceptions are *slyly, shyly;* also *paid, laid,* and *said.*

F. *-Able/-ible:* You learned that, normally, words that have an *-ation* form will have a form ending in *-able.* One exception is *sensation/sensible* (also *sensitive*).

In spite of all you have discovered, there are still some frequently misspelled words that just do not fit any of the principles you have learned. This section gives a list of most such words, along with hints on how to remember them:

across [What is on top of a church? A cross]
advice [noun: good advice]; advise [verb: I advise you]
among [I am on e amon g many]
analysis [Why (*y*) do you need an anal y sis?]
article [A diamond is a valuab le artic le]
basis [one]; bases [more than one]
category [What cat ego ry is your ego in?]
cemetery [Do they put you in ceme nt in the ceme tery?]
committee [two of everything: *ms, ts, es*]
comparatively [There is a rat in comp arat ively]
conscious, conscience [Is science trying to con us?]
crisis [one]; crises [more than one]
curriculum [one]; curricula [more than one]
criterion [one]; criteria [more than one]
definitely [Are you de fini tely fini shed?]
description [de + scribe: something you write down]
embarrass [two *rs* and two *ss*]
exaggerate [two *gs* needed to keep the previous *a* short]
fascinate [Sci ence fa sci nates me]
interest [An item of inter national inter est]
interrupt [inte r + r upt = two *rs*]
literature [four syllables—lit er a ture]

necessary [A ⌞cess⌟pool is ne⌞cess⌟ary in a rural house]
occasion [two *cs*—a chameleon; single *s* to keep the *a* long]
opinion [three syllables; sound it out: o PIN yon]
opportunity [See the ⌞port⌟ if you have the op⌞port⌟unity]
parallel [Those two *ls* are parallel lines]
personal (PER son al—concerning a person: her personal problems]
personnel [per son NEL—employees of an organization: The personnel want a raise]
possess [A very possessive word—it holds on to its *ss*]
precede [Only *proceed, exceed,* and *succeed* end in *-ceed;* nearly all other words
        ending in this sound end in *-cede*]
prejudice [It means to pre-judge; no *d* after *pre*]
privilege [It is ⌞vile⌟ not to have any pri⌞vile⌟ges]
procedure [Even though *proceed* has a double *e*!]
professor [Do you con⌞fess⌟ your doubts to your pro⌞fess⌟or?]
pursue [If some one stole your ⌞purs⌟e, you would ⌞purs⌟ue him]
quiet [Not noisy; do not confuse with *quite* or *quit*]
recommend [re + commend; to commend again]
repetition [re + petition; to petition again]
rhythm [Notice the central *h* in each syllable: r⌞h⌟y t⌞h⌟m]
separate [There is ⌞a rat⌟ in sep⌞arat⌟e]
success [two *cs*—one for the hard sound, *suc-*, the other for the soft sound, *-cess*]
supposed to [Put that *d* in!]
surprise [Winning a trip to Big ⌞Sur⌟ would be a ⌞sur⌟prise]
through [THRU]; thorough[THUH row]
tragedy [No *d* after *tra*]
used to [Put that *d* in!]

This module has, necessarily, just skimmed the surface of English spelling. You must still rely on your ear, your memory, your personal spelling list, and a good dictionary. Know your weaknesses and check each paper carefully to eliminate them.

MASTERY TEST

Since the section on exceptions has also helped you review much of what you have learned in this module, we will move right to the mastery test. Look back over any sections you still feel unsure of before beginning the test.

Part I. In every line below, one (and *only* one) word is misspelled. Find that word and respell it correctly in the blank at the right:

1‡writing   adviseable   sincerely   safety   _____

2‡hopping   shiping   loneliness   referring   _____

3‡quarreling   committed   beginning   acheive   _____

4‡decieve   niece   foreign   vein   _____

5‡courageous   reducable   pronounceable   negligible   _____

⁶‡athlete privilege equiptment beggar   _____

⁷‡grammar legislator similiar narrator   _____

⁸‡professor aggressor influence conquorer   _____

⁹‡accelerate acommodate irregular immediately   _____

¹⁰‡colaborate succeed dissatisfied unnaturally   _____

¹¹‡annoyance tragedies extravagant convieniance   _____

¹²‡correspondence invisable truly seize   _____

¹³‡across apartment shyly payed   _____

¹⁴‡analysis catagory conscience definitely   _____

¹⁵‡occassion precede separate supposed to   _____

Part I (*alternate form*). On your own paper or in the blanks above, spell correctly   †
fifteen words your instructor pronounces aloud.‡

Part II. In the blank below each sentence, rewrite it as it should be:

¹⁶‡Its a sad day when a mother in laws only pleasure is wondering who's house
shes least welcome at.

_____

_____

¹⁷‡Score's of citizens lined up at the Capitols main entrance for admission to
the sessions of the ninety first Congress at which the Vice President might have to
cast the tie breaking vote's on bills that would effect the rights of every women.

_____

_____

_____

¹⁸‡They're are only twenty three counties in the West where your still bound
by their anti drinking laws, which were past before Coolidges era.

_____

_____

_____

¹⁹‡Ray Brushback, the Astros ex pitcher, has lead a happier life since he
excepted his release from the teams roster.

[20‡]The principal reason for Ray's contentment is that their is now less tension in this one time aces life then when he was loosing to many spine tingling ball games. Now his life is alright.

_____

_____

_____

†   *Part III.* (*Optional*) In the blanks below, spell correctly ten words dictated to you by your instructor from your personal spelling list:‡ (If the misspelling is a homonym, your instructor will give it to you in a sentence; write in the blank the words before and after the homonym in the sentence, as well as the homonym itself.)

_____   _____   _____

_____   _____   _____

_____   _____   _____

_____

ANSWERS

INTRODUCTION AND PROBLEMS SOLVED BY SOUND

[1]there, obvious, writing, than, spelling, error, average, fragment, redundancy, paragraphs, misspelled, your, right, between, rightly, wrongly, opinion, ability, intelligence, affected

[2]Same

[3]similar, accidentally, privilege, government, laboratory, athlete, February, temperature, quantity, equipment

[4]Vowels

[5]a, e, i, o, u, (y)

[6]Consonants

[8]Yes

[9]Hope

[10]Hate

[11]The second column

[12]Long

[13]mĕt, kĭt, dŏt, jŭt; mēter, kīte, dōte, jūte

[14]hăt, hāte, pĕt, Pēte, gāte, lĕt, īce, stĭck, hōme, cūre, cŭb, bĭt

[15]consonant

[16]never

[17]always

[18]glŭt, rīme, flūme, wrĭt, īcon, whīning

[19]No

[20]Vowel

[21]sliding, famous, writer, raking, investigator

[22]No

[23]Yes

[24]Yes

[25]homely, spadeful, sincerely

[26]dining, spiting, spiteful, homeless, homer

[27]vowel

[28]consonant

[29]p

[30]bitten, stopped, slapping, batter

[31]No

[32]sinking

[33]planter

[34]No

[35]cupful, sadness, manly

[36]reddest, stacked, fatter

[37]slope, wade, strip

[39]Yes

[40]re FER, con FER, de FER, OF fer, pre FER (If you had trouble with these, do the box that follows in the text.)

[43]re FER, de FER, OF fer, BEN e fit, CON ference

[44]Offer

[45]First

[46]inferred, occurred, happened, excelling, quarreling

[47]signaling, omitted, opener, buttered

[49]con FER ring, CON fer ence

[50]jumped back to the first syllable

[51]preferring, preference, inferring, inference

[52]Yes

[53]Yes

[54]*ie*

[55]receive, ceiling, conceited, deceive

[56]In all four words, there is a *c* just before the *ei*.

[57]*ie*

[58]*c*

[59]*i, e, c*

[60]brief, niece, siege, priest, receive, perceive

[61]No

[62]*ei*

[63]forfeit, rein, sleigh

[65]Yes

[66]*e, i,* or *y*

[67]No

[68]j

[69]No

[70]yes

[71](g)igantic, reli(g)ious, (g)elatin, (g)yp, tan(g)ent

[72]forcible, reducible, eligible, invincible

[73]serviceable, manageable, changeable, noticeable, replaceable

PROBLEMS NOT SOLVED BY SOUND

[1]They are all pronounced the same or almost the same.

[2]unaccented

[3]same

[4]*-at-*

[5]*-or* in all blanks

[7]The accent shifts to the next-to-last syllable.
[8]definition, definite; practicality, practical; narration, narrative; symbolic, symbol
[9]your . . . to . . . by . . . writing
[10]No
[12]It is too [excessively] early to tell which of the two [2] two-headed [2-headed] monsters is too [excessively] dangerous . . .
[13]There is a rumor that the Russians will allow some emigrants to leave their country [the country belonging to them]. Since there is a shortage of food in Russia as well as a lack of housing there [at that place] . . . ,
[14]She was a woman [one person] of rare charm and grace.
[15]So was her mother. They were both unforgettable women [two persons].
[16]Where [at what place] were you when the lights went out?
[18]Chief (greatest, most important): The *principal* is the chief official of the school; the *principal* cause is the chief cause; the *principal* of a bank account or a loan is the chief part of it; the *principal* export is the chief export.
[19]The principles [rules] of good business demand that we invest the principal [chief] portion of our funds in the Swiss Merchant Marine Company. If the dividends are good, we can leave the principal [chief part] untouched . . .
[20]When I saw Sue's tan, I was then [at that time] convinced that she had a better tan than [compared to] Fran . . .
[21]The police found Bronsky dead in bed from lead [the metal] poisoning. A hunch led [brought] Detective Tracy . . .
[22]Fidgwick, who is usually loose [as a goose] and relaxed in chess games, somehow became nervous and began to lose [rhymes with whose] his concentration . . .
[23]A verb
[24]A noun
[25]The first effect [noun]. . . . But soon her new responsibilities affected [verb] her . . .
[26]verb
[27]. . . we passed [verb—went by] Hondo Hall . . . I passed [verb—went through] that course with an A+, because it dealt with the past [noun].
[28]. . . everyone except [excluding] Hugo. I hope everyone else will accept the invitation . . .
[29]changes its appearance
[30]accelerate, accent, accept, accident, accommodate, allot, allure, annul, appear, appetite, apprehend
[36]consonant
[38]donkeys, portraying, annoyance
[39]flies, cried, tries, carrier, marriage, tragedies, business, hurried, happiness, magnification, realities, liberties
[40]*y, i*
[41]angrily, relays, enemies, carriage, horrified, loneliness, livelihood, x-rayed, valleys
[42]carrying, hurrying, magnifying
[44]alterable, restorable, demonstrable
[45]repressible, impressible, comprehensible
[46]-*ible*
[47]installable, reformable, reversible, taxable [taxation]

TWO MARKS THAT AFFECT SPELLING

[1]It is impossible to tell.
[2]b.
[3]c.
[4]father-in-law, re-established, retire-ment, vice-president, thirty-eight, one hundred twenty-five, thirty-year, old-age, pre-retirement
[5]Contractions
[6]We're sure you'll love the expanded first-class service on our Guano Airlines superjets. You're in for a big surprise. There's an entirely new cabin decor, and our hostesses will provide your every comfort: They're ready with drinks, steaks, magazines, and pillows. We'll make you say, "Here's an

airline I'll fly again; it's Guano for me!" Guano's the one for you.

[7]It is Charlie's problem.

[8]belongs

[9]Nouns

[10]Yes

[11]Yes

[12]'s to Hattie

[13]Tomorrow is Hattie's birthday.

[14]Charlie's

[15]Charlie's

[21]driver's, men's, children's

[22]captain's, driver's, mayor's

[23]Hunter's,

[24]professor's, Shakespeare's

[25]secretary's, director's

[28]No. *Means,* for example, does not take *'s*

[29]None

[30]No

[31]No

[32]No

[33]None

[34]No

[35]No

[36]No

[37]A high school athlete's fondest dreams concern athletic scholarships to colleges. If a school's basketball star averages twenty points a game or makes an all-star team, that boy's phone rings constantly and his mailman's bag is stuffed with offers from colleges.

[40]Ali

[41]the Celtics

[42]one twin

[43]the twins

[44]a state

[45]fifty states

[46]the quintuplets

[47]Yes

[48]The quintuplets' mother was near exhaustion.

[49]nations' ministers

[50]five nations

[52]a dozen houses

[57]None

[58]it is

[59]it's

[60]It's plain to see that the government has abandoned its responsibility to its youth.

[61]Your first downhill run on skis will be something you'll never forget. It's frightening to be pulled higher and higher up the mountain in the chair lift. Everyone who's ever skied has felt the same. You'll find that it's almost impossible to get off the lift without falling when you're a novice.

MODULE 15

REVISING AND PROOFREADING

Previous modules required: This module can be done at any time during the course, but incorporates material from nearly all other modules and is most effective when done last.

THE FINAL PRODUCT

How many times did you rewrite your last paper before you turned it in? After your last rewriting, how many times did you read through it for mistakes or omissions you had overlooked? If you are like most people, once you finish the "good copy of a paper the last thing you want to do is read through it again—usually for fear of finding more mistakes or weaknesses that will force you to do still more work on the paper. But this is where to many students stop—just where they might have made those final improvements that would have made a fair paper into a good or even superior one. Such people are like an English Channel swimmer who stops with the cliffs of Dover just a hundred yards away, saying "I just don't feel like swimming any further." All his twenty hours in the water have been wasted. So will most of the hours you spend in writing a paper be wasted unless you force yourself to go through the paper two or three more times—even after you have typed it—to catch last-minute slips. (This is called *proofreading*.)

No paragraph is ever perfect. Even professional authors, reading sections of their own writing in print, have moaned, "Did I write that junk?" Writing rarely comes easy, even to professionals. In fact, one of reasons they are professionals may be that they revise and polish their work so carefully, like a master cabinet maker polishing that fifth coat of varnish on a bookcase he has handcrafted. On the facing page is a section from a college professors typed draft (each writing or rewritting of a paper is called a draft) of an article that was later published. Before this there were two handwritten drafts, and after this another typed draft, which was then proofread several times. Look over his revisions; see whether you can discover why he made some of them.

All these remarks are meant not to scare you but to help you see that you may be a much better writer than you think you are.

You have had ample practice in revising throughout the previous modules. Now let us focus on proofreading. How good a proofreader are you? In the first two paragraphs of this module there are five deliberate errors—words or punctuation left out, spelling mistakes, or inconsistencies. Did you spot any as you read? Reread the paragraphs; try to find all five and correct them in pencil by circling the error, drawing a line from the error to the margin, and writing the correction in a circle, like (thiss).‡　　　　　　　　　　　　　　　　　　　　*this*

What should you proofread for? Everything that you have learned in this book or that your common sense may notice. Some possible weaknesses, like forgetting to paragraph or arranging your details in the wrong order, you should have caught in the earlier drafts. But even on the final draft you will hand in, there will probably be several easily correctable mistakes that you have overlooked.

Here, then, is a checklist for proofreading your next-to-final and final drafts. Proofread, proofread again, and proofread once more, for:

A. *Typing or copying.* A recent study found that a third of all papers in college English classes like yours were handed in with words simply left out at two or more places. Even if someone else has typed your paper, you are responsible for catching the errors. Watch particularly for omitted words, apostrophes, or commas; reversed letters; words copied twice (like this this); words mistakenly written for other words (such as *is* where you mean *in*). Be sure that you close every set of parentheses, quotation marks, or interrupting commas that you open (not "like this, but "like this").

B. *Consistency.* Did you capitalize *President* in one place and write *president* elsewhere? Did you spell *judgment* in one place and *judgement* in another? Are there illogical shifts in your tenses (*goes-went*) or your point of view (*I-you-a person*)?

The energy crisis

Why does this occur? Quite often because, in spite of dozens of ② ③ lessons on the topic sentence of a paragraph, the student does not think of his whole in terms of paper / a central idea on which he must use his organization and details / must focus to develop.

~~women's lib~~, abortion, the abolition of grades, etc. - formless
sludge with no center. Often the students central idea sentence
is merely a restatement ~~to~~ of the topic/ "The central idea of this
paper is about women's lib/" - or a vague noun clause that presents
a question rather than an answer - "The central idea is how the
U.S. can prevent world starvation," or "The cnetral idea is ø why
there is so much disenchantment with college." But how can we
prevent starvation? Why is there disenchantment? These sentences do not say.

Moreover, even when he is forced to write a central statement of his central idea he often cannot phrase it in a way that it will so help him to guide him to the point he is trying to make.

(three-step discovery)
(short, unit)

I am still amazed at the number of my freshman students who treat the concept of a central idea as some kind of previously ~~ ~~ a revelation

I suggest the following ~~steps,~~ applicable to either the senior high school or college freshman level, to teach first, the
effective central ideas. The first step shows the to conceive of a paper in terms of ~~the~~ the form of a central idea; and
need ~~for~~ a central idea ~~and~~ second, the ~~way to write an effective~~
The third, the way to write an effective one. For these points to be driven home to the
~~one. For the students to realize the need, the teacher shows the~~
and remain with them, the teacher must proceed inductively, leading the students to discover
~~need through an inductive approach rather than merely ~~by~~ telling~~
these concepts rather than merely *in my college freshman class*
~~that a central idea is needed.~~ In teaching such a unit, I begin
with paragraph-size ~~XXXXXX~~ papers and work up to ~~the~~ full theme,
since the principle of the central isea is the same for both. *(Though texts use different names - topic sentence and thesis sentence.)*

To ensure a truly inductive lesson, the teacher does not ever tell they class

The first step is for the teacher to give the students,
short
without any comment, two selections to ~~x~~ read; ~~The class is~~ ~~they x are~~
~~not even told~~ that the central idea is the topic of the lesson.
I use two selections from Charles Lindbergh's The Spirit of
ten
St. Louis (New York: Scribner's,]953). The first is a ~~ten~~-sen-
beginning with
tence paragraph ~~with~~ a clearly stated central idea/ "A pilot
doesn't feel at home in a plane until he's flown it for thousands
However, the) selection, though
of miles" (p. 191). ~~The~~ second, also in paragraph form, is act-
and developed by examples.

C. *Pauses and stops.* Read the paper through (aloud, if possible) to see that you have a comma at every pause necessary for clarity and a period or other stop mark at every stop. A wise English teacher once suggested reading each paper backward, not word by word but sentence by sentence, in order to spot fragments and run-togethers more clearly. Try it.

D. *Spelling.* By now you know the kinds of words you are most likely to misspell. Unless your paper is written in class under a time limit, there is no reason not to check all the spelling. Some of the most commonly overlooked misspellings are the well-known homonyms *to/too, there/they're/their, its/it's,* and *your/you're.*

E. *Wording.* Your final check may still catch some wobbly words: vague ones, like *thing, many, a lot of,* where more precise words are needed; unimaginative ones, like *get,* where alternatives are plentiful; out-of-tone ones, like *guys* or *a bunch of* in a formal paper; and the same nouns, verbs, or modifiers repeated too often or too closely.

F. *Clarity.* To steal from St. Paul, "Though I speak with the tongues of men and of angels, and have not clarity, I have become as sounding brass, or a tinkling cymbal." On your last read-through, if something is not clear, change it! All the topics you have studied in this book and with your instructor are important to good writing, but "the greatest of these is clarity."

If you are worrying about the appearance of your paper when you make all these last-minute changes, remember two points: (1) Most instructors prefer an accurate paper with several neatly penned corrections to a beautiful-looking paper handed in with errors known to you. (Naturally, a paper that starts to look sloppy should be recopied.) (2) Excessive corrections and revisions on your final copy can be avoided by more careful proofreading of earlier drafts.

MASTERY TEST

Part I. Do whichever of these your instructor assigns:

A. Take one of your papers that your instructor has indicated as not too carefully revised or proofread. Go over it carefully, making all the revisions and corrections you find needed. Recopy, proofread, proofread once more, and resubmit it.

B. Form a team with another student. Before you submit your next writing assignment, but after you have given it a final proofreading, you and your teammate proofread each other's paper, indicating lightly in pencil all corrections and other suggested revisions. Reclaim your own paper; decide whether all the changes your teammate has indicated are valid; then write the valid ones in ink and submit the paper. At the bottom of the paper write "Proofread by [your teammate's name]."

Part II. The following is the actual text of a paper submitted in a freshman English class. Proofread it several times, making whatever corrections and other revisions you think necessary in the writing. Do not attempt to change the writer's ideas, except to try to clarify garbled sentences or vague expressions. Make the changes neatly above the lines or in the margin; if the paper becomes sloppy, recopy the whole paper, including your revisions.‡

"Warning: The surgeon general has determined that cigarette smoking is dangerous to your health," is on all packs of cigarettes but people still smoke. Did you ever wonder why?

Most teenagers start smoking because their friends do it, or to make them feel older. Adults do it because they are bored. Picture yourself at a party and you don't drink your hands are empty. What should you do to fit in with the crowd hold a glass and pretend its a drink? Well thats pretty silly, so the next best thing is a cigarette. Atleast you will fit in with the crowd, but there is another type who has both hand occupied with a drink and a cigarette. I guess they figure if I drink, I might as well smoke.

All smokers know that cigarettes are harmful to their lungs, but this doesn't stop them. I believe that people just don't care any more about their selves. Years ago people tried to live longer and not to do any thing that would damage their health but now things have changed. I feel that people that their is nothing to live for and if your going to die it has to be from something even if its not cancer. Also people are relizing that life is not so easy. Prices are going up jobs are hard to find and who wants to live in a world where things are difficult to come by.

Many people know that after you get a certain age your not going to get any farther in this world so they live the life the same until its gets motonous then their ready to give it up. I believe if the world wasn't so corrupt and things weren't so hard to get, more people would take better care of themselves.

MASTER LIST OF WRITING TOPICS

The list below contains topics which are suitable for most of the writing assignments in this book. The list is divided according to types of topics. Follow your instructor's guidelines in choosing topics.

I. EXPLAINING

How to cook lasagne (chitterlings, sukiyaki, etc.)
How to win at hearts (poker, etc.)
How to get an A without knowing anything
How to cheat successfully on an exam
How to make him/her say *yes*
How I "get away from it all"

How to perform _____ (a certain maneuver in sports, etc.)
How to tell off the boss without being fired
How to avoid being cheated (at cards, in buying a car, etc.)

How to make a _____
How to say *no* gracefully

How to _____ (do something)
How to make a fool of oneself
What is "in" and what is "out" in current clothing styles for college men/women
Current trends in rock music

II. DESCRIBING

An Italian (Polish, Jewish, etc.) family holiday dinner
My "get away from it all" place
An unforgettable person I have known
Where I grew up—there was no place like it

_____ at night

Revisiting _____ after ten (twenty, etc.) years

My father (mother, grandparent, etc.)
The great man/woman I once met
A place you would not believe
A person you would not believe
My room (clothes, car, etc.) as a reflection of me
The Harlem (Appalachia, Boston, Texas, etc.) few people know
Athens (Naples, San Juan, Hong Kong, etc.—any foreign city where you have lived) com-

    pared with _____ (the American city where you now
  live)
A state that wild horses could not make me live in
The ugliest person I ever met
The most dishonest (hypocritical, nasty, etc.) person I ever met
The most kind (unselfish, wise, etc.) person I ever met (other than a spouse or relative)

III. TELLING AN EXPERIENCE

A news-making event I witnessed (or participated in)
An unforgettable party
A memorable encounter with the opposite sex
The time I came to know what love (death, marriage, sex, prejudice, fear, hypocrisy, cruelty,
    loneliness, growing up, responsibility, poverty, inequality, rejection, pain, friendship,
    etc.) really means
The time I really blew it
My first day in the United States
My first taste of city (country, suburban) life
I will never do *that* again
The thrill of _____ (something you have done)
I could never do it—but I did
Surviving unemployment
Surviving a ghetto childhood
Surviving a suburban childhood
An ironic incident
An unforgettable dream
"So simple even a child can do it"—the instructions said
Living on my own

IV. PERSONAL

The me nobody knows
I am different
I am not different
Me—ten years from now
Me—through another person's eyes
Why I sometimes think I am crazy
Why I sometimes think I am the only sane person around
The man/woman I marry will have to be . . .

Why I hate _____

Why I fear _____

Why I love _____
The TV character most like me
Me now, compared with my childhood vision of me now
My adolescent vision of college compared with the actuality
My dreams (fears) as I begin college
I never thought it would come to this
Men/Women and I
Where I would live if I had the choice
The hardest thing about being a teenager was . . .
A year I want to live over
A year I would never want to live over
My "good old days"—how good were they?
What "turns me on"
What "turns me off"
The music that moves my soul

The effect on me of _____ (a photo, painting, sculpture, film, etc., shown by your instructor)

V. OPINION

"They don't make movies the way they used to"
An unforgettable acting performance
An unforgettable motion picture
The worst motion picture I have seen this year
The best and the worst war (Western, cops-and-robbers, black, etc.) movie I have seen

The movie _____ compared with the book (or compared with an older version of the same movie)
The lives of people like me on TV, compared with our real lives
A movie that had a special meaning for me
A believable TV drama (or comedy)
TV quiz game shows—what they reveal about Americans' values

VI. CAUSE AND EFFECT

My city (county, etc.)—how its present condition came about
My educational weaknesses—whose fault are they?
How the current situation in the Middle East (Southeast Asia, Northern Ireland, the U.S. economy, the condition of the migrant workers, etc.) came about

VII. ISSUES

Welfare—blessing or curse?
Women's lib (gay lib, etc.)—great progressive movement or ridiculous fad?

Men *are* superior
Women are not equal to men; they are superior
Abortion—should there be any restrictions on it?
Abortion—should the father have a say in it?
"Urban renewal equals black removal"—true or false?

The assassination of _____—is the official story true?
Expansion (salaries, players' rights, the playoff system, etc.) in professional sports—does it need changing?
No coed dorms for me
Do the police favor certain groups over others?
Does busing help minority-group children?

Our next president (governor, mayor, etc.) should be _____

Change the rules of _____
Baseball—the world's dullest spectator sport?
Cigarette sales to adults should (should not) be restricted
TV stations should (should not) be allowed to show anything they wish
Blacks should (should not) form separate communities instead of trying to live with whites
Interracial marriage—should it ever be tried?
Preferential or quota hiring of minority-group persons is fair (unfair)
The most forgotten minority group

Few people think _____ and _____
are alike, but they are
Should single people be allowed to adopt children?
What should the courts do with juvenile criminals?

VIII. THINKING DEEPLY

What I really want from life
What are my obligations to the human race?
Why does the world hate instead of love?
Can politics ever be made honest?
The world of witches, spirits, and demons—does it exist?
Can whites and blacks ever live peacefully together?

Can the human race avoid destroying itself by _____?
Was man meant to live in cities?
Should minority-group people keep their own culture or try to live like "typical" Americans?
Are city poor better off than rural poor?
Would I ever allow myself to be mercy-killed?
What effect is Vietnam having on the values of returned veterans?

IX. IMAGINATION

My dream dwelling
My dream car

Heaven
Hell
My city—year 2001
My dream man/woman
My dream invention
The sport I dreamed up
What I would do with a million dollars
My first official acts if I were mayor (county supervisor, governor, etc.)
If I were white
If I were black
If I could make a movie

Clarity, 8–14, 141, 292–308. *See also* Coherence; Parallel structure
  and economy, 252, 292–308
  proofreading for, 480
  in punctuating series, 333–334
  in speaking, 91
  through combining ideas, 205
  through eliminating fragments, 394–395
  through eliminating run-togethers, 401–407
  and word choice, 83, 86
Clause, 208–209
  definition, 208
  distinguished from sentence, 208
Clear reference. *See* Pronoun
Coherence, 57–61
Colloquialism, 84–87, 96
Colon, 339
Combining ideas, 204–243
  with trimmed groups, 269–270
Comma, 321–338
  in addresses, 336–337
  in *and*-link sentences, 254, 255, 335–336
  for clarity, 326–332, 335
  consistency in using, 337
  in dates, 336–337
  in direct address, 337
  excessive, 334–336
  function of, 314
  with *if*-links, 336
  with interrupters, 324–332
  after introducers, 323–324
  optional use of, 322–323
  with qualifying expressions, 337
  with quotation marks, 341
  relation to reading speed, 337
  in run-togethers, 403
  in series, 333–334
  after *therefore*-links, 214
  in titles of persons, 336–337
Comma fault. *See* Run-together
Comma splice. *See* Run-together
Communication, 82
Compactness. *See* Economy
Complement. *See* Completer
Completer, 167–172
  mistaken for subject of following clause, 322–323
Completer forms. *See* Pronoun
Composition, 50. *See also* Theme; Paper; Essay
  length of, 252
Compound nouns. *See* Noun, double

Compound sentences. *See And*-links, combining ideas with
Compound verbs. *See* Verbs, double
Conciseness, 300, 301. *See also* Economy
Conclusion
  qualities of, 73–74, 77
  signal words for, 60
  writing, 66–68, 72–78
Condition
  with *if*-links, 231, 238
  with *therefore*-links, 213
Conjunction. *See also* Link
  coordinating. *See And*-link
  subordinating. *See If*-link
Conjunctive adverbs. *See Therefore*-link
Consistency
  proofreading for, 478
  in use of contractions, 90
Consonant, 431
  before *y*, 456–457
  doubling
    before ending, 435–441
    with prefix, 452–454
  endings beginning with, 434–437, 455
  sounds of, 432
Context, definition of, 109
  determining meaning from, 109–112
Contraction, avoidance of in formal writing, 87, 88–90
Conversation, informal. *See* English, informal
Convincing, 48–49, 53. *See also* Persuasion
Coordinate conjunction. *See And*-link
Coordination. *See And*-links, combining ideas with; *Therefore*-links, combining ideas with
Copying, 478
Correlative conjunctions. *See And*-link, of two parts
Crutch words, 94–96

D

Dangling modifier, 257, 258
Dash, 340
Deadwood, 293–308. *See also* Redundancy, Economy
Declarative sentence. *See* Sentence

Dependent clause. *See* Subgroup; *Who*-group, *If*-group; *What*-group
Description
  order in, 62–63
  signal words for, 60
Detail
  distinguished from generalizations, 26–29
  need for, 49
  off-topic, 55–57
  use of, 51–55
Determiner, 148, 174. *See also* Article
Diction. *See* Word choice
Dictionary
  avoiding memorization of, 104, 106
  word meaning from, 107, 109–111
Directions, writing, 8–12
Do, 164
Doing, words of. *See* Sentence, description of; Verb
Doublespeak, 292
Doubling principle. *See* Spelling

E

Earmuff principle, 326, 340–341
Economy, 83, 251–287, 292–308
  combining ideas for, 205
  dropping *that* for, 226
  through eliminating crutch words, 96
  through eliminating roundabout expressions, 97–98
  in using modifiers, 182
Effect, 451. *See also* Cause-effect
Emphasis, 297. *See also* Parallel structure
-*En*-form, 160–163, 165, 265–266. *See also* Verb
  distinguished from full verbs, 192–193
  mistaken for full verb, 395
  as modifiers, 192–193
-*En*-form master sentence, 161
-*En*-group, 265–268
  combining ideas with, 266–270
  punctuation of, 323
  sequence of tense with, 268
  trimming to, 265–268, 270–272
-*En*-link, 266